# MOVING WORDS

## Literature, Memory, and Migration in Berlin

In the decades since the fall of the Berlin Wall, Berlin has re-emerged as a global city in large part thanks to its reputation as a literary city – a place where artists from around the world gather and can make a life. *Moving Words* foregrounds the many contexts in which life in the city of Berlin is made literary – from old neighbourhood bookshops to new reading circles, NGOs working to secure asylum for writers living in exile to specialized workshops for young migrant poets. Highlighting the differences, tensions, and contradictions of these scenes, this book reveals how literature can be both a site of domination and a resource for resisting and transforming those conditions. By attending to the everyday lives of writers, readers, booksellers, and translators, it offers a crucial new vantage point on the politics of difference in contemporary Europe, at a moment marked by historical violence, resurgent nationalism, and the fraught politics of migration.

Rooted in ethnographic fieldwork, rich historical archives, and literary analysis, *Moving Words* examines the different claims people make on and for literature as it carries them through the city on irregular and intersecting paths. Along the way, Brandel offers a new approach to the ethnography of literature that aims to think anthropologically about crossings in time and in space, where literature provides a footing in a world constituted by a multiplicity of real possibilities.

(Anthropological Horizons)

ANDREW BRANDEL is an assistant research professor and the assistant director of Jewish Studies at Pennsylvania State University.

# ANTHROPOLOGICAL HORIZONS

*Editor: Michael Lambek, University of Toronto*

This series, begun in 1991, focuses on theoretically informed ethnographic works addressing issues of mind and body, knowledge and power, equality and inequality, the individual and the collective. Interdisciplinary in its perspective, the series makes a unique contribution in several other academic disciplines: women's studies, history, philosophy, psychology, political science, and sociology.

For a list of the books published in this series see p. 271.

# Moving Words

*Literature, Memory, and Migration in Berlin*

ANDREW BRANDEL

UNIVERSITY OF TORONTO PRESS
Toronto Buffalo London

© University of Toronto Press 2023
Toronto  Buffalo  London
utorontopress.com

Printed and bound by CPI Group (UK) Ltd, Croydon, CR0 4YY

ISBN 978-1-4875-4368-6 (cloth)     ISBN 978-1-4875-4370-9 (EPUB)
ISBN 978-1-4875-4369-3 (paper)     ISBN 978-1-4875-4371-6 (PDF)

Anthropological Horizons

___

**Library and Archives Canada Cataloguing in Publication**

Title: Moving words : literature, memory, and migration in Berlin / Andrew Brandel.
Names: Brandel, Andrew, author.
Series: Anthropological horizons.
Description: Series statement: Anthropological horizons | Includes bibliographical
   references and index.
Identifiers: Canadiana (print) 20230220916 | Canadiana (ebook) 20230221033 |
   ISBN 9781487543693 (paper) | ISBN 9781487543686 (cloth) |
   ISBN 9781487543716 (PDF) | ISBN 9781487543709 (EPUB)
Subjects: LCSH: Literature and society – Germany – Berlin. | LCSH: Literature and
   anthropology – Germany – Berlin. | LCSH: Ethnology – Germany – Berlin. |
   LCSH: Berlin (Germany) – Intellectual life – 21st century.
Classification: LCC DD866.8 .B73 2023 | DDC 943/.1550883 – dc23

___

Cover design: Val Cooke
Cover image: *Water Music*, 1957; oil on canvas, 51 x 71 cm; private collection (detail).
© Zao Wou-Ki / ProLitteris, Zurich / SOCAN, Montréal (2023).

We wish to acknowledge the land on which the University of Toronto Press operates. This land is the traditional territory of the Wendat, the Anishnaabeg, the Haudenosaunee, the Métis, and the Mississaugas of the Credit First Nation.

University of Toronto Press acknowledges the financial support of the Government of Canada, the Canada Council for the Arts, and the Ontario Arts Council, an agency of the Government of Ontario, for its publishing activities.

# Contents

*Acknowledgments* vii

1 Introduction: Berlin, City of Letters  3
2 The Prosody of Social Ties: Poetry and Fleeting Moments in a Workshop  32
3 Exile in Translation: The Politics of Remaining Unknown  56
4 In the Footsteps of a Flaneur: A Grammar of Returning (to a Street)  93
5 Selecting, Collecting, Connecting: Making Books and Making Do  122
6 Life in a Net of Language: Literature, Translation, and the Feel of Words  149

*Notes*  177

*References*  239

*Index*  265

# Acknowledgments

I have incurred incalculable debts in the writing of this book.

*Moving Words*, work toward which has occupied my life for the last decade, began at Johns Hopkins University, and I owe so much to my teachers there. I took every course Naveeda Khan offered, and it was in her seminar rooms that I first learned to think anthropologically. This journey would have been impossible without her advice, her encouragement, and her ever-crystalline insight. Clara Han's guidance and support throughout these years have left an indelible mark on me as a scholar and as a person. Every word I ever write will be shaped in some way or another by my intellectual friendship with Veena Das, for whose equal measure of brilliance, generosity, and care I cannot sufficiently express my gratitude. You are the teacher I always hoped to find. I owe many thanks as well for all the lessons learned from Deborah Poole, Jane I. Guyer, Ranen Das, and Sidney W. Mintz, who passed away suddenly in 2015. I miss his wit and wisdom. Wonderful friends made my time Baltimore rich in so many ways. I am thankful to have shared those years with Aditi Saraf, Amrita Ibrahim, Amy Krauss, Anna Wherry, Anouk Cohen, Bhrigu Singh, Bican Polat, Caroline Block, Fouad Halbouni, Gregoire Hervouet-Zeibar, Hitomi Koyama, J. Andrew Bush, Mariam Banahi, Maya Ratnam, Megha Sedhev, Miki Chase, Neena Mahadev, Pooja Satyogi, Serra Hakyemez, Sidarthan Maunaguru, Sruti Chaganti, Vaibhav Saria, Victor Kumar, and Young-Gyung Paik. I still never send a thought into the world unless I have discussed it at some length with Ghazal Asif and Swayam Bagaria. At that time, Hopkins was a place of incredible interdisciplinary energy. I benefited immeasurably from conversations with faculty and peers in German, philosophy, and what was then the Humanities Center, and from the opportunity to study with Eckart Förster, Hent de Vries, Paola Marrati, and Rochelle Tobias.

This book is, among other things, a labour of love for my friends in Berlin whose names appear throughout these pages, sometimes pseudonymously, who have taught me how to live with literature. When I arrived in Germany for fieldwork, colleagues at the Freie Universität, at the Institut für Europäische Ethnologie at the Humboldt-Universität zu Berlin, and especially Ursula Rao and the Institut für Ethnologie at the Universität Leipzig, were among the first to welcome me and provided opportunities to discuss my research at the earliest stages. Paulo Farqui and Samantha Grenell-Zaidman on different occasions spent time with me in Germany and enlivened the work. I cannot sufficiently express my thanks to Christin Cieslak and Manisha Döbler for their work at various stages with interview data and in navigating bureaucracies.

I have been incredibly fortunate to have friends and colleagues willing to engage with my work and push my thinking forward. This book is very much a product of conversations with Adam Reed, Elizabeth Ferry, Emily Apter, Estelle Ferrarese, Lotte Buch Segal, Janet Carsten, Jocelyn Benoist, Michael D. Jackson, Michael Lambek, Michael Puett, Piergiorgio Donatelli, Nayanika Mookherjee, Sharika Thiranagama, and Tobias Kelly. It will no doubt be clear from the work that follows how much I have learned from and am inspired by Sandra Laugier. I could not ask for better fellow travellers in academic life than Canay Özden-Schilling, Cynthia Browne, Dwai Banarjee, Eric Hirsch, Nancy Khalil, Tom Özden-Schilling, and Yana Stainov, from whom I always learn so much.

Shalini Randeria has been a most cherished mentor, friend, and collaborator. Her invitation to spend a year writing at the Institut für die Wissenschaften vom Menschen came at a crucial time, not least because it afforded me the opportunity to be in dialogue with Ayşe Çağlar, Ezgi Yildiz, Filipe Calvão, Karl-Heinz Kohl, Holly Case, and Rannabir Samadar.

Teaching on the Committee on Degrees in Social Studies at Harvard proved one of the most rewarding experiences of my academic life. I am so thankful for the friendship and support of Bonnie Talbert, Hannah Winslow, Jona Hansen, Kate Anable, Katie Green, Lauren Doan, Nicholas Prevelakis, Sean Gray, and Shane Iverson. Nicole Newendorp lent me courage and a careful eye in the final stages of writing. My students have been an inspiration, particularly my advisees and participants in my seminars on the city and on language and power, in whose company I read and reread many of the texts I engage here. I am a far better reader and teacher because of the intellectual community I found at Harvard. In particular, the time I spent reading and debating with Brandon Terry, Charles Clavey, Daragh Grant, David Lebow, Don

Tontiplaphol, Gili Kliger, Katrina Forrester, Rebecca Ploof, Rosemarie Wagner, and Tracey Rosen has profoundly shaped my thinking, and much of what appears in the following pages is a response to lessons I have learned from them. I am also grateful for the program's generous contribution toward the subvention of this book.

The publication of *Moving Words* coincides with my move to Penn State University, where I have been fortunate to be welcomed by incredible colleagues across the College of the Liberal Arts. The Program in Jewish Studies has provided me with the intellectual space and support I needed both to bring this work to fruition and to begin to see the different possibilities it has opened for my future work.

I am enormously grateful to Jodi Lewchuk, my editor at University of Toronto Press, and to Michael Lambek, the series editor of Anthropological Horizons, for supporting the project and for their keen insights. An earlier version of chapter two was previously published as "The Prosody of Social Ties: Poetry and Fleeting Moments in Global Berlin" in *Current Anthropology*; I thank the University of Chicago Press for allowing me to reuse that material.

I would not know my way about in the world without my mother and father, Debbie and Norman Brandel, and without the balance my siblings Eric, Jamie, and now Amie bring to me. Kayla has ridden highs and lows of this book with me, held my hand, read every page. Her belief in me and her love make it possible for me to keep moving. And to my Ruth, for whom I prayed, I hope your life with be filled with joy, peace, and beloved books.

This book is dedicated to the memory of my four grandparents: Vittorio Orvieto (Z"l), Elias Brandel (Z"l), Dina Kornreich (Z"l), and Ruth Löwensohn (Z"l). The shattering of their worlds by Nazi violence led them and their families on paths that ran through Germany, Poland, Italy, the Netherlands, Czechoslovakia, South Africa, Australia, China, Ecuador, Palestine, and later the United States. It is only now, when they are gone, and I am older, that I am beginning to more fully appreciate their efforts to smuggle books, to carry with them stories, poems, nursery rhymes, and fables. Their memory will always be a blessing.

# MOVING WORDS

*Chapter One*

# Introduction: Berlin, City of Letters

One of a large and growing number of young artists who came to Berlin in pursuit of a literary life, Fabian arrived shortly after finishing university, attracted by what he had read of the city's history and its reputation for supporting creative work. We arranged to meet on the corner outside a popular bookshop near Savignyplatz in Charlottenburg, where he had been working for the better part of a year with his collaborators – his partner Grashina, a visual artist and writer who was born in Berlin, and a local publisher named Richarda – on the inaugural issue of a literary magazine. He was excited to tell me the first print run had already sold out in a few neighbourhood stores, that they were leaving to start work on the next issue in another city and would return only after a few months.

Their project was to document life on a single street; in this case, Kantstraße, the street that bisected the square where we stood. They wanted to trace how stories seemingly from different times and places arose with varying intensity with every step they took along the concrete. The group had been inspired by the stories they read of Franz Hessel, a flaneur who wove his own way through Berlin in the twenties, and by Walter Benjamin's well-known 1929 review of his *Spazieren in Berlin*. They had made walking the street the cornerstone of their creative practice, meeting the people who lived and worked there, listening to their stories, and drawing what Fabian described as literary connections between them. Those they met also became collaborators in the production of the magazine, offering interviews, photographs, or artistic works of their own. From their point of view, Fabian explained, the street was a fragment, though neither in the sense that it was a part of a coherent whole nor in the sense that these connections could be cobbled together in any linear way. Rather, the fragment alluded to the force of contingency and of possibility, to the fact that no totalizing imagining of what the city was or could be was possible.¹ It became their motto, a way of interpreting the often-incongruent worlds and histories they discovered, and the different ways they could cross one another. "Now we retire to the land of speed, coasting along on a modern odyssey," Fabian wrote in that first issue,

> The nomads, who look back on their own footprints, are long gone ... in the sallow light of the neon signs, slowly passing by as in fleeting still-life paintings, we can observe every corner, embracing them all making them more beautiful and worthy with our glance ... this city is an accumulation of completely unrelated artefacts. We delve into their beauty and try to reorder them anew. In this land of our time, the logic of the linear is replaced by the logic of fragments, the desire for fragments.

When I asked what made these connections literary, he pointed to an open window across the street on Paulsbornerstraße. "Nabokov could have lived in that apartment, and that would explain how you can hear the sounds of the trains in the novel. But it does not really matter whether this one turns out to be his. It could have been." I found myself thinking about a passage in *La Pensée Sauvage* where Lévi-Strauss remarks on the strong and arbitrary emotions inspired by tours of the houses of Goethe or Hugo, how the main thing was "not that the bed was the same one on which it is proved Van Gogh slept; all the visitor asks is to be shown it." For Fabian, the literary pointed to the untenability of drawing lines too sharply between what we take to be real and what fiction. "Between dreams," as he put it once, "and routines." The group's experiments took a variety of forms: maps made from the names of writers arranged like city streets (Nabokov lay at the intersection of Eise Ury and Helen Grun); a poem about the history of Berlin's Chinatown in the form of a takeout menu; a series of newspaper clippings about Berlin's Russian emigre population with dark black lines drawn through the text. More recently, Fabian had been giving walking tours, returning to Kantstraße each week to retrace their earlier work, and to see what new might emerge. The tours were hosted in conjunction with a local group of writers and critics, most of whom had come to Berlin in the last decade and who shared an interest in walking as a creative medium.

It was the tour's organizer, Paul, who put me in touch with Fabian when he learned about my fieldwork. Paul occasionally published works by local writers, and when I signed up for Fabian's next tour, he suggested I read a short piece that historian Manan Ahmed had recently written about finding ghosts in Charlottenburg.² In his essay, Ahmed describes how he was already familiar with firangi stories, with jinn and with churail from his childhood in Doha, when he came to Berlin. But unlike these, and unlike even the white ghosts of London, the ghosts in Berlin turned to him and spoke. The first time one spoke to him, "she said words I did not understand. She struggled to find another language. I did not know any that she knew. She lived nearby. Just three doors down." Ahmed began to learn about the neighbourhood from the ghost, a Polish survivor of the Shoah who points out to him that Nabokov's house on Paulsbornerstrasse was nearby, and Ahmed himself goes on to trace "the ghostly city outlined in Nabokov's Berlin crime novels." Only later does Ahmed encounter himself, or the version of himself who lived in Charlottenburg, as a ghost. When he first arrived in the city, he lived "mute and deaf," but now, another him had found a voice:

> I made no eye-contact. I saw no one. No one saw me. No one said anything to me. I walked un-noticed. A citizen of Berlin invisible to his neighbours, his fellows. Slowly, I began to show myself. I remember a gentleman in a car – desperate – yelling an address at me. I answered him. Relieved, he took off. He was the first person who saw me in Berlin … Emboldened, I started to show myself elsewhere. I began to find those brown and black spaces where ghosts hung out. I began to move in a crowd. They notice you in a crowd. Four brown people are noted on the U-Bahn. One day, there were eight of us and then we really got noticed. Being a ghost in Berlin had its advantages, sometimes.

Nabokov himself came to Berlin from Cambridge in 1922 and lived there until 1937. The outbreak of Civil War in Russia had led nearly half a million people to seek refuge in Berlin, and this influx helped cement the city's growing reputation as a centre for émigré intellectual life, especially in literary publishing and criticism. After the war, hyperinflation of the mark, fuelled by reparation payments and punitive trade policies, led the German bourgeoisie to look eastward. Lenin meanwhile was eager to acquire cheap books because of a shortage of ink and paper in his own country. German capital backed Russian publishing houses to acquire overvalued foreign currency. Russian language periodicals were cheap and widely circulated. By the middle of the 1920s, hundreds of new small publishers, salons, literary cafés, and readings circles had emerged on the scene.[3] In his favourite story from that period, aptly titled "A Guide to Berlin," Nabokov describes a series of everyday scenes from across the city – the black utility pipes that line the walls of the apartment building, giant tortoises being fed at the zoo, the unusual hands of the streetcar conductor – all sketched by an unnamed immigrant writer for a likewise unnamed friend while sitting in a pub called Löwenbrau. "It is of no interest," the writer's friend replies in the end, "what do trams and tortoises matter? And anyway, the whole thing is simply a bore. A boring, foreign city, and expensive to live in, too." While he listens to this opprobrium, the writer catches a glimpse of a child in a mirror in an apartment across the way, sitting on a green couch, looking back at the pair. "I can't understand what you see down there," the friend continues. "What indeed!" the writer thinks aloud, "how can I demonstrate to him that I have glimpsed somebody's future recollection?" The sentiment refracts an earlier moment in the story, when an encounter with a trolley becomes the impetus for reflection on the passing nature of things.

> The horse-drawn tram has vanished, so will the trolley, and some eccentric Berlin writer of the twenty-first century, wishing to portray our time, will go to a museum of technological history and locate a hundred-year-old streetcar ... Then he will go home and compile a description of Berlin streets in bygone days. Everything, every trifle, will be valuable and significant: the conductor's purse, the advertisement over the window, that peculiar jolting motion which our great-grandchildren will perhaps imagine ... I think that here lies the sense of literary creation: to portray ordinary objects as they will be reflected in the kindly mirrors of future times to find in the objects around us the fragrant tenderness that only posterity will discern and appreciate in the far-off times when every trifle of our plain everyday life will become exquisite and festive in its own right: the times when a man who might put on the most ordinary jacket of today will be dressed up for an elegant masquerade.

This literary work, which Nabokov later describes as "the capacity to wonder at trifles,"[4] continually rubs up against the friend's sober scepticism. Each encounter with ordinary objects, with workmen's swinging mallets, or Christmas trees, or cobalt-coloured mailboxes, is a reminder of the contested nature of things. From the start, literary critics have debated whether, or in what sense, any particular object the writer describes was found that way, made by Germans, part of the equipment of their boring, foreign city; or whether it was already Russian, transformed by literary magic into a missive to the future; or even, since we are reading it now, if it were already a recollection.[5]

His last Berlin novel, *The Gift* (Dar), tells of a young poet, Fyodor Godunov-Cherdyntsev, whose family comes to Berlin after the October Revolution and whose literary career begins with a scarcely noticed book of poems, evolves through the production of a critical biography lampooning Lenin's favourite writer, Nikolay Chernyshevsky, and culminates with the synthesis of everything earlier in his desire to write a "classic novel, with 'types,' love, fate, conversations."[6] A book, as many commentators have pointed out, rather like *The Gift* itself. These literary forces also seemingly conspire to bring him alongside his love, Zina, one of the few readers who bought his first book of poems. The great Nabokov scholar Brian Boyd describes the Berlin of *The Gift* as filled with "characters from other eras or other climes (Siberian exiles, Tibetan lamas, Russian Old Believers on the shore of Lob-Nor), a host of St. Petersburg and émigré and German figures, historically real, actual but disguised, purely fictional or doubly imaginary, secondary, subsidiary or downright peripheral, made to live in only a line or two, or allowed a hundred pages to themselves."[7] In a justifiably famous and terse foreword written several decades later in 1962, however, Nabokov warns his reader that, though they share many qualities, he is not and never was Fyodor Godunov-Cherdyntsev, that he did not, at least at the time, have the "knack of recreating Berlin or its colony of expatriates as radically and ruthlessly" as he had done with other places in his later writings, and that we should therefore not confuse designer with design. History, he confesses, does nevertheless shine through artistry from time to time.

Literature continues to carry people to and through Berlin on irregular and intersecting paths. Some, like Nabokov, were great writers. Others remained relatively unknown or had only oblique relationships with the formal literary landscape, having been excluded or having chosen not to participate. Many I met during my time in the city were newly, or relatively newly, arrived from the other parts of Europe, the United States, or southern Germany, and were frequently of economic privilege and chasing after bourgeois fantasies of creative freedom. Some were artists who, despite having lived their whole lives in Germany, were constantly told they did not count or that they counted by virtue of their belonging elsewhere. Still others were among the rising numbers of refugees seeking asylum from a "welcoming" class of left-liberal artists and activists, and from a state eager to perform reparations for Nazi atrocities and to access pools of labour, even as it increasingly adopted exclusionary policies and rhetorical stances. There were celebrated and "seditious" poets, cheered by an aging public in converted villas, made up primarily of older "real" Berliners who had participated in one way or another in the political foment of 1960s or of the 1980s, and some of whom now found themselves increasingly pushed to the margins of "their" city. There were those too who fell through the cracks, those who were waiting for the right moment in which to speak, and those who refused the terms of their invitation entirely.

This book is an endeavour to think anthropologically about crossings of this kind, in time and in space, where literature provides a footing in a world constituted by a multiplicity of real possibilities. It describes some of the ways literature was seeded in everyday life in Berlin at a moment when the city's reputation as a world capital for global art and as a cosmopolitan destination for migrants and travellers was growing, the culmination of a transition to what had been branded the "New Berlin."[8] Across its chapters, I track how the movement of literature and the movement of people through history and geography came to inflect one another, and I try to understand what it was about Berlin that gave rise to so many multivalent threads of encounter. It shows how literature was not a domain of life set apart from reality; that even fiction was lived as a region of the real. And it explores in what sense characters like Fabian and Nabokov, Ahmed and Fyodor could be said to share a world or a city each calls Berlin.

One conventional way of reading these stories is by opposing literary worlds and those with which we are otherwise familiar; the Berlin of *The Gift*, of Fabian's magazine, and Ahmed's ghost stories, with the Berlin of the real world. Interpreters have conventionally assumed that the two constituted fully formed perspectives on reality, normally opposed to one another, but entangled in the person of an author or a reader. The idea is that literature, or even literary uses of words, obtains to an extraordinary, rarefied domain of social action, offering an escape from reality and the humdrum of everyday life. Literature is often seen as a register that breaks with the ordinary sense of a word or phrase and which can express an otherwise inexpressible experience. It has been imagined that relatively strict boundaries can be drawn between these worlds and that we might know well enough which objects, which practices, and which signs belong where and what protocols to follow to separate them.[9] Behind these assumptions lays an even deeper conceit, that it was possible to axiomatically insinuate a gap between words and the world; that language was constituted by mere or inadequate signs, external to inner experience and to the world in which literature is one more or less felicitous point of view.[10] In other words, that language stands between us, like a screen dividing inaccessible, supersensible substrata, that there is more or less "touch of the real" to it.[11] This ideology relies on a picture of language that takes public and private experiences as stable and strict alternatives.[12] It thinks of words as pointing beyond themselves to an autonomous region of immediate experience.

A parallel claim was regularly made about the worlds of the migrant and of the German, who though they shared a city, nevertheless were thought to belong to potentially commensurate though essentially different realities, shaped by the particularity of their historical forms of life, their language, and that language's philosophical grammar. In public talk (and in scholarship), one found an enduring (if at times tacit) presumption that these boundaries could be known in advance, that there were texts, practices, and people that belonged by their nature either to German or to Germany, or somewhere else and to some other language. The assumption was that there are, at least theoretically, unmixed languages from which we start that can be mapped in most cases onto the borders of a polity. Even where these possibilities were taken to be hybridized or shown to be themselves heterogenous, this way of speaking itself belies the belief that at bottom, linguistic worlds remain combinations of already formed, and ultimately hypostatized, identities. More often than not, their differences resolved into tropes of racial types and national traditions,[13] what Zora Neale Hurston referred to as the convenient typical. One could read about writers who straddled life in two places or languages, or who, like the exiled or Heimatlos, remain existentially caught in-between otherwise already fashioned, unmixed worlds. According to this logic, "foreign" and German worlds could only ever be externally related, inaccessible to one another except by means of imperfect approximations and by forging equivalences that necessarily deform one or both. Linguistic and cultural practices were made commensurable by making them count as literature.[14] Boundaries were naturalized, even by those who considered them porous and shifting. They remained the point of departure, an unavoidable if regrettable heuristic.

The people I came to know moved through spaces where a dominant, liberal linguistic ideology took these divides to be a given, and often summoned literature to bridge otherwise separate worlds by more felicitously evoking distant cultures, by communicating something they supposedly share.[15] Within this discursive regime, literature was treated like a class of expression more closely approaching an ideal language, and which meant that it was capable of better responding to failures in ordinary communication, the usual difficulties we have expressing ourselves and understanding each other. Writers and texts were rendered iconic of traditions, bearers of culture (Kulturträger) or tradition,[16] providing a glimpse of an ever-receding world on a distant shore. A condition of being carried over that divide was that texts and people alike performed scripts of authenticity in exchange for "welcome" under the sign of cosmopolitan projects like world literature. Paradoxically, as other anticolonial critics point out, these translations held out impossible standards of authenticity,[17] structured according to European and Christian models – an "ordeal of language"[18] in which acceptance or denial of such demands carries profound political stakes. The stories of the people I met, however, ultimately contest both sets of claims. Many felt they lived their lives in the company of literature. Its characters walked the same streets, and one could visit its times and its settings. Relationships with neighbours or kin or even oneself could take on a literary quality.

Suppositions about the external relationship of literary and real worlds on the one hand and German and migrant worlds on the other were deeply connected in Berlin, a city whose reputation as a *global* city is inextricably linked with its life as a *literary* city. Berlin's status as a world capital for literature and for expatriation has ebbed and flowed over time, but the recurrence and potency of their coincidence is essential to understanding the micropolitics of everyday life in the metropole. Cities like Frankfurt and Leipzig have arguably been more important for the national literary landscape. But in popular discourses in Germany and beyond, Berlin has come to represent a certain potential, or yearning[19] for globalized cultural production that is integral to the politics of mobility. Understanding this identification has become more urgent in recent years, in the wake of the Chancellor Angela Merkel's infamous declaration that "multiculturalism failed, absolutely failed" [Multikulti ist gescheitert, absolut gescheitert][20] and in the face of resurgent populist nationalism across a German-led European Union.[21]

More than any other German city, writers from around the world seemed to find themselves in Berlin. And as the most enduring symbol of national culture, the institutions of literature were regularly leveraged to facilitate and govern the movement of peoples and to re-mobilize histories of difference-making. Though a swell of nationalist, anti-migrant sentiment has spread again across the continent, literature's historically privileged status has meant that migrant *writers* had been afforded, at least nominally, rights to the city and even expedited asylum status, while others are regularly and visibly excluded. The terms of writers' "inclusion" were unsurprisingly uneven and deeply fraught, and looked rather different from those of others who come to Germany by other means. But this story's position at the heart of a liberal political discourse of welcome made it essential to ongoing discussions of the wider migrant "crisis" today.

Berlin's claims to worldliness were tightly bound to this story about its literariness as well, since conventional sociological definitions of the global city[22] do not yet fully bear out in this context, or at least did not during the time of my principal fieldwork.[23] The rhetorical emphasis was instead on the supposed flourishing of linguistic and cultural difference. The difference between Berlin and Germany, critic and linguist Yasemin Yildiz writes, is that "'Berlin' is written in many languages, in many different places, and circulates at times far from the city itself."[24] I knew many Berliners who cited Mark Twain's infamous lament, half-joking, partly with pride and partly in anguish, that one could learn anything in Berlin except for German. I argue that these nationalist disavowals of the nation are especially salient in a context where one is expected to habitually perform repudiation of the nation to commemorate past crimes of nationalism. This is what it meant when writers reminded me repeatedly that "Berlin is not Germany," at least whenever talk turned to the politics of migration. In other words, if Berlin was a global city because of the presence of migrant artists and foreign cultural objects, this rhetorical distancing from Germany allowed for oblique nationalistic gestures.

Most often, the diversity of the culture market was read as a sign of national catharsis, testament to the fact that Germany was working through its troubled past, the establishment of what in Germany is called a culture of welcome (Wilkommenskultur) as reparation (Wiedergutmachung), simultaneously prophylactic and apology. The braiding together of a literary view of the world with the politics of national memory meant that it was possible to express an "acceptable" national pride in a context where overt demonstrations of nationalism were usually considered an affront to historical guilt.[25] In the forums and salons, reading groups and seminars I attended, invitations were often framed explicitly in a comparative register, as an interest in the plights of others because of a particularly German burden of having committed and suffered the worst of all possible human atrocities. In practice, these ubiquitous and monumental acts of memorialization served to obscure the more everyday racialized exclusions perpetrated by and in its shadow.[26] This is not just because they distract from concrete forms of violence. At their very heart they enact powerful erasures. If cosmopolitanism was posed as a response to the threat of return of fascism, it nevertheless functioned via a paradeigmatic translation of historical contexts by making them commensurate with and measuring them against the suffering of Shoah and its modes of remembrance, itself made into an impossible metaphysical standard.[27]

The conjunction of national practices of remembrance with migrant history remains understudied in professional academic circles. The archives of migration call, Yildiz and Rothberg argue,[28] for a "reconceptualization of memory as transcultural that leaves behind residually and unwittingly ethnicized models of remembrance and founds itself instead on a social and political form of collectivity." These conjunctions are by no means new. Talk about Berlin, and by extension (and rhetorically under cover) Germany's and Germans' capacity to host and support the flourishing of worldly creativity belongs to a two-century-long history of ideological transposition. In the eighteenth and nineteenth centuries, an ascendant cultural bourgeoisie (Bildungsbürgertum) crafted a national imaginary in its own image by promoting a series of central metaphors of "inwardness" (Innerlichkeit) – concepts such as Geist, Kultur, and Bildung – to the status of "lexical totems" of German identity.[29] In the absence of a fully centralized administrative state, resistant to the encroachment of Napoleonic power associated with classicisms,[30] and struggling to compete with colonial expansionism, German elites associated national greatness with cultural (rather than economic or political) achievement. Literature, and in particular world literature, became a way of articulating a national aspiration for global domination; despite political weakness, Germany's "openness to others" meant it could still claim a role as "the center and arbiter of world culture."[31]

This cultural greatness was in turn justified through genealogical ties (linguistic, philosophical, and racial) to parts of the world beyond the prosaic planes of Europe, and in particular with the cultural heights of ancient India and Persia, over which England and France could not lay the same spiritual, biological, and philological claims.[32] The movement of literatures relied on a powerful idea that languages and the cultural worlds they implied were discrete entities, internally homogenous, and separated by borders that were "obvious and based on lack of mutual intelligibility,"[33] that they were property, typifying of those who spoke them, and that equivalents could be found across them. Among the world's languages, German was particularly supple, romantic nationalists ventured, capable of bearing within it a fidelity to other worlds without losing itself in the process. Johann Wolfgang Goethe, for example, wrote that it is "part of the nature of the German to respect everything foreign for its own sake and to adapt himself to foreign idiosyncrasies. This and the great suppleness of our language make German translations particularly accurate and satisfying." Johann Herder claimed that in Germany, unlike in France or Italy, the muse's fundamental character is her capacity to imitate: "To this end we have in our power an admirable means, our language; it can be for us what the hand is for the person who imitates art."[34] Even Edward Sapir says that "with Heine, one is under the illusion that the universe speaks German."[35]

The implications of this worldview far exceeded rarefied domains explicitly marked as literary. B. Venkat Mani has documented how in Germany a "Faustian pact with books"[36] took the whole universe to be "arranged like a library, the world indistinguishable from the book.[37] "Not only books," observed the Romantic poet Novalis, "everything can be translated." Although material conditions have changed, this ideology is alive in different forms today and is inseparable from contemporary modes of managing of human mobility that extend far outside self-consciously defined literary spaces.[38] Germany continues to invest considerably in its translation regime. The domestic literature market sees ten thousand translations a year, accounting for almost 14 per cent of new titles, a plurality of which comes through Berlin. UNESCO maintains that German literary works are the most translated in the world, thanks to a concerted effort on the part of the state and institutions such as the Goethe Institute, whose mission is the promotion of German language and "cultural exchange." Many of the people I write about who were engaged in literary projects earned most of their wages doing translation work, literary and otherwise. It was part and parcel of everyday routines and ordinary habits of thought, earning a living, tending to chores, even walking the street. Its practices were ready at hand in a thousand daily performances, and very often it was a principal resource to which people turned to make sense of their encounters with different times and places. Nowhere was this more profoundly felt, more urgent, than in the ways literary translation shadowed thinking about migration. The desire to bring texts to Germany via translation cut across the ways people imagined human mobility: sometimes with the grain, sometimes against it. But this held as much for movements in time – the impress or feel of history and national memory, its modes of presentation, often its contradictions – as it did for those in space. The intertwining of these two dimensions is a major theme of this book.

**Difficult Pasts and Cosmopolitan Futures**

While literature might seem an unusual entry point into questions of human movement, at least for an anthropologist, its tendency in Berlin to arise in important moments in talk, to be a touch point in the ways people thought about and discussed difference, and its power as a social institution make it unavoidable. Sociolinguists working on globalization and migration regimes have for some time argued that the study of human mobility cannot be disentangled from the mobility of linguistic resources across space and time,[39] and have shown how processes of standardization and hierarchization continue longstanding projects of empire and nation-building. Cultural anthropologists meanwhile have been contributing enormously rich ethnographic descriptions of the forms of governmentality emergent from the European "migrant crisis" and to migration and refugee studies more generally.[40] Among the most important trends in the field has been the effort to resist the categorical fetishism reflected in German and European discourse, and to offer sustained critique of the representational economy through which their borders are policed.[41] At the same time, anthropology's own "politics of life," its rush to contribute to care, its attempts to "do good" often re-inscribe hierarchies reminiscent of "apolitical" humanitarianism.[42] Mobility is increasingly managed as migration[43] through regimes of care of which anthropology is commonly a part and which produce the "morally legitimate suffering body" against universal standards to be apprehended by biopolitical techniques of governance alongside the labour of nurses, doctors, and NGO workers. Miriam Ticktin has potently argued that the force of this moral legitimacy, which compels action in the name of humanity, relies on constitutive exceptions and exclusions – for example, of the exploited, labouring body that constitutes the rule – and so engenders new forms and practices of violence.[44] Building on this work, I take literature to be another site through which this new humanity is produced.

Like Ticktin, I am interested in how changes in political economy, colonial history, and new structures of international governance have made care work into a privileged site for enacting politics. If in France biopolitical regimes of care are particularly resonant, in Berlin, care for cultural differences was a significant preoccupation. Cultural institutions, and in particular literary institutions, played an outsized role in shaping the politics of migration. Their conspicuous absence from much social science literature is therefore curious. The questions such practices posed were of course different from those in clinics or in bureaucratic offices, but the relationship between them is crucial to the operation of such regimes. In the sites where I worked, the question that arose again and again is whether literature can prove a site of resistance in addition to control. Were there literary practices, the editors of recent issue of *Parse* asked, "that [did] not unwittingly serve to objectify and (re)fetishize the otherness of migrants and refugees whose material and practical circumstances already render them objects of the power of the systems and apparatuses of bordering?"[45] If so, the question is what these practices look like.[46]

In January of 2012, an Iranian refugee named Mohammed Rahsepar hanged himself in a reception centre in the southern city of Würzburg. Following his death, a group of young asylum seekers sewed their lips shut in protest, leading to a widely reported spread of tent vigils throughout the country. In March, a group of fifty left Würzburg and walked for a month across Germany to Berlin, coming to rest at a tent protest in Oranienplatz. The O-Platz protest continued to galvanize action against deportation and the Residenzpflicht (a legal restriction of movement that forced thousands into cramped camps), and quickly became a symbol of political mobilization among liberal and left-wing groups. Just five years earlier, in 2007, *Der Spiegel* had announced Berlin's comeback as a Weltstadt,[47] a world city. But this status now took on a new valence. As millions arrived on Europe's shores seeking asylum, Chancellor Merkel couched her initial response in terms of Germany's moral responsibility to open its doors to refugees, given its earlier crimes. She also spoke about Germany's economic prosperity and political stability, and its commitment to the rule of law. Merkel at first paid a political price for the "openness" of her position, leaving her to defend her right flank from increasingly popular far-right parties about which so much as has been written of late. While her government did accept a greater proportion of refugees than other countries in the European Union, the law was quickly mobilized against vulnerable asylum seekers in a number of ways, while migrants confronted countless daily barbs and injustices.

These events set off a bevy of book publications, public art events, critical essays, and award nominations, a veritable industry of literary projects dedicated to "making sense" of the situation. Literature was just one of the prominent ways the regime distinguished desirable and undesirable migrants, and writers played a prominent role in shaping public perception of the situation facing minoritized people more broadly. The literary texts that circulated through the city at the time theatricalized this politics, its ways of looking, talking, and listening, reinforcing the casual ways difference was perceived. In 2015, Jenny Erpenbeck's novel *Gehen, Ging, Gegangen* (translated somewhat awkwardly as *Go, Went, Gone)* took local and international literary circles by storm. The novel follows the story of Richard, a retired professor, who reads Proust, Dostoevsky, and Ovid and socializes with other intellectuals. Lamenting his fate (the loss of his wife, his abandonment by a young lover, the end of his career), he learns about a group of ten African refugees living in Oranienplatz who have decided to go on hunger strike to protest the European Union's asylum policies. Seeing that they too are "out of work," Richard befriends some of the men, who he learns have followed different trajectories from Burkina Faso, Nigeria, Ghana, and Niger. He gives each a Greek name – Tristan, the Olympian, Apollo – and teaches them a few words of German, provides them with bus passes, accompanies them on chores around the city, and struggles to learn about the conditions of their flight and the places they left. He realizes his questions elicit answers "he neither expects nor knows what to do with."[48]

Newspapers described the novel as offering a "crash course in refugee studies," and as "reflective entertainment." The *Berliner Zeitung* wrote that the book's ambition was to make "the fate of Berlin's refugees visible [sichtbar]." In a review published in the *Frankfurter Allgemeine Zeitung* titled "We Became, Will Be, Are, Visible," literary critic Friedmar Apel describes "almost comedic" scenes of "understanding and misunderstanding," a reminder that literature is "the medium of understanding, [in which] the foreign and the own-most [das Eigen] prove to be two sides of a context." One well-known reviewer writes that "having grown up and lived in East Germany before reunification … Richard and his friends are closer, perhaps, than many Europeans to understanding the uneasiness of the refugees' lives." Most academic and journalistic accounts of the protests, at least in Europe, emphasized an eruption into consciousness made possible by literature.[49] The circulation of images from the camps was said to suddenly, as if for the first time, make the conditions facing refugees in Germany apparent. In truth, I did not know anyone in Berlin for whom such novels and articles made something newly appear out of thin air. What they did produce were small shifts in perception. They naturalized stories about learned, well-meaning Germans who could be brought to see the error of their indifference and, in fact, whose ignorance about cultural others cut across the failings in their own kin relations. Or stories about the commensurability of "foreign" experiences to those of East Germany, how life in divided Berlin seemingly prepared its residents to see aspects of life elsewhere.[50]

While literature can certainly affect aesthetic shifts, different ways of looking at and talking about the world, new (and not so new) arrivals and the violence directed against them have been hypervisible in German politics for decades. If anything, hypervisibility was often conjoined with invisibility to produce commoditized icons of difference and to effect minoritization.[51] This book calls for attention to literature's role in producing these shifting optics.[52] Among the arguments I pursue to this end is that visibility is too often taken to be

Introduction: Berlin, City of Letters  17

a straightforward political good. Visibility can be a risky prospect, and invisibility is not always dissolvable into bourgeois anonymity promised by modernity. Even more distressingly, this language of crisis itself, the claim of a sudden eruption into consciousness, becomes another way of summoning "the ever-reinvigorated and convulsive recalibration of strategies" of bordering.[53] This language centred on the event responds to what Nicolas de Genova describes as "a permanent epistemic instability within the governance of transnational human mobility, which itself relies on the exercise of a power over classifying, naming, and partitioning migrants/refugees, and the more general multiplication of subtle nuances and contradictions among the categories that regiment mobility." My concern then is less with the opposition between grand ruptures in what can and cannot be seen[54] and more with peoples' ordinary struggles to make themselves intelligible, including to themselves, and which cannot be formed but in relations with others.

Literature could still be a site of profound struggle and reflexivity, though, thus far, rarely (if ever) through dramatic breaks from the vicissitudes of everyday life. Some writers took the opportunity instead to explore the continuities between literary work, the everyday politics of translation, and the temporality of crisis. For example, Teju Cole addressed an audience on the occasion of the Internationaler Literaturpreis (a prize awarded by the Haus der Kulturen der Welt for a first translation into German). He spoke of a resonance between the etymology of the English word *translation* and the German word *übersetzen* – to carry over or traverse – and the images of Flüchtlingshilfer[55] carrying the bodies of refugees out of the water. He retold a well-known story of a German boat captain arrested for carrying asylum seekers onto her boat and which, because it takes place on water, reminded him of an earlier story, when in 1943 Danish Jews were helped to flee across the water to Sweden. For Cole, good translation, like good literature generally, is linked to such efforts, because both involve a moral courage in which an act of carrying over is taken up by virtue of a claim on shared human form of life. Arriving on the other shore is often a "return journey … to some part of its scattered family like a prodigal child." To have one's work translated, for Cole, was to recognize within it something it already contained but which could not earlier have been seen. Far from any loss in translation, he says, the German translator of his *Open City* carried the book back into German. He quoted from Dany Laferrière, who, when asked whether he was a Haitian writer, explained that he "took the nationality of [his] reader." "Is the work of literature connected in any way to the risks certain citizens undertake to save others? I think so ... because acts of language themselves can be acts of courage."

> Great claims are often made for literature ... [but] there's no true correlation, in the scientific sense, between literary practice, and the way we treat others, so long as we define them as others ... I wonder if there isn't in fact a greater likelihood that those cultures that pride themselves on their literary achievements are also the ones that bomb others. It seems sometimes that we have libraries here so that we may shower death on them over there ... what we can go to literature for is both larger and smaller than clichés about how it makes us more empathetic ... Literature cannot, no matter how finely expressed, change the minds of the little fascists who are once more overrunning this continent. So then what is it good for? ... Literature can save a life, just one life at a time, and that life is yours ... good literature has saved at least one life. Mine. And not once and for all, but only at certain moments ... Inside this small thing called literature I have found reminders to negate frontiers and carry others across, and reminders of others that carry me too. That's quite a scary thing. Imagine ... that you have to carry someone else, or have to be carried by someone else.[56]

Like the texts themselves, the institutions of literature played a critical role in this management regime and in its resistance.[57] Despite tightening legal conditions, writers were granted special privileges. Facilitated by organizations like the German PEN Centre, writers could apply for expedited asylum status; were eligible for special grant monies, housing and training programs; and could mobilize an extensive activist network of support services. Accessing these pathways, however, required that writers perform their suffering and their alterity according to anticipated forms of expression, evidenced in the kinds of questions people asked, in the standards of translation afforded their work, and in the scripted expectations for performances of difference and suffering. Chapter three explores how, in the face of this scrutiny of their language practices,[58] writers responded in a variety of ways. There were writers who accepted these terms of intelligibility for themselves. And there were those who refused or resisted these stipulations, choosing instead to remain unknown, to wait, holding for the right context in which to express themselves.

*Cosmopolitanization and Literary Marketplaces*

Conditions were particularly ripe for literary migrants in part because writers and readers could, I was often told, sustain themselves more cheaply in Berlin and because new journals, publishers and salons could manage with less capital and donated labour. This view reflected normative assumptions about who could earn a livelihood in what ways, who could move and how,[59] and many people who articulated these views were likewise wholly aware of the contradictions involved. But there was a feeling shared by many that things were possible in Berlin that were not in Paris or London or Munich. When the Berlin Wall fell in 1989, wide availability of cheap housing, relatively low costs of living, and a reputation for subversive writing and publishing began to draw thousands of artists to the city, and especially to the central East. These shadows proved attractive for many new arrivals.[60]

Buildings and state-owned businesses were rapidly converted to new uses, in several cases to house sponsored cultural projects. While population growth was on the decline in many parts of the country and continent, rapidly gentrifying neighbourhoods like Prenzlauer Berg started to experience birthrate expansion. Subsequent demographic changes have been marked. Since 2004, the rate of foreign migration to Berlin has increased approximately by half, more or less uniformly across all boroughs, alongside the rate of transient visitation, in both cases largely in parallel with a significant increase in the share of twenty-four to thirty-four-year-olds in the city.[61] The city not only boasted high rates of positive net migration (one of the highest in Europe), but also substantial rates of population turnover. Much of Berlin's newfound economic productivity was tied to growth in creative industries reliant on transitory young newcomers, both for the labour they provide and discursively as part of Berlin's appeal.[62] At the time, the city has continued to hold high levels of debt, and the housing market, especially for qualified low-rent options, has been curtailed by a massive shift away from rental properties to what are called Wohnungseigentum – condominiums – resulting in a reduction of the number of available properties by 125,000 in ten years.[63]

One of the most striking features of the economic situation in Berlin though was that impersonal market forces had not yet devoured its thousands of independent bookstores, publishers, and salons. Large institutional projects often sat alongside smaller, humbler, and more mundane scribbles that were easier to miss. Far from the large black-glass buildings that hosted international literature festivals, an NGO advocating for better education and employment opportunities for women, Baufachfrau, had begun turning Berlin into a "sustainable" and "ecological" library, hollowing out trees in Prenzlauer Berg and equipping them with bookshelves so that residents could exchange books with neighbours and passers-by. In cafes, books were used as shelves, holding up other art works or plants. Under bridges in Alexanderplatz, poets read their work outside into portable microphones, as crowds shuffled into street buses, while musicians played on the tracks. On the S-bahn, groups of artists jumped from the platform and rode along to the next stop, playing music, singing, reading poems or selling papers, and quickly escaped before the controller came to check their tickets. Like in other parts of the world, in neighbourhood bookstores, scores gathered to have dinner, drink, and share stories. In living rooms, reading groups discussed the new list of Booker prize winners, exchanged sympathies for lost family members, and complained about their jobs. Walking tours recovered literary artefacts of the city and read them aloud to groups of onlookers. Writers sprawled couplets and aphorisms on urban ruins, walls were adorned with plaques marking the homes and favoured haunts of famous writers, and streets were named for celebrated authors.

For all its power and reach, many still felt that global capital had not exhausted all possibilities for social experience.[64] Independent booksellers often thanked strict fixed-pricing regulations and shared wholesale distribution technology for their survival. Without the structural iniquities borne of differential access to stock, cost, and delivery times, neighbourhood stores, they felt, succeeded by forming lasting relationships with their patrons. Books are regulated differently from any other market in Germany. They have a special legal status defining their "conflictual character" as cultural goods and commodities and specifically structured copyright protections. All facets and sides of their production and sale are represented by a single trade association, the Börsenverein des Deutschen Buchhandels. Within the juridical regime, bourgeois economic analyses, and in everyday talk in bookshops, aesthetic and cultural value were thought to offer resistance to capitalist encroachment, evidenced (apparently) by the relative stability of neighbourhood booksellers (Kiezbuchläden) and publishers, the "diversity" of products sold, and the face-to-face relations some describe as the "village in the global city." The Börsenverein is itself explicit that "cultural diversity in Germany is largely shaped by the existence and activities of the many smaller independent publishers." This diversity is supported in turn by the large number of writers and readers who pass through Berlin as literary tourists, to collect awards, read their work, facilitate translations, or meet with publishers.

Classics of social theory have taught that literature in the era of mass-print technology services a national "fantasy of communion" not borne out in everyday life,[65] and that life in the city under capital is straightforwardly marked by an acceleration that leads to homogenizing anonymity and alienation or else to supermodernity proliferating "non-places."[66]

But in Berlin, the gamble was that neighbourhood bookshops could still be posed as sites of struggle against these tendencies. One of my majors concerns in this book is to show how the stranger sociality of reading publics[67] generated by print capitalism, at least conventionally conceived,[68] intersects these face-to-face networks. The transitory nature of urban life under global capital also meant the regular production of relatively fleeting social ties. But even this situation was considered well suited to certain sorts of literary projects,[69] and in this way, could not always read as a straightforward sign of the degeneration of sociality and alienation. In chapter two, I show how certain forms of verbal art like slam poetry, often identified with Berlin's migrant populations, flourished in part because of their affinity with these conditions. Rather than assume, however, that ephemeral relationships were necessarily degraded or failed versions of enduring, albeit alienated ones, I make a case that a more felicitous account would be sensitive to a heterogeneity of meanings. My interlocutors connected forms of sociality emerged from literary circulation outside strict market exchange with the sonic materiality of language – the ways being present to hear voices, shifts in tone, volume, and pitch were essential to the movement of texts and to the kinds of relationships this movement engendered.

The class-inflected nature of these processes had downstream structural effects as well. It has been suggested that beginning already in 1989 and accelerating in the wake of the great recession, experiences of material disenfranchisement, especially among the working classes, are increasingly expressed in nationalist and populist language because capital, the upper classes, and the political elite have all been "cosmopolitanized." In other words, their class interests no longer align with welfare-state formation. The narrowing of the domain of the political, its hollowing out by expertise, flows from the globalization and financialization of capital.[70] What is more, the process of cosmopolitanization so ubiquitously identified with Berlin was premised on fundamental exclusions, especially of those who rely on state programs. In his pathbreaking ethnography among young right-wing extremists in East Berlin, many of whom relied on welfare-for-work, Nitzan Shoshan describes how the labour involved in rehabilitating German nationhood "grounds the very specters that it struggles so strenuously to exclude at its very core and betrays its own inevitable incompleteness." The management regime that holds these youths and their illicit expressions of nationalism at the margins of society is meant to quarantine "the dangerous potentialities of emergent national imaginaries in the reunited Berlin Republic." The fractal recursions through which these bounds of legitimate politics are produced and policed, Shoshan shows, go hand in hand with new forms of social marginalization that issue from global de-industrialization and financialization.

Though most of my time was spent closer to the centre of the city than the Treptow-Köpenick neighbourhood where Shoshan worked, the two sets of stories are deeply, even dialectically, interconnected. Such exclusions lie at the very heart of the success of the narrative of cosmopolitan Berlin, even as this story's success undermines itself. By 2014, international media had decided that the allure of Berlin had passed, a sentiment quickly echoed in the German press. "Berlin soll nicht mehr cool sein"[71] one headline read, "der Strich traf mitten ins Herz."[72] The popular assumption was that as the cost of living in Berlin increased, artists, and particularly vulnerable artists, would need to find somewhere to relocate. So far, however, this has not come to pass, the city's reputation had not been supplanted, and gentrification has continued unabated. Rent has more than doubled in a decade. Utility costs, privatized by liberal city governments in the 1990s, have also dramatically increased. Housing rights continue to be a major issue, as artists and left-wing squatters have openly clashed with city officials over access to property.[73] And in the same period, far-right political activity has become increasingly visible in the city centre over time. When neo-Nazi marches reached the city centre in 2016, literary institutions took the lead in staging public discussions and education programs in response. Neighbourhood bookstores in particular were instrumental in fomenting political action. Shop owners used customer lists to mobilize protests and held town hall discussions in their stacks. Several had their windows broken and their walls graffitied.[74] Several people told me this was only natural, that bookshops were spaces where social life changes because people gathered there and encountered multiple voices.

**An Ethnography of Literature**

In these ways and others, literature was integral to the ways people ordinarily thought and talked about how language works, and how they perceived difference (historical and cultural). It was crucial for the formation of an ever-shifting public lexicon used to mark difference – both in the reuse of older terms like a Leitkultur (a "shared" set of values), integration, and diversity, in the generation of new terms like "Migrationshintergrund" (migration background) that track these boundaries across generations, and in "postmigrant" interventions aimed at complicating who counts under categorizing regimes.[75] As Sharon Dodua Otoo[76] observed in a recent column for the Goethe

Institute, these racializing discourses tend to proliferate nouns in particular. Nouns like "Rasse" (race), "Ethnie" (ethnicity), and "Hautfarbe" (skin colour) are used according to this linguistic ideology, she writes, as if they were "immutable characteristics" of persons, as if they named essences, as if they labelled the furniture of the world. Debate broke out over the use of the term Rasse in the provision for equal protection under the law in the German Constitution.[77] Activists and political leaders argued that the use of the term gave the impression of fact prior to a process, a supposition itself grounded in racist ideology. Many called for replacing the word with a participle; Otto suggests Rassifizierung, racialization, would be a fitting change.

These nouns and their logic were embedded in the language of the liberal cultural institutions for which Berlin is now famous, that claimed the city – in the words of one salon's operator and promotional materials – as a "free port for literature," a place where "arose innumerable encounters with what Goethe called 'world literature': a network of awareness and recognition of the other as an equal." But if a governing ideology assumed that crossing sharply marked boundaries required an extraordinary event of translation, a bit of literary magic, this book shows how in practice, languages and literatures were already (and always had been) found in the company of other languages and literatures, and that literary crossings, mistranslation, and quotation were normal conditions of life in language, not aberrations from it.

I argued earlier that literature often figures in social theory and in public discourse as a barrier marking boundaries of intelligibility, or conversely, as a bridge between worlds. In either case, the guiding assumption is that context is relatively bounded, stable, and pre-given. My own sense of these scenes, however, is that they instead demonstrate that context is never given in advance – that each use of literature is a coming into being of context. The stories in this book emphasize that context is continually being built in human worlds, that it is indeterminate and immanent to the human forms of life through which it is produced and reproduced. This is true even of the sense of being fenced off or separated from experiences of myself or another, from the possibilities that others inhabit.[78] Rather than think that what was at stake in these moments was a resolution of frames of reference, whether literary or everyday, German or migrant, I show how worlds were in the process of being made, how multiple possibilities were experienced in the neighbourhood of one another. Put differently, the examples in this book show the interpolation through which context is built and in which the possibility of a future together is on the line. Context is not so much a rigid frame drawing a boundary between words and the world but a weaver's loom that brought a world into being. The city comes to define the shape of the literary as much as literature comes to define how Berlin is experienced.

If traditions like ethnopoetics have offered important routes to understanding literary performance through ethnography,[79] Adam Reed has pointed out that among cultural anthropologists working in European contexts, studies of this kind continue to be relatively few and far between, in part because the particularity and normativity of the concept of literature in many cases was elided by its absorption into categories like textuality. What work has been done has found varying success in navigating the "dangers or normative pulls of traditional approaches," not least their assumptions about agency in meaning-making.[80] Part of the difficulty arises from concerns about how to think about literature without imposing a concept of literature: a concept that has proliferated globally by means of empire and capital, with their attendant claims to universality and translatability. The challenge becomes how to track the specific ways the concept is embedded at once in local, regional, and global circuits.

Most of this work to date has justifiably focused on local poetic systems or traditions of speaking, writing, reading, and performing. Ethnographers have taken pains to show how poetry and literature are embedded in the social and have called attention to creative practices through which aesthetic traditions come to have political effects.[81] Anthropologists working in a range of contexts have described how particular political projects come at times to be mapped onto specific forms of writing or speech. But in Berlin, no clear mapping of poetic forms to political formations was tenable. The role of explicitly stated rules and the authority to impose them is significant in establishing and sustaining a literary tradition, but the outcome of the experiments with context that I describe was not determined necessarily by the fact that they reproduced (or failed to reproduce) an anticipated form of expression typifying of one or the other tradition.[82] Instead, this book tracks the shifting conditions under which literature moves and moves us, and how contests in what counts as literature tell us something about the limits of the concept within human life. It asks what is happening between traditions, where the idea of traditions as bounded is simultaneously reproduced and contested. It calls attention to the fact that languages and literatures are always found in the company of others, and to the normativity of what counts as a language, or as literature, in these contexts.[83]

I encountered these practices during ethnographic fieldwork from 2011–16, and intensively from 2013–14, during which time I lived in neighbourhoods in both the old East and West of the city. This project grew out of initial effort to study the local reception of a handful of texts from India during the long nineteenth century. The longer I lived in Berlin, the more I saw that this earlier moment of exchange continued resounding in crucial ways in bookstore catalogues and walking tours, translation seminars and public events. My research took me to a wide range of sites in the city, from well-funded state-sponsored institutions and international festivals to small-scale informal networks of bookshops, reading circles, workshops, and poetry salons. I spent the better part of the first year trying to chart the tangled literary circuits that ran through the city. I attended storefront readings and joined several book clubs, worked with writers at professional workshops, and made weekly visits to bookstores and publishers in nearly every district of the city. I made a method of cataloguing the books I found on shelves on daily walks, collecting notices and flyers for readings, and advertisements for new and old collaborations. I interviewed culture officials and participated in hundreds of events where literature was read, performed, and debated. Different contexts called for different languages, though most commonly German, English, Turkish, and Arabic, and there were certainly times when languages were used that I did not know, and I have tried to describe those moments and their political implication as clearly as I can. Though my focus was not solely on the famous writers living or dead who traversed the city, they did nevertheless often appear in my fieldwork, and I treat them here as I found them, like other characters, as companions in the lives of others I came to know, and so in that sense, as contemporaries with whom one might get along, argue, love, despise, forget, or introduce.[84]

The bulk of my time over subsequent years has been spent in a series of sites to which I found myself drawn: a salon and asylum program for exiled writers; a popular workshop for poetry that maintained a digital archive of recorded performances; a young magazine-and-walking-tour project; a bookstore owned by its authors; a family publishing house specialized in translating texts from and about India. Each of the next four chapters focalizes one of these sites, and in each, I found mentors and guides who helped me to acquire a sense of literature's possibilities. They also challenged me to rethink my assumptions about what fieldwork might look like, about the materials I might collect, and about the forms these relationships and their description might take. I use the term *site* not to suggest that these contexts are spatially fixed containers within which the action of the story unfolds,[85] but to call attention to the specific ways practices are embedded within and helped to constitute the very "background against which we see any action."[86] The sites were by no means representative, and I do not mean to extrapolate from them in any general way. I was drawn to them because each opened new ways of thinking about and putting pressure on common assumptions about what literature does in practice. Each sat slightly uncomfortably with some aspect of received social theoretic wisdom on and from Europe, and so in each chapter, I have tried to show how we might challenge their suppositions from a view of actual uses of language.

*Grammar, Context, and Meetings*

The interpretive approach I develop draws from a tradition of thought that understands the whole of our life in language as contextual and calls for investigating the uses of words in the particularity of expressive situations. Rather than take certain classes of words as means through which we fasten language to the world, in my view language in its entirety is already world bound. When we recognize what West calls the contextual "quality of all human activity," when we give up "the quest for certainty," what comes into focus are the conditions under which we speak to one another.[87] I want to resist the temptation, still dominant in scholarly thinking, that we must begin by fixing a definition of literature, or firm expectations about the forms it might take or the places it might appear, as if what literature is or means could take the general form of a proposition.[88] I take fieldwork to be an effort to go looking, to see where and when people felt things could be described as literature, not because they followed a rule but because it struck them as natural. We discover what literature is (and what it is not), what it means and to whom, in practice, in an intuited sense of its rightness, its fit in these contexts (which some linguists call its esthetics), and never once and for all.[89]

My emphasis on the particularity of expressive contexts and their microphysical conditions is meant to offer resistance to the idea that different experiences have to add up to a singular, coherent whole.[90] I am resistant to the idea that we need an explanation, a definition, or a master concept to draw connections, to link this example of literature with that one, and what unites these two may in turn be something other than what joins the second and the third. "What really comes before our mind when we understand a word?" asks Wittgenstein. "Isn't it something like a picture?" This picture might "suggest a certain use to us, but it [is] possible for me to use it differently. Then this use of the word doesn't fit the picture … But doesn't it fit? I have purposely so chosen the example that it is quite easy to imagine *a method of projection* according to which the picture does fit after all."

While we learn words and teach words in one context, Stanley Cavell explains, we "expect others to be able to project them into further contexts. Nothing insures that this projection will take place (in particular, not the grasping of universals nor the grasping of book of rules) just as nothing insures that we will make, and understand, the same projections."[91] This means that every use of literature is in this sense exploratory, a test of the flexibility the concept can tolerate.[92] One example and another speak to each other: they are in conversation (they "correspond," as with letters). They can also contest each other, they can fail or lapse into cliché. Which resemblances between contingent examples count also depends on the circumstances. The connections between one use and another are like a weave of "family resemblances … as in spinning a thread we twist fibre on fibre. And the strength of the thread does not reside in the fact that some one fibre runs through its whole length, but in the overlapping of manning fibres."[93] Each bears multifarious relations with others.[94] When we use a concept like literature then, it communicates "an awareness of 'possible meanings' of the potential and capacity in language (and so in ourselves)."[95] Particularity speaks to possibility. Instead of proposition and its derivations and deviations, or an original and a facsimile, these movements in language are always already ongoing. And each activates a network of neighbouring concepts. In the cases of literature I discuss, this includes concepts familiar to scholarly literature, like prosody, voice, and humour, but also seemingly more mundane concepts like walking, friendship, and eating. These constellations too may be somewhat different in each case, and we can never quite know in advance where an investigation might lead. My effort in this book is to describe something of these networks, not in order to make claims about the concept of literature *as such* but to show how it moves.

Language ideologies might elevate and reify certain cases of literature and by extension ideas about language use and identity in general.[96] But the criteria that govern our use of a concept and our capacity to project it into further contexts are continuously grown from our participation in our forms of life.[97] These criterial relations are given in what I refer to throughout this book as philosophical grammar.[98] For Wittgenstein, "grammar tells us what kind of object anything is," what an expression is for. It describes, it tells us what is possible and what not, to say and to mean. A grammatical investigation of this kind helps us to get clear about the connections between uses in context, among which similarities might appear and disappear and reappear, without suggesting that every case has one singular quality common to all. Grammar, moreover, is not independent of its speakers but is something we do. Wittgenstein notes in the *Philosophical Investigations* that "the *speaking* of a language is part of an activity, or a form of life." Used in this way, grammar should be conflated neither with linguistic grammar (though the latter can often guide our investigations) nor with a closed repertoire of static forms given prior to use, but instead signals something where a detail can travel, fading away or remerging in new contexts, plots and arrangements.[99] It marks "the locus of the difficult work of aligning oneself with the language one inherits but in a way that is always open to disputation, clarification and innovation."[100]

Despite talk of a literary turn, anthropological thinking still stands to gain considerably from engagement with specific literary practices on this measure, and especially in relation to recent efforts to see ethics as intrinsic to life.[101] Since literature is part of what it means to have a life in language, when we examine literary experiences we scrutinize life in and of language itself; it is one way of exploring what we say when.[102] Literature can illuminate moral life in particular ways, writes Cora Diamond, not because it helps us to analyze moral concepts in general, but because it helps us to perceive, clarify, or describe the "shape of certain possibilities in human life." It achieves this not only or even primarily in virtue of what its characters *do*, but in its capacity to put at issue our "descriptions of life, of what matters, makes differences in human lives," and to shape "the language of particularity" itself.[103] Claims on and through literature allow us to recognize the "description of gestures, manners, habits, turns of speech, turns of thought, styles of face as morally expressive." It can provide an education "in how to picture and understand human situations,"[104] not necessarily in the way of providing arguments as judgment but by refining our sense of what is important.[105] For Diamond, our very capacity to use "a descriptive term is a capacity to participate in the life from which that word comes; and that what it is to describe is many different kinds of activity ... although the terms we use will have a place in a network of evaluative thought, to participate in the life in which the terms are used does not mean we must share those evaluations." If anthropological descriptions are part of "learning to *live another form of life*, and to speak another kind of language,"[106] this was also an issue that my interlocutors were actively involved in thinking through and not one that began when I arrived.[107]

Because literature can respond to a potential for invention within grammar,[108] it can help clarify connections and "give voice to the experience of what we take to be ethically or spiritually significant."[109] In the words of one poet I knew in Berlin, trying out words in different situations could provide the means to "get clear about how we see what we see," to see where and when our words are at home, where they have friction, and where they do not. This means that literature is not only another metaphor for social processes, though it can be this too. It is also an experiment within the forms of life from which it is borne and through which belonging is negotiated. It was one way people found their footing in the world, one way it was given life and remade, and it was one way people were excluded from that life. It provided resources for contesting and transforming these agreements, our very ways of speaking and seeing. It confronts us with the fact that even in creative language practices, our struggle to find our own voice is always in words we borrow from others, words that were there before us, and that we inherit.[110]

The relevant contexts in this book were constituted by practices unfolding at what I think of as meeting points – conjunctures at which different senses of what counts as literature, or German, or migrant, or even the real, touched. My concern therefore is with how the feeling that we inhabit different worlds emerges from within forms of life and is not, by contrast, a given about a state of affairs.[111] Diamond makes the case that "the real is (among other things) that which we take to be at stake in conflicts and that means that the concept of *what is real* has a complexity beyond what can be elucidated by examining its role 'within' language-games or modes of thought." If this is so, then where two seemingly irreconcilable or contradictory senses meet – that is, where the sense of what is real is on the line – even in situations of considerable differential in power, the space opened by their conflict cannot be determinatively given in advance. These meetings have a grammar of their own, and it cannot be explained simply by appeal to prior forms of life, as if they provided a sure ground.[112] As I argue in chapter six, it was the *feel* of words, their touch, their taste, an intuition of their rightness, that guided use.

What was at stake in these meetings was not an ultimate resolution about the definition or significance of any of these terms but rather an agreement in criteria, in the kinds of things that could be expressed and accepted as human possibilities, the fragile conditions of conversation.[113] Any articulation in language expresses a claim to shared validity, and this holds even if we speak different languages, draw on distinct literary traditions, or tell different stories.[114] If a claim in language is a search for criteria it can also understood as a search for who is implicated in this claim.[115] In Berlin, where different possibilities so regularly touched, the question that arose time and again was how far the "naturalness of certain ways of being in the world that are recognized in one's culture"[116] could be projected into the lives and practices of those in different social groups. Under what conditions would their claim be acknowledged and under what denied? In what acts or gestures did it become clear our concepts could or could not be made to fit the descriptions of someone else's actions? What, moreover, does imagining different forms of life as human forms of life reveal about what is entailed in one's own?[117] Where are the differences between knowing another language and finding our feet in it?[118] How far could a concept like literature extend and under what conditions? How and when does literature makes claims on us, "express us and expose us"?[119]

The limits of a form of life, the point at which differences "cease to be criterial differences," Veena Das argues, is the point at which it becomes "impossible to imagine a future together." This possibility of incommensurability shadows everyday life as it is lived, and not only in "the philosopher's reflections on it."[120] My picture of anthropology takes neither concepts nor worlds to have rigid, pre-fashioned bounds we later cross but instead trains attention on the specific contexts in which movements in and of language unfold. This requires investigating the grammar of meeting points. It calls for us to give up reliance on the language of outsides as the starting point for thinking about human movements. An approach of this kind requires dramatically recasting conventional approaches to thinking about human mobility because it does not take categories of governing regimes to be already the case. It is one way of working against an indolent "methodological ethnicity" or nationalism in studies of migration, one that takes racialized and ethnicized categories as units of analysis, rather than outcomes of power-laden processes.[121] In its place, I offer descriptions of what it means to live a life in language, where being at home in the world means being in motion, as well as how these movements resist and even transform the arresting efforts of hegemonic discourse.[122]

I began with a series of interlocking scenes in hopes of provoking questions about what it meant to call Berlin a literary city and a "colony of expatriates." As Nabokov's unnamed interlocutor observes, what is at is at stake is nothing less than what is of interest, what counts, and for whom. I said that the meaning of literature cannot be grasped by means of a general preposition. I have argued that to discover what counts as literary, we have no choice but to go look in each case. What stories like these bid us to learn to accept is the impossibility of grounding language's relation to the world.[123] But the second point I take from them is an insistence on the fact that we *live* with literature, that it is lived as a component of the real, and that it is involved in process of making life liveable, and, at times, denying it. As Paul Friedrich noted, it "permeates ordinary language ... poetic language is actualized in all domains of life, even the logician's study, and is common in cafeterias, bars, streets, at kitchen tables and conveyor belts – wherever one argues, persuades, seduces, reports, creates rapport, or otherwise communicates – and particularly in moments of playfulness, humour, trauma, crisis, and strong emotion."[124]

The examples I pick up in this book, the characters, texts, and scenes sometimes pass another by and sometimes connect, not all the time, but now and again in a gesture, or a word, or a reading, or a sound. And perhaps they slip away again. The form of fieldwork itself, to say nothing of the writing, took on this quality as well. It meant at times focusing intently on a single figure, or word, or scene, and at other times drawing back. My hope is that these chapters will be read in a similar spirit, speaking to one another in different ways and with different force, as a conversation, or a garland of fragments.[125]

Chapter Two

# The Prosody of Social Ties: Poetry and Fleeting Moments in a Workshop

Einmal – nicht lange – müßtest du hier sein.
Wo das aufregend gefährlich flutet und wimmelt
Und tutet und bimmelt
...
Aber weißt du: jeder verkehrt hier mit allen,
Nur nicht mit stillen Menschen oder mit toten.

– Jaochim Ringelnat, "Berlin"

Berlin has often been described as a place of near constant ambient transformation[1] – a fact reflected not only in its concrete structures, but also in its soundscape and in the ephemerality of social ties this condition seemed to engender. People were constantly on the move. In a contribution to a serial titled *Letters from Berlin*, translator Lucy Renner Jones likens the city's inhabitants and its ever-changing storefronts to squirrels darting across the landscape. She herself had come to the city in the nineties and "since then life and work have changed dramatically. After a few quiet years, scaffolding began to go up all around us, and we were woken up by the sound of pneumatic drills at seven o'clock sharp, even though our freelancer existence meant that we would start work at ten." The streets and the people in them were transforming, but she had managed to stay on only by staying on the move, like a squirrel. "I find it hard to see the transformation of this area as progress," she laments, even as she notes the people denouncing tourists and gentrification were themselves "incomers" ten years earlier. A pecking order of abuse has emerged, ending with the Swabians, a term that refers to people from the southwestern part of Germany but in Berlin has morphed into a wider moniker for gentrifiers. Jones relates a story about learning that 85 per cent of the population of her neighbourhood had left in the preceding decades, and how it led to setting herself a task of finding someone who hadn't. Eventually she found a couple who lived in a legendary Wasserturm (water tower) in Kollwitzplatz who had been in the city since the 1950s and who came to Prenzlauer Berg because it was seen as a place for agitators and students. They tell her that the Lebensgefühl, the attitude toward life, has changed. What once was a neighbourhood where people sought solidarity had been defeated by "competition and vanity." What was once had been home to a "motley crew of people" had become, under the influence of capitalism, a place where "everyone wants peace and quiet." "The new Lebensgefühl in Prenzlauer Berg as time goes on is adapt or leave," Jones writes, "develop a new lifestyle and tastes, or nest elsewhere. And for those of you just come to visit, be sure to listen out for the sound of plastic coffee-cup lids dropping from the trees in the parks. Some would say it's the sound of gentrification, others the sound of progress."[2]

A subtle feature of these descriptions is their reliance on sound and sound metaphors to capture something essential about the experience of fleetingness. During my time in Berlin, I found that sound and ephemerality were often conjoined in descriptions of the literary forms associated with urban migrants and transient visitors, in particular with oral genres of literary performance occasionally called live literature. One journalist, writing about one of the country's most important literary events, described what they saw as a renewed Lust am Vorlesen, a desire for reading aloud, rather than in solitary encounters with print. "Literature in a canape format (Literatur im Häppchenformat)," they ventured, accommodated both "increasingly strict 'time-budgets'" and the "communicative orientation of society [kommunikativeren Ausrichtung der Gesellschaft] that prefers reading together."[3]

Institutions specializing in performance of literature are, as elsewhere in Germany, ubiquitous and take a range of forms, from traditional salons to author readings in neighbourhood bookstores, though some, like poetry-slam competitions, are closely associated with Berlin. Slam performances found a home in smoke-filled rooms at lounges and music clubs throughout the city in the 1990s, but at the time were concentrated in Prenzlauer Berg, combining dance and participation with the more formalized, rules-oriented, and moderator-and-jury forms of slam. This neighbourhood was one of the first to gentrify with the surge in expatriation in the time since.[4] In just a few years, slam performance moved out of dark Kiffkeller (a room for smoking pot) and turned to hybrid forms to push this element of spoken-word to larger and more diverse audiences.[5] Writer and slam-interpreter Sulaiman Masomi suggests that the interactional, dialogical form of poetry re-enlivened the centrality of didactic criticism rerouted through the new-mediatic recalibration of the relationship between acts of writing and acts of speaking.[6] For Masomi, the technological shift was coincidental with the Wende, the historical "turn" around re-unification, allowed for a re-centring of literature on the event of interaction, such that the "authenticity of the art work in the age of mechanical reproduction is secured through the performance, accompanied by an intimate co-presence."[7] The eventization of society (Eventisierung der Gesellschaft) was part and parcel, he argues, of modernization. Cultural geographers have similarly described Berlin as a city where the "experience economy" transforms space by means of performative events.[8] At the same time, the valorization of "hybridized" cultural forms as markers of ethnic style takes such expressions to be "authentic" representations of "minority popular culture" that emerge relatively spontaneously.[9] Such a view can be misleading though, not least because it elides the contexts from which these forms have emerged and which are mediated by institutional frames eager to profit on commoditized, reified cultural differences.

While these organic theories take on a wide variety of forms, I focus here on a series of encounters mediated by a single node in a wider network of such institutions – a literary workshop for poetry in Prenzlauer Berg, the reputation of which has changed in the last decade – to develop this sense that oral literary events are particularly well-suited to social life under conditions of modern acceleration, to the proliferating, transient encounters that an aspiration to make Berlin a "global" city seems to demand.[10] For the workshop's director, this importance stems from the experience of being present to hear a human voice articulate a word and which gives fleeting encounters their meaningful quality.

This suggestion, however, looks rather different depending how one was positioned within hegemonic discourses. Tracing these different claims as they cross through a single site allows us to complicate dominant characterizations of both literature and urban life as part of a necessary, flat movement toward an increasingly alienated modernity: in the first case, where writing technology is seen as overcoming the fragility of oral texts, enabling the maintenance of national imaginaries; and in the second, where the rapidity of life in the city is marked by isolation and anonymity. A shared space like a poetry salon often emerges as a site of contradictory desires for social life – desires that are expressed not only in diverse stakes in and claims on literature but also reflected in disagreements *about* literature, particularly its capacity (or failure) to serve as a conduit for cultural translation. These interconnected scenes describe a heterogenous "local economy of knowledge"[11] about poetry within a shared social world constituted by these conflicts. Conflicts, that is, in how people talk about literature and, in turn, how these myriad ways of talking play an important role in how people make sense of their world and their position in it. As Julie Cruikshank has argued, it is necessary in such contexts to describe both how these performances serve the ideological interests of the dominant system – "emphasizing incorporation of colonial influences, commoditization of culture, or perceived 'inventions of tradition'" – and how performers and audiences confer meaning on their work. In this spirit, my aim is to track how different people negotiated this nexus of interests.[12]

Though conventional analyses of the relationship between literature and modern cities often treat fleeting relationships as inferior to more enduring ones, fleeting socialities are significant in their own right. A more nuanced picture of life in Berlin requires a view of their crossings with more stable, if alienated, social forms. We cannot take for granted that the selection of texts (or relationships) for the effort required to make them durable is a necessary sign of judgment about their relative value, nor that it is necessarily the semantic content of a text that such effort endeavours to preserve. Instead, I want to develop a picture of what I call the prosody of social ties in order to suggest we move away from strict oppositions between ephemeral and durable forms, or weak and strong tries, and toward notions of tempo, pitch, stress, and cadence – concepts essential to the poetic, and which can be borrowed for anthropology analyses in such contexts. By prosody, then, I want to signal the importance of the weft and warp of these elements, the material aspects of speech as social action, and the centrality of voice as an embodied claim.

Prosody is also essential to understanding how the multiplicity of languages in use in poetic performance spaces was experienced, particularly where audiences did not understand the language of the performance.[13] In the scenes below, simultaneous translations are produced alongside performances but are understood by audiences members (and performers) to do something other than what happens when they hear the sounds of poems in languages they do not speak. Poetry performances, and particularly their prosodic elements, make different alignments of voice different ways of staking a claim in a form of life.[14] People spoke of literature as a bodily practice that gave life to language in ways that were sometimes durable but, just as often, rather fleeting. And this fleetingness of voice and the claims to sociality it implied carried different promise among those implicated in the event of its performance. Just as some sought out and formed lasting relationships through participation in literature, others found their punctuations, breaks, and interruptions even more important.

## Scenes from a Literary Workshop

When I first met Anne Marie in 2012, she had been living with her partner, Taimur, in a small apartment in the area of Kreuzkölln, a borderland between two boroughs (Kreuzberg and Neuköln), only a few subway stops from Prenzlauer Berg and one of the most important new battle grounds in the ongoing tension between young émigré artists, working-class former inhabitants, and anti-capitalist crusaders. At times, these tensions tipped over into physical violence, vandalism, and hate-speech.

Anne Marie was raised near the city and returned in her early twenties to try her hand at writing after a few years working in the technology sector. Taimur was raised in Pakistan, educated in part in the UK, and made his way to Berlin after publishing a short collection of English poems. The pair each worked only a few days a week at café near their apartment, and Anne Marie brought in extra money – as did many in similar situations – as a freelance translator of technical documents and, occasionally, small works of literature. The money they earned afforded them a small shared apartment and groceries, and the rest of their time they dedicated to writing workshops and small collaborative projects with friends in the city that seemed to form and dissipate every few months. Anne Marie had spent her childhood in nearby Brandenburg, but returned as an adult when she decided after leaving her job to take up writing. Someone she had met in the street outside a reading had told her about a major event in Prenzlauer Berg, and she invited me to come along. While she maintained her relationships with friends she had known in school, she increasingly found herself interpolated within migrant communities that dominate the literary landscape in this part of the city.

We met one afternoon outside the Kulturbauerei, at one time a brewery, refurbished in the preceding decades as a home for cultural events in various media, and among the formerly state operated businesses that were salvaged by a unified German state in the period after the fall of the Wall. In the spring of every year since 2011, thousands of urban dwellers have crowded the corridors of the old facility to hear readings from authors, discuss trends, get autographs, and talk to publishers. The building is several stories tall and occupies several square blocks, like a fortress blotting out views of anything else, including the sound from the nearby urban thoroughfare. Whichever entrance you used, the pathway opened onto a massive open space, a courtyard between the outer buildings lined with white tents and packed with people bending over, glaring at books. Somehow the walls seemed shorter from the inside. Performers walked by on stilts, and you could smell food cooking on an open fire in a pit near the middle of the mass. Publishers had their names written on the backs of sheets in the tents, and books were sprawled across a clean table as writers and readers ask what they might like and hand cash across. Beer and wine were poured into large drafts, and people in the middle talked loudly, while people near the edges leaned over one another to hear what is happening. On one side, a black box had been set up, inside which, behind a glass screen, a young poet sat with a book in their hands reading into a microphone. Passers-by, three or four at a time, stopped to put on headphones outside the box and listened to the reading. A small white sheet of paper outside listed upcoming readers and the selections they chose.

Near the box a wide but short stage was set up with a black couch and two speakers sitting, talking into a microphone. The younger of the two has just finished a novel, and he reclined back into his seat as the silver-haired interviewer told the audience that he'd be reading from his new book later in the evening in a nearby salon. The speakers crackled as drops of rain fell, but the crowd filled in the benches set up in front of the food station anyway. Several people were huddled under a *Berliner Pilsner* umbrella; others simply ignored it. Behind the crowd two small theatres have been converted for readings, and across the way a large auditorium was packed as one of the headliners took the stage to promote their new work. Sounds filled the space, competing for attention amid the cacophony, but each was carefully attended to by those caught by its fragrance. People walked through such spaces as if through a garden or museum taking in the landscape before something called for closer inspection. Berlin Buchnacht is a literary festival like many others that dominate the cultural landscape of the city, many of which are better known or better attended. But its structure marks a shift in the affect of participation in such events. Rather than the spectacle of the major festivals – with quiet audiences wearing name tags and holding waxy brochures, university emblems, held in bourgeois institutions funded by foreign governments or corporate sponsors – events like these spill out into life on the streets.

As we are walked through the event, Anne Marie and Taimur recognized a writer with whom they once spent an evening reading from his work, with a small group around him. I asked whether they would like to go over. This elicited a smile from Taimur who started us off in the other direction. Anne Marie told me that "this is what it's like all the time here":

> That's why people want to be in Berlin. For poets you know, the liveliness [Lebhaftigkeit] is like ink. This kind of wild [fetzig] movement, frenetic, but you are meeting different kinds of people all the time, that shifts something in how you are using words. Maybe you don't recognize it yourself when you are working. It is ok if you do not always create stable ties, things don't have to have that kind of pressure, you can be free to try something out and move on something else. There's always something going on somewhere, you know, in a different area. But you know, with my older friends, they are starting families, they are working in some kinds of technology jobs, it's another kind of life. As a Berliner, in some way of course I don't like that people are pushed out, because it ruins what really made it Berlin.

These were sentiments I had heard expressed repeatedly by young writers I knew. The same organization of social life that drew them to the city threatened to destroy itself. As we walked toward a small salon space at the back of the Kulturbauerei, Taimur lit a cigarette and closed his eyes briefly to catch the last line of a poem being read behind us. As Anne Marie went on ahead to find seats, I asked Taimur if he planned to stay in Berlin indefinitely. "I am comfortable here," he replied, in English now, "it's good for starting new projects, but I will leave for sure. It's ideal for when you want to live this life, but sometime I will want something else, slower, less change, going from this to that. A bit longer. She will stay, for sure" he said motioning his hand ahead of us where Anne Marie had gone, "this is her home. I don't know what comes next for me yet."

*The Doubled Appearance of Poetry*

Around the corner from the main courtyard of the old factory, down another stone-paved walkway between yellow-brick buildings, the salon was one I frequented during my fieldwork. It had become known for making the relationship between the sound of human voices and literature its special focus. Far from the old West Berlin stages crowded today by an older and more homogenous demographic, poets at different stages of their careers shared works in progress, collaborated, translated, improvised, and recorded their proceedings for an archive of texts, translations, and voices. For twenty years, this workshop tried to centre dialogue about poetry and created a space for the return of voice in not just literary arts but in allied practices as well. Poems might be accompanied by music, dance, and photography, a multi-disciplinary commitment that had precedence particularly in East German contexts, where this openness to material form was used to subvert and evade political controls. Through hosting public events, competitions, performances, and discussions, the workshop's organizers aimed at what their director called the sharing of poetic experiences. They worked especially to support young German poets and expose them to other traditions. Since 1998, the *open mike* competition has become one of the premier outlets for young (under the of age thirty-five) poets in Germany. While judges from the national landscape came to administer the competition, it was the performance in front of an audience that often garnered more attention, as listeners voted and announced their selection in the popular Berlin newspaper, *die Tageszeitung*. The winners toured German-speaking countries reading their work and discussing their experiences. A key node in the network that supports open mike, the workshop invited participants and officials from the competition to experiment together with the audience.

I only very rarely saw Anna Marie there. When I did, she would call me over to introduce me to others she had met in writing groups or reading circles, though they were invariably people she knew only tangentially. But on this evening, she nudged me toward the front of the room, in the direction of a tall, broad-shouldered man frantically shaking hands. He introduced himself as Thomas Wohlfahrt, the salon's director. He invited me to his office the following week when he'd have more time and laughed that he was (with the exception of a small cast of young employees and interns) the one consistent face in the room. The crowd changed as often as event posters. Thomas had been formally trained in German literature and musicology in Halle and Wittenberg, earning a doctorate in 1985. For several years he worked as a researcher in an institute for literary history in the Academy of Sciences, before moving to the West to work in a local theatre house and in support of literary prizes, until an invitation came in 1991 to take up the helm of a literary workshop in the Grotewohlhaus on Majakowskiring – once the home of the Berlin section of the East German writers' association – where it had been squatting since the fall of the Wall.

Since its relocation in 1994, the Werkstatt had focused on poetic forms in their relation to other media and hosted roughly 150 artists from around the world each year. In 2016, it was renamed Haus für Poesie. "Before we were here, however, there was no central point for poets in Germany. Certainly, there was no voice for our poets internationally, it had hardly a place." When we met again, I asked him about an interview he'd recently given, in which he had called for a "reorganization of the memory of poetry into a kind of library" [in einer Art Mediathek das Gedächtnis von Dichtung reorganisieren]. "I've travelled a lot around the world, you know, and really the German poet and poetess really has something to say, it's some of the best out there." The interviewer had asked him whether he agreed that poetry was something fragile, something that needed small gatherings, and whether that small circle stood opposed to the larger ambition of a centre for poetic voice. And then, like now, he replied by appealing to the experiences of poets elsewhere. "Look at how big our events are, it is both … it is about access to poetry."

There was something remarkable about the statement that any branch of German literature had not found a place in international literary traffic. Yet the absurdity of the claim falls away as we attend to what he really meant when he spoke of poetry. The journalist had it backwards. Fragility did not register what was at stake in poetry as opposed to, say, in the novel form. "What makes a poem a poem is sound lines, rhythms and the sensuousness of spoken language." Thomas said. "This is our primal engagement with the world, there is something very reassuring in it. Every child likes to hear it. Let us think of poetry as an event of voice, breath, body, and the senses. Whether the listener understands everything at once isn't always so important."

Poetry, for Thomas, was a worldly endeavour. "Poetry has different needs to be encountered. If it has to be heard, sharing it takes something else – how do you describe that then? I think that's what he meant to ask." I pressed him, anticipating the sort of academically structured response to which I had grown accustomed. "It is about this re-organization. There [has] always [been] this combination with music, dance, and it had an element of meaning, a cultic act [kultischen Handlung], and later a religious act. There are other theories of the emergence of poetry, that it came from the 'stop-function' – like that, tak, tak … we have many synonyms for it, but it was always linked to the voice. With book printing things changed, you could read alone, it had given up the social place, the marketplace – you know, because the poet would go to the market or have a gathering of people and declare, in a sense, what they were composing. So, memory techniques were linked that way, in sounds, rhythm, rhyme, the movement, the sharing came from this kind of memory. Say a famous poem like the *Odyssey*, you too could have them [in your body]."[15]

But this was removed from poetry by chirographic techniques. There was a shift, which Thomas called a "functional change" in the techniques of memory to the "purely aesthetic." Now "[poetry] is perceived as beautiful." But it is not that linguistic messages are encoded by such experiences, nor is there a desire for the endurance of the poem itself, but rather a desire for the routes of its sharing. This distinction is crucial for understanding the hope that one might have for a "centre" for poetry, as well as claims about the multiple scales at which poetic sharing takes place. As poetry left the "social place" – the gathering of community, he would say – it deteriorated. The public he imagined was not a sterile meeting place for rational strangers. It had the qualities of the intimate, the private, "the living room." It was marked by an opening up to others of what had earlier lived in an "inner-space-situation" [Innenraumsituation]. It transformed the "hermetic, the sensitive, the sentimental, if you will the heart-pain stories" [Herz-Schmerz-Geschichten]. In 1999, the Werkstatt began a project trying to imagine transactions between these forms of memory and community. It came in the form of a digital archive through which one could explore the ramifications of new media technology for this politics of poetic voice. Beginning as a project to document the "melodies" of different poets and their traditions that came through the Werkstatt network, their digital presence paired translations with recordings of performances in sixty-eight languages and boasted tens of thousands of recordings and translations. It began, moreover, from the awareness of a general decline in the publishing industry's interest in poetry and the contemporaneous rise of the "event-character" of the German poetry landscape. Once again, he told me, we can hear "a tangle of voices" [Stimmengewirr], as the "primordial elements" of sound and rhythm, "whose real terrain is song and dance," have been revived. Their archive thereby, Thomas says, "counteracts the falling apart of writing and sound which leaves the poetic field in an unhealthy state":

> Whenever it is heard, the poem works and goes via the body into the body. And if you take this seriously, then what is in between? What is in between is actually something that the book alone does not provide, but which is made available through [is at the disposal of] the performance of the poet, namely the instrument. And that instrument is the human voice. This is the rise of the human voice. So therefore, we might compare the poem to a score. Few people can from the notation alone translate for themselves sounds and rhythms. Thus, we need the symphony, the orchestra, the band, the pianist, the guitarist, the tuba player. The instrument lifts it, *awakens it to life*.

This notion of awakening of words to life points us to a very different relation to language than might be anticipated. The social life of poetry, Thomas seemed to venture, like the poem itself, could not be described by appeal only to stable relations; it requires that effervescent communities also come into being. Absent this sense, one would come to know poetry only in part, like experiencing music only through notation. This embodied act does not, however, merely replace the written text or its modes of circulation. The two vectors cross one another in the poem and go on to found different sorts of relations. I asked Thomas one evening whether community comes into being *through* the reading of the poem:

> It is produced and because it is produced, it is there ["present"]. It functions like a community; they listen and are there [dabei]. And we produce something even when hours earlier we did not understand the language in which the poem was written. Even thousands of people can sit and listen and understand. So, I am very sure that voice is the essential element of poetry Playing with the alphabet, the written pulls out meaning ... but it is fundamentally different. So, for me the poem is always best when it has a double appearance [Doppelauftritt], to read and to listen.
>
> Are there two works, one written and read, the other spoken and heard, and two communities?
>
> In one sense, there are two, in another, there is one. It has a unity, we call it a poem, but it has many lives.

This doubling occurs at multiple register, and the forms of sociality engendered through each register were distinct. They also expressed different modes of intimacy. But most surprisingly, neither the message nor the sense of collective effervescence awoken by such poetic performances is burdened by concern with its temporal fragility. It begins and ends in a kind of enlivened present. For the poet, to speak then of the reorganization of memory, as I understand it, is to think with the memory of the body, of the breath, rather than the text conventionally understood, or with a picture of sociality that requires endurance for its authenticity. Or perhaps it would be better to say that this reorganization is akin to a recognition of the multiple vectors that traverse the poem and the relations it posits between words and bodies.[16] The formation of relation flows through public oration, signalling a relationship otherwise inaccessible. The speaker, or more precisely the speaker's co-presence with the addressee, is likewise the channel – but through, rather than against, the sounds that fill the space. Such a relationship is not between just between two partners in speech but also within the crowd, in opposition to some other public not present. Poetry was not always intended as message, but the transformation of message to embodiment.¹⁷ Such embodiment marks the singularity of the speaker's voice, through which we find an alternative picture of politics, and in opposition to her capacity for signification.¹⁸

*The Fleetingness of Social Ties*

When Anne Marie and I met again it was several months later. She and Taimur were no longer together, and he had moved to Belgium to work for a small technology firm. She had been spending the last few months travelling and working for a small journal, attending readings and public events when she had time. We came to the Werkstatt in Prenzlauer Berg to hear one of China's great poets of the post-Cultural Revolution era, Yang Lian. One of the "Misty Poets" (Ménglóng Shīrén) who fought against the oppression of the arts during the height of tensions in the PRC in the 1970s, Yang had become a popular poet in Berlin, regularly visiting to read his poems or deliver talks on the political history of China or the poetry one writes in exile. His playful smile settled a lightness over the room. In a recent essay on exile, Yang had written that it was an "inborn feature of poetry to be able to stop at any line: a poem must be continued and mark the constantly failing but courageous attempts of human beings." For him, journeys in language take two directions simultaneously: "Every sentence emits sound from somewhere in myself and enters into dialogue with the surrounding world. When depth itself affects the grammar, something 'new' will naturally emerge. This long journey has no end, because the effort to explore the ultimate limits of darkness can never be exhausted." This mean too that he felt his poems would be "foreign" even to Chinese speakers, that something in them resisted "translation."

People chatted as they collected into tightly packed seats. A few lingered at the ticket counter, where pamphlets and translations were spread out and two women took coats and distributed water. I took a seat near the middle as Thomas walked out from the back and along the far wall to whisper something to one of the two Germans on the stage with Yang – a translator and a professor from a local university. This ritual was enacted on the vast majority of stages across the city, with each of the roles filled by a rotating cast of performers from a local network sufficiently large that no one person could know all the other members, but small enough that some mediating event could nearly always be found. Thomas welcomed everyone from a microphone beside the stage before turning over the event to the two conversation partners on the stage, who introduced Yang's biography and the theme of the readings and discussion (the poetry of the Cultural Revolution). Yang bounded to the podium to read. "Tǎ zhōng de yīyè," he said smiling out to the crowd, in one smooth breath. His voice was youthful, energetic, but experienced, confident. Like most of the audience, I understood no Chinese. (A few weeks later, when the words and the recordings were made available through their database, I found the text in German.) The first two notes of the poem hit hard, and he took a moment before completing the thought. I noticed it crash into people's bodies as they sat upright with a start. There's a lingering break between a *de* and *ér* in the first line. The next two lines came quickly, as Yang's arms stirred. By then, though, the bodies were poised in anticipation, rigid and alert, during the break in rhythm.

A momentary breath after the first syllable, and Yang returned to the pacing he had acquired just a moment earlier. Anne Marie leaned over slightly and whispered that "one falls into the rhythm, like one falls into the patterns of a story" – not by meaning or tones, but in timber, breathes, intensities. She laughed when he chanted loudly. By the second set of breaks, Yang's speed picked up, his arms opening up widely outstretch. He moved his chest upwards like a wave, occasionally pushing his face past the microphone, allowing his voice to usher forth unmediated by speakers. He darted to the side, dancing on his toes as the translator, taller, milder in manner, leaned over the podium in his place and unfolded a white piece of paper. His voice was softer. There was less movement in the words. My neighbour wondered in a loud whisper whether the tonal structure of Chinese demanded more be done expressively with other features of voice. The German breaks around punctuation, it sounded rounder, the breaths longer, steadier, slower, more subdued.

> The darkness is all that we seek. Window however
> are wild animals [wilde Tiere] with a glaring glance.
> A snow, once seen, divides the distance from eye to eye [*Ferne von Auge zu Auge*]
> Birds wide wisp on pale naked bodies,
> and stones swirling until they enclose themselves, become the angle,
> thus our flesh is enclosed unto itself.
> Only the night is necessary, a night of skin,
> all ears for the storm, never quiet enough under the rock.[19]

At earlier events, whenever the poet finished reading, the audience would ask questions. There was little time this evening, except to ask about the situation in China today, whether his style was similar to others of his generation, and what lessons Germany might take from Yang's experiences. No one asked about message. The crowd broke out for cigarettes and wine in the space outside, a few lingering to ask Yang questions or to greet Thomas. We stood in circle with others outside as Anne Marie smoked, and a man who introduced himself as Yuri asked us what we thought of the readings. Someone in a black jacket borrowed a lighter and interjected that she thought Yang had an incredible "vocal effect" [stimmliche Auswirkung]. She described the sensation of moving along with his words with everyone, as if we had all been together on a boat, riding along waves. "Who cares even what the words were, it could be nothing at all, that's the point, no? We are on an adventure now together." Yuri took the opportunity to begin a narration of his recent past in a recognizable and confessional mode. He had been an alcoholic, had a falling out with his mother, and had been living as a monk in China, but had come back when he began to feel he was really a Christian at heart. He lit another cigarette and asked us about ourselves. Such a performance of intimacy among strangers would, in most other contexts, have been considered strange, a form of speech usually associated disparagingly with Americans. Yang meanwhile had left without much fanfare, shaking hands with Thomas and disappearing into the shadows with two others. In a dialogue with Gao Xingjian, a novelist who since the late 1990s had similarly lived in exile from China, Yang described a common misconception that literature was something "necessary" for society or reality. But for Yang, literature was something that simply had to be expressed: "You don't take into account whether people will understand or accept it, you care only about whether poetry can allow you to 'exist.'"

We quickly found ourselves in another grouping, as clusters of conversation shifted and reformed. Adalene, Catrin and Edouard were all in their thirties and had come together from France, having grown tired of what they described as the relative restriction of life in Paris. The women both found jobs doing translation work between English, French, and German, and Edouard made storyboards for a game producer. They had met Chih-Wei, who worked at the university and had lived in Germany nearly his entire adult life (since coming for an undergraduate education) at a reading the week before in their local bookstore. We traded stories about life in Berlin until they invited us to a small bookstore in Kreuzberg where the proprietor invited people for dinner in the basement among the stacks once every two weeks.

The second-hand shop catered to non-German speakers and functioned as a library for its patrons. But its basement opened each week, and its owner cooked homemade food for whoever wanted to come (and offer a few euros to defray costs). When we arrived at the dinner event the following week, Sophie (a self-professed British Anglophile) was perched behind a long and low table. The line was long, but she welcomed each of us, asking where some had been the past few weeks, about family members and new jobs. One by one we left a few euros so she could cover her costs, a few more if we took a beer from the fridge behind where we stood, and then made our way down an old staircase behind a bookshelf halfway into the shop. The basement room was large but already getting crowded. A line formed in the back to fill plates with dishes Sophie had spent the day preparing. People shared stories, talked about books, some returned, and some never did. The room was full, as it nearly always was.[20]

As we sat at a table near the back of the room, books falling occasionally from shelves onto our plates, I asked the group about their experiences hearing literature performed. Their experiences in Germany had, unsurprisingly, been rather different. For Catrin and Eduoard, echoing a common story, the alienation of life in other cities had driven them to Berlin, where they felt freer to take up creative work but also more "exposed" to the world. For Adalene, a day job as a translator provided enough money to spend four days a week working for a nascent international literary magazine. In the past year, she had become an editor and taken on more responsibilities for the publication, which earned just enough money to continue. But the changing cast of characters that made the work worthwhile also threatened to derail the project, as editors struggled to maintain continuity. "Who's going to do the budget, who is going to bring the copies to the shops, it's a problem. We are always having to reinvent. It brings energy, creativity, but you have to reinvest. Not just in the work but our social life."

Chih-Wei was more tentative. "I am invisible, after twenty years." Berlin bore a promise of visibility that other cities did not, but it was no guarantee. "In the US, you can just be hit in the face. It's something else here, some of them don't see I exist. Some do, sometimes. This is the most I can ask for. People say all kinds of things, about my education, my German. You see people pulling down the corners of their eyes, and no one calls out their racism. That's everywhere. From time to time, I think I will leave. But people are always leaving at least, others coming. In a reading, or a bookshop, there is some shared ground." We left slowly, stopping on each corner to smoke and trade stories. As we came to the underground station, we shared contact information scribbled on shreds of paper and agreed to have a standing meeting at the bookshop. But Anne Marie warned, "We won't see them again." And we didn't. Talk of transience took many forms, the divergent valences of which ought not be lost in thinking about its consequence as a category. As I spent time with Chih-Wei, who felt regularly invisible to Germans, I began to understand how small slights could often be more damaging than highly visible or dramatic ones. In such a condition, the benefit of ever more opportunities for new encounters and connections became clear. For many ostensibly well-meaning Germans (or else, for their American and British peers with whom they were also at times at odds) frequent encounters with different kinds of others serve to bolster an image of themselves as cosmopolitan and as artists. For the rest of the city, ephemerality meant something else. We might thereby distinguish the privilege of remaining anonymous from the condition of invisibility. Whereas the European subject is ever visible, it is dissolvable into the anonymity of the crowd associated with modern sociality (epitomized by the bourgeois dandy strolling down the boulevard). Those who are marked out in opposition to such a subject never entirely benefit from that anonymity, and yet can have their humanity denied by making them invisible. For some, the prosodic nature of social life is the means toward self-cultivation as cosmopolitan subject; for others, it is a condition of survival.

Chih-Wei sent me a message a few days later, inviting me a restaurant he liked in the neighbourhood where we both lived at the time. He shared that he had been feeling frustrated with Berlin and was starting to think about trying life in another city. It had been weighing on him, he said. "It is not that they cannot see me – they know I am there, they always know I am there. But they don't see me, as a person. They see and don't see, and don't see that they don't." I asked him where he thought he might go. "The problem is I don't know. I suppose the benefit of saying here is I can keep trying." And then he took out a small scrap of paper with two lines written on it: "Can you see me / or just my face?" "I've been leaving a few lines here and there on these pieces of paper. Maybe they blow away? I don't know. Maybe someone picks it up. It says something about someone, I think. Whether you can see other people. I worry for them. They must be killing something deep inside. Maybe they are lonely themselves. What can I do about it?"

What made these experiences in Berlin so wounding then was not the fact that he was invisible, a fleeting image or sound, but that he wasn't – that he felt he could not be seen as someone, that he was being actively denied, that he could be seen without being seen as a human being. His sense was that those around him were "soul-blind,"[21] and that his refusal amounted to killing something in themselves. What would it take to cultivate this sort of selfhood, where one seems to will that the other did not exist? It must be rather different from our ability or inability to perceive an aspect in an ambiguous image, where something new might dawn on me, like a fact about my culpability in oppressive regimes.[22] It would have to amount to a denial of something about who I am, and that my inner life belongs me by virtue of my life with others, that it is in some sense not possible for me to be alone – hence their loneliness.[23] But what is striking too in Chih-Wei's small gesture of leaving bits of verse in different places, or his hedging of his desire to leave, is that the possibility of recovery is held out by very fleeting things that can be carried off by a gust of wind. Perhaps this is a way of expressing a conviction that, at least, the world may yet be remade, and us with it.

**The Privileging of Durability**

The incorporation of this affirmative logic of fleeting ties has broad consequences for anthropological and linguistic theory. The insistence within Western theories of language use on the primacy of meaning has led to the assumption that the durability of message in public memory stood in for, or at least referred to, the endurance of social relations in their institutional guises. This relationship between social organization and text was premised on the re-definition of "text" through the separability of words or strings of words from the context of their utterance.[24] Material images deployed by poets the world over, Karin Barber[25] has shown, at times point to an imagination of the texts as having presence that outlasts time entirely, a testimony to histories otherwise subject to death. Texts are marked by their double existence as tethered to the context of and yet potentially separable from the instance and condition of their utterance – social facts as action. The textuality of the text is thus given in interpretable coherence, as a cluster of signs that can detach itself from the immediate context.[26] It is imperative to consider not only how or whether texts endure as metaculture, but how and why they are selected for the effort required to make them durable. The same might be said of the social organizations understood to be grounded in and through texts, which likewise require work to make durable.

Historians of the book have extended this dual opposition between ephemerality on the one hand and durability and value on the other by showing how value judgments might be enacted through the transformation of the material form of the work, thus allowing for the preservation of the text in new objective guise.[27] But these experiences call out for challenging the assumption that selection for durability is indicative of a judgment that these texts mattered, as opposed to those texts (and relationships) that remain ephemeral. My sense is that we are better served by developing a vocabulary through which to recognize multiple simultaneous paths of circulation, not only of the text but of social relations, without hierarchizing them.[28] How can we register this heteroglossia without assuming either that the effort at making a text durable is a necessary sign of a value judgment or that these judgments mirror one for one the distribution of power? What's more, if the opposition between orality and literacy no longer seems to us correct, it must be in part because of the inadequacy of these terms to the very different practices of circulation and their social stakes. There is clearly value in fleeting relationships because they allow for more recombination, but the nature of that value is different for Taimur, who sees it as integral to poetic work; for would-be cosmopolitans; and for Chih-Wei, for whom it makes recurrent injuries more tolerable.

The scenes above also suggest that we have to dislodge the notion that the message of poetic speech is the root of our determination of its relative merit (the effort it demands). Repetition of the speech event is not necessarily the ambition. Rather, it could also be what Thomas calls the sharing of poetry, which such performances seem to proliferate. If there is a text that survives by dislocation, then it is not to be found in either signs or the manner in which they are uttered, but rather the exchange itself. The units of that exchange seem to be mobile even if the linguistic text is not. Not particular relationships, but the form of the relation. Thomas's conception of poetry (the prosody of the text grounds the mobility of the [form of] relation) is thus an important inversion: where the classical picture in anthropological linguistics begins with the dislocation of the text from the pragmatic conditions of its utterance, Thomas seems to venture that "textuality" might just as well refer to relation and not the string of signs. Of course, conventional texts circulate through this space too, and Thomas himself participates in that movement through the publication of translations and recordings. Thomas proffers that something is not shared when words, even the sounds of their expression, travel, unless bodies travel too. This notion of the textuality of the relation allows us to square Thomas's language of "library" and "memory" with the classical picture, so long as we understand him as operating across these two registers – memory for code in one direction, and for form of encounter in another. When Thomas speaks of a reorganization of the memory then, I understand him to index not bodily techniques as mnemonics, as in ritual or in rhetoric, but where the bodily effect is the end itself.[29]

*Beyond Stranger Sociality*

The encounters among those whose lives intersect in Thomas's Werkstatt testify to the exceedingly complex political consequences of these overlapping vectors. For example, the reactions of audience members to readings and Thomas's description of the voice as the medium of exchange between bodies both confound the assignment of spaces as categorically private or public, intimate or distant. The tacit assumptions about what kind of spaces are important for creative-language work and about what constitutes memory have, as in other contexts, often led to antimonies in the structure of the relation of voice to text. The rigid boundaries between the sounds of voice, the linguistic text, and political reality are themselves ideological constructions.[30] The location of voice at the interstices of affect, bodily practice, subject formation, technological mediation, identity, and ethical formation has been essential to its re-emergence as a central concern for semiotics[31] and a desire to dislocate Enlightenment hierarchies of the masculine and feminine, the colonizer and the savage.[32] Outside Europe, control over the tonality of one's voice, for example, has been shown to be an important site through which one might fashion personhood or embody a transformative aspiration.[33] But voice also suggests the ways in which words are given life, in the surprising animations or awakenings of language or else in the withdrawal of such animacy, in its potential to make communion possible through acknowledgment but also to destroy us through refusal.[34] If the people I met in Berlin talked about prosodic relations, these possibilities were often contingent on a picture of poetic performance as bringing something to life. When Thomas speaks of the "awakening of words to life" or Anne Marie of Lebhaftigkeit as ink, they are attuning us to the literary event's capacity to transform everyday life, not only through shifts in our systems of meaning-making, but also in the relationship between bodies in space. The affirmation of life is a promise of its continuity but also something that takes place in moments of shifting intensity.

Literature, like art more broadly, is often lauded for its capacity to fracture publics, providing for a democratization of claims to the space of the city.[35] But in this context, the dominance of the creative-cities discourse has translated into a frequent adoption of governing norms that in some cases extend access to rights to the city but often serve to simultaneously re-inscribe neoliberal models of citizenship and belonging.[36] And as we will see in the next chapter, inclusion is often predicted on performing scripts belonging to a universalizing European typology.

It does not seem appropriate, therefore, to begin from a supposition of clear demarcated binaries. Instead, we can start from the entanglement of everyday life, out of which, doubtless, various kinds of separation are often posited. Of course, we know that inhabitants of the city are not solely strangers from different worlds, and the speed of their encounters does not necessarily imply a radical ontological separation.

In everyday life, their paths do cross and alter one another's trajectory, and it is, in a sense, their inhabiting of a shared world that allows for the pervasiveness of ordinary violence associated with conditional welcome. When Chih-wei is wounded in different ways by the denial of his presence, it is not because he senses another world from which he is cut off. His existence can be denied only from within what we might call a form of life: that is, by his material encounter with and refusal by another. If poetic events give life to language, if they allow one to claim a voice (in the sense of belonging to a form of life),[37] the value for Chih-Wei in their fleetingness and multiplicity is clear.

Analyses of urban life in places like Berlin have been stymied by long-standing assumption that modernity tends uniformly toward stranger sociality, associated with the rapidity of urban space, with a mode of resistance to traditional authority's insistence on stasis, or with alienation understood categorically. Early urban sociologists like George Simmel thought the city epitomized the modern form of conflict between individual consciousness and society: the "violent stimuli," the "rapid crowding of changing images," the continually shifting presence of strangers that pervade metropolitan life, all begot an "intellectualist character," a kind of defence mechanism against the sovereignty of the city.[38] The development of this attitude moreover had everything to do with the rise of the money economy, from the capitalization of social life, alienation, and the "indifference to difference" that made every stranger like every other. The ensuing collapse of spatial, geographical distance by modern technology and exchange meant the "reproduction of distance internally as spectacular separation."[39] On the other hand, "modernity is the transient, the fleeting, the contingent," a feature of life on the street that de Certeau described as a "mobile infinity of tactics" positioned against an otherwise imposing and occasionally intractable spatial arrangement.[40] In more recent writing, this leitmotif has been reinvigorated through the language of "non-places" in which multiple "remnants" of cultures press together and where the whirl of the metro is emblematic of the crossing of solitudes.[41]

Literacy and literature play a central role in the formation of this picture of modernity. In part, it was born from analytical attitudes that pitched reading as an activity that reifies difference and distance in an oppositional relation of audience to speaker,[42] or between autonomous, liberal subjects in political communities[43] who long for a communion that remains always just out of reach in actual experience.[44] It is print capitalism, after all, and the proliferation of texts in the vernacular that gives rise to imagined communities. These multiple registers of circulation are mediated, moreover, by the formation and maintenance of (reading) publics, a third category of social body between or beyond its definition as bounded space of the audience on the one hand and as social totality on the other – an alternative sense, it is claimed, known to us intuitively within the bounds of modern culture.[45] It is a self-organized body constituted by virtue of mere address (and not enduringly) and thus is simultaneously personal and impersonal. In our participation in a public, we are identified as the addressee not by virtue of individual identity but rather through our participation in the indefinite body of the discourse, "in common with strangers."[46] The temporality of this circulation gives the historical rhythm to the life of the public. When defined by the particularity of their address,[47] such counter-publics make "expressive corporeality the material for the elaboration of intimate life among publics of strangers."[48]

And yet a field of fleeting and variously overlapping publics seems inadequate to the reality of social life in places like Berlin.[49] If what circulates is not simply the textual product, but the form of the relation, then the performance of literature in Berlin amounts to an experimentation with forms of access and enclosure. But such scenes also complicate our notions of access to cultural commons (and its relation to publics) by revealing multiple textures of engagement with cultural resources. It is the stitching together of these registers of circulation that is important to describe, the weave of variously overlapping publics with the rhythm of small, fleeting encounters, the corporal experience of listening to poetry being read, even in a language one doesn't understand, with the dizzying alienation of capital-mediated sociality. Their crossings, the pressures they exert on one another, their similarities and differences in tone, is what I tried to suggest we can think of through the language of prosody.

*The Literary Moment*

In the examples I have cited, we find a variety of social and textual forms, each articulated in a single, if fractured and contested, field. Reading publics of thousands are connected through a temporally and spatially diffuse set of articulations. Bound together by moments of attention to a relatively fixed manifold of signs – like Yang's poem that we heard that night in Berlin but which has also been read by untold others in different places and at different times – such a social body is certainly marked by relative durability (like the texts that ground it), whether or not we understand them to be fantastical. In the case of our workshop's circulation of recordings, the aural content moves in a similar register. New media technologies made the externalization of memory for oral texts possible a century ago, and so we must distinguish now too between these and live performance. The durability of these texts we have said is understood to be contingent on their dislocability from the context of their utterance, and this too allows the social forms that emerge from such circulations to remain durable despite distance. The relationship between members is not one of particular identities of individuals with whom one is in relation, but an amorphous, perhaps totalizing social institution, the bounds of which we cannot know. The resignation of Anne Marie and Taimur's relationship to one that can only be short-lived is clearly not a sign of its devaluation. Much the same might be said of our encounter with Parisian friends in the bookstore basement. Or with Anne Marie's disappearance, then reappearance amid a different audience in the salon on different days. There needn't necessarily be a sense of lack in relationships of this kind. These particular relationships disappear, just as one accumulates more of the same kind, and a form of relation continues.

Written texts also circulate in other ways, through gift economies, in face-to-face exchanges among friends, with trusted proprietors, through relations that can be enduring and intimate in different ways, and whose meaning is particular to the context of their articulation. Multiple forms of relating can thus be identified within the same circulation; a reading public, an audience, a cherished friend. The nexus of textual relations is immanently multiple and requires that we be willing to track the various trajectories of circulation and their attendant forms of sociality simultaneously. The emphasis on separation has been premised on a privileging of durable relations as the ones that count, a subtle reintroduction of the higher status of writing culture. Not only do we have to conceptualize ephemeral social ties without regarding them as merely degraded or failed forms of enduring ones, but we also need to dislodge the assumption that the form of the text refers to a single relational form, one to one. For obvious reasons, this cannot be achieved if our analyses continue to rely on overarching master concepts.

There are those in literary theory who, for important reasons, have sought to invert the hierarchy of textual relations.[50] But such provincializing gestures cannot be enacted solely by turning a structure on its head. As the ethnographic data on life in Berlin makes clear, we would be better served by thinking of these as crisscrossing vectors within a contested field of claims to and through literature. Description, resistant to a quick ascent to very large concepts, in this way provides a necessary theoretical counterpoint to allied disciplinary approaches to the study of literature. This perspective also allows us also to problematize an often-tacit insistence on the homogeneity of the public form that still haunts "applications" of a Eurocentric imagination of the possibilities for modernity. Instead of overturning but preserving binary oppositions, I have tried to show how the intersection of these different temporalities, socialities, and configurations of power are not easily disentangled.

I have tried to make a series of suggestions, beginning from the assertion that the reality of intimacy need not be opposed necessarily to the realm of the imaginary or the fictive. I have argued that this premise of a literary life in Berlin goes hand in hand with a form of intimacy marked not by its reliance on endurance but by ephemeral and corporeal connections. By the same logic, I have suggested that this fleetingness or event character is also not a reflection of the fragility of memory, as many scholars have assumed, but rather a shift in its substance. Rather than look for the performance (both its channel and its effects) within the conventionally understood "text" of poetry, it is the mode of sharing that becomes mobile. Finally, I have tried to maintain that we understand such avenues for literary action not in opposition to those accrued around writing forms but rather as existing in a state of heteroglossic play. The dual nature of these performances attests to those simultaneous possibilities for poetry.

"Poetry," Gaston Bachelard once wrote, "is the metaphysics of moment ... it must deliver, all at once ... the secret of a soul."[51] Poetry rejects the temporality of the scaffold, of preambles and principles, by marching against doubt – "at most, it calls for a prelude of silence." It comes in the wake of echoes of prosaic thought. Its time, Bachelard, remarks, is vertical as everyday time is horizontal. That is to say, by accepting the poetic instant, "prosody allows its reinsertion into prose ... social life, ordinary life."[52] The time of poetry, for Bachelard, contains, "a multitude of contradictory events enclosed within a single instant."[53] It imposes an order among these simultaneities, but one that runs perpendicular to the time of prose, and in so doing gathers up depth. In the example of reading Mallarmé (a "direct" assailant of horizontal time) Bachelard uses the metaphor of pebbles cast into streams, whose ripples shatter and distort images and reflections.[54] The smile and the regret remain in free play, neither overcoming the other. Hence, Bachelard's claim that poetry does not unfold but is, rather, knit. The epiphanic instant[55] is the coming together of the event and eternity, which is itself a reflection of the material encounter of two people.

> Someone exists in the world, unknown to you, then, suddenly, in a single encounter, before knowing him, you recognize him. A dialogue begins in the night, a dialogue, which, through a certain tone, completely involves

the persons. "Michel, is that?" And the voice answers, "Jeanne, is that you?" Neither one needs an answer, "Yes, it is I." For if the questioned person were to transcend the questioning, and forego the infinite grace of the encounter, he would then descend into monologue or confession ... into the dull narrative of wishes and woes.[56]

In Berlin, a literary form of life deeply troubles the usual assumptions about the relationship of durability and social life; in poetry readings, prosodic elements opened a range of crossing and mutually contesting significations. Rather than assume that ephemeral relationships or texts (those associated with the transience of populations) were necessarily degraded or failed versions of enduring (albeit alienated) ones, a more felicitous account would be sensitive to a heterogeneity of meanings and valorization. Thomas, Chih-Wei, and others connected forms of sociality that emerged from fleeting events with various aspects of the sonic materiality of language – the ways being present to hear voices, shifts in tone, volume, and pitch were essential to the movement of texts and to the kinds of relationships this movement engendered.

*Chapter Three*

# Exile in Translation: The Politics of Remaining Unknown

And what happens to me when I withhold my acceptance of privacy – anyway, of otherness – as the home of my concepts of the human soul and find my criteria to be dead, mere words, word-shells? I said a while ago in passing that I withhold myself. What I withhold myself from is my attunement with others – with all others, not merely with the one I was to know.

– Stanley Cavell

At the end of one of Berlin's S-bahn railway lines, near the southwest border where the city becomes Potsdam, there is an old brown mansion surrounded by gardens that for more than four decades has been home to one of the capital's most prestigious literary forums. This stage and its guesthouse were the setting for some of the most important (and contentious) conversations in local literary history; its walls silently listened to some of the twentieth century's most celebrated writers, including the renowned Gruppe 47 behind so much of the city's Nachkriegsliteratur, the effort at German literary renewal following the Second World War. It promotes itself as a site where there "arose in innumerable encounters what Goethe called 'world literature': a network of awareness and recognition of the other as an equal." Designed to be a transnational (Länderübergreifendes) centre for literature with support from the Ford Foundation and the State Senate, the Literarisches Colloquium Berlin hosts a number of highly innovative workshops and support programs for translators into and out of German.

One evening in 2013, I sat in the back of the dimly lit reading hall as Liao Yiwu read from a new book. It was the first time I had the chance to hear the celebrated poet in person; he wore a simple white linen shirt with a Mandarin collar and looked down over thin-rimmed glasses, dramatically chanting the story of his time in state prison in

Tumen, where he learned to play the dongxiao (a bamboo flute) from an elderly monk called Sima. "I became his last disciple," Yiwu told us. In prison, he recalled a mounting pressure to record his story and those of the people he met; if he did not, he would forget and their memory would be lost – that recording now exists primarily in German translation. Three times he wrote down the words that became the manuscript that became *Für ein Lied und hundert Lieder* (For One Song and a Hundred Songs), and three times it was seized by police. The sound of a gong quietly rang in the background played out of speakers tucked away in the corner of the ceiling. His German language translator, Karin Betz, sat to his right and read her version of his poems out loud when he was finished, in a practiced and calm cadence. He answered questions from the audience through an interpreter named Yeemei Guo about China today, about the violence he experienced, about Daoism and its aesthetics, and about poetry. They asked him about his relationship to "traditional" Chinese writing, his impressions of life in Europe, and how it differed from the place he was forced to leave. And they asked what Germany could learn from him. Yiwu reflected on the particularity of Berlin as a context for his continued literary activities, about living on a street named for the poet Hölderlin, and noted the ironic significance of Heidegger for the poet's reception. At the end of the conversation, Yiwu played the xiao for us, and roared a short final chant.

As a young man Yiwu read Western poetry and rose to prominence as an official writer of the state. But when he published two poems in 1989 calling the Chinese system of communism a cancer, he came under suspicion. After the violence at Tiananmen square that summer, Yiwu began repurposing older aesthetics of oral poetry and chanting, challenging the state by recording his poems rather than writing them. In 1990 he was arrested and placed on a life-long blacklist for seditious writing, but internationally his reputation grew. He was invited to an international festival in Germany (first in Frankfurt, then in Köln), where his work had grown enormously popular, but Yiwu found himself under a state travel ban. Despite a formal invitation from the Haus der Kulturen der Welt to participate along with an official Chinese delegation of one hundred writers, Yiwu was barred from attending by the state. In response, he wrote an open letter to German Chancellor Angela Merkel, pleading for help in February 2010. "Dear Madam Merkel … My Name is Liao Yiwu, I am a writer from the bottom of Chinese society." He chose to write her directly, he said at the time, because of her influence, because of the love the German reading public had given to his books, and because of her personal experience:

you once lived in dictatorial East Germany, and perhaps you were trampled upon, humiliated, had your freedom restricted, and have some understanding of how I feel at this very moment. When the Berlin Wall fell you were 35 years old, I was 31 years old; that year the June Fourth massacre also happened; the night it happened I created and recited the long poem, "Massacre" [unofficial English translation of 屠杀, Tusha]. For this I was arrested and imprisoned for four years. In 1997, we founded the underground literary magazine *The Intellectuals* [unofficial English translation of 知识分子, Zhishifenzi]; in the inside front cover and inside back cover of the first issue we published two exciting photos: one was from 1970, of Willy Brandt, Chancellor of the Federal Republic of Germany, representing the German people, kneeling, admitting guilt, and repenting at the monument to the innocent victims of World War II, in Warsaw, Poland; the other photo was from November 9, 1989, when the people, ecstatic, broke through the Berlin Wall ... As individuals, perhaps we once had a shared history? Maybe I am destined to experience, sooner or later, what you experienced in the past? God really looks out for the Germans.[1]

But when February gave way to March, Yiwu was still unable to leave China. He next wrote a letter to his German readers (in Chinese and German) apologizing for his absence, still in his home in rural Chengdu. He sent along his poems – the ones we heard that night in 2013.

To my dear readers in Germany whom I have never met, how many other sages like my master are there among the Chinese people now? I do not know. How many innocent political prisoners are still imprisoned? I also do not know. Before the June Fourth massacre in 1989, how many old blood stains have been wiped away? I still do not know. But writers like me from the bottom of society still have to write, record, and broadcast [our stories], even to the dismay of the Communist Party of China. I have the responsibility to make you understand that the life of the Chinese spirit is longer than the totalitarian government. Below I entrust my fellow writer in Germany Miss Liao Tianqi to read my piece, "*Chuigushou jianhao-sang zhe Li Changgeng*." The main character of this piece plays the *suona*, a Chinese musical instrument made of copper. The pitch is high, intense, and sharp like a knife. It contrasts distinctly with the *dongxiao* that my master taught, but the spirits of the instruments are the same. These two instruments, with the addition of wailing mourners, are also used to remember the dead and to console the living. In this China which is free for neither the living nor the dead, my readers, your attentive listening to this story will also comfort me at the edge of the grave.[2]

By July of the following year however, Yiwu, had made a harrowing escape through China's border with Vietnam, bribing a criminal gang, who in turn bribed customs officials, ultimately making his way to Berlin, where he now lives and works. In 2012, he was awarded the Peace Prize by the Börsenverein des Deutschen Buchhandels in commendation for his service in the fight for the freedom of others. And in 2019, he gave an interview with the German historian Irmtrud Wojak, in which he reflected on his first arrival in Germany nearly a decade earlier. "Many friends have tried to persuade me to stay in Germany, but I did not want to stay here," he confided on that occasion:

> I still have many friends in China, I cannot speak German and so I went back. But immediately afterwards followed the Arab Spring, which also hit China and the political mood was very sensitive. I grew scared again that I would never be allowed to leave China again, although my book *For a Song and a Hundred Songs* would be published soon in Germany, and then the Chinese version in Taiwan. My publisher told me that they were worried about my safety, even postponing or canceling the publication. That was a turning point for me, for the publication of my work I would absolutely wager something again.[3]

Wojak asked Yiwu at the end of their interview whether there was something he would like to say to "us"? "The things I tell," he answered, "I always have to repeat." His interpreter, Peigen Wang, had been complaining to him that he constantly repeats himself:

> I have no choice. My job is writing and testifying [Zeugnisablegen, lit. providing evidence] for the world, for history. The reason therefore that I keep repeating myself is that in a democratic society, freedom, democracy and human right ... And I find that this is no attitude to have. So, I must mention and emphasize these things in conversations and in my writing again and again. I have a certain notoriety in Germany and I find it is also relatively easy to be heard. Therefore, I must simply use these powers to hold up and to defend the values that are so important and so valuable in our society. For example, I have repeatedly spoken about Li Bifeng [a writer imprisoned in China since 1998], and even written about him, and indeed many Germans have been struck by my stories. Some Germans have even gone to China, traveled to Chendu where Li Bifeng is detained to visit him in jail. I find this very good. Once Chancellor Merkel was on a visit to Chengdu, when she suddenly expressed to the accompanying official that she wanted to visit Li Bifeng. That simply terrified these officials.

I liked that very much and that is reason why I always repeat the same questions or the same stuff.

I share Yiwu's story and words at some length to highlight the logic of commensurability through which it operates; the alignments of his speech with normative expectations (in this case, registers anticipated within particular institutional settings).[4] This process moves by forging barter-like equivalences (Tiananmen Square for the fall of the Berlin Wall) in which the dominant language serves as a template, at the expense of the shifts in force or feeling that words carry as they move into different contexts. Yiwu accepted the terms of these translations, at least in the context of a petition for political protection. Like other writers, especially very great writers, who find themselves living in exile in Germany,[5] Yiwu has been able to leverage literature's historically privileged status to claim rights to the city and even expedited asylum, grant monies, and institutional support at a time when others are so regularly and visibly being excluded. He won residency with the aid of his publishers and through state-sponsored programs run by organizations like the Deutsche Akademische Austauschdienst (DAAD), whose Berlin Künstlerprogramm offered financial support and a visa for a year-long stay, funded by the German Foreign Office and the Berlin state senate. The program describes its missions as staving off the threat to diverse "cultural traditions" posed by "uniform levelling out in the process of globalization." The perspectives of "other nations [in art] on conditions here," their flyers elaborated, "are to be seen as a *decisive incentive to self-reflection in our society.*"[6]

Writers like Yiwu are taken to serve as examples of national traditions, or what the DAAD calls national perspectives, under a pluralistic scheme proper to world literature that assumes a correspondence between common features of cultural works and the worlds they are made to represent. Within liberal discourse, language practices were thought typifying of the people who speak them, and their legibility requires performance of "metasemiotic stereotypes"[7] or "emblematic identity displays,"[8] where the attribution is to not an actual, external stock of cultural knowledge, but an assumption about one.[9] This can take the form of what Ellen Basso termed an "ordeal of language," in which we recognize the "inherent contradictions in the 'texts of self' one is required to perform." Facing the scrutiny of our language practices, the ways we speak (or do not speak) can make us accomplices in (our own) domination. In such cases, the anticipated scripts do not necessarily determine the content of performance so much as the shape of what might count as a literary tradition and the ways difference is marked within them – in other words, what sort of performances can be understood from within a form of life as an example of the concept of literature. As one official from the largest international literary festival in the city, Internationales Literaturfestival Berlin (stylized *ilb*), put it to me, selection for participation in German literary worlds comes down to a matter of "aesthetics," here understood as "political relevance":

> It is crucial for the work that we would like to imagine that it has a particular moment – addressing themes that enter into European discourse insufficiently, or even just in an aesthetic way: forms of storytelling and writing that open new perspectives on the world ... we try to be a corrective to the German book market.

The gaps in European discourse "anticipate" the expressive forms into which "foreign" writers can slot themselves if they are to count as writers at all. For writers to see themselves in those imputations, to count, to appear as real, to be recognizable, their words have to take on another aesthetic guise.[10] This is what gives the work its particular character.[11] Being out of place is registered as a condition of translation. For performances to count, they must simultaneously fit the concept and yet register as not-quite-at-home in their formal aesthetic qualities. This contradiction is essential. And because in Germany world literature serves as a favoured metaphoric template for the movement of peoples, even carving out specific routes along which people have been able to move, writers like Yiwu who find themselves in need are forced to perform these scripts again and again, to countless journals, activists, publishers, and critics, to secure – in fact even to petition for – asylum.[12] Translations under such a regime are indicative not of movement "beyond or without borders" but of specific ways of enforcing and regulating mobility and immobility.[13] Such putative distinctions in literary practices do more than set a neutral background for encounter. They are interested enforcements of "a particular place for literature in the world."[14]

Behind ostensive gestures of inclusion lies a powerful assumption about translatability, a thought that all human languages are infinitely translatable, that every experience can be made legible through a logic of market exchange, by finding local equivalents for European categories.[15] While ostensibly ontological differences proliferate, literatures are assumed to be interchangeable *as literature* because they congeal an abstract quality common but external to each. The abstraction and equivocation necessary for exchange of this kind effects what a hegemonic view treats as a licit deformation on both ends.[16] On the one hand, there is threat of blending, of homogenizing; on the other, the threat of losing something in translation, something that we have not fully understood. This network has operated through a tendency Emily Apter describes as a "reflexive endorsement of cultural equivalence and substitutability, or toward the celebration of nationally and ethnically branded 'differences' that have been niche-marketed as commercialized identities."[17] But while concepts like world literature have generated considerable debate in comparative literary studies in recent years,[18] less attention has been paid to what it might have meant to actually live under this discursive regime.

Anthropologists too have sometimes advanced arguments that all languages, and all cultures, are infinitely translatable into one another.[19] If language determines the limits of expressibility, and every language is wholly translatable, then anything left aside or mistranslated or "lost" must therefore be inexpressible, beyond the bounds of sense. Should we however assume that transcendental propositions are the only, or the best, bearers of truth? Perhaps instead what we need is a more robust account of the friction of translation, those aspects of language that resist or pose a question of translation rather than the inexpressible?[20] In Germany, while a writer can take advantage of the special status afforded writers and their books under German law,[21] they have to be legible *as writers* according to normative standards modelled in *these* forms of life, and simultaneously "identify with an impossible standard of authentic traditional culture," a situation that leaves them permanently half-othered.[22] Below I argue that this sense of one making one's self legible through equivalences shares much with a dominant, trauma-theory–based understanding of testimony. Both pose experience as outside language, as normally inexpressible, and as issues of knowledge.[23] At the same time, as much as such interpretations illuminate about the "discursive power or desire of the observer" and the similarity detected between "foreign" practices and those "at home," the possibility of drawing connections seems to suggest a "background of common sense that we might identify as part of the human way of life."[24] There were also those I came to know who refused or resisted these stipulations, or who were never offered them in the first place.

I juxtapose here Yiwu's story with that of a poet I knew named Najet, who had come to Berlin from Tunisia and who was – at least initially – willing to bear remaining unknown rather than accept this situation. As she awaited the right context in which to be acknowledged, she found herself cut off from everyday life, from language, and from kin. How should we read this "certain kind of silence"?[25] Rather than see this as a failure to acclimate, I think of her gesture of waiting as a politics of refusal. Her manner of finding a life in the city troubled a dominant view of literature and political action in which truth reveals hidden conditions, in which the "writer in exile" bears the burden of his or her entire class symbolically and of the entire nation rhetorically, and for which writers such as Brecht are the model. Literature, within this discourse, involves a manner of "carving up the world," an arrangement of what can or cannot be seen. But by refusing conditions of translation and, by extension, everyday life on the terms on offer, she can wait for moments in which she finds words to express herself on her own terms. Najet's position does not simply negate the dominant form of talk; she offers an interpretation of it through shifts in the region of voice, shifts to what Foucault called the "double" of a term:

> It is not a question of installing, as people say, another scene, but, on the contrary, of splitting the elements on the same scene. It is not a question, then, of the caesura that indicates access to the symbolic, but of the coercive synthesis that ensures the transmission of power and the indefinite displacement of its effects.[26]

It is this doubling I want to trace. I move back and forth between a fragmentary lingual life history as it was shared with me[27] and scholarly and public debates about language, exile, popular culture, and translation. When Najet and I spoke, it was often English and German, occasionally with smatterings of French words. I have included among these scenes a few scattered selections of her poetry either in the original English or in my translation from the published German.

**A Salon in Wedding**

I first met Najet through a mutual friend, an intellectual and activist who grew up in East Germany, named Christa. Early in my fieldwork, Christa helped me navigate the variegated literary terrain of the city, its political contours, and its dense tangle of networks. She had studied philosophy and philology, earning a doctorate in 1977, and worked as a translator of English literary texts into German, publishing more than 150 major novels for the German market since the 1980s. In 2006, in recognition of her achievements, the German branch of PEN asked her to help organize the International Congress to be held in Berlin – eighty years after the fateful meeting of the same organization predating the rise of Hitler's regime. She was invited that year to serve on the board and was quickly placed in charge of the growing writers-in-exile program. Throughout the Nazi period, International PEN had helped countless writers and artists escape persecution, and after the Nazi purge of "tainted" literature, a German PEN centre was founded in exile in 1934 in London. The modern German charter stipulates four aims: 1) whoever participates in PEN should see literature, always in view of its national origins, as a common medium of circulation for all nations; 2) should help keep literature from the ravages that national and political suffering can cause; 3) should help establish good understanding and mutual respect among nations, for the ideal of a world without the hatred of races, classes, or peoples; and 4) should promote the unimpeded exchange of ideas within each nation and between nations, oppose the oppression of freedom of expression and arbitrary censorship, establish the freedom of press, as well as stand against their excesses, lies, and disfigurements of the facts, and therefrom assume the necessary progress of the world to a higher organizational, political, and economic order, which requires free criticism of the government and administration.

In return for the world's response to the plight of German writers between 1933 and 1945, the state, in the person of Minister of State for Culture and Media Michael Neumann, granted federal funding for a writers-in-exile program in 1999, offering scholarships and aid for five to six refugees to live in Germany under expedited asylum status (generally granted in under two months) and to receive paid healthcare, security, counselling, language training, and networking opportunities.[28] The program provides up to two years of funds and housing for writers from anywhere in the world who need refuge. Only a few writers are in the program at any time, housed in four cities throughout Germany, but most live in Berlin. In her time with PEN, Christa had overseen the careers of more than twenty-five Stipendiaten. Almost none of the writers in the program had applied by themselves to come to Germany; many were recommended by NGOs, often Journalists without Borders, Amnesty International, or International PEN itself. Others had made their way to Christa via colleagues already living in exile. Her personal history allowed her to move through the German literary-political landscape with an ease that would have been nearly impossible for someone born anywhere else. But it also meant that she was positioned as a cultural intermediary, and she tried to make herself into a conduit for their encounter.

She no longer held that post when we first met, opting to hand over the reins and focus her attention on a subsidiary project, a literary salon aimed both at opening up a reading public for new arrivals and creating a space to explore various politics of exile and writing in the context of those experiences. Outside the bureaucracy and the more ossified

Exile in Translation: The Politics of Remaining Unknown    65

regime of formal world-literature institutions, she had more room to manoeuvre. When I first became involved with Salon Exil in 2013, three Stipendiaten were living in Berlin: one from Tunisia, who had been in Berlin for some time; and two newcomers, one each from Georgia and Vietnam. If possible, Christa tried to find funding to help the families of writers escape as well, finding them bigger apartments or larger stipends. Christa often emphasized that she was unconcerned about how great a writer seemed. "We are responsible for those who are really in danger," she would say. "We want to provide a literary dignity to authors." "Today," her website and flyers read, "we speak of exiles primarily in connection with artists, writers and journalists" as those most directly impacted by the crushing of the freedom of expression. The condition of exile can endure, often for many years. "It is not easy for anyone to live in exile," she explained, "but for authors, it is especially difficult, because their work is more acutely attached to their native language than that of a doctor or an engineer, and the thoughts they express, the images in which they express themselves, are rooted in the cultures of their homelands." Such artists are uprooted twice:

> First from the soil that nourishes her writing, and thus also from the extensive networks of common history, common myths and narratives, which they share with their readers. Secondly, through the loss of resonance with her own reader community [Leserschaft] that influences her writing and is in turn influenced by what she writes. For writers exile ultimately means the extinction of her own identity as a writer ... and thus as part of public life.

To make this situation "somewhat more bearable" [etwas erträglicher zu machen], the salon staged an "encounter" [Begegnung] with potential readers.[29] Another encounter was staged simultaneously, in the form of conversation about exile. The salon met semi-regularly to hear new writing. We collected donations in a small tin and charged a euro for a glass of beer or wine. But since nearly everyone who came was already a friend, hardly any money was charged. Most were friends of Christa's with personal experiences of displacement – those who were children during the Shoah and who had returned to Germany as adults, or else East Germans who, though they had not themselves moved, often felt that they were strangers at home after the fall of the Wall and in the wake of Berlin's rapid recent transformation. Though the later were increasingly displaced from the city centre by newcomers, particularly if they spoke no English, they were by and large, at least in my experience, able to preserve their social networks. Many were highly credentialed. This group often functioned as intermediaries for those who made their way to Germany now from elsewhere, who had limited proficiency in German, or lacked the paperwork necessary to secure more permanent accommodations or work. They helped buy groceries and acquire cell phones. Among the non-Germans in the group, there were those who always intended on returning "home" and were simply biding their time in Berlin, waiting out political conditions. Several did make it out. Claudia, for example, was a journalist from Sierra Leone who reported on crimes committed by the Supreme Council of the Armed Forces Revolutionary Council during the civil war in the 1990s, including a massive plot to massacre rebels; in response to her reporting her house, and later the offices of the newspaper she founded, were burned to the ground. She lived in Berlin for five years, and by the time I met her, was back living near Freetown, where she had returned a year after the disarmament was completed. Najet, by contrast, had no such horizon of return nor really any desire for it. There was no home to return to, she once told me, at least anywhere people would know her experiences without her having to voice them. "My Tunisia," she said, "has been destroyed, there's nothing to go back to now even if I could." She made it to Germany after a group of acquaintances helped her to change her passport and flee to Weimar in October 2012. Friends then put her in contact with Christa. They knew her as a "person who wants to help," Najet told me much later. Christa "saw a lot in her life, and she is a fighter, and she loves to help fighters."

The first time I heard Najet's name it was after a long meeting of Salon Exil, where one of Christa's friends, a Jewish writer called Maik, told us about his own time as a refugee, about his birth in Shanghai to dissident Marxist parents in the 1930s and his transit through Switzerland to Danzig as a boy. He spoke about his mother's participation in the resistance and her work in military intelligence, and later his career as a translator and authority on Shakespeare. Maik felt at home, he told us, in German and in English, the latter often serving as lingua franca for discussions, though it occasionally excluded some of the former East Germans who had taken Russian instead. We moved from the salon to a café for a drink after the meeting, where everyone laughed and traded knowing stories. But Najet sat quietly on the other side of the table in the corner, her chair pulled slightly out, slowing drinking water and taking a handkerchief to her nose. After we'd been eating for a while, Christa brought over a tall German man to meet her, who told her he'd like to arrange a time to film her talking about her experiences, and to which Najet nodded but didn't commit, apologizing for having been sick again lately and very tired. She excused herself not long after. Back at Christa's apartment, she gave me a small green book that had finally come out in hardcopy, *Fremde Heimat: Texte aus dem Exil*,[30] for which three of Najet's poems had been translated from Arabic into German by another friend, Leila Chamma. By the time they were published, Najet had stopped writing in her mother tongue, cut off from those publics first by force and now by choice. She had been thinking of writing a novel in English.

Written during a brief visit to her home in Tunisia in the winter of 2008, the first of her poems translated into German is rendered "Sehnsucht," longing. It begins with an invocation of a light, a voice. But in the second stanza, we learn the narrator is perhaps addressing pain itself. "I am facing you, pain, falling upon me, be my ink on the paper" [Zugewandt bin ich / dir, / Schmerz, / fall über mich her, sei meine Tinte auf dem Papier]. She is lonely, "without a homeland, without a name, without [her] loves." She "extends her soul" [in the familiar inflection, dir, to you] and beseeches "be my jacket in this death, be a ship that avoids the port." Everything is salt. The taste of coffee, even the letters, in her eyes, on her lips, leaving the tongue to dream of sugar. Like waves crave the rock into which they slam their pride. Twice more she draws parallels to earlier sensory metaphors: like a boat craves "handkerchief loving women," like eyes to water. And she is herself drawn then to the dream-images (Traumbildern) to which she entrusts a secret, a lost secret, because the bottle that kept it is now smashed. Another poem continues a thought:

On the street of Freedom
behind my mirror image
entrenched
I play my defeats
of a woman
who my Tears hate
A woman who witnessed my taming
saw
how one unprogrammed me
how I complied with the rules
how one trained me
broke myself
…
My poem, in mourning
accompany me
send out letters
to lick up the mud of my defeats
…

> On the street
> yet only
> my I
> and its reflection
> me, the Word

I wrote to Najet after that evening to ask if her we could get together. She told me she still wasn't feeling well, she was tired, but that I could come by the following week.

## A Child Poet, a Mother, an Unknown Woman

People in Berlin often asked Najet about Tunisia, how it was different from Germany, whether she preferred her life in Berlin or whether she longed to return home. As I left Najet's apartment late one evening after many hours of talking, she began to cry. She took my hands and told me that a writer from a newspaper had called her earlier in the day and that their interview lasted only a few minutes. She said that "these journalists don't want to know true things, simple things." She was living around the corner from the Lichtburgforum where Salon Exil met, in a typical Berlin building with a courtyard, grey walls, and white windows. I was late that evening for our visit because I missed the first train from my flat in another part of town. As I approached the door, I noticed that her name wasn't on any of the placards where one normally rings to be let in. It read simply PEN Zentrum. After climbing three flights of stairs, she greeted me in grey sweater, blue pyjama pants, and worn slippers. She hadn't left the house at all that day. Ushering me inside, she pointed to a stool where I could leave my shoes and bade me sit in her bare living room. Two blue chairs and a blue couch, an orange shag rug, a broken old TV, large windows grazed by a young tree, a work desk with an old flat-panel computer monitor, a fax machine, and a cordless phone. The phone rang twice in the time it took her to fetch some coffee, but she let the calls go to the machine since the messages were more often than not for some former resident, and in languages she didn't speak. She'd come to PEN not long before we first met, in April of 2013. "Berlin is a place for me, it is better than America or Paris, I started to think of staying. Of course if they allow me," she told me, laughing. "Here it is now because now they have democracy they have kind of freedom, they have more expression," she said, as she returned from the kitchen.

> You can talk, and that is a little bit different. I think for me it is too much different. But for the German, I think sometimes I see some people that

are not really happy because they don't know what is suffering, what is real suffering, because those people if they lived in Africa or some Arab countries they will discover the difference. In the places even you can't say normal things about your being, or what you want. Maybe that is because they have a lot of democracy and a lot of freedom and that is why these people they can't see they are free.

When I asked her if she had found good local readers apart from the journalists, she told me that she had given a few readings from time to time in bookshops that Christa had helped to arrange.

> N: When I go and I read, people like because they tell me and that makes me very happy. And of course, when I go and I read and people like it, that is my life. My life is my writing. My experience, writing and my readers. And when I go, they always like. I met a man once and I talked about my experience and he told me, "Did you write some novels about this?" and I said yes, and he told me "In which language?" I said "In Arabic," and he said "Give me your number maybe I take one or two to translate." But he didn't write never called back. Maybe one day somebody comes … what I read translated in Germany it isn't giving the real face of Arab society. Because it is about this revolution and the Arab Spring but they don't know, some people they want to make to be famous or something, try to make some book. What I saw that's translated, not only to German, but to French, to English. Americans are interested to write about the Arab Spring and they have translated a lot of novels. But I saw that and it really makes me laugh sometimes. But when you read the text in Arabic, it is not true. Sometimes I laugh.
> A: What are they interested in?
> N: I think when they read only about politics, or about Islam, or those kinds of books, they have money they translate things and they put them everywhere, but I don't think that shows the real problems of the people. I think there are some people who write true about these problems, and they don't wait for prices or pay, they only want to write about the reality. And that is what needs to be shown to the people in the world. Because as we know about French people, we know about American people, we know about German people, we read everything. And even if we don't practice the language, we read it translated. In Arabic, I was shocked when I read Shakespeare in Arabic and then read him in English and I was shocked, I thought, "Poor Shakespeare!" some people have made crimes. That's why there are some people now they want to translate my work from Arabic to German. But not professional. I like somebody who is like a real translator. But those they ask money. And

> I met some others they want to translate for me. It is good for me, good for me.
>
> A: And in Tunisia, are people reading you now?
>
> N: Not me, I chose to stop. I stopped writing in Arabic recently. I like now to work here in Europe.
>
> A: So in English?
>
> N: I wrote in English, some poems, and a novel. Of course, most of my writing is in Arabic
>
> A: But now some has been translated to German?
>
> N: Some of it has been translated and maybe some more will be translated and I wish one day some novels because I like the German people to know about us. About how women live in our society. How things are with our society. They know about us – I discovered I mean they know about us from our politicians to give the grey face of our society. But our society is not politicians. We are us. We have traditions. We have problems. We have many things. Nobody knows them. And I write about those small things. And I want that for the German people to know us as Tunisian people. And how we live.

Some years later, as paperwork was coming due for her to continue refugee status in the country, she explained to me the difficult process of meticulously translating documents from German into English and then her answers back into German, working carefully so as not to introduce any errors. The expectation all the time, she said, was that she would speak and write in German. People often asked her to read her poems in German translation, but she usually refused:

> It is better if someone else should read it because I feel pity on my poem. One day I was presenting in a theatre, and they asked me to read in German, so I read three poems in German. And I felt as though I was doing a crime against my poems. I was not happy. But they wanted me to do that ... It is better for me to read them in English, or Arabic. But when they ask me to talk in German, I will not find the words. I will stop and think. Maybe I will say something else, or something I do not know. I respect the German language. I respect all languages. But I cannot read my poems in German. They tell me, "Talk!" but I can't talk. What shall I say? I want to say something about they are discussing and about what they are saying in English, but they want it in German.

Najet's life intersected politics in a number of ways. Her mother, a Muslim, was against Bourguiba. So was her brother, "but he was not a Muslim," she made sure to remind me. Her father was a Bourguinist, "despite that he had done many bad things to my father," she told me.

> I don't know why sometimes, I don't know why people like him ... One year he became sick, he has to not let Tunisia between the hands of his family to tear the country. He was ok, he was fine. He educated the Tunisian people, he gave over freedom, he made a lot of beautiful things ... but he did not want to relinquish power, so he was also making mistakes, by the time he became old I was against him, against his politics, his system, his way.

Najet grew up in the north of Tunisia, in a town called La Marsa, a suburb of Tunis, "a place by the sea." Her rise to prominence as a poet in Tunisia was miraculous. As a young girl, her father did not permit her to attend school. He was against formal education for girls. "He had the mentality of the *master*," she told me. Next door to her childhood home was a school run by the Sueur Blanche, a Catholic order of nuns. Najet would sit all day by the window, watching children come in and out, and imagining what studying would be like. The sisters took notice, and one day, the priest came to talk to her father, ultimately convincing him to let her attend. She began her studies in French at age six, but her mother sent her on Fridays to the mosque to study Arabic as well. Najet hated it there because the man in charge who called himself a sheik and an imam was "not a true Muslim. He is a cheater." She was not allowed to speak French at home. "The French army killed my mother's father. She hates the French language and everything French, because he was a combatant and they killed him." She laughed. She enjoys teaching me about the history of Tunisian Arabic and the historical politics of language in the region, over which she had extraordinary breadth of knowledge. Najet began to learn English at fourteen years old, drawn to it for the doors she said that it promised her it would open. I asked her once if she always knew she wanted to be a writer. "Oh early!" she told me. "I was born like that." She began to publish her poems at the age of nine, and by eleven she was winning local and national prizes. "It was very hard to publish at that time in newspapers," she explained. That year a festival was held for Arabic songs, and a call was issued for poets who wanted to participate, instructing them to submit their writing in an envelope without a name or address, which were only to be included in a separate sealed envelope. Winning a place in the festival meant appearing in print in a section of the newspapers normally reserved for the great writers.

> That's why when I won three prizes, my name was not on the poem because if they knew they would never choose me because there were great poets and they were shocked when they saw me. I was only a child and one of them said, "It is only a child! What's this! You shouldn't add that to [include her among] us! We are great poets!" And there was a man who was in the jury – he is still alive, he is a great composer – and he told them, "We found good poems and that is enough for us. We didn't see that is a child now. And what is interesting for us, it is only the poems."

Just like that, Najet became a celebrity. "I came by the window, not by the door," she would say. The difficulty of being a woman writer, she went on, "started from the house":

> It started from the house because my father was against that and each time when I published a poem he hit me hard. He punished me. And a lot of pain. Each time. I can't read my poems, I can't go, he said he wanted many times to stop me from studying and from going outside. But I fight it hard. One day he cut my hair, all my hair, to make me not go outside. And he tore all my clothes, to not let me go outside, stay at home, and not go read my poems and go outside. Despite that, I left, and I read my poems. I didn't mind.

From an early age Najet says she felt the need to fight. I asked her once if this was always part of her plan as well, to fight for the freedom of women. She corrected me: "Men are not free too. They are suffering. There are workers. There are children. For everyone." As a child, she said that she became aware that fighting meant opposition to the dictatorship and aligning herself with the communist opposition. One of her teachers secretly provided her with copies of the works of Karl Marx, but they were taken away from her by police who overheard her proud boast of reading his work. Though it would be several more years before she could study Marx in detail, "thoughts of the rights of the workers ... started to grow" in her mind. Another teacher warned her that the communists were disingenuous: "They are not true ... they are cheaters here, they are not true ... don't work with them. They are not good." But it was not until she was arrested as a young adult for her part in proletarian consciousness-raising demonstrations that she found herself with no allies – "They let me face my destiny ... since that time I discovered what ... is communism in Arabic societies. It is not really true. It is something like you bring a Bedouin and you make him wear a costume," she said, laughing again, "a French costume or something like that. And since I started not to be a communist or anything like that. Only a person who fights." At university, where Najet began studying journalism, she developed a parallel autodidactic program, devouring Trotsky and Che Guevara:

> I started to discover a lot of things. A lot of things. And I decided since that time to be free. In my writing, in my literature and my poems and my novels – it is my pen. Not a party. Not communism. Not anything else. I'm free, and I fight for humanity. Only that … When I started to write, I was fighting in the house, I fought my father. In the culture arena I fought those people, poets and writers, who refused to see a woman as a writer … they didn't want a woman to write and to fight and to say things against some things in the society. That is something that shocked them. They started to do a lot of things to stop me. And each time I felt very badly, and I cried and I went home and I told my mother, "They did that and they did that," and one day my mother one day told me, "If you are weak, stop and study and don't go and don't write and don't go. If you want to be a writer, you have to fight. You have to not cry." And so, I went again.

At twenty-four, Najet was married, and took a job producing television programs about the history of Maghrebian literature. By 1981, she had begun to find herself at odds with the Bourguiba regime. In 1982, her first book, published in Arabic, was released in the Tunisian market, as well as a number of political writings in then-banned local newspapers. Police began harassing her on a weekly basis, sometimes arresting her for one day, other times showing up at her house. She frequently found herself followed in the street. A year later, the situation grew dire, and she left the country with her husband. Though she was not at the time officially forbidden from returning, police visited the home of her parents and threatened her mother:

> They told her, "Your daughter is very clever and she's better than 100 men because she [ran] away, she knows how to run away from our hands." And she told them, "Why you are looking for her – she's only a girl and one, just one of them?" And he was a man I [knew well], he made a lot of affronts to me and to my mother … And even had he tried to do … things. And he told my mother, "You don't know what is your daughter … maybe you think that your daughter is only a girl. But she is not only a girl; she meant a *lot* to us."

Though she couldn't always bring herself to say the words, the nature of the threat was clear. She held a tissue firmly, shook her head, and looked down again. For two years Najet remained in Yemen. "And after that we went to Cyprus. Two years in Cyprus too. After that Algeria, and after Algeria, Morroco. And Sudan. And Beirut. And Oman." She started to laugh again. "And Baghdad." In 1984 she gave birth to her first child while in exile, and then a second while in Algeria, and a third in Morocco. I asked if each of her children had different passports "Yes, when I [went] to change the passport, they said, 'How many times are you married!?'" She laughed. From her travelling exile (a condition common among those who have found themselves similarly on the run), she continued to write. During the time of Ben Ali, encouraged by news of changes, Najet visited La Marsa to see her family. In the meantime, her marriage had fallen apart, and she struggled to convince her husband to assent to a divorce. It was finally granted in 1998, and her father subsequently threw Najet and her children out of his house. She lived on the street with her children for several years:

> And in the time of Ben Ali, I went there, at first only for a visit. I stayed one month [in La Marsa]. And I read about a lot of things, about he makes change, he gives freedom of speech, he gives a lot of freedom … And I was happy, I said maybe it will be ok. Because he started to say a lot, he started even to make some associations for actors – because the actors and artists before him they were without any rights … for me, when I came back after the divorce, the minister of culture, when I went, and I told them I am a writer and I want a job. Now I am here, and I have three children with me and they want to eat. And they didn't give me anything; they told me, you are on the "blacklist" and go away. And I said to them, "But things are changed!" and they said, "Nothing has changed. They are still the same. The police is the police. Everything is the same." And I tried to go, I went to the Ministry of Education to be a teacher or something like that. And they tell me go away. I would have even worked as a secretary or something like that, and they always tell me to go away. And at that time, I started to teach in three schools, by the hour, I have to teach a lot of hours to take some money, and I have to write a lot of articles and I sell them to the people. Sometimes they don't put my name over my work. Even I sold my poetry. I sold my songs, my creations. To feed my sons. And that is something that scratched me. I said I am in my country, and I am a foreign person. Nobody wants to help me.
> 
> And I went in the street with my children. I have to work. I have to fight. – Did you find an apartment? – No, no, no apartment at the beginning,

something only to sleep on. And the children who were living at a high level and suddenly they found themselves in a bad situation. And it was hard for them. And they suffered with me a lot. And me I was working all the time to have the money to feed them. It was not easy. But after three years, I started to find my way, I started to work in good magazines in the Emirates, I sent things.

Though for a time, Najet lived free of explicit threats from the state, she found herself with little work and unable to assert rights over her writing. She began again to write in opposition to the government, at first spurred by artists' inability to stake claims on the products of their labour. Shortly thereafter, she began to circulate articles criticizing the exploitation of young girls in the propaganda machine. Through her work, she came to the attention of women living in the neighbourhood where she stayed, and encouraged by their petitions, she began operating a series of workshops and courses for women who had not had the opportunity to get a formal education. For a while, she taught large groups how to paint, how to weave, and how to write. "They were very happy, they told me so. They listened to the radio when I did something, and they were proud of me." But when political revolt again came to Tunisia, Najet found her courses empty. People ignored her on the street and shopkeepers refused to sell her groceries. The authorities told her at that time that she could no longer publish or appear on the radio.

> And of course, they menaced me. And if I stayed, I would be killed like many they were killed. Right now, they still don't know which one killed them and the people that killed those people, they are living and free. And we are in the forest. Some people they think now there is more democracy … It isn't that. It isn't enough. Because when you are not safe … you can't live, even the poor people they became poorer, and some people became very rich.

The decision in the end to come to Germany meant accepting poverty. The situation, she said, made her ill with some regularity. But there were few options left. And it meant leaving her sons. One eventually came to Hamburg and had a child with a partner, but travel became difficult with work and so they rarely saw each other. Two remained in Tunisia, but she did not have the money or space for them to visit, so they spoke on the phone and shared photographs. A few years later, we were discussing two novels she recently finished and for which she wanted to find a publisher but was having trouble. I asked her about the shift in the forms of her writing:

> I am still writing poems. But at this time now I am sixty-five, I will leave maybe after some years, I don't know when, and I don't want to leave my words scattered here and there, I have nobody to care for them, that's why I have to publish and I am happy to see my writing happy, and doing well in the world, that they are ok before I go. I don't want to leave them without a mother, alone.
>
> ...
>
> For me, my sons, they are my books. These novels, they are my girls, these poems they are my boys. Really. I love my books like I love my children. I love them, and I worry about them. And I want them to be fine, like when you want for your son or daughter to marry. The book, it is you. That is why you can understand your books more than you son. They are good children. Then they fly away, they go off, that is life.

A character from one of the novels she had been writing, she went on to say, had been particularly difficult to live with. "She makes me nervous; sometimes I go to a café only because that is what she wanted. They live with us. For me, the characters in a novel, they live with me. I see her, I think about her, what she will do, what she wants. The novel lives with you. And the personalities stay with you. Sometimes it is hard to get rid of her." Her sons and her other children lived with her in different ways, but both situations could prove painful. Their proximity also gave the stories a particular charge. The sentiment reminded me of one of her poems, "A Café through the Window," which she wrote in 1984 but which was translated into German ("Ein Café Durchs Fenster") only in 2015 as part of a collection. She had read it aloud a few times over the years, just recently at an event on the migrant "crisis" in Thessaloniki:

> Should I forget you
> or the sorrow?
> My way leads into the night
> wallowing
> the rest of grief
> into the future
> Two siblings call
> my name:
> cigarette
> and vague idea

I crush the thought
with my teeth
and spit it
full of pain
onto the lively street.
Optimists
push carts in front of them
with their future,
whispering
eyes empty
stretching their noses
toward the jasmine branches
the sun colored their lips
dark
like each
happy woman.[31]

## At the Limits of Expression: Translation, Trauma, and the "Mastery" of the Past

At the outset I suggested that in the performative contexts that writers like Najet often find themselves, the governing expectation is that writers can (and do) make their cultural backgrounds and the suffering that necessitates asylum intelligible to audiences.[32] Built into dominant conceptions of both translation and violence (cultural and literary) is a particular view of human intelligibility. What I mean by this is that expressions of suffering and cultural difference are often taken to try bounds the expressive limits of language. These are questions of what I can know – and what I cannot – about a reality that is not mine.[33] This was initially how I understood Najet's complaint that "they do not want to know the true things." In an effort to assuage the anxiety that language might be inadequate to an external reality, to secure "our" knowledge of the event of violence, one response might be the accumulation of evidence in the form of testimony. Lest after all, the event be forgotten. But an important feature of this demand for testimonial speech is that it is shadowed by a profound sense of partiality, the simultaneous necessity and impossibility of finding one's footing in such expressions. Najet's words offer an interpretation of the situation.

There is a crucial knot in popular discourse in Germany in the idea that exilic consciousness, exemplified by victims of the Shoah, tells us something fundamental about how language works in general, about our capacity to speak and be understood, and more specifically, tells us something essential about the (im)possibility of translation. The guiding assumption is that poetry and literature can – perhaps should – be read as forms of testimony. The connection between ideas about translation and the condition of displacement is not only formal. In Germany, writers like Primo Levi and W.G. Sebald are often said to have broken the silence of the immediate post-war period by inaugurating a style of representational documentation that, at the same time, could never really be represented adequately. Parry and Sontag called this the ethical conundrum of life after the Holocaust, a demand that we agree to both of these seemingly at-odds facts: that its horrors exceed our capacity for expression (Levi himself says it is a unicum) and that we are morally obligated to try anyway. Since the 1950s, public and scholarly discourse in the West frequently identified the possibility of acts of cultural translation with the figure of the Jewish writer in exile. The Jewish victim became an icon of conventional theory, a metaphysical exemplar of exilic consciousness who bears the impossible burden of making themselves legible. They stand in for life in language in general. The singularly horrifying plight of European Jews has been flattened into a sign of suffering in general against which all experiences of exile, even all modern alienation or uses of language, are made to measure, just as European forms of life provide the template for culture in general.[34] The depths of these experiences are simply "beyond" expression. Casting the Jewish victim as the exemplar amounts, strangely enough, to an avoidance.[35]

Understanding how the genre of testimony operates in the public imaginary therefore is essential to understanding the politics of translation, as expressed here in the form of questioning put to Najet or to Yiwu. Under an interpretive regime of testimony, the experience of an unmasterable past is read into a sign of life in language in general and is considered especially relevant to thinking about the (im)possibility of translation. The trauma-therapy response that grew out of the experience of the Shoah, the attempt to master the past (and by extension, cultural difference) by means of knowledge, is posed within that discourse as doomed by its very nature to fail.

Testimonial speech is considered partial because of an enduring sense that private and public experience are kept strictly apart, as though the words through which one expresses oneself were separated from (immediate, private) experience. It follows that experience is always, at least potentially, beyond one's capacity to express.[36] This instability, this anxiety that we might fall out of life in common, that we might not be understood, shadows everyday life. Human language is continually threated by inexpressiveness. I eventually want to argue that Najet's words test agreements in forms of life, that they amount to a claim of voice, a claim in language I feel myself expresses me, in this case, in translation. From this point of view, "if I do not speak," Sandra Laugier writes, "it is not that there is something inexpressible, but that I *have* nothing to say." If then I am voiceless, it is because I have come to a point where I am no longer "speaking for others [for their consent] and allow[ing] them to speak for me." Even the sense of privacy is not a given from this point of view but is borne from a life in language that can always be denied and thus has to be achieved again and again.[37] What was at stake for me then in listening to Najet's words, and in observing the ways other listened, is not the outcome of our search for the expressive limits of language given in propositional form by universal human reason, but the fact of desire for or temptation to the inexpressible.[38]

As writers like Najet and Yiwu are read through the machinery of translation-as-testimony, the remainder, whatever is left untranslated or cannot be brought into overarching narrative, is either substantivized as the unspeakable portion of trauma (for which we cannot bear fully witness because we survive) or racialized as unreachable cultural experience (implicitly beyond the bounds of sense). This view of human intelligibility is also evident in much scholarly writing on European testimonial cultures. Giorgio Agamben thinks that the quality that marks testimony as a form of speech is its lacunae. Bearing "witness to trauma" the fleeing emigrant "does not possess the truth but is rather part of an ongoing quest for truth, a quest that involves an audience able and willing to endure the silences that accompany all Holocaust testimony."[39] Lawrence Langer similarly describes how "deep memory"[40] fails to find the words that would allow the survivor's story to be imagined or expressed, and so the story comes to rely on common memory, which presumes a linear narrative of redemption (through the catharsis afforded by public expression) and which can circulate within the public sphere. The survivor who is capable of speaking is thus the double of the Müselmann, the victim who grows too weak to survive and has as such marked themselves for extermination. The survivor who provides testimony can never fully speak to the experiences of those who died, and so in an important sense, the claim to universal intelligibility is bound up with the assurance of its failure, in its incapacity to capture the true extent of the horror of the trauma.

While earlier historians thought of trauma as a transcultural and transhistorical concept, more recent evaluation has shown how Auschwitz was a historically and culturally specific turning point in the nature of collective memory. While other forms of violence *could* be measured according to recognized standards of judgment, the Holocaust was so extreme that any measure would be inadequate. The Shoah is thought to have resisted conventional measures afforded by then-available psychological, political, and cultural methods, and forced a recalibration of concepts of violence now applied to experiences forward and backward in time for which there had "previously been no language or public interest." Because there remained nobody, no full survivor, to "retrospectively redeem or bear witness to the totality of the crimes," the sense of inaccessibility this reality engendered came to define the discourse. After Auschwitz, the inadequacy of the model becomes, in the guise of the concept of trauma, the "ultimate cipher of traumatic unspeakability ... the lodestone of modernity in general."[41]

Through this anxiety about the accessibility of experience, exile seems naturally to pose questions about language and the depth at which experience resides. It is characteristic of this discourse that the figures who broke open questions about national catharsis and the existential nature of exile are writers, because being at home, according to Hannah Arendt, means being at home in language. It is life in language that counts. "We exiles," she writes, "more than nationality, we lost our mother tongue, which means the naturalness of reactions, the simplicity of gestures, the unaffected expression of feelings."[42] For Najet too there was no going home. "My Tunisia has been destroyed," she says, and yet she holds out for a future life in language.

As I explore in the next chapter, the loss of the mother tongue amounts ironically, for Arendt, to the loss of poetry and a descent into cliché. The exile's denaturalization of the mother tongue forces the speaker to realize they do not "speak the logos," that one's language is "just one language among others."[43] Without the logos to secure it, a worry appears that something is doomed to be lost in translation (even when translated well). For Arendt, and indeed for much subsequent work on testimony, what counts, say, as political is what can be brought into narrative as distinguished from what in my experience cannot be put into words.[44]

Under the sign of trauma, this loss amounts to a return of the (repressed) experience as a symptom that can be overcome when it is brought to light, even as it threatens to recede from view.[45] One could read Yiwu's insistence on repeating himself, on the necessity of repetition to stave off becoming indifferent to democratic values, as mirroring a conventional concern that if Germans forget the Shoah, history might repeat itself, as if Holocaust denialism were only a matter of having enough (or the right) information. In both cases, the first repetition comes to stand against the threat of the other; namely, the return of history. Repeating historical narratives, securing and repeating the evidence, is the only thing keeping the reoccurence of the inexpressibly violent event at bay. Securing that history as event keeps it, so the story goes, from being absorbed into everyday life. German historiography in the post-war period has focused extensively on the resultant symptomology and, at least for a while, mostly took the form of questioning to what extent society masters the past, including its potential to be blocked by these compulsions. Many have told compelling psychoanalytic stories about this compulsion[46] and rendered a variety of diagnoses, in some cases offering important critiques of the assimilation of the historically particular into overly general theories of language.[47]

My disquiet has to do with the promise of solutions. Trauma-theory approaches of this kind are structured by a masculine "impulse to construct a coherent narrative of the event as a route to healing and recovery."[48] With the aid of the analyst, the suffering person works to secure knowledge of the event, give expression to suppressed experience of violence, which usually figures as something lost or hidden, and in so doing achieves catharsis, even for those who are aware that the process is interminable[49] and thus lined with tragedy. For Lacan, for example, the process leads from "empty" to "full speech." Through "interaction with the subject's discourse, the analyst's discourse, and the discourse of the Other," as Clara Han explains, "full speech emerges, the effect of which is 'to reorder the past contingencies by conferring on them the sense of necessities to come, such as they are constituted by the scant freedom through which the subject makes them present.'"[50] The conventional vision for a future German cultural identity free to play, in the psychoanalytic sense, partakes of the sense of coming into full speech as a capacity to "rework experience" into narrative.[51] And this is precisely how testimonial speech works – by transforming experience for those who were not there so that it can be imagined, but which is ultimately "based on a denial, at the same time, of all other parameters that in fact determine the sense of the everyday of these extreme situations"; for example, by making it appear within in a well-ordered plot.[52] This reworking stiches experience into historical events but remains ethnographically fictional in the sense that there are fragments of ordinary experience not easily absorbed into coherent narratives.[53] Those experiences that cannot be narratively re-worked, that are absorbed into the non-event of the everyday, are elided by master narrative, a fact priced into testimony as its necessary failure.[54]

## Listening for Voice

Let us return then to the interpretation of interpretation on offer in Najet's story. If Najet's words should not simply be read as an object of knowledge external to language, it remains to be said, what do her expressions do? And relatedly, what sort of moral striving is at stake in the determination not to return everyday life on the terms offered?[55] What is at stake, in other words, in refusing the penetrating desire of others to know me and to be reconciled with them, and instead to wait, to not write or speak? What compels us to accept certain words and not others, if not logical propositions?[56]

One way of approaching these questions is by returning to Najet's position that some translations on offer were unacceptable while others were not, as well as her suggestion that many of the people she spoke with were not interested in knowing "true things." In the first case, while there were translations and interviews that she refused, this was not because she felt her experiences were, by their nature, inexpressible. She was waiting for a moment when she found that the translations expressed her. Relatedly, she can write only in English, and perhaps one day in German, at the same time that the "mother tongue" tongue feels suffocating to her. But notice too that Najet's rejection of offers and her annoyance at journalists is not about the accuracy of the translations (at least if we think of translation as a matter of finding equivalent words), nor does she contest the historical nature of their accounts. But something in their manner of taking interest was not right. I asked her once how she knew a translation was right. "I am not the expert in German," she told me, so in that way, "I cannot always tell you if this word is correct or not. But there are those who translate each word by word, and maybe it is correct, but it is not right, because they do not read the whole work, they don't want to understand what it is saying, and that I cannot accept." Rather, Najet said she preferred working with translators who would come back to her to ask how a word was used in a particular line. But this too could pose issues. Translators would sometimes come to Najet to explain a metaphor or word choice. "I became like a teacher," she told me, "but then they change the words. Once I explained something, they took it away. They didn't know the mythology of the words. So, I think I will stop being a teacher in the future."

Similarly, the sentiment she expressed about truth could also be read in at least two different ways: either that they should want to know something else instead or that the architecture of knowing was itself the problem. We can draw out this difference by way of Najet's contrast between the "grey face" of knowledge with what she calls an awareness of "the small things." Her poetry, one might say, calls out for listening to these small things over and even against the neat frameworks captured by the usual political narratives.

Perhaps it is better to rethink the question of translation as a matter of voice, as an articulation of a claim.[57] One cannot say, as we have seen, that the "original" poem, those written in Tunisian Arabic, is necessarily where she feels *her* words reside – an assumption that is deeply embedded in monoglossic ideologies invested in a discourse of authenticity. Her poetry makes clear that the words one uses are the ones one finds and makes do with – that is, that we find they fit and hope they will be received or picked up again, since that is what it means for them to be alive. Neither is the turn to poetry for her a way of expressing something for which there simply are no words otherwise. We read in her poems that her expressions are what they express and not representations or images. The question is how – or really whether – I recognize myself in these words, in this moment and in this situation. But what is at stake is not a matter of certain grammatical classes or even intentions. A sentence might be meaningful, and yet we can find it used in a context where "there isn't anything which is the thought which I express in uttering these words."[58] So it is a question of finding the right context, finding that we are "the subject of one's words," that we have the ability "to tolerate being expressive, or meaningful."[59] Being at home in language, if we might recast Arendt's provocation about the mother tongue in this way, is not even necessarily a question of specific languages one speaks, or which words one selects (as if it were the property of words "in themselves" that they are better or worse), but whether or not an inner and outer come into alignment in speech, such that I might stake a claim in these words, in this context – a claim that is both mine and that these words hold for others. Words come to life in their movements among us. Among whom? That is what is discovered in the claim.

To clarify, let me take an example from anthropology that has stayed with me for many years, and read it alongside a few lines of Najet's poetry. Veena Das, in her work on abductions and sexual violence against women during the widespread communal violence of the Partition of India in 1947, feels compelled at various points to return to the writings of Saadat Hasan Manto and Rabindranath Tagore. "Some realities," she writes, "need to be fictionalized before they can be apprehended."[60] Das relays scenes from the great Urdu writer Saadat Hassan Manto's story "Khol Do" ("Open It"), written in the context of the Partition, in which the grievous violence on the woman's body is portrayed through the subtility of a gesture rather than a direct description of her violation. The protagonist, Sarajjudin, whose daughter has disappeared in the unruly crowds, finds a group of Muslim volunteers who are going around, offering help to locate people. He begs them to find his daughter, describing the conditions under which she disappeared. In the next scene we see his daughter, Sakina, in a jeep with the volunteers who have won her trust by evoking the name of her father and offering her a jacket to cover herself so she feels less exposed. In the third scene we see her in a clinic, with her father maddened by grief on her side. The doctor enters the room and, feeling stifled by the heat, says, "khol do" – open it, gesturing to the window. There is a movement in the corpselike body of the daughter as her hand moves to the string of her salwar (loose pants) and fumbles to unloosen the strings for, in khol do, she can hear only the second command. Her father cries out, "My daughter is alive, my daughter is alive." Das reads the father's exclamation as a willingness to take his daughter, however degraded, however violated sexually; and not as a sign of a sullied reputation and a disgrace but as a promise of life. She writes,

> In the societal context of this period, when ideas of purity and honor densely populated the literary narratives as well as family and political narratives, so that fathers willed their daughters to die for family honor rather than live with bodies that had been violated by other men, this father wills his daughter to live even as parts of her body can do nothing else but proclaim her brutal violation ... In the speech of the father, at least, the daughter is alive, and though she may find an existence only in his utterance, he creates through his utterance a home for her mutilated and violated self.[61]

The expression "my daughter is alive," though it may appear to be an indicative statement, in tone and pitch might be better read as a gesture of acknowledgment in defiance of the societal norms that would have made her an outcaste. The father's expression breaks with a scripted tradition of narratives characterized by an "archetypal motif ... of a girl finding her way to her parents after having been subjected to rape and plunder and being told, 'Why are you here – it would have been better if you were dead.'" While these refusals may not have been quite so common as they seemed, Das argues, the normative pressure they asserted was clearly testament to "the power of stories." At the same time, Manto's story itself allows Das to "pawn her voice" to a literary text in such a way that it allows certain blockages to be moved. Of her own effort to receive the words others share with her, she writes, "I hope I shall be evoking the physiognomy of their words not in the manner of a thief who has stolen another's voice, but in the manner of one who pawns herself to the words of the other."[62]

Two points are especially salient. The first is that the philosophical grammar of certain expressions calls out for acknowledgment – not for knowledge – and so its denial is not so much an intellectual failure as a spiritual one. If acknowledgment is withheld, it is not a matter of my "ignorance of the existence" of the other but of my "denial of that existence."[63] Rather than referential statements about a hidden inner object, the words "body forth" in the way they compel the hearer.[64] "You are not free to believe or disbelieve me," Das writes, "our future is at stake."[65] There is at the same time no guarantee that my words will be received. And there is no way to "separate my pain from my expression for it."

Najet expresses a related thought in the stanza I translated earlier in this chapter, in which she writes, "On the street / yet only / my I / and its reflection / me, the word." What Najet taught me to see is that what blocks an expression may be posed as acknowledgment but offers instead a usurpation of voice, which can then, in turn, fall on her to refuse or accept. Part of what makes the exchange so troubling is that the words are posed as hers. When, for instance, a translation is suggested to her that she senses is "not interested in the true things," what makes the offer so wounding is that on the surface the translation appears as though it is offering her own words back to her, but she has a feeling of hollowness, that it is not her or what she knows that is expressed in the line or the word. Their denial of her existence is articulated to her in what appears to be a case of taking interest. The second crucial point, which follows from the first, is that turning to literature to move a blockage (which Das refers to as pawning voice) cannot be said to work because fictive statements are more efficacious indicatives. I said earlier that poetry does not respond to a failure of ordinary language, that it is a mistake to assume for it the status of special class of utterances better hooked into reality, since this view belies an assumption that normally there is a gap between an expression and what is expressed. But then how does the pawning of one's voice to fiction or to the anthropologist, or to the translator, work?

The distinction between pawning and stealing voice comes from a short passage in Cavell's *A Pitch of Philosophy*,[66] where he discusses John Stuart Mill's conviction that women are equal to men in intellectual originality. Mill writes, "Who can tell how many of the most original thoughts put forth by male writers, belong to a woman by suggestion, to themselves only by verifying and working out? If I may judge by my own case, a very large proportion indeed." Cavell describes Mill's confession as a vision of "high Western culture as plagiarized, speaking with voices other than those it owns," which can be distinguished from not listening at all. The image of voice (and of philosophy of or as) in pawn-broking, by contrast, tells us what is of importance in the sense of what counts: "the concept of what we count, especially count as of interest or importance to us," as in recounting, settling of accounts, or giving an account (of oneself). Finding that we are at home in language, that words express us, is finding both that we make a claim on the right to speak in the name of others and that our expressions are articulated in words that we have borrowed – they were there before us, and looking through them, we (might) find the right words. By pawning voice then, we understand a sense in which we discover these particular borrowed words express us in this context, whereas stealing voice snatches that opportunity up – I am spoken for.[67] In both cases, the speaker speaks in the name of others – words are not in either case mine, as if they were a private possession – but in one situation they are claimed as an inheritance, and in another that claim is pre-empted. A claim to voice implies a pawn: having a future together means others will have to pick up and carry my words.

I am thinking now of two lines of internal description in several of Najet's poems I cited earlier. The first is where she invokes pain to be ink on paper and then moves onto a description of her life alone "without a homeland / without names," and in which everything tastes of salt, that salt is in her eyes, though her tongue alone dreams of sugar. She writes, but she has lost a taste for life. The use of breaks in the opening lines of the stanza and the familiar dative pronoun (Zugewandt bin ich / dir, / Schmerz) leaves the addressee somewhat ambiguous, whether it is pain itself or someone else. The salty taste of letters recalls the paper onto which the ink falls. The last lines of the poem reads, "A secret, / that has been lost, / since my bottle with a dream inside / is smashed." In the second example, the speaker asks the poem to accompany her, to "send out letters / to lick up the mud of my defeats." And she concludes a thought, in the final poem with the image of grinding a painful, optimistic thought in one's teeth and spitting it "full of pain / onto the lively street."

These lines suggest to me a double movement, one in which the speaker breathes life into words, so that they may provide company, attest to our losses, carry forward our dreams or our pain into the street. In each of the three examples, we do not know where our words will go. As in Das's case, that pain should itself become ink or that a dream may reside in a bottle conveys the sense that experience and expression are bound up with one another, so that if someone had found the bottle on a beach somewhere or read the note, what they would be holding would open up the possibility of acknowledgment. But there is also a feeling that one mourns the failures of one's words, is even angry with them; that words get lost, that they haven't been picked up, that the bottle is smashed. As Das writes evocatively, "Does the whole task of becoming human ... not involve a response (even if this is rage) to the sense of loss when language seems to fail?"

I want to return to the thought that there are at times offers of words that are posed as an acknowledgment but in which we cannot find our voice. The offer lends itself to two genres of response – one in which I accept the terms (I find these words take hold) and another in which I withhold acceptance so that I might opt to wait for another opportunity. But these different possibilities also interact with other another. They do not simply pass in the night. In fact, they seem to bear an internal relationship to one another. The difference shows up not just in different people's stories (as in Najet or Yiwu's, where neither life can be taken to adopt, once and for all, either of these postures) or different scenes, but even within a scene or a line, where one can detect small shifts in the region of voice – not in the "identity" of the person speaking, but through small shifts where in certain moments words come to life, while at others they seem "frozen, numb, without life."[68]

In each case, everyday life is threatened by rupture, which in popular culture – for example, in what Cavell famously termed "comedies of remarriage" – is usually figured through domestic disharmony.[69] But the terms held out for reconciliation are deeply uneven and gendered, where reconciliation "inevitably takes the form of the woman's education by man" – her accepting a return to domestic life on his terms, her being created as a new person from his rib. In the case of the exiled writer, this education looks on the surface to be a movement in the opposition direction – that is, the foreigner educates Germany about their experiences – but because they accept life on the terms laid out by German discourse, they are created from its rib. One genre of response – the one I have described Yiwu as taking – begins from the threat of rupture and the narrative concerning reconciliation; life returns to normal, but on terms set by Europe.

Najet takes a different route. As a derivation of the genre of remarriage, her response negates some of its key features. We find "a certain choice of solitude (figured in the refusal of marriage) as the recognition that the terms of one's intelligibility are not welcome to others ... what the idea of unknownness comes to is ... matching the continuing demand of the woman in remarriage comedy to be known, reads back, or forward, into the various moments in which I have gone into the meeting of skepticism and tragedy at the point, or drive, of an avoidance of – terror of, disappointment with – acknowledgment."[70] It is this domestic that is constantly under siege for Najet in a way that it is not for every writer: in the disruption of her writing as a child; in the interruption of daily life by official harassment; in her divorce; in being thrown out by her family as a result of the divorce; and in Germany in her apartment where nothing is hers and her children are entirely displaced.

One situation can suffocate the other: ordinary voice (Cavell writes, "my limited presentness to the world and others in it, the small differences and intimacies my existence projects") by the metaphysical voice ("interpretable as the advent of skepticism, hence of the subjects of comedy and tragedy"). Stealing and reclaiming of the woman's voice is the subject of the genre. In both cases, however, the status of solitary unknownness is preferable to the "marriage of irritation." The "terms" of one's unknowability are not "welcome" to others. That knowledge as an object of desire can take a number of forms, as can the desire – for example, as a longing for "ratification."[71] Recall in Najet's story the routinized violence of her father, who reacts to her voice, to her writing, with physical violence. He is, for her, a microcosm of the masculine in society, an expression of both a desire to stifle her speech and the physical violence of disciplining control. Her resistance is marked by her capacity to bear the dissolution of the world they shared.

Both acceptance and withholding work out what Cavell calls, after Emerson, the "problematic of self-reliance and conformity."[72] Yet if Yiwu's case posits a relation of equanimity between all as a possibility for the future by means of poetry (or the work of metamorphosis) and an exemplary pair (in this case the typified foreigner and their host), in Najet's, this expressiveness and joy is to be found in relation to one's self.[73] It is, to put it another way, a response positioned relative to a problem of scepticism to excess. Nothing less than her human existence is at stake. The threat of such a doubt is not to her knowledge but to her very being (or being known). Such a distinction, I said, takes on a gendered character. Her unknownness becomes an object of desire for the masculine impulse – that is, for her knowledge or knowledge of her – generating perhaps a species of cruel optimism.[74] This reading inverts, however, not the relation between the masculine and the feminine but turns us instead toward the relationship between the child – who is coming into a form of life – and mother. I am thinking here of the nearness of Najet's two sets of children and the situation they face – her books she is afraid will not live a happy life if she were to die too soon, and the fact that what brings this to mind is that she cannot see her biological children. It is the child gazing upon her mother that opposes a conventional description of exile as a tension between two cultures – hers is not a problem of "not belonging" but of belonging on the wrong terms; she is "at odds with the [culture] in which she was born and is roughly in the process of transfiguring into one that does not exist, one as it were still in confinement."[75] The absence of children in the remarriage appears like a price for a happy return to the domestic. The creation of the woman becomes self-reliance.

> But where does the woman's ability to judge the world come from? … It comes from the woman's being confined or concentrated to a state of isolation so extreme as to portray and partake of madness, a state of utter incommunicability, as if before the possession of speech.

Her power is in her choice of this half-world. We might refuse the inherited picture of sacrificial pain in favour of sitting with the recognition, on the part of the woman, of her own isolation, bordering as it ultimately tends to on the brink of madness.[76] This is a distinction between the imagined desire to be known, to make one's self known (identified with human desire in general), and the capacity on the part of the women in the melodrama to remain unknown, which he calls "the capacity to wait."[77] This waiting is not a failure to be known but instead a (re)claiming of one's existence, an assertion of self-reliance, teetering between melancholy and ecstasy. She gives expression to her recognition of an inability (willingness) to be known, to understand that her words might (or will) fail or fall or short of the plentitude of her experience.[78]

In Najet's case, shifts between "voiceless" and "voice" not only internalize heteroglossia[79] but also amount to a capacity to bear one for the other. What makes the literary such a dangerous space is that it promises itself as a cipher through which one can overcome the distance to the pain over the other even partially; it is the threat of an amnesia of the scepticism that haunts the human condition in our solitude. These shades of difference are everything. The politicization of the experience of exile as a discourse on freedom and human rights presupposes the availability of their experience – an experience that also is supposed to undergird the very possibility of writing in the first place: the importance of exile to literature, and not just literature to exile.

**Shifts in Region**

"In Berlin I feel more comfortable, I like the cinemas, getting North African food, and the graffiti remind me of the murals during the Arab revolution." The words printed on the page caught my attention. I was away from Berlin visiting family when I saw the image of Najet with her hair done up, laughing and smiling, standing in the middle of a bookshop reading a little green book with the word *Meerwüste* across the top, her new book in German. Two years after our first meeting in her apartment, Najet's countenance appeared to have completely changed. The photo referred to a tour by the Goethe Institute, which is proudly displaying her book in their library, and which she joins walking through the Prinzessinnengarten, stopping the guide to ask about small details: what the birds like to eat and why the seeds are planted in just this manner.

But the article captured two stories – one of which is subverted by the desires of the other. A quick summary of Najet's life appears and then the usual bureaucratic language of assimilation – "language," it read, "is the key to integration." The journalist writes "[Najet's] entire life has been shaped by language" and so naturally she takes German courses, an opportunity afforded her by the joined forces of German PEN and the Goethe Institute. Najet is juxtaposed with another Writers-in-Exile alumna, an Iranian journalist, who declined the language program because she wanted to ultimately return home and felt herself caught in a purgatorial trap. But while Najet's words service the needs of the discourse of aid and integration, she has indeed managed to write now, she is smiling, and her poems have found a home in German, with help from Leila (her translator from Arabic), Christa, and Mary, whose family had a publishing company. But by the time her newest book was set to be released (*Vulkanworte auf dem Leib aus Schnee*) six years later, the publishing house had closed. PEN again stepped in with funds from the government, paid for translation, and another local publisher was secured. Najet insisted that this most recent work should be published as a trilingual edition, so an Arabic translator was secured, and Christa made translations from English and edited those already in German from Arabic; she also contributed a short interlude so that it became a book, in Christa's words, "with two beginnings."

At the same time, Najet tells me that people have stopped asking for interviews. Critics tell her that her English won't suffice for publication. "Your English," a publisher explained, "is not Elizabeth's English." "There are many different Englishes," she replied. "My English is like me; it is my English. When I speak in England, or Boise, or Chicago, or I read in a university, people understand me, and they like what I have done." But Najet still finds it difficult to find an outlet willing to work with her English language prose. As news cycles have changed, she insists, the audience has moved on to another story. Najet calls this the appetite for fast-food literature.

I argued that while the writers I discussed here opt for alternative politics, one posture is not the complete negation of the other but rather a refusal of its force. And this refusal is enacted in small ways and incomplete ways. In an interview with the German portal, *Qantara* – an Arabic word for "bridge" adopted by a network of institutions, including the news outlet Deutsch-Welle, the Goethe Institute, and the Bundeszentrale für politische Bildung (the Federal Centre for Political Education) – Najet captures the double bind of the multiple politics of writing:

> In my throat nests the pain of all those to whom I lend a voice. For their sake, I have to be as strong as a bird – a bird with powerful opinions. Only the strong can put up peaceful resistance to violence.[80]

The "true word," she says, is the "free word." Both God and the police can set "traps" for words. The interviewer asks her first to reply to the ongoing Syrian refugee crisis before turning to Berlin. "A label like 'writer in exile' can also become a kind of prison," she says to Najet. "Sometimes you don't have a choice," Najet replies. "I'm not in prison; I'm in a wonderful city, a place I love, which is beginning to become a part of me … Every place has its own perfume. So, the poems I am writing at the moment wear the scent of this city." She is careful to mark her gratitude to Germany and to Berlin. At the same time, she acknowledged very subtly the limits of those gestures – if there were a better choice, a freer choice, she'd take it. And her expressions are different for Christa and her work than for the society at large – Christa, she told me once, "makes it possible for us to rebuild our lives – we are not just surviving but living and writing." She wants her work to be read in German, but her willingness to find routes to expression is not tantamount to complacent acceptance of what I earlier called remarriage. It has generated something new, using the language that might have been a prison to different ends. The "perfume" of Berlin that clings to her new words is something other than acclimation or transcendence: it refuses the dialectics of seen and unseen, written and unwritten, in favour of bearing unsettlement, a forever incomplete return to the domestic, not as a failure but as a gesture of resisting the force.

I said my concern was with marking a shift in the relationship between a term and something else. This shift is not an escape from a particular language but a movement within it to another region of voice. As Hélène Cixous once said of the call to écriture feminine, this was a mood, a stance that resisted the machine that had been "operating and turning out its 'truth' for centuries." To write herself meant "return[ing] to the body which ... has been turned into the uncanny stranger on display," a writing that "cannot be theorized," a "working (in) the inbetween."[81] In these small moments, in small shifts, the testimonial regime is refused and new possibilities are opened up by waiting. One genre doesn't replace the other. And neither "solves" the doubts that line our concerns with intelligibility to one another. The gendering is in the nature of the doubt, whether on the one side, about my knowledge of some foreign-to-me experience, or on the other, of making myself intelligible, of finding someone "to whom I might trust my words," which is to say, who acknowledges rather than knows my experience.[82]

*Chapter Four*

# In the Footsteps of a Flaneur: A Grammar of Returning (to a Street)

For there are no new ideas. There are only new ways of making them felt, of examining what our ideas really mean (feel like).

– Audre Lorde

We all know the curious way in which unpleasant memories suddenly throng on us, and how we do our best by loud talk and violent gestures to put them out of our minds; but the gestures and the talk of our ordinary life make one think we are all in this condition, frightened of any memory or any inward gaze. What is it that is always troubling us? what is the gnat that will not let us sleep? There are spirits all about us, each moment of life has something to say to us, but we will not listen to the spirit-voices. When we are quiet and alone, we fear that something will be whispered in our ears, and so we hate the quiet, and dull our senses in society.

– Friedrich Nietzsche

For Fabian and his collaborators, moments of the past could be retrieved through their traces in material artefacts, as solid as buildings and fragile as old posters, photographs, or discarded menu cards, or in crumbling monuments hidden from public sight. This was a literary work, they ventured, enacted through a special logic of walking that they saw themselves as reinhabiting, relearning, reinvigorating from the past, though now emerging against the backdrop of a history that has proven difficult to absorb. Through this literary approach to moving along city streets, the group encountered characters not merely as frozen figures within the bindings of a book but as real or fictional personages to think and live alongside. Their efforts in turn led them to pose questions about their own approach. What is it to return to a way of returning, say to a street, or for that matter, a book, or a phrase, as a recovery; what sort of threats might it carry and what promises?

In 2013, along with his girlfriend, Grashina, and friend Ricarda (now the group's publisher), Fabian founded a literary magazine around the concept of exploring one city street at a time. Fabian had studied philosophy and had been involved in film and music projects throughout Berlin for several years. Like many of the younger German artists I knew in the city, he was caught by awkward conditions of life there, eager to "explore" the world through the guise of its cultural products, less burdened by the tick of nostalgia for East Germany that marked the speech of previous generations, somewhat, if imperfectly, conscious of and concerned by the nation's colonial heritage, and still anxious to find a way of thinking through the weight of cultural memory and what it might mean to bear it.[1] They worked odd jobs that sufficed for them to make do on rent and groceries, though they spent most of their time on passion projects that turned little profit, selling just enough copies for the magazine to reproduce itself and to occasionally add a feature or two. As a reading public developed, the group agreed quickly on what they called "literary" or "subjective" perspective on urban space, a concept they later identified with the flaneur, and *Flaneur* became the young journal's title. Their idea was to walk and re-walk a single street again and again, as way of uncovering otherwise scant traces of past events and to inaugurate collaborations with those who lived there now. They were also aware of the dangers of re-walking in language, that treading over the same words again and again could acquire the sense of cliché, and that cliché carried precarious connotations. The critic James Woods writes that "clichés, borrowed language" are "bourgeois bêtises" excoriated by the likes of Flaubert; "Bovary's conversation is likened to a pavement, over which many people have walked." This for Woods is why so many modern and postmodern writers "employed and impaled cliché." But re-walking the streets was, Fabian ventured, one way of productively moving through the past literarily. A tiny detail brings space to life in new ways, even if it did not always yield the uses one hoped. And as literary method, it expressed something about what it meant to live in language. But these were not only metaphors. They were concrete manners of uncovering and creating connections.

Their initial print run was humble. The team was not expecting an immediate demand and ordered only a few hundred copies from their printer. Despite their modest vision, *Flaneur*'s first issue on the life and history of the nearly two-and-half-kilometre Kantstrasse sold out in just days. Surprised and delighted by the reaction of their readers, Fabian and another mutual friend developed the idea of a walking incarnation of the issue as a literary tour, a re-imagination of the concept that seemed nevertheless a natural extension. Their picture of the flaneur was as work of art that moved between mediums and between times and spaces, and in so doing negotiated a new form of "historical and archival production."[2] Walking the streets with Fabian and his colleagues was an experience in which, at each moment, figures from the past swelled up owing to their associations with particular buildings or specific spots through a kind of literary labour that Fabian and *Flaneur* performed. Each moment, it seemed, contained multiple times. This walking enacts what Fabian describes as literary connections between places and times, effecting a "creative play of place."[3] These decisions made into a practice of walking (and perhaps writing) allowed events and experiences to emerge from the past, not just from an individual's memory but also the collective's, adding mnemographic depth to the lived experiences of a place. The densities that accumulate vary according to various forces, the character of the memories, the material of the street, the ambitions of the author.

For anthropologists thinking about the street in different parts of the world, connections with memory, place, and storytelling practices have been close at hand. Marc Augé, for instance, thinks of the aberration of memory as a counterpoint to urban solitude in shrinking spaces. In a moving afterword to Augé's book, Tom Conley writes that the anthropologist "discerns like the dots adjacent to the names printed in red ink over the fabulous detail of buildings and streets on most subway maps, points of crossover and intersection. They are the thematic chiasms, Freudian 'switch-words' that both mark junctures and turn the wheels of memory in the mental machinery of everyone who descends into the metro."[4] For Augé, forgetting is integral to the actualization of memory as a means of reimaging space, reawakening it to life – and it is unsurprisingly literature that teaches this duty to forget.[5] In a very different context, Deepak Mehta and Roma Chatterji[6] describe acts of walking the streets in Dharavi as narrators from the neighbourhood talk about the impact of riots just a few years prior. As they walk and come upon certain objects, places, or edifices, space comes to life in their talk, as interlocutors describe the effects of violence "on buildings, they show where people fought, killed, or sought refuge." While at first the ethnographers can see only a bustle of people doing chores and shopsellers, the people they walk with see "an ensemble of past events and future possibilities," not as static features of the landscape, but as something they make and remake in acts of telling; for example, through assigning proper names. Unlike when violence was discussed sitting in a room, where the space of violence could be "easily located" and mapped on boundaries of the neighbourhood, while walking, stories were punctuated by cross-talk and interruption, pasts disappeared and reappeared, and boundaries were (re)drawn, in relation to the particular contexts of the tellings. "It is almost as if walking," they write, "is an act of remembrance being embodied in speech," an act that allows multiple kinds of differences to be articulated – in their case, between Muslims and Hindus.

In Berlin, the weight of German memory culture, the relative distance of events, and the local histories of the flaneur character all meant that walking took on yet another valence.[7] The journal's methods and its name were explicit claims of return to another moment, a version of the flaneur that had become an influential icon of social theory. Moritz Reininghaus wrote in an introduction to a new edition of Franz Hessel's 1930s flaneur text *Spazieren in Berlin* that Berlin was now a "capital of walkers," not just a place of a handful of striking solitary figures. The "real Berliner," he went on to say, distinguish themselves today primarily by the skilful way they form arcs around the homeless, the newspaper salesmen, the child or animal rights activists who want a signature, and the groups of tourists. The rhythms of red traffic lights adorned with the familiar little man (the Amplemann) present impediments to free movement, and dangers and obstacles to the walker's aesthetic pursuits abound. In April 2014, the German radio program *Forum SWR2* similarly convened an on-air debate about whether we might think of the flaneur as a form of life and if so, whether it had gone extinct or if there were still relevant ways of inhabiting the city. Another local artist, Tina Saum, had also recently founded what she called a "laboratory for Flanerie," a collaborative art project with installations, audio tours, and organized walks, that invited participants to use a range of senses and "experiment with different modes of perception and narration in order to tell the story of a city in different ways." For Saum, Flanerie had now again been revived [wiederbeleben], even if the figure of flaneur itself had not (perhaps, she seemed to suggest, for the best), as it is historically wont to do. To this the moderator replied that already in the 1920s, it was a revival, as Benjamin's review of Hessel, "Return of the Flâneur" [Wiederkehr des Flâneur] made clear.

In this moment, however, stakes were compounded by new debates about public memory, in particular over the inclusion of victims of German violence besides European Jews and the place of these voices within a broader landscape of acknowledgment – claims that extended not only to those who suffered the Nazi regime, but also to those long overlooked or overshadowed targets of German colonialism.[8] Scholars and activists pointed out that the conjunction of these violent histories was anything but incidental, and their refusal, part of the stifling supposition about the uniqueness of the Holocaust, remains integral to contemporary racial logics.[9] These are questions "quotidian intellectuals," especially subjects of racializing discourses, had already been theorizing for some time despite their erasure within many journalistic and academic accounts.[10] These discussions led to another slate of new memory projects, art installations, museums, and protests (including recent successful calls for repatriating looted items held in cosmopolitan collections like the one housed in Berlin's Humboldt Forum). The capacity of memory for bringing together different times could now be seen as a source of its "powerful creativity, its ability to build new worlds out of the material of older ones."[11] Returning *again* made it possible to see what had been covered up. At the same time, these efforts were quickly met by reactionary concerns that the expansion of participation in the memory regime would mean that expressions of guilt were becoming banal, a worry that allowing newness to enter into retellings (a newness of what had always been there) would weaken the impact of the "original" claims, or that they signalled a dangerous "normalization" of the Holocaust.[12] The desire to make history present, and an anxiety about how, could turn in various directions, sometimes in single gesture; the newness of a gesture could seem simultaneously as reinvigorating a discourse always on the verge of becoming stale, as a solution and, at the same time, the problem of itself.

In the previous chapter, I argued that memory discourses centred on the Holocaust often came to overwrite other experiences of suffering by setting an impossible standard. Hannah Arendt observed that fascists "were totally convinced that one of the greatest chances for the success of their enterprise rested on the fact that no one on the outside could believe it." The unimaginable burden of memory after such unbelievable violence becomes a dangerous "strategy of words," or perhaps against words – a hell, Didi-Huberman says, "made by humans for the *obliteration of the language of their victims* ... to speak of Auschwitz in terms of the unsayable, is not to bring oneself closer to Auschwitz. On the contrary, it is to relegate Auschwitz to a region of "metaphysical adoration, even of unknowing repetition of Nazi *arcanum* itself."[13] In Berlin, literary language, in this case, like re-walking a street, was also often seen as a resource for keeping such language alive in face of this strategy of destruction.[14]

Fabian's work posed the issue differently by asking whether, given the ubiquity of certain forms of memory talk in Germany, there was any room left for newness to emerge, perhaps by going back to more of the same? Or were all attempts to "work through the past" already pre-figured?[15] Connecting literature to the street, and more specifically to re-walking streets, allowed him an entry point into the past cognized as return without mere repetition. In this way, the project challenges us to dwell a bit longer on forms of revisiting in our ways of walking and of speaking. Can we use a cliché and mean it? Can I say something new in quoting? Are returns of the past doomed to resolve into banality? The group's method – and even its own relationship to past flaneur literature – was itself such an example of such a challenge; these uses of the flaneur concept could not be understood simply in terms of a universal process of modernity or "flaneur attitude" that transcends national and historical boundaries.

Instead of starting from the idea then that our ways of talking about the past are beholden or potentially (in)adequate to metaphysical facts about the past,[16] I want to suggest Fabian's project is better understood by focusing on the philosophical grammar of that talk itself: that the possibilities for expressions about the past are entailed by present forms of life that are in the midst of being remade.[17] I am not convinced that when we investigate statements about the past that the crucial issue is, as Elizabeth Anscombe once put it, "what we *know* in knowing anything about the past"; in other words, that a question of metaphysical versification is what is at stake.[18] As Anscombe suggests, the purpose of describing the ways people talk about the past is in order to stop looking to a past *fact* for *justifications* of how we talk.[19] Such an inquiry begins at those moments where one has exhausted justification, and one simply does.[20] The point of scrutinizing what people say about the past is not to discover *what* people say, then, but what people *say*, including how one determines whether they are in a position to say it.[21] The question becomes, What kinds of utterances about the past have grammatical sense in what contexts? When do they work, and when do they fail?

**How to Talk about a Street**

A thought returned to Fabian during one of our walks: "What if something as seemingly stable and real as a city street were instead a fragment, some place between an empirical reality and a fiction, a dream and a routine, a present and a past?" It was an intuition that returned frequently in writing and in conversation, that we could not say "This is Kantstrasse" but should rather say "This could be Kantstrasse." This refrain was to become the banner motto for the tour and the magazine alike. Reflecting back on the origin of the magazine, Fabian recalled Ricarda's experiences as she awakened to a particular experience of the streets she had always known but now saw through new eyes:

> Ricarda was travelling back and forth between Berlin and New York at the time and coming back to her old neighbourhood in Charlottenburg, she realized that, for the first time, she started walking the streets of her childhood with open eyes and an actual interest for the place she grew up in (the first glance is a very flaneurish perspective …) G(rashina) and me came on … and we worked out a concept that would take the street as the fragmented [micro]cosm that it is. We were not much interested in providing guidance … taking the street not as a logical linear construct, but a territory that most of the time is only accessible through various historic layers, by embracing the randomness and the disturbing parts of it, by looking at it subjectively and allow ourselves to reorder things in a rather literary sense that finds itself at the edge of facts and fiction – all stories do I believe.

Fabian described Flanerie as a technique of thought.[22] It is a strategy of experiencing a place that Fabian often referenced in opposition to others, such as those of the journalist and the travel guide writer. Indeed, for Fabian, it was not just about the aesthetics of walking but also a way in which to inhabit the world, or at least the city. As Benjamin famously suggests, losing oneself in a city requires some education, an art he called Irrkunst (art of erring). For Fabian, this art takes on another valence. "We are always mirroring ourselves," he often said, "you get rid of the idea that you have to tell the truth." He described this mirroring as a projection, a literary play with the connections between material objects, characters in the world, and historical events that isn't beholden to the truth. The street for him becomes a screen, where a literary labour is free to play with the elements it finds there, and thus these new relations, for Fabian, bear the marks of their creator's subjectivity – they are a kind of therapy. Yet the relationship between the fictive and the real is more complicated than it appears – as I will explore below, *Flaneur*'s work rests on extensive research, gathering stories, plumbing archives, conducting interviews, collaborations, and concrete experiences with the street's denizens. It is not entirely untethered from the world as he finds it.

Fabian regularly insisted on the tangible nature of the interaction with the street as a mode of turning back and on the resistance he found in the matter of the street as part and parcel of the adoption of the spirit of the flaneur, even if its materiality is distinct. Each version (walking for research, the text as walk, the tour) seeps into the other in occasionally unexpected ways. Fabian's understanding of the flaneur technique changes with his experiences working on new issues: new stories are provoked on the tour from participants, and while he is writing for one issue, he is planning the next and selling the last, all while revisiting Kantstrasse. To trace how these literary connections were forged, let me turn to a series of stories, elements of Kantstrasse, as they were picked up, arranged, and re-arranged; first in the team's research, then in a written text, and finally as the text is brought back to the street on a tour. In each case, it was the relations between elements that find new incarnations; a bricoleur-like play with what are nevertheless relatively motivated components. There are multiple returns of Flanerie in this story. It emerged in the early days of Fabian's project, their ways of returning to the flaneur's expression in the 1920s by writers who *Flaneur* engaged continually and explicitly during our walks, at times as ancestors and at others as artefacts of a different world. Focusing on Fabian's various walks along a major Berlin thoroughfare, Kanstrasse, I first trace how Fabian conceives of his project in terms of forging literary connections between concrete elements he finds on the street. By comparing his research, the texts he produces, and the re-imagination of the text back into a physical walk (as a tour), I want to trouble distinctions between the literary and real without fully collapsing them into each other. In the final sections, I examine how an internal limit of the literary forces shifts in the registers of Fabian's language; in particular, how the ethical project of engaging a difficult history surfaces in ordinary forms of speech.

## The Making of a Walk in Words

For Fabian and *Flaneur*, the process of producing an issue begins with the selection of a street to explore. With a map of the city in hand, the group walks the streets, allowing each to make an impression on them, some bad and some good. It could be anything that draws them in. George-Schwarz-Strasse was often the example, as everyone shared a feeling of uneasiness there, a sensation they described as "cinematic," like a horror movie where a kind of imminent danger hung over the place. It takes two months to gather materials from the street – half of the issue will consist of work produced by the team, while the rest is contracted to local artists. With funding secured from their publisher, Ricarda's private funds (and recently, from the Goethe Institute as part of its ongoing efforts to export German culture), work begins in earnest when the walking begins. One day, an Italian journalist came to interview Fabian about his work, asking whether the first view of a place when the team arrives was somehow privileged, free of the judgments that burden later walks. "Is it undistorted?" he inquired. Over coffee, Fabian explained to me why the journalist had misunderstood the project. "Well, I do think it's very powerful, and there's a kind of naiveté in the child's view of seeing something for the first time ... but I think it's not a distortion, because that is, exactly what it is. Even if you're a child ... you're already a container filled with all sorts of influences." In the flaneur technique, every perspective is as much a part of the picture as every other. "All of these stories are super personal, and that's why people can understand them somewhere else. It is because they are subjective and not objective."

Kantstrasse was an obvious choice. It was a familiar street in a familiar city, but one with compelling layers of history. Kantstrasse itself was built at the end of the nineteenth century as part of an effort to make the Charlottenburg district feel more Parisian. Running east-west from the Kaiser-Wilhelm-Gedächtniskirche near Breitscheidplatz to the district court, the street has had many lives; as a centre for theatre and arts at the turn of the century, de nomine "Chinatown" (or Cant-on-strasse) in the 1920s, site of a Nazi jail in the 1940s, and architectural experiment in the 1950s. After the Wall fell in 1989, the city's centre of gravity shifted eastward, leaving the street less crowded, and its once ahead-of-the-times aesthetic now a strangely unoccupied exhibit of bygone sensibilities.

Much of the first month is taken up with walking the block, wandering into stores, and spending time with whoever enters. Each person Fabian meets, he asks to arrange a time to sit and talk over coffee; his desire, he explains, is to become "part of the street." In the course of researching Kantstrasse, Fabian had sung with a men's choir for Easter at the local Baptist church, hung around his favourite coffee shops and evening haunts, spent hours eating and drinking with locals, and playing football with children from local schools. One follows on sparks of friendship as a method, he told me.[23]

One afternoon in Charlottenburg, Fabian found himself walking, head down, and noticed scuffed Stolpersteine outside an apartment building at Kantstrasse 120–121. These "stumbling stones" were monuments created by Gunter Demnig, marking the homes of victims of Nazi violence, and Fabian had, unlike those passing by too busy to look, stumbled upon a such a mark of violent history. Bending down, he read the inscriptions: "Here lived Julius Tauber, b. 1906 – deported 29.10.1941. Lodz/Litzmanstadt. Died 28.10.1944." Alongside the first, a stone for Erna Ewer. How did these stones get here? What happened to this family? Did they survive? He decided not to let this story lay here unattended and returned home to search for the victim's family. Archives in the Berlin district office provided him a skeletal story – Erna lived with her daughter, Ruth, son-in-law, Julius, and grandson, Michael, and was deported to Poland where she was killed. Her daughter, Ruth, survived Auschwitz, ultimately immigrating to the United States with her son, Michael, who had also managed to survive. Through diligent pursuit of connections and some luck, Fabian succeeded in finding the boy Michael's phone number (still in exile across the Atlantic) and decided to call. When the now-old man answered the phone, Fabian's face dropped in surprise.

In the conversation that ensued, Michael described the house in great detail – "there is a large door, three panels with windows, walk straight there is an elevator, one of the old ones with a gate and lever … upstairs you'll find the apartment just off the landing to the left, it faces the street." Fabian hurried back to the street and followed a resident into the building. He followed Michael's memories through the hall, slowly making his way up a small staircase and resting his hand on the banister, pausing briefly at each door. When he arrived at the unit where the Taubers once lived, he knocked gently. A man of probably thirty answered in a thick Swiss accent. "Was darf's sein?" [Can I help you?] Fabian told the man he had come to see the apartment where Nazi victims had lived and wondered if he could look around. But the man's face remained blank, unmoved; he found the request strange, and Fabian was forced to turn about. The walk ended.

Michael, it turned out, had sent the stones to be placed on Kantstrasse in 2010 but had not been there to see them. Passing his eyes over them again as he left, Fabian decided to polish the bronze stones. He took pictures before and after and put them in the issue.

*Small Texts and Footsteps*

While working on an earlier project, Grashina had begun a technique of collecting tiny observations, random encounters or conversations on snippets of paper, which she then compiled randomly throughout the text. These traces of a walk "[tell] a story without really telling a story," she told me. Grashina decided to continue jotting down thoughts or encounters, "[scattering] these pages throughout the magazine to create an atmosphere of an actual petit flaneur strolling through the magazine." The idea to place them alongside, around, or throughout the other pieces in the volume rather than giving them their own conventional text block came later.

Grashina wrote her fragments while they were working on the magazine, but they were not inserted until the end of the design phase.

Accordingly, Grashina's fragments were dotted throughout the text as Fabian put together, in the final hours, his own sort of walk in words, a recurring piece called *Traces of Resistance*, which served as an artefact of the process of putting the entire issue together. It was Fabian's way of making his way through the story of writing the issue: a walk, then, not just in texts but through them. The two sit side by side in the final version, two routes through a space, with hers dotted throughout *Flaneur*, on the sides, tops, and bottoms of pages, climbing through crevices between words, slinking their way alongside the movement of other pieces, down side streets. His, "heavier … very philosophical, descriptive and poetic," hers "more direct." At the bottom of the final page of the Kantstrasse *Traces*, one of Grashina's tiny texts culminated her walk alongside his, in her own font and position:

> "Manfred, how are your hemorrhoids? You feeling any better?"
>
> His drinking kept him from getting to the hospital to get those nasty fuckers cut off * My question calls forth an annoyed sigh from the bar lady * Others erupt in excited chatter * His hemorrhoids are apparently the topic / No operation * "I've cut down on drinking and smoking" His butt – fine.

*Traces*, through which Fabian gives an account of how an issue comes together, began from the intuition of a shared spirit of resistance among characters with whom he worked on Kantstrasse. As *Flaneur* developed, it became increasingly obvious to him that his own project was also about a kind of resistance. Inhabiting the flaneur technique requires resistance to the traps of other patterns of thought: "If you go into that travel guide trap you automatically go back into colonial thinking, because you want to make something "handy" or you want to make something "enjoyable" you want to sell a place or point out all the exotic features, but not go too deeply, because it could make the place weird, or creepy … so for me it's about resisting that, especially now we're going places where we have never been before." Of all the pieces in *Flaneur*, *Traces* is the lengthiest, requires the most time to complete, and is the last to be submitted. Work begins as soon as the street is selected and continues throughout. It is not finished until the rest of the issue has been completed, themes have begun to emerge, and direction to the stories given. This language emerged in Fabian in particular after a visit to Canada, where much of the discourse the group encountered centred on the history of colonial rule. At the same time, it echoed a pattern of speech he'd learned as a student of cultural studies in university, where he encountered Benjamin early on but whose approach he now abandoned.

"Resistance is a basic human condition," Fabian explained to me:

It's very powerful ... focusing on the resistance you really get those characters, because you capture them at a more extreme level of their identity ... that doesn't mean that they might have regretted twenty years later, or as I've said some of these links that I do are kind of literary truth, not all of these characters would maybe agree with links I'm trying but I also think it's nice to draw these parallels because all of a sudden, you see this historical situation and there was this resistance and it led to this or that. But to link something that happened in the '20s with something in the '90s where you can't see the direct, logical line but there is something that's ideal, but it becomes some universal in that you tell a story and you find something human, and in the other story too and you get some recurrent pattern.

*Traces* is a series of words and a collage curated under a motto of urban life – an epigraph from Hessel ("We can see only what looks at us. We can do only ... what we cannot help doing"):

This manifesto of resistance draws lines between different lives
that are connected through the street until
"the woods are all black but still the sky is blue."

The allusion is to the first volume of Proust's *À la recherche du temps perdu*. The text was translated in the 1920s by Benjamin and Hessel, and the immanent critique produced from this labour led to the developments in Benjamin's thinking about memory and time in the 1930s. Twenty-two numbered fragments follow, a two-page collage, and another twenty-eight fragments. The text is a meditation on the street, on an attitude to the street of which it is, itself, an example. It is itself a walk, another version of flaneuring on Kantstrasse. We begin this time with a reflection on a song stuck in the flaneur's head, and an "old Romanian" singing a picture of history. It's the faces of the people on the train that trigger the thought and the "half-forgotten melody." The song "lies on the threshold of oblivion ... that remains anticipated but never occurs." The voice comes from another world. It tells the listener that "we lived at the same time." "We are dependent on these shadow pictures; they are the clay that binds us together, because we alone have no connection ... Our knowledge, be it only a removed one – makes us allies, comrades, linked. This is the history of a street, a documented statement of connections."

Each subsequent segment adds a link – a name, a story, or a work of art – arranging this cast of figures in two columns side by side. Sometimes a heading precedes a segment – other times only a number. Twenty such lines into the piece, a reflection written in Fabian's voice:

> Maybe flaneuring is the opposite of reading books. Or rather, two different sides of the same page. Maybe this is what the reader does, when he leaves the room and wanders (his) streets. In a book everything is already laid out, in the street the flaneur has to go in search of images first. ("The pictures, wherever they may live" W.B.) Walter Benjamin says that the city opens up to the flaneur like a landscape; it encircles him like a room. (Acceleration; past; remembrance) Bertolt Brecht says that reading books and going wandering in faraway lands means, "out of the room and into the stars." (Lightspeed; irresistible; the present as the future's past)

The fragments resume where they left off on the other side of the images. The Kantstrasse *Traces* ends with the quotation with which it began. The relations between elements of the street, the different values ascribed to spatial arrangement (as representations of real topographies, political boundaries, or semantic connections), between the concrete street and the fragmentary nature of intertwining lives is inverted in the collage presented in the middle of the text. Greyscale images appear like an old still. Names are arranged as streets, often at right angles and indicating multiple folds in time and space. This mapping of social relations into the form of city streets is reminiscent too of the concrete Berlin streets I knew, more often than not named for great writers, artists, and intellectuals.

*A Walk on Kantstrasse, February 25, 2014*

I met up with Fabian as he was leading a tour, a mixed group of locals and tourists, Germans and expats, around the Charlottenburg borough of Berlin. Down the grey stairs of the train station at Savignyplatz, I found myself in a familiar corridor of a street, bustling restaurants on one side, bookshops on the other, opening up onto the grass square bordered on three sides by stores and on the fourth by a main road. A bronze August Kraus cast of a boy pulling a ram, well-maintained lawns, trendy store windows, and stone apartments grace the streets. The assembly gathered outside a bookstore, the Bücherbogen ["Book arches"], and we took turns introducing ourselves as new members joined the party: a German-American journalist living in Berlin; a recent British expat who left a corporate job to take up life as a writer; a German doctoral student, studying literary and musical history; a young German couple who frequented such tours; a theatre director here after a stay in Taiwan. Fabian was gearing up to leave for a research trip (the first for *Flaneur* abroad) to Montreal's Rue Bernard, so this was to be the last outing for a while.

Our two-hour excursion was billed as a literary tour of a major thoroughfare in the former West Berlin. As we walked toward Kantstrasse from Savignyplatz, Fabian explained that the wide streets of Charlottenburg were intentionally reminiscent of the Parisian boulevard, part of a vision von Bismark had for the city as Germany entered a new era on the world stage at the dawn of the twentieth century. The area enjoyed economic success as it built itself up on the French model, with spacious parks and residential housing and a booming commercial district around Kurfürstendamm, Berlin's Champs-Élysées. When the Prussian government passed the Groß-Berlin-Gesetz in 1920, Charlottenburg (along with six other former towns) was annexed to the greater Berlin. Since the turn of the century, Fabian explained, the area had (also like Paris) become a meeting place for artists and thinkers, many of whom frequented some of the more well-known stops on our walk. Names like Brecht and Döblin brought a Parisian cache to the area. "This," he went on, "is how places and times move." The period prior to the Great Depression would be celebrated as a "golden age" for the area around the Ku'damm, as it blossomed into the epicentre of bohemian artistic life, including for the newly imported flaneur aesthetic (no longer in fashion in Paris), enlivened by the presence of writers like Hessel and his friends. During the period of division, these streets were the symbol of the economic boom in the West, and in 1968 of the leftist student uprising. But since the fall of the Berlin Wall, the centre of the city had rapidly shifted east, leaving empty and uncannily anachronistic "modernist" architecture in its wake.

Fabian's attention darted around as he considered where to pause for another fragment, occasionally stopping to read a marked passage from the magazine. Conversations formed and broke up as we told stories, shared favourite books, traded business cards. When interest waned, Fabian dragged us along somewhere new. We came to the Theater des Westens, where an old blue-and-white plaque for Trude Hesterberg reads, "The Wild Stage ... laid the foundation stone for modern, German, literary-political cabaret." Her production in the basement of the theatre was the first of its kind run by a woman, and it was there that Marlene Dietrich would hone her craft. After her role in *Der Blaue Engel* (a part for which Hesterberg also auditioned), Dietrich returned to Kantstrasse a star – the composer of the score, Friedrich Hollaender, reopened the theatre in 1931, three years after it had been forced closed. This, Fabian confided, was the story he preferred about the place. After the Nazi seizure of power in early 1933, Hesterberg joined the Party and a cohort of artists in "defence" of "German culture," opening a new cabaret that proved a commercial disaster. "It ruins the place once you know that."

Stopping soon down the road, Fabian reminded us of Truffaut's *Jules et Jim*, based on Roche's first novel, exploring his relationship with Hessel. "The writer Isherwood was also here at that time and while he is here he met Paul Bowles in this neighbourhood, who was taking part in the vibrant gay community in 1931." He pointed across the street toward a bodega: "There was a club there, perhaps it's where they met ... Isherwood wrote a kind of fictional autobiography called *Goodbye to Berlin* and names the protagonist Sally Bowles. And this character inspires another in a novel by a writer you might know, Truman Capote, *Breakfast at Tiffany's*. Let me just read these two quotes." Fabian pulled out his copy of *Flaneur* and turns to a page marked by several yellow notes and reads. "OK the first one from Sally Bowles: "I can't be bothered to explain, darling. Here, read this, will you? Of all the blasted impudence! Read it aloud. I want to hear how it sounds"; and then this one from Holly Golightly: "Would you reach in the drawer there and give me my purse. A girl doesn't read this sort of thing without her lipstick. Maybe this will come in handy – if you ever write a rat romance. Don't be hoggy, read it aloud. I'd like to hear it myself."

Fabian called us over to an iron gate and lowered his voice, pointing to a large hotel, Kempinsky, and told us not to go too close. The original owners of Europe's oldest hotel group had been German Jews, but who were stripped of their holdings during the Arianisierung (the policy of finding Aryan replacements for less desirable business owners). Afterced the Wall fell in 1989, descendants of the original Kempinsky asked for recognition on the building but were denied by new corporate management for fear the story would impact business. In the 1990s, when a small plaque was finally erected, family members were not invited to the public unveiling. "They don't like it when I tell this story," Fabian announced, turning around to the empty lot by the gates. We were standing, we now discovered, outside the footprint of the former centre of Jewish life in the city, where now all that stands is a crumbling tower in the back corner of the lot. "I pass this every day and never knew what it was," someone murmured from the back.

The neighbourhood changes as we come to our final stop outside a residential building, and Fabian arranged us in a semicircle, making room for shoppers and residents passing through. His affect changed as he knelt down to point to a scuffed, nearly hidden Stolperstein on the ground. Fabian told the crowd the Taubers' story, his voice quiet and contemplative, especially as he described his phone call with Michael. He pointed to the Swiss flag hanging outside a window above us. The tour ended here, though we walked together back to the station near Savignyplatz where we met. Several of us exchanged information and agreed to talk again soon.

This was how we walked Kantstrasse.

### Art, Voice, and Memory

In the past two decades, geographical and sociological work on urban life has increasingly and successfully traced the interplay of public art projects and urban restructuring,[24] the relationship between symbolic economies and the cultural determination of public space[25] distributed as claims to participation in the city. More recent anthropological interventions[26] have explored how artistic production not only marks urban landscapes but also gives rise to new forms of political action that fracture publics and refuse integration, while affirming "rights to the city," thus demanding a rethinking of democratic practice and the production of the city in aesthetic and political terms. Bourriaud's[27] picture of relational art as one in which the artist enables a community, a way of living, has found a home in such conversations through the implications of witnessing. In Berlin this idea carries a double weight, not only because witness makes possible a Rancièrean community of sense, but also because it remakes the act of witnessing itself.

*Flaneur's* chimeric construction seems to suggest that some experiences must go beyond words. "Multiple translations" between media make it "possible to address the deformation of language that a traumatic event creates, moving the body in pain to occupy other modes of habitation."[28] The world of the trauma is not simply reconstituted, but rather "is being coproduced here as a shadow world, a world made stranger by speech that is untethered from its source. The memories that are recalled take on the character of the uncanny – they belong to another I, one that I no longer recognize." This performative possibility of achieving something that cannot be registered otherwise, is, I think, helpful in understanding the kind of work that Fabian's literary labour achieves, in juxtaposition with other domains of language that fail to register even those pains they seek ostensibly to mark. Moments contain multiple times, pasts, presents, futures, "much as a drop of water might be swarming with organisms that it has gathered from different places."

For Fabian and *Flaneur*, inspiration was to be drawn from their ancestors of the 1920s, Benjamin and Hessel, friends who walked in the city and whose own encounters with and writing about the street has been the subject of scholarly and public attention for some time. Two other figures are likewise often referenced – the Parisian founder of modernité Charles Baudelaire and the Swiss novelist Robert Walser. Each was for them a variation on flaneurish thought, whether as an object or form of literary criticism (as in Benjamin and his accounts of others), a genre of writing (in Walser or Hessel), or a tour-and-paper magazine. "Flaneurs share an interest in looking into the past, with the writers who came before them," Fabian told me once. Yet while the spirit and component elements of these variations stay the same, the relations between them are constantly transforming across time, media, and space.

On the streets of Paris in the long nineteenth century, the trappings of modern life came to be associated with one walker in particular, the Baudlerianian dandy, whose strolling down the boulevard expressed bourgeois leisure and life in a city more generally, where one could disperse into[29] anonymity, lost in the faces of the crowd. Through Baudelaire, the great poet of modernity and Paris, the flaneur became the sign of the alienation of capital, torn between his positions as "disengaged and cynical voyeur on the one hand" and an artist deftly entering the lives of his subjects on the other. The artistry of his jaunts enabled the flaneur to effect collapses and erasures, not just across geographical space but also time. They incarnated anachrony into the material of the street, folding the modern into the past through memory, rejecting the "self-enunciative authority of any technically reproduced image"[30] in favour of the literary encounter, thereby remaining out of step with the crowd that was the condition under which he had been born and to which he owed his literary existence. Despite the particularity of post-Revolutionary Paris, however, the flaneur was to soon dissolve into the category of modernity in general, due in part to modern life's "saturation" with the perceptival attitude he embraced.[31]

When the flaneur re-emerged in Berlin in the 1920s, in the words and persons of writers like Hessel and Benjamin,[32] the figure was again out of place, literarily, politically, or otherwise, something foreign, outmoded and ill-fitted for the realities of an interwar economy. The city was rapidly expanding, its streets reimagined by von Bismark, made broad and long on the model of Paris.[33] As the capital and showpiece of the Weimar Republic, Berlin boasted bright lights, a vibrant club scene, elegant shops, bustling automobiles, and new monuments to antiquity and capitalism alike. Surrounded by the city, Max Weber observed in 1910 that "the distinctive formal values of our modern artistic culture could only have come to be through the existence of the modern metropolis with its ... wild dance of impressions of sound and colour, impressions and experiences which have an effect on sexual fantasy, all variants of a spiritual constitution, which brood voraciously over the seemingly inexhaustible possibilities of means to life and happiness." The streets seemed to many observers designed for walkers looking to take in the phantasmagoria. The historian Eric Weitz quotes from a local newspaper that in Berlin that "for not much money you can get a breath of a wider world." Following in the footsteps of the city's famous flaneurs, he describes walking the city as opportunity to "feel" politics and history, and "above all else, to sense modernity: the sight, smell and taste of traffic congestion ... the press of crowds jostling one another on the streets, train platforms, and subway cars." Stefan Zweig says of the same period that "Berlin transformed itself into the Babel of the world."[34]

This famous second iteration was no mere copy of its Parisian predecessor. The flaneur had been transformed, acutely aware of its own emergence from different historical and material conditions. According to Siegfried Kracauer, against such a backdrop the flaneur tried to call urbanites away from emerging distraction industries in favour of a more embodied, immediate, and mindful inhabitation.[35] If the flaneur of old walked to observe to the world while remaining himself invisible, disguised among the crowds, such a discreet witnessing took on a new burden in the era of fascism, preserving for the collective consciousness the sight of terrible violence. The strategy of writing memory from the street-level view allows, as de Certeau famously showed, for an everyday *rhetoric* that breaks the dominant narrative: these procedures, this rhetoric of walking, combines various styles – that is, symbolic manifestations of ways of being-in-the-world, and uses, crystallizations of these communications as "actual facts."[36] This allowed the walker to tell a story in the gaps of official discourse, spatial arrangements, and symbolic orders, a power all the more crucial in a place that is, on the surface, so determined not to let the reality of fantastic stories of violence slip away, but which in the very act of establishing *the* story of the past reveals its unwillingness to let those experiences breathe. This time the figure was short lived, forced out of a world shattered by the rise of Nazi fascism.[37]

Benjamin's early work on Baudelaire developed out of the physiognomy of the bohème marked by a position of political revolt against the emperor Napoleon, a conspiratorial aesthetic, and ultimately an identification with the splenetic ragpicker. Baudelaire's fate is to be caught in a dulled state of opposition to the rule of his own class.[38] What makes

Baudelaire such an interesting case for Benjamin is his inability to do anything about the condition of contradiction, marking him out from Poe's detective stories. Instead, Baudelaire has no choice but to bear these aporias in his very being.

In an uncanny set of views of the city in the *Berliner Kindheit um 1900* (a work in photographic philosophy Benjamin says constituted his "political view of the past"), we see through the eyes of the child in memories and at a moment of particular precarity, arranged and rearranged several times by editors in the time since Benjamin's untimely death. In his forward, Benjamin confides that it was in 1932 that he began to realize he might not see his childhood home for a long time. "I had learned the procedure of vaccination many times in my inner life," he wrote, calling up images he says most viscerally churned up feelings of homesickness while in exile – those of childhood.[39] Longing is to the mind, he goes on, what the vaccine is to the healthy body.

The boy Walter's walks are an escape from his privileged upperclass surroundings. He is out in search of the nooks and crannies of urban space, untapped resources for the child's imaginings. No doubt it is the adult Benjamin's voice who intercedes on Krumme Strasse, lamenting the self-satisfied wall erected around his neighbourhood, a kind of prison of bourgeois pride. On the street with a bend, with an old pool, and stores selling all sorts of sundry items, Walter finds not just an escape but a manner of sexual awakening as he strategically ducks between windows, even scanning accounting books as an alibi before finding more illicit material for his gaze. He had timed his adventures to the absence of traffic, taking his time even as "rosettes and lanterns … celebrate the embarrassing event."[40] Sex and class are bound together for the child. Benjamin describes in "Berlin Chronicle" how Ariadne the sex worker seduced wealthy sons across the boundaries of class. The young Walter collects postcards, images that spiral out not in lines but around curves, that sometimes zoom in and others out, and through which the adult Benjamin then walks again, as if they held some political promise that he could reclaim.

Benjamin's *Eisenbahnstrasse* begins with an epigraph declaring the dedicatory naming of the street composed in his fragments: "This Street is Asja-Lacis-Strasse, for the engineer who broke through the author." Here too is a desire to map his life, constructed by what he describes as a (late in life) learned practice of getting lost. In this way it was Paris, where he spent much time during his exile, which taught Benjamin about Berlin. We find a street punctuated by activity and reflection. Time here too is crystallized in various ways, into buildings and economic analyses, urban debris of various kind, to highlight in every case what is rejected from history. His occupation is with the actual and the ephemeral. Howard Eiland notes relatedly how, by the time of the *Passengenwerk*, the figure of the flaneur had become central to Benjamin's dialectical conception of awakening to the past, in which different times vibrate with one another:

> At streetcorners, before housefronts and shopfronts, in proximity to particular doorways, particular stretches of cobblestone, particular entrances to the catacombs, particular cafés and cabarets, he experiences an uncanny thickening and layering of phenomena, an effect of superimposition, in which remembered events or habitations show through the present time and place, which have suddenly become transparent, just as in film an image may bleed through one or more simultaneously perceptible, inter-articulated images in multiple exposure. It is a dreamlike effect, with the moving imagery characteristically yielding, in the flâneur's case, a "felt knowledge" that is not yet conceptual.[41]

Ironically what marks Walser by contrast as "so Swiss" for Benjamin is shame. "As soon as he takes up the pen, he's seized by his desperado mood [Desperadostimmung]. All seems lost to him, a torrent of words breaks out, in which each sentence has the task of forgetting the past."[42] The walker's stumbling through blackness keeps us in the present by erasing whatever came just before, save for the occasional glimmering light of hope that dots his path in the form of the figures he meets. These "garlands of language" are like the depraved heroes who appear out of that darkness. Such figures, he argues, come from the forests and valleys of Romantic Germany. "[Hebel's] Zundelfrieder from the rebellious, enlightened petty bourgeoisie of Rheinish cities … Hamsun's characters from the prehistoric world of the fjords – it is people drawing their homesickness into trolls … what they cry is prose. Because the sobbing is the melody of Walser's loquacity. It tells us where his loved ones come from."[43] This is a process of healing, a cure. Walser's walk is punctuated by people, as well as by nature, by rupture and continuity, but in each moment there is a reflection of some larger structure of life. Each encounter is self-contained and discrete though somehow also reaches out beyond itself. Each is a moment, an example of the flaneur experience and a meditation on it. If Baudelaire's action/inaction concerns a blunted revolution and reveals contradictions in the rule of the cultural bourgeoisie, the flaneur of the Deutsche Sprachraum pertains to a vaccination of the soul. The space of the city where he grew up becomes for Benjamin a screen against which he can draw and confront both his past and his future.

The Berlin that Fabian inhabited was again rather different. The streets and buildings that lined Benjamin's Berlin had in many cases been destroyed by war. Urban historians disagree on the exact figure, but estimates range from 80 to 90 per cent of the city's buildings were damaged or destroyed. During the period of division, an early expansion of building projects gave way in many cases to dismantling and abandonment, and after the Wall, many state-owned buildings were repurposed and at times, reconstructed. Walking itself had to change as well.

In the production of the journal, Fabian's walking followed in the footsteps of serendipity, allowing history and distance to be overcome in small eruptive moments of connection. In *Traces*, fragments arranged first by logical steps, and then suddenly transplanted in that form into spatial distributions, mirroring the arrangement of the streets we walked in both previous incarnations. Fabian's encounter with the living, human voice of history in the present, in the character of Michael Tauber, came to resemble the ways in which space is traversed by Hessel in one of the stories from our tour. On a sunny day in Berlin, Hessel is carrying an umbrella and, when his friend Franz Blei asks why, he replies, "It's raining in Paris." When we "stumble" over a stone then, the distance to that past moment is collapsed, much like the distance to France. Perhaps other times and other spaces are, in world of the flaneur, are not necessarily other at all. Time and space are, for Fabian, not distinct directions but belong instead to the same category of collapsible distance, a separation that can be rearranged interchangeably, this time for that place.

There is then a crucial difference between Fabian and his forbears in the pervasive awareness of the looming spectre of uncertainty as a trope in the ordinary worlds they inhabit. In Fabian's words, we see that the collapses, in or between time and space, of blame or identity don't quite fully work out. Recall that on the naming of streets Benjamin writes "this street is called" and Fabian "this could be." The Stolperstein on which we trip into the past is neglected and needs polish, the Kempinsky family goes uninvited to the plaque ceremony, the current resident of Tauber's house is unmoved by the story of its former occupants. Fabian points out that while it's raining for Hessel, it is not for Blei. These ruptures or disjunctures are mirrored by Fabian's insistence on resisting the single story of the street, the "colonizing" narrative.

These worlds, streets, lives, texts, and stories are similarly fragmentary, singular and complete in themselves and yet also open and shifting. Fabian's Berlin is suffused by a "culture" of guilt. Shame is announced everywhere, constantly, and around every corner. Our neglected memorials and forgotten stories take on the meaning of showing the limits of such efforts to make amends for the past, even as ever more plaques, stones, and statues spring up. From a privileged vantage point in history, one could say that Fabian's sublimation of space and time is an artefact of being able to assume those processes as already there from an earlier moment. But one could no longer collapse Berlin and Paris – the insistence on the particularity of *German* guilt makes that quite impossible. And in the same way, one cannot simply re-inhabit ancient pasts, because of the suspicion that trails any attempt to look backwards for anything but darkness. The threat of a taint is too great. Yet avoiding such lived expressions masks another kind of violence and everywhere reveals a subtle limit of a confrontation with history.

## Standing Languages of Memory and Cliché

The politics of memory and its relation to the work of art in the contemporary global city is a theme that remains central to both sociological and literary thought, much of which is, like Fabian's project, indebted to Benjamin. And it is no surprise that any number of approaches to memory work have emerged in the past few decades, particularly in relation to trauma, through an engagement with urban experiences. Among the most influential has been Andreas Huyssen's[44] suggestion that the alignment of the city as the site of a certain kind of memory work through art arises from emergent crises in the ways the past has been kept in the past, the security of which was ensured through material traces in the built environment. If history allowed for the stability of a transitory and present modernity by fixing a narrative of historical time, memory, in the hands of poets, seems occupied with the hauntings of that past. It is memory, not history, that is hypertrophied in the contemporary moment, as an act more and more commonly associated with our actions in the present. If history is no guarantor that the horrors of the past will not be repeated, the argument goes, why should our "notoriously unreliabl[e]" memory be any better?[45] The solution can rest, Huyssen continues, neither with Nietzsche's creative forgetting (perhaps one wonders why not?), nor with a preoccupation with the future, namely in a triumphalist, neoliberal discourse of globalization.

Memory work in the age of hypertrophy might just as easily lead to a melancholic fixation on trauma, to a self-indulgence of the present.[46] Here the dominance of trauma is taken as a symptom of its position at the threshold of remembering and forgetting and threatens to eclipse the larger functions of memory work. As I argued in the previous chapter, this threat is manifest in the ways the Holocaust has been read as a metaphysical model and could lead to the making-traumatic of the whole history of modernity, victimizing subjects universally and somehow denying their agency. Huyssen, like many in Europe, puts his faith in the redemptive power of human rights discourse (rather than psychoanalytic categories) because its "function" is to allow people to break from traumatic repetition. Art seems to share this function. He remains convinced that memory discourse and its forms of labour are "absolutely essential to imagine the future and to regain a strong temporal and spatial grounding of life and the imagination in a media and consumer society that increasingly voids temporality and collapses space."[47] Implicit in such a framework, however, is a picture of modernity and life in the city that reproduces elements of the discourses we seem otherwise keen to avoid, notably that technology and globalization are now shrinking space and evacuating time; tropes thoroughly critiqued by anthropological and sociological literature on the category of modernity and which my ethnography in Berlin suggests to me we ought finally to move beyond. As we saw in the previous chapter, despite the critique of trauma theory, the alterative proposed by scholars of cultural memory seems unable to break free from the strict dichotomy of speaking and silence. Ethnographic studies on memory in Berlin, while important for having revealed the multiplicity of place[48] in the era of transformation, and the tensions that rest at the heart of construction,[49] have likewise rested on the opposition of public/private, space/time, personal/impersonal, or memory/history.[50] But perhaps these categorical oppositions are always insufficient, at least from the vantage of those for whom the promise of art to free themselves from the "repetitions" of trauma also carried at its heart a limit – a limit often missed by researchers who have focused primarily on how memory work "pervades *real* public space."[51]

These connections come into clearer focus as we notice that the concrete figures of the metropole's built environment are increasingly treated as palimpsests of space.[52] If memory studies have been positioned against the criticisms of deconstructivism, particularly in architecture, then concerning the imperialism of écriture, I am entirely in agreement that it is not just concrete structures but life itself that can be made literary.[53] I remain unconvinced, however, that there need be a redemptive potential of such a life. Literature's capacity for newness, from Fabian's point of view, was built into the concrete, into ordinary habits like re-walking a street, and is not an escape from what is beneath our feet. Scholars often approach memory work as a negotiation of a problematic tension between binaries bound together, like space and time, public and private, remembering and forgetting. But *Flaneur* offers one way of shifting the terms of analysis by suggesting these categories are deeply interwoven. They are neither collapsible into one another nor strictly different experiences in an oppositional struggle. What would it mean to think of the language of memory as unfolding, as defined by a constant work, without needing to work toward a durable structure of time?

We can take the relationship in the other direction as well – that is, from concrete street to forms of talk. Fabian's focus on re-walking is instructive, in that it provides material for recasting assumptions about the nature of returning. When is the use of a borrowed phrase or a word a re-use and also an *over*use? When does it become meaningful, and when meaningless? By showing how re-walking the same street again and again can be a mode of discovery, Fabian is also telling us something about language.

The pervasive worry in public discourse has been that an overuse might make talk about the past banal. But it is worth parsing further the relationship between the ordinary, the cliché, and the threat of descending into banality. In Arendt's famous formulation, banality is associated with a loss of the mother tongue, in which "one cliché chases another." As Barbara Cassin explains, "The productivity, inventiveness, and authority one displays in one's language come to be ... 'cut off' the more one forgets. 'Cliché' is the term we need to focus on here. The banality of evil – think of Eichmann, the specialist – is not without relation to the banality of the language one speaks." But everything hinges on how we understand what it means to invent in a language, which Arendt associates only with the mother tongue, and thus comes to the fore in the condition of exile, read as the inversion of Eichmann's situation. "The German language will still be a mother tongue for exiles, but it was no longer one for ordinary Nazis: this is the result of the decoupling of language and people pushed to the extreme. For lack of a mother tongue, when the mother tongue is no longer a tongue, a language, there is only propaganda."[54] This is a worry for the exile too, that they will end up able to speak only in clichés in a language because it is "not one's own," and leads some exiles to "cling" to their mother tongue. But is it something about the reliance on chains of clichés – the forms themselves of talk – that is at issue, or is it, rather, the ways they are used? What is it, moreover, to feel a language is one's own? At times, Arendt seems to suggest that it was not the use of clichés per se, but that Eichmann could only speak in cliches, that was at issue; he "was genuinely incapable of uttering a single sentence that was not a cliché" – he "consoled" himself with them. At others, it seems like cliches (or least, this utter reliance on them) can be distinguished by way they cut off meaning – they no longer count as language at all. Cassin writes, "The cliché must not be mistaken for an ordinary use of words, for ordinary language: on the contrary, each word of ordinary language is full of all the associations and meanings that have accrued to it, in the back of the mind ..."

> One can thus speak one's mother tongue using clichés: here is the proof! If invention is really something proper to oneself, like the "mother," then one would have to conclude, in all good logic, that one's tongue is no longer a "mother tongue" as soon as one no longer invents anything in it, indeed, that it is no longer even really a "tongue" for all those politically and humanly idiotic listener- transmitters crippled by banalities and lacking in any reflective or critical judgment.[55]

To return to the question I posed at the outset, can a cliché ever be something I mean? Could it even be read as an invention? If, for Arendt, banality is an emptying out of thought, it is precisely because this was an ordinary possibility, that Eichmann was an ordinary man (and not an extraordinary evil), that he was subject to justice.[56] This fact removes from the figure of the Nazi perpetrator all "ontological monstrosity." Eichmann is banal because he is a mediocrity (joined with his simultaneous sense of superiority conferred by the events in which we took part). This is different from a picture of the ordinary as an "ontologically sufficient" condition to produce banality (that is, evil), but rather to show that it exists as a real possibility within the ordinary. If this is right, it would mean that in and of itself, the banality of evil is "empirically almost unfounded, ultimately insufficient for taking account of the participation of millions of men and women in the programmatic killing of dozens of millions of people on every continent, across the globe."[57] Perhaps then what is needed is a move away from a perspective that looks to know what an expression means (or that it is meant or, if not, overused) from the phrase itself, and toward an investigation into ordinary lives themselves. Repetition, especially when enforced by a memory regime as overwhelming as Germany's, can certainly deaden words that normally have a life within a form of life. But just because a turn of phrase is ordinary or repeated, even again and again, doesn't mean it necessarily ceases to be meaningful.[58]

If we do not start from an assumption that the use of clichés is indicative of banality (and thus evil), what else could such an utterance be doing? Why assume after all that every example of a cliché (or banality) has one thing in common?[59] In each instance rather, Fabian's work asks us to go and look at how it is being used in *this* return. We can think of the situation in such contexts as one in which there are "standing languages"[60] available through which to talk about the past, but which we may or may not feel express us. But whether there are words or not within a standing language is never settled once and for all. There is no master list of possible expressions. In Berlin, the standing language about memory could be suffocating: On the one hand, the worry that to keep memory alive and prevent history from repeating itself, one is under pressure to find new authentic ways of expressing oneself. On the other hand, attempting to determine whether past ways of talking about the past worked threatens a descent into a banal double of fascism. But stumbling over a stone could also lead to a surprising phone call. A chance collaboration, a serendipitous alignment of words, could be effected by the same string of words or streets that earlier yielded nothing.

**A Mirror of Burden**

The summer after we first met, I meant to ask Fabian what he thought about this question of guilt, and the flaneur's power to reveal the contradictions in the language of shame deployed so often within German public discourse. But Fabian brought up the issue before I had a chance. The "advertising ethic," Fabian said, has taken over everything. It seemed to him that "people are not used to the flaneur technique – we're in a marketing dictatorship, everything is full of positivity, and a lot of it looks like journalism but it isn't ... These things have to be learned, these cultural techniques have to be learned, the literary techniques as opposed to journalistic approaches." But what about the world *Flaneur* lives in, the one being projected on to the places they visit? Like Walser's pen, this loosed a torrent of words:

> This euphoria, there's not much space for the past – and maybe that's necessary from their perspective, because if you're on the forefront of building a city and selling a city, maybe you kind of have to be focused on the future. It's hard for them.

It is hard, that is, to lament the passing of time and to acknowledge their disappointments and failures. The conversation turned to the media hype over Berlin during the past decade, the enormous influx of tourists and expats from the young artist class. Yet the affordable and

# In the Footsteps of a Flaneur: A Grammar of Returning (to a Street) 119

avant-garde world that attracted these visitors also threatens to destroy it. While on the one hand, cultural production became the linchpin for the transformation of Berlin into a world city, this boom has lead in subtle ways, yet again, to the reproduction of exclusion of other groups:

> You might have heard about the bashing of the Schwabisch [wealthy southern German newcomers] ... there was this [tabloid photograph of] graffiti that said, "don't buy from the Schwaben" and they took a picture of it and put it right next to a picture from 1933 of "don't buy from the Jews." ... Under this whole "we have to protect our city" there are certain kinds of racisms, certain kinds of anti-Semitism, certain kinds of stereo types – they are all of the sudden legitimate, you can get away with them, and that's where the far left is always very close to the far right. I think it has to do with disappointment.

The crux for Fabian rested between action and rhetoric. Words and memorials flood the city, but economics and persistent structures of exclusion tell another story about life there. The flaneur, the writer, the walker, demand we look at the multiple fragments, the ruins that lie everywhere on the ground. But if, as Fabian thought, such literary techniques of living in the city are forgotten, dangerous and hegemonic stories can settle in – a condition one worries we are watching unfold in the highly publicized rise of radical-right parties across Europe. Each fragment, the textures of which we find hidden, is in need of literary recovery.

> We get used to rhetorical guilt. We changed our use of language, certain words have been abandoned ... [but] you don't believe it anymore, the words don't have any value anymore because they are so overused, it's a bit like these memorial ... it's like a huge PR campaign, running around and being guilty. And it has worked so well because people believe we've dealt with our history. But did we really? ... We managed to create an economic system in Europe that works for *us*. And no one mentions it. Because we're busy running around telling this myth of the hard-working German who is aware of their history ... But now the conservatives ... have to defend themselves ... they say, "we are for the EU because we are aware of history" So even this economic system they've created around themselves turns into something they are doing to pay back for history.

But even this entire pattern of speech partakes in a rather ordinary series of utterances bordering on the point of cliché, a common feature of ordinary conversation, borrowing from official discourses, past histories of aesthetics, and public intellectual labour. What has been added in the grandchildren's generation, those who, like me, find themselves thrown into a world two generations removed and yet made to constantly bear a kind of witness in our flesh, is a desire to throw off the "excessive" burdens of guilt. The desire to unburden oneself from guilt, however, bears the double threat of forgetting history, which could lead to the repetition of such violence, generating a moral conundrum that is often gingerly navigated.

I highlight the everyday nature of this utterance to put pressure on the limits of the literary to *express* the tensions that emerge as aporias in ordinary speech. As Benjamin reveals about Baudelaire, or Fabian reveals about Hessel, these disconnects of literary speech are a feature of such language *and* its opposite. Encounters with the limits of literary speech in the register of the everyday tell us something important about its purpose in this domain of life, in this case a way out of a certain dilemma by dislocating the terms of engagement. The shift in his language reveals again that a certain contradiction is inherent in the confrontation with social guilt, because as soon as we have succeeded in "dealing with it," we have failed. But what about the pages of *Flaneur*, the fleeting moments of allowing oneself to be swallowed up by the literary relations, rather than concrete ones, between times and places?

If this technique provides us a mirror, a way to project unannounced burdens, forgotten struggles, and buried disappointments, here it seems we have uncovered the task of Berliner flaneur. The discourse that on the surface seeks to keep alive memories of violence to protect us from falling into familiar traps covers up other experiences (including of suffering), re-inscribing violence into the structure of social life. The literary project works by revealing that no fragment is secure from the force of doubt that creeps up at every instance. Small ruptures threaten more scepticism, the limits of not just everyday expressions, but poetic ones made to exceed the limits of ordinary speech, reifying again the intimacy of daily life and great events. The flaneur seems in this way as concerned at heart with question of reclaiming the human voice (in history) that we have lost in the dissolution (as we later come to find) into the collective and the ephemeral. The pattern of the flaneur, I have tried to argue, is not about one form or another, but about a certain imperative to ask a question, about freedom and the human voice. Literary approaches to the street and to history allow us to abide (without resolving) a tension that seems inherent in the German confrontation with the past – the desire to work through the past rather than process it, for a forgiveness without forgetfulness.

The longer I lived in Berlin, the more I found myself needing to walk. Nearly every day I walked a larger and larger circuit around my neighbourhood. Sometimes walking in Berlin, like writing in Berlin, can till the ground and churn up ghosts we'd thought long since exorcised.

Chapter Five
───────────

# Selecting, Collecting, Connecting: Making Books and Making Do

When Rixdorf Editions officially started printing its first books in 2017, James had been living in Berlin for eleven years. Before that, he had been living in London, where he worked for an international bank when he decided to learn to German, though he couldn't recall how he chose it. Determined to leave banking, he moved into what was then one of Berlin's poorest neighbourhoods, part of the soon-to-be gentrified Neukölln, an area earlier known as Rixdorf, and took up work as a commercial translator. "I recognize that it's cliché," he told me one afternoon in April, "but I also see why people do it; I've very much reinvented myself."

> I had never imagined being a translator. Then as I really got further into German, it presented itself as an option … I know a lot of people that are translators and writers and I'm fairly certain that it really is the city, the purely material circumstances which allow people to create, which is changing. Before, no one ever came to live [in this neighbourhood]. It's just amazing how that's changed. Those conditions are changing, but still, and I think about the people I know, the translators, the writers, the editors, people that are otherwise involved in publishing, there is a dynamism, there's also space and time to work on projects. It's also changed. It was so decentralized before. You have publishers in Hamburg, Stuttgart, say Munich, and now increasingly come to Berlin, at least with an office and sometimes moving entirely. I think that lends it a general sense that this is a city where things happen in books.

For several years, he worked erratically on a personal blog as an outlet for what he described as an "obsession with minor cultural figures on the edge of cultural history." He described those initial forays as something like an impulse. "I think this is partly perverse, something contrary, in my nature." Living in Berlin, James found himself drawn especially to the biographies of local bohemians who were writing during the reign of Kaiser Wilhelm II and whose stories had been eclipsed both by the focus in popular culture on the Nazi era and in the rush to reclaim Weimar-period writing as the locus of pre-Holocaust possibility. It was their very absence, at least from Anglophone cultural memory, and the fact that they were "hidden in plain sight" that attracted him at first. As he read on, he sharpened his "sense for these neglected stories."

> It became more and more apparent to me that it wasn't just one or two writers. It was a matter of following instinct, I think, and that's something that I've developed more as coming to Berlin. It's a place where you can follow your instinct and my instinct told me there's a story here.

The first book he set out to translate was Magnus Hirschfield's *Berlin's Third Sex*, a pioneering account of queer life in turn of the century Berlin, often cited as an important early example of advocacy for queer rights in Europe,[1] among the first books burned by Deutsche Studenschaft and which, to James' surprise, was not available in translation. But unsure where to publish his work, and unconvinced about the appropriateness of the presses he did know, he grew excited at the prospect of setting up his own imprint. Without experience as a professional literary translator – or in publishing for that matter – he reached out to a local publisher he admired, who warned him about the financial hurdles. "I really admired her approach, so I went to see her, and she laid out for me the challenges, the logistics. I probably could have canvassed more people, but I think maybe in the back of my mind, I was worried I was going to be talked out of it." Undeterred, he found an affordable printer in Poland and commissioned a designer friend named Kara to work with him on cover art. She had worked with printed products before and so had a sense for relevant questions: where the copyright information went, how to align chapters headings, how to do colour correction. He knew he wanted to print smaller books that could be carried around, and that they had to have a signature style. The pair landed on a consistent black frame to highlight the period postcards James also collected from antiquarians and fleamarkets, which had been sitting in a box until Rixdorf provided an occasion to use them. By the time we met, Rixdorf had already published eight books and sold its first few thousand copies. Still Rixdorf has absorbed considerable savings, and much of its revenue went back into the business. Without external funding, and without the considerable capital necessary to expense promotional efforts, including travel, James was all too aware he was unlikely to turn a profit or even necessarily recoup his costs. "It is simply a compulsion," he avowed, "I just followed this compulsion, immersed myself within it, trying to orient myself in or through these names and places and works." For James, simply holding a book could create that connection. "I seek out places associated with the authors," he told me another time, "certainly the ones who worked in Berlin."

> A few nights ago, a friend suggested we eat at a Chinese restaurant way across town in Wilmersdorf, an area I very rarely visit, and when I got there I realised it was directly opposite the site where Else Lasker-Schüler had written much of the *Three Prose Works*. My connection is clearly literary, but I think anything, any interest, that can serve as a silent guide through your environment, setting secret guideposts for you along the way.

James is one of thousands of independent publishers and booksellers living and working in the city, drawn in part by its material conditions and in part by its literary reputation. One popular aspect of this story is that Berlin's capacity to attract large numbers of creatives from different parts of the world has been predicated both on a history of subversive and avant-garde cultural production and – perhaps more concretely and more commonly – on the wide availability of cheap housing after the fall of the Berlin Wall and relatively low costs of living, at least initially and especially in the former East. Buildings and state-owned businesses were rapidly converted to new uses, in several cases to house sponsored cultural projects. In turn, much of Berlin's newfound economic productivity has been tied to growth in creative industries reliant on transitory and often young newcomers, both for the labour they provide and discursively as part of Berlin's appeal.[2] At the same time, this liberal expansion has come at the cost of the so-called "transition losers" (wenderverlierer) who did not fare so well in the new political order and have increasingly been pushed to the outer neighbourhoods of the city.[3] And while one can still hear this story repeated in Berlin, rent has more than doubled in a decade. Utility costs, privatized by liberal city governments in the 1990s, have also dramatically increased.

Set against this backdrop, the enduring viability of independent publishing houses despite the enormous condensation of capital in the global industry, as well as the relationship between their success and regimes of movement (human and textual), is a complex phenomenon. The industry has generated nearly ten billion euros in trade annually and two billion in exports, comprising more than 22,000 enterprises (nearly 7,000 separate retailers) and an enormous translation machine (importing almost 12,000 titles annually).[4] In Berlin, as in many cities, increasing diversity of linguistic practices in the last twenty-five years has translated into growth in the number of shops and publishers specializing in languages other than German (though by far the most common is the global hegemon, English), occasionally in the original, but more commonly in translation.[5] In the early days of my work, I tried to chart their various specialties, their relationships, and some of their histories, though this proved daunting, and I eventually settled on a smaller group in which to spend my time. I spoke to customers and owners and took pictures of changing stock on shelves week to week. I wanted to know who came in for what, and why this shop and not one of the countless others. By and large, booksellers specializing in "non-German" literatures outside of the city's central districts were not especially reliant on tourism but drew the bulk of their clientele from locals. As with other commodities, literary markets relied on the portability of labour and its products, though unlike many others, the success of these products, particularly in Berlin depended on the textual labour bearing the sign of having been produced elsewhere.[6] As James explained to me, it was the local material conditions and history that made the Berlin's independent houses and shops possible, but the "oddity of being a publisher of books other than in German is that everything is somewhere else."[7] This means too it can prove difficult to find readers and even stores willing to carry the books, and without the resources to promote their list, small operations typically struggle to break even.

While stories like James's are familiar across national landscape, attention was long focused on Leipzig and Frankfurt, traditional capitals of the industry. But already between the 1880s and 1920s, Berlin emerged as another centre of the industry, until the Nazi propaganda machine dismantled it in the 1930s. The isolation of Berlin during the period of division (and its position, along with the other traditional publishing capital, Leipzig, in the East) simultaneously dislodged it from the activity of major players, while allowing it to grow as a hub for small establishments. The economic downturn of the 1970s and weakening surveillance regimes lead to a youth counter-movement effected through secret meetings and unofficial publications run through small-batch printers, mirroring the rise of anarchistic politics in the West.[8] This reputation made certain neighbourhoods popular early on in Berlin's transformation.

According to state figures, in the years since the fall of the Wall, Berlin rapidly rose again, overtaking all other German cities for the production of new works, accounting for 14 per cent of all first editions by 2006, and housing more than 300 independent publishers, including seven of the top 100 grossing nationally.[9] City officials I met often repeated what was to be found in their official literatures, that the success of the industry in these terms is built on the strong network – "An infrastructure of literary institutions has been developed in Berlin, starting prior to but accelerating since reunification, which is without equal worldwide," the city's *ProjektZukunft* suggests. "Berlin is Germany's capital of authors" one document boasts, 186 of 661 national PEN members live in Berlin, 500 of the 4,000 members of the German authors' association, the *Verband Deutscher Schriftsteller*.[10] "Authors from Berlin," it continues, "do not just have the weight of numbers on their side; they are also influential and the defining factor for the image of contemporary German literature. This is particularly true of the middle-aged and younger generation." Berlin's state government also specifically targeted special subsidies for book production and circulation (up to 35 per cent on investments for both domestic and foreign companies).[11] Payroll and loans could also be subsidized at the state level, and tax rates on books were the lowest of all large German cites – the government additionally provided considerable grants to literary institutions and to authors and translators to encourage new works.

Many pointed to the 100,000 books published annually in Germany (several times greater per capita than similarly sized economies) as one of the benefits of the system. These laws level the field (increasing diversity) by ensuring (comparatively) small profit margins on bestsellers, and leading backlists now to typically account for only very small percentages of total sales (as low as 3 per cent). German economic analyses of the impacts of the current laws have, following official languages, assessed regulations on two axes, "cultural diversity" and price, across six stages of book production: authoring, copyright, wholesale, licensed retail, consumption, and regulatory environment (for the promotion of "cultural diversity").[12] In each case, economists found that the current structure had either negligible or indeterminate effects on price for each category, and positive effects across the board for "cultural diversity." And officially, even an undesirable fluctuation in price or net revenue would be tolerable in the name of variety and circulation. European nations where fixed-pricing agreements have been lifted (as German booksellers also often pointed out) have seen rapid concentration of capital, closure of huge numbers of smaller and independent sellers, and an increase in prices for all books besides bestsellers. Even with these measures in place, Germany's largest wholesaler, Koch, Neff and Volckmar, filed for bankruptcy in 2019. An increasingly small number of publishers account for a larger and larger percentage of sales.[13]

If the movement of books and people through this regime, like any under capital, is affected through various forms of abstraction,[14] among the bookmakers and sellers I knew in Berlin, there was also considerable investment in the idea that there was something particular about literature in this situated particularity that chaffed against abstraction, or at least held out that possibility despite the encroachments, that there was still something about life in Berlin that made literary lives liveable. Literature was regularly described to me as a site of if not resistance to, then at least friction for, global capital, even if in only very small ways (for example, by avoiding large chains and maintaining personal relationships with bookmakers, sellers, and authors or by making publishing decisions that ran self-consciously against perceived economic calculations).[15] This broad view was also inscribed in the language of law that regulates the industry, and describes the book as leading simultaneous though distinct lives as a "cultural good" and as commodity. My aim in this chapter, however, is not to adjudicate their claims or their success in "resisting" capitalist logics. Indeed, all my interlocutors acknowledged that there was no such thing as a "purely local economy."[16] In what follow, I am interested in the grammar of this talk itself.

While the bookmakers I knew wouldn't claim that they lived outside capital, they did feel that their works were productive of social relations that took on a far wider range of textures, and moreover, that these real, material, social lives of the objects they produced were lived simultaneously.[17] Instead of beginning then from the idea of a closed relationship between text and social reality, that words primarily *refer* to the world, or else that a gap exists between regions of social life (say, economic as opposed to aesthetic judgments) through which texts travel, what I found was a sense that words themselves have a life, and that a text, and not just authors, exert agency.[18] Moreover, for many of the people I knew, the motivation for selection involved not just aesthetic judgement or economic rationality but also things like kinship obligations and compulsions.[19] But if bookstores and publishers are more than simply places to buy books, what kinds of textual affiliations do they manifest? What is the texture of the relations that move through them? How do the wider social imaginaries of print capitalism intersect these relations, and in what sense did people think of these forms of circulation as having a different character than alienation or strange sociality?

One way forward is to think of the selection of books as part of a material, textual process. If the ethnographic study of textuality has been well established in the discipline, "texts are also things," as Karin Barber[20] puts it, which is to say they are "social and historical facts" expressed in context-dependent forms whose objectification can (and should) be studied empirically.[21] Anthropological attention to the production and circulation of texts has contributed enormously to thinking about writing and performing, and more occasionally reading, but there has been less work on the material manufacture of texts.[22]

The processes of collecting texts, selecting among them, arranging and editing them, and putting them into various material forms can be as central to their creation as texts as the work usually ascribed solely to authorship, more narrowly and conventionally conceived.[23] As with other things, the book appears as an object of a certain kind through "the relations people have with another,"[24] which are made evident as the sort of things we might know, only through a concerted intellectual effort; in other words, through what Marilyn Strathern describes as a particular act reification.[25] The objectification of relations through which books appear as objects in this way constitutes persons by creating specific relations. The making of the book thus reveals something of how we think of the self and relation to objects in the world.[26]

## Regulation and Autonomy in the Book Trade

Bookmakers and sellers often thanked the specificity of the German regime for their endurance. The livelihood of Berlin's independent bookshops and publishers is possible, when it is possible, in large part because of the special set of regulations enacted by federal and regional laws in Germany. The central institution of the system is the Börsenverein des Deutschen Buchhandels (Association of the German Book Trade), a single-membership body that regulates both wholesale distribution and retail sales across the industry, for nearly seven thousand publishers and booksellers and around one hundred wholesalers. Founded in 1825 (as the Börservein des Deutschen Buchhändler, "book traders") the Börsenverein operates on a three-tiered representative government system: publishing, wholesale, and retail each maintain representation at an annual members' meeting during the summer in Berlin, distributed between regional branches. Among its collective bargaining achievements have been special VAT categorization (approximately half of other commodities) and reduced postal rates for shipments of books.

Two legal regulations are especially relevant, each of which has been subject of considerable collective action. The *Gesetz über Urheberrecht und verwandte Schutzrechte*, federal copyright law, came relatively late compared to the rest of the region when it emerged in 1710 (the law was not enacted until 1837 in Prussia and the end of 1965 in Germany). Since its inception, however, the German variant has been extraordinarily open. Two features are particularly noteworthy. For one, very low thresholds are required for the claim of author's rights over fine art, while applied arts standards are much higher (except, however, for typeface setting and design patterns, which constitute a legal exception).[27] This distinction itself reveals a particular "object-ideology," a "formulation of materiality" that distinguishes "concrete expressions" from the ideational content, in which only the form is subject to ownership as property.[28] Second, the law itself, in contrast to many other European states, emphasizes the inalienable right of the producer, and denies, de jure, the possibility of both corporate copyright of any kind and the transference (except by inheritance) of the right of authorship. The period of time that must elapse before the rights over the artwork enter the public domain has, in the past century, been the longest of any member nation in the European Union. Some aspects of the book were easy to give away, and others weren't, a distinction that tells us a great deal about their relative importance for social identity.[29]

In 1888, the nascent Börsenverein introduced a mandatory fixed-pricing agreement to be enforced for all member groups. Despite opposition, the policy remained in effect and dominant throughout the book industry until the partition of Germany following the Second World War. In 1958, newly established anti-trust legislation included special dispensation for a book-trade fixed pricing scheme, in the form of mutual price maintenance contracts (with the stipulation that all such contracts had to be extensive, including all potential sellers), leading, seven years later, to a novel incarnation of the Börsenverein's initial scheme. In order to streamline implementation, the Börsenverein introduced the Sammelrevers, a special contract form that functioned as an umbrella agreement for all parties of a book's production and circulation, often signed by a joint legal representative of all parties involved. This opt-in fixed pricing scheme remained in place until 2002 (and in any event, already covered the near entirety of the book market, as much as 90 per cent of all titles). Following the formation of the European Union in 1993, trade agreements covering the Deutsche Sprachraum – Germany, Austria, and Switzerland – were signed to prevent the disruption of fixed-prices through international trade and re-entry, but EU law quickly superseded the agreement and declared it invalid. In response, the reunified German government re-nationalized fixed prices for the book trade in 2000 (the other former members of the three-party agreement quickly followed suit).

In 2002, the European Union government reversed its decision on the constitutionality of contractually based fixed-pricing for books, only to see the German parliament enshrine the fixed-pricing scheme as law, eliminating the possibility of opting-out and punishing violations by a fine of several thousand euros. By the standards of contemporary neoliberal governance, fixed-pricing laws are an important aberration. The official rationale (and one repeated by the vast majority of participants in the market whom I knew) was that books have a dual and conflictual character as commodity (Ware) and cultural good or asset (Kulturgut), two lives lived in the same object d'immanence, though not reducible to it or one another.[30] The Börsenverein positions itself, on this basis, as promoting the welfare of the book as an asset to culture, to diversity (Vielfalt) and freedom of expression (Meinungsfreiheit). According to representatives of the institution I spoke with, the Börsenverein operates under the assumption that books are an inalienable feature of the development of culture, and that a network of booksellers and goods with greater variety is essential to the effective distribution of that culture, a reality secured economically by the fixed-pricing structure.

Diversity in the industry was measured in several different ways. At the largest scales, it involved tabulating not only formal aesthetic features or the identities of participants, but also the *volume* of disambiguated participants – for example, the number of booksellers and publishers in the market of a certain size who are not owned by large conglomerates (and not the differences between them), the specializations represented in a particular market area, or the number of titles whose sales contribute most of the revenue. But it could also mean something closer to home, like the growing number of regular patrons whose names or faces a proprietor could recall, or the opportunities proprietors provided to meet new, unfamiliar writers or read unexpected books. In other words, the possibility of generating new kinds of encounters was mediated by the social life of the neighbourhood, by the fact that fact that small, local businesses remained viable despite the crush of global market forces.

Take, for instance, a comment from Carla, a trained ethnologist now working as a volunteer in a book repository, who emphasized an ethical dimension of the continued patronage of local independent shops.

> I only go for my books in my Kiez, I know the owner well, and those online sellers, they run labour camps out there on the other side of Europe where people work in deplorable conditions. I'm not in a hurry, if I need something and they don't have it in stock where I go, he will order it for me; they have their own databases, some kinds of software, he will just have it sent directly to the shop for me.

The system Carla mentioned links local retail shops to wholesalers, who generally fill orders within twenty-four hours. Her objections were both to the impersonal, mechanistic experience of books as mediated through computer screens, as well as the dominance of global capitalism. This was as important as the quality of the books and the selection on offer. Locals arranged the city, or at least the major central zones, into twenty or so Kiez-areas (a north German term for a small community or area within the city). While the word has different connotations throughout Germany, even among relatively nearby major cities and the outskirts of the state of Berlin-Brandenburg, *Kiez* in Berlin is conventional language for an emerging local area without regard for official, administrative boundaries, though the city bureaucracy increasingly takes these designations into account for districting. The idiom of the Kiez was one way Berlin residents expressed the preference for the local, but also registered that the picture of locality sat uncomfortably with the effects of cosmopolitanization. One writer I knew well explained what struck him as a contradiction between, on the one hand, the aspiration to make Berlin what he called a "city of the world" and the pride the youth take in such a designation, and, on the other, the desire to never leave their Kiez.[31]

> There is this thing where you always want to be the big city, the multicultural place, but at the same time you really want to be in the Kiez against the sell-out. You want to sell what you are, and you want to be appreciated ... they are proud of being a desirable place. At the same time there is this, "we really want to stay in our villages," because the Kiez is nothing else than the former village culture, there's the church, there's the market and the houses around it and some things you need, they're all little villages ... and I think that's a big problem if you want to be a city of the world.

Yet at the same time, social life in the city is organized into units that friends sometimes called *villages*, seemingly at odds with the spirit of a modern public. The same culture that Berlin proudly markets itself as fostering, of welcoming people from the world over (and especially artists and other voracious consumers and producers of culture), appears in paradoxical opposition to the need to remain in a close, socially bounded space. The booktrade, I will suggest, is a crucial site of this interchange, in which the Kiezladen, the neighbourhood shop, in particular functions as an important node in the networks that determine value.

Many felt that Berlin had retained some of this quality of a "village in the city" even as other times it appeared to cease, or at least, was under imminent threat.³² Bookshops were important sites for the maintenance and production of social ties in the Kiez that extended beyond the circulation of books themselves. That bookstores should be the scene of such encounters may seem anachronistic against the backdrop of a global industry that finds itself increasingly under attack by other media, mass-consumption mentalities, the dominance of internet sales and growing e-book market. But in Germany, and especially in Berlin, social networks across demographics regularly grounded hyper-local socialities in the physical space of the bookshop (as we saw in chapter two).

Every week since I began my fieldwork I have received a newsletter from several of the local bookshops I frequented during my time in the city. I was able to catalogue several hundred in a small archive during my first two years of research. Their tone was often familiar; they relayed small stories about patrons or authors who had come to visit and were friends of the proprietors, joked about local news, reflected on the state of the world, or advertised upcoming events. "Dearest friends," one from 2015 began,

> We thank you for the many wonderful moments we shared over the past year and look forward to the next. Berlin, Charlottenburg and with them Savignyplatz are changing. Retail spaces are available and hopefully no chain stores are in the starting position. Thank you for believing in "support your local dealer." [This phrase is in English in the original.] We have a good feeling that retailers and innkeepers with unusual ideas will continue to settle on the square in the future. This is all of our neighbourhoods where we want to feel comfortable.³³

Another, this one from 2014, reads,

> We are dedicating June to women who have shown their husbands what is what ... The summer was friendly earlier, the plums juicier, and there was more free parking. But such is not our lament – whoever would agree with that would be missing a lot! Unfortunately, Frau Magnot is ill these days, and cannot visit Berlin to join us [to celebrate a book in her honour]. We wish her a speedy recovery. Your everlasting spirit is an example to us.

Over the course of my time in Berlin, I spent time in a handful of Kiez across the city over the next years, some in the former West, some in the en vogue East. Certain names recurred often in conversations and had storied reputations: younger people told me about *Die Gute Seite, Dorotheenstädtischer, Stadtlichter, Büchertisch* or any of the other small shops in Neuköln and Kreuzberg (occasionally a more self-consciously avantgarde institution in Mitte); older Ossies (East Germans) might recommend *Bei Saavedra*; expats loved *Shakespeare & Sons, St. George's*, and *Another County*. Many in the know talked about *Marga Schoeller Bücherstube*, the story of which was especially deeply engrained in local lore. The daughter of a paper maker who became an apprentice at a publisher in Munich, Marga took over the store on the famous Kurfürstendamm – later known as Buchhandelsmeile, booksellers' mile – in 1929 when it was a branch of what was then a prestigious chain, Buchholz, with seed money from her parents. It quickly became a meeting place for anti-Nazi intelligentsia, in part because she continued to sell, from a hidden cellar, leftist books that were banned or publicly burned and because she refused to sell Nazi publications. After the war, she was the first licensed bookseller in the new Berlin, and the store was almost immediately re-established as the gathering place for left-wing writers.[34] It was also among the first in the city to boast a sizeable English-language catalogue, and this proved a decisive turn. In the ensuing decades, Berlin's sellers, even those not specialized in "foreign" literatures, increasingly have lists that cater to long-standing German interests in English literature (in translation), and target the international community that makes up a greater (and rising) portion of sales.

Along with the nearby Marga Schoeller, I went often to the autorenbuchhandlung before I finally spoke to the proprietor. Neither shop was in the neighbourhood where I lived; I switched three times on the transit system and rode across the city every week just to spend afternoons among their stacks. The autorenbuchhandlung opened every day at ten in the morning except Sundays. One could easily get lost exiting the S-bahn station. Coming from the east where I had been living, if you turned around you would end up behind the square, one block down the road. You would then have to walk out to the main intersection and come around fully through the square and back down the small alley where there were two entrances – one to the café and the other to the store itself. I made this mistake regularly despite having frequented this particular shop since my first week in Berlin. The autorenbuchhandlung was just a few steps from the train stop, past a juice stand on the right and an Italian restaurant on the left. The front door opened up to the cashier and a large, central room with a wide selection of contemporary books laid flat across several square tables and tucked neatly into shelves that covered the walls. Often a poster out front listed which author was coming that week to read from their latest work, and sheets of white paper propped up with plastic displays announced developments of late; lists of finalists for important local, national or even international literary awards; or worthwhile events in Berlin. Two small golden-haired dogs would sneak out from the back room to greet visitors, barely half the height of the tables but never jumping up or disrupting the books.

A small hallway at the back of the room was lined with Reclam books, small yellow reprints of classic texts often sold for a handful of euros. To the left was another slightly smaller room, its back wall boasting important works of the twentieth century, Thomas Mann or Rainer Rilke, and occasionally display editions of Johann Goethe or Friedrich Hölderlin. Opposite this selection stood a wall of English language printings, some original, while others were translations, but many popular books. Back through the main room on the side was the literature café – a plain room with a glass case of cakes and a coffee machine, scattered neat tables for one or two, clean prints on the walls. During the afternoon, one or two people might sit alone, reading and sipping tea – at night, a few times a month, when an author came to read from a new work and spend an evening with patrons, the room was regularly filled to capacity. The other side of the shop was a small café where during the day patrons ate or drank coffee and read their new books, and in the evening, chairs were arranged for readings.

During the day, the manager, Christoph, sat behind a long counter at the front of the main entrance and waited for customers. When I came in from time to time, he would nearly always ask about a friend who had joined me once, a local opera singer with whom he spoke at some length about music books. When he wasn't at the counter, he was in the back checking on the stock. Once a customer had settled into browse, he'd quietly dart over and introduce himself. About half the time, he already knew them and their interests, had something to recommend near the front of the store. Sometimes, an author who was scheduled to speak that evening in the shop would come by earlier and meet some of the regulars, and Christoph would introduce them to customers. Customers would meet and discuss texts with the writers they were reading or learn about new authors from a trusted source. Similarly, the relationship with the authors was enduring; authors were reliant on the bookseller to put them face to face with their public. They valued the bookseller for the intimacy of their relationship with the public, and the patrons, in like fashion, appreciated the aesthetic acumen that proximity to authors brings.

Christoph was part of a group that had taken over from the original owners a few years earlier. "They had noticed a need to bring publishers and authors together ... when we came in 2007, 2008, we bought a share and took over the catalogue, you know some of the original authors were no longer there, some had died, but we started the events, every seven-fourteen days, and brought in 'English books' [he said in English], and books for young people, and we started this – the first customer magazine [Kundemagazine] in Germany, the only one, the only one." The autorenbuchhandlung was founded in the 1970s by group of prominent local writers to "keep alive autonomy of the literature business (Autonomie im Literaturbetrieb wach gehalten werde) by aligning the interests of producers, publishers, sellers, and audience." The job of the bookseller, Christoph explained to me, was essentially to facilitate these relationships not just through sales but in establishing relationships. The intimacy of these relations, he felt, was not solely a market tactic, though it did also function as one. Their transactions led to the establishment of trust in the stewardship of taste. Patrons trusted the proprietor's recommendations (which also relied on a knowledge of their preferences). The shop was very intentional in its desire only to support *worthwhile* texts, to exert a curatorial influence, to protect and strengthen what was "special and essential" [Besonderen und Essentiellen]. In their Kundemagazine, they described this work as the need to be "inquisitive, but also critical, benevolent (wohlwollend), but also judgmental (wertend), literature is a universal host that invites other arts to join in a fruitful exchange … this is our model and it spurs us onward." Such aesthetic determinations matter, in turn, because they come to be enduring features of life in a community, and the cycle continues.

By 2008, many of the founding members had grown too old or passed away, as had many authors who comprised the society through their friendships with early leadership. The political moment had also changed, and new conversations were taking over in Berlin. Joachim Fürst and Marc Iven were identified as suitable successors as leaders of the new group by the bookshop's founders. The new collective took over fully aware, as they said on many occasions, that literature now found itself in competition with a growing number of media, a "short-lived-consumer praxis" (kurzlebiger Konsumentenpraxis) that replaced enduring and personal relationships, and globally booming internet sales. In an anthology put together for the shop's anniversary, titled *Geistesblüten* (spirit blossoms, also the official name of the Kundemagazine), was the statement, "We author-booksellers (autorenbuchhändler) want to face that challenge by including book titles we believe are essential, even decades after they appeared, because they form the topsoil of our culture. Reading is no fad, it is an attitude [toward the world, a posture]." Literature, they felt, invited an exchange of thoughts, much the same as the shop: both are spaces in which intimate interchanges take place. Literature is their "model"; we join others, they say, on "literary expeditions (literarische Entdeckungsreisen, voyages of discovery)." When the shop was founded in 1979,

> the station title of the Berliner U-bahnhof at Friedrichstraße had been stripped. Here there was a pedestrian overpass from the West to the East of the divided city, and at the same time, the only place in West Berlin where one could buy toll-free cigarettes and alcohol ... There on Charlottenburg's Carmerstraße, tens of men and women met, who yet had nothing to do with our childhood lives, but who later would mean the world to us.

The group grew and included several of the most widely influential writers, scholars, editors, and publishers of the period: Heinrich Böll, Uwe Johnson, Marianne Frisch, Allen Ginsberg, Briggitte Kronauer, Wolf Lepenies, Martin Walser, Ernst Jandl, and other giants of German literature. They decided, they wrote, that after seventy years, since the Confederation, it was high time to oppose the trend of large bookstores and batch commodities (Stapelware). The formation of an artist's society (Künstlersozietät) was well underway; their aim was to combat the "*general flattening* of the book trade," and to stand up for the strengthening of the special and the essential, to "give literature as art a protected space, and world literature a new, unconditional home."[35] So these writers founded branches in Munich, Frankfurt, and Berlin. In his opening speech on the "famous, green tile stove," Günther Grass stressed not just literary but mercantile[36] acumen. The text version adds, "The fox knew already then that the hunt begins in the construction and advocated the *City*[37] as a location." In the words of well wishes from two booksellers to the autorenbuchhandlung and their customers, as readers, the shop was to enable "that concentrated pleasure that only literature can provide." Christoph added, "They showed that the literati are real writers of history."

According to *Geistesblüten*, "autonomy in a literary world" allowed the shop to emerge as a site for discussion, not just of literary texts but also political events and daily turmoil, including those facing the surrounding neighbourhood. Portraits were presented of authors, publishers, and critics; nights were a time of literary play. In addition to the list of names, the story of the bookshop thus also appended a list of events, presentations, debates, discussions: Günther Grass *Die Rättin* (1986); Hans Sahl *Das Exil im Exil* (1990); Oskar Pastior *Ingwer und Jedoch* (1985); Susan Sontag *Ich, etc.* (1988). In *Geistesblüten*, the list occupies half a page. In the thirty-five years since its founding, communal participation was a form of care they described as the "lifeblood" (Herzblut) of the autorenbuchhandlung: "care for an engagement with literary understanding of our time." The authors associated with the shop donated their back catalogues and came to speak regularly with patrons. The ending of Günther Grass's contribution from "Transatlantic Elegy" is particularly salient:

> Hear the legend from over yonder
> There was a thousandfold librarian
> Who preserved the literary legacies

The metaphor is clear – the bookstore is a sanctuary for books and for people, to save them both from the pyre, as a famous plaque bears witness in the public square at Bebelplatz in Mitte, where not so long-ago Nazi student groups threw books into the street and burned them, and a few years later did the same with people. The plaques carried an inscription of Heinrich Heine's famous and haunting premonition: *Dort wo man Bücher verbrennt, verbrennt man auch am Ende Menschen* – where people burn books, in the end people also burn. The threat to literature and to life tarry along hand in hand; so must our protection of them. When booksellers talk about freedom of expression and the necessity of culture – cornerstones, as we shall see, of the discourses they produce – they do so in a way that gestures to a recent history of oppression, at the hands of the Gestapo and Stasi, and violence against both words and flesh. The bodies of books and their literary value, the bodies of people and their social value, are not just metaphorically borne together, but substantively – the walls we erect protect the speech carried on our breath that is our life. More than once in recent history the city has moved to hide books and people side by side in hidden corners and crevices, beneath baseboards, or away in attics.

What counted as good literature, I was regularly told, had to cut across, even against, financial interests.[38] As sociologists have long pointed out, performing this independence could be an effective strategy for building symbolic capital, and in turn, driving profits. Through her discussions with publishers, writers, and critics at the Notre Dame Berlin Seminar, Marike Janzen has similarly shown how this sort of claim to autonomy could also be used to garner symbolic capital, and in turn generate profits.[39] One particularly compelling example is the case of Andrea Rötzer, who had been an accountant with the publishers Matthes & Seitz in Munich, who restarted the imprint in Berlin in 1999. Rötzer describes how he was intentional about publishing half their books at a financial loss, which was affordable because of the gain generated by accumulated social prestige. This sort of "Mischkalkulation," or mixed calculation, included judgments about how to offset losses through the sale of more popular titles, often considered of lower literary value. This was possible, Janzen argues, because of a massive national investment in literature, which the state deemed essential to the formation of good, liberal citizens and their cultivation as autonomous agents capable of engaging in the bourgeois public sphere.

The state invests more than one billion euros in subventions to support these calculations – as Janzen notes, a figure fourteen times higher per capita than in the United States. This was in addition to local state support, which in Berlin included low-rate loans and additional funding.[40] Rötzer received considerable funds both in the form of loans, including from the Kreditanstalt für Weideraufbau, which was established to direct Marshall Fund monies to development projects, and Berliner Wirtschaftsförderung, a self-described public-private partnership to support the "be Berlin" marketing campaign for the city. Rötzer was happy to acknowledge that these investments offset costs in order to take on projects that would generate symbolic capital through claims to autonomy, which in turn translated into financial gains. For example, in 2015 the press was able to afford a gamble on a massive 817-page novel by Frank Witzel, *Die Erfindung der Roten Armee Fraktion durch einen manische-depressiven Teenager im Sommer 1969*, brought to them by a friend of Witzel's, and which had, until that point, been turned down by 137 presses. The book ended up winning the Deutscher Buchpreis, and demand quickly exceed the press's printing capacity, a rare though not unprecedented success.

The same conditions that expanded the field could also close doors. And the manoeuvring through the regime was not only motivated by aesthetics, as K.D. Wolff, a well-known publisher and activist explained to me. The former leader of the Sozialistische Deutsche Studentenbund (the Socialist German Student Union), he founded Roter Stern in 1970 (now Stroemfeld Verlag Buchversand) in West Berlin and is perhaps best known in literary communities for a historical-critical edition of the complete work of Hölderlin.

> At first, we put out small booklets, etc., around the political topics that we worked on, that is anti-imperialist struggles (Vietnam, Black Panthers), young workers groups, etc. After 1972 we quit publishing agitational literature, and decided we would only publish books that we ourselves would buy. We met D.E. Sattler who would later be the editor of our Frankfurt Hölderlin-Ausgabe more or less accidentally in 1974, this changed our life, we studied editorial methods etc. during the next 20 years we developed the best editorial classics program in German literature.

Our first booklets were still typeset in lead, the Hölderlin edition was only possible because we could ourselves use an IBM Composer 82 with a very small memory (8000 bytes only, enough for about one page – by now, of course, everyone can typeset with good programs with personal computers). When we started there were hundreds of small leftist bookshops, now altogether perhaps a few hundred sell our books at all, of all the leftist bookshops perhaps a dozen do still exist.

On his sixtieth birthday in 2003, a group of Wolff's colleagues and friends produced a book of messages to Wolff, which they titled *Stardust: Post fur die Werkstatt*, celebrating his contributions to the industry, which he shared with me in 2014. Writing in the collection, Urs Haymoz shares the story of his first meeting with Wolff in 1992, at the invitation of the latter's brother Reinhardt to come and help with some financial matters, in the private library of Klaus Heinrich, a professor in Berlin. The experience in the West was a "total scene-change," Haymoz writes, who until then had only been busy with the "depressing balance sheets" of East German businesses on the brink of collapse, including those already handed over to Treuhandanstalten, organizations established by the Volkskammer in the last year of East Germany to take over and restructure organizations as private companies for the impending reunification. When Haymoz asked Wolff about what difficulties they faced, the latter answered dryly, "We're broke." Haymoz recalls telling Wolff he did not know much about the publishing business. Looking through Roter Stern's financial books, it became clear that without a massive financial investment, they would have to close. While a few titles were turning profits, they did not cover the costs of the majority that did not. They owned a considerable backlist that could be sold off, but not quickly enough to cover their debts. But Wolff was reluctant to change their model other than to try to reduce costs during the project-planning phase and increase efforts focused on direct sales. Even with these changes, Wolff needed a million marks in capital to keep the doors open.

They did however have what Haymoz describes as a series of "assets": their historical editions (which Wolff wouldn't let go without pressing need), and their authors. For political reasons, Wolff had parked his authors' rights in a second publishing house in Switzerland, rendering them inaccessible to even aggressive creditors. And he had a committed team, "the core of house," who would never leave. Haymoz says that assets like social networks don't show up on balance sheets. Bankruptcy was nevertheless inevitable, and the press was reborn through its Basel sibling as Stroemfeld, with the support of a Förderverein, a semi-formal association of backers that opened up access to new funding opportunities. In a "nasty" capitalist environment, Hayoz notes, a small publisher survives publishing high-quality books on a "constant pendulum swing between publishing euphoria and financial collapse," and only with the support of a network; "balance sheets in the cultural sector are obviously to be read according to non-material rules." One scene, he writes, sticks out in particular. The house had been working for many years on securing a contract for one of its renowned historical-critical editions. The editors were saddled with a substantial degree of the financial burden, and the editorial board were eager to familiarize themselves with the financial situation of the press and were understandably concerned about the real possibility of a ruinous outcome. The balance sheets were, in those early days, hardly in order. So the balance was eliminated, "um die zur Auftragsvergabe notwendige, mittlere Lebensdauer des Verlags ordentlich darzutellen." In the midst of crucial talks with the editors, the publisher's balance sheets were written off, and in its stead, the Förderverein provided a list of supporters. Amazingly, the ruse worked, and Stroemfeld won the contract. Wollf and Stroemfeld/Roter Stern, writes Haymoz, "overcame the gravitational force of balance sheets – unspectacularly, without the help of the Börse."

**Collecting Attachments**

Manoeuvring through this regime could likewise take on a rather intimate quality. Transactions in bookstores, like publishing decisions, could be a way of locating oneself in social worlds, whether at large scales like the nation[41] or more humbly within families. It is one way people make sense of their experiences of self and their situation. In his work with members of the Henry Williamson Society, Adam Reed has shown how something like an interest in a minor character, for example, can be an important way in which people confront their place in the world, their feelings of neglect, or their anxiety about imminent death. But unlike a solitary event of reading, reading together – especially rereading – members of the society described to Reed how shared practices made this sort of interest or attention possible, a labour that allowed them both to have new experiences of the text and engendered a zeal for coming together. This "lived engagement with characters in the world"[42] provided insight, moreover, into their (the characters and readers alike) situatedness in a range of temporal regimes, as in the difference between, say, an act of absorbed reading or (more commonly in Reed's case) rereading, readers' research into characters, or the group's regular gatherings.

The material object could play a role quite like a character. For Reed's interlocutors, the fate of physical books was often seen as an index of the wellbeing of their cherished author, who, in turn, stood for an entire ecology of encounter.[43] The value of the book, in other words, rested in its capacity to substitute for the person or persons. The fewer books in circulation, the greater their neglect, the fewer the pathways for readers to chance upon Henry, and by extension, other readers. Members of the society were encouraged to create markets for his books, to persuade local libraries to purchase the complete works, and to maintain their own collections. Even as collectors, however, Reed notes that for Williamson's dedicated readers, the relationship with book-objects was less like property ownership (or an appropriation of an object to a stable self) and more like guardianship for circulation. Many even felt that they themselves belonged in a certain sense to their author and his capacity to organize relations. If the assumption is usually that collectors are after books for their atypicality, their unique story, or their "absolute singularity,"[44] here a book's "biography of transmission" could contribute to the sense that individual copies and their particular form of ownership could "liberate books from their status as text or work and public commodity."[45] Value was thus accrued through the object's location within meaningful arrangements that were subject to unending work, and not, as Benjamin might have it, through a question for original context and with it, authenticity. In the words of one of Reed's interlocutors, a collection abides a "constant cycle of dissolution and reintegration."

Note that for the collector, the book's status as commodity does not line up cleanly with the question of the equivalence of copies, since they all mark a relation to this author and this set of relationships. The distance that (commodity) exchange enforces in our relationship to things (or as Cavell puts it, "mystification in their measurement for exchange")[46] then, is not a given, and again *pace* Benjamin, the denial of equivalence is not the only route to our reacquaintance. Similarly, while we might say that it is "*oneself* that one collects," it ought not be taken for granted that we know what sort of relation to the "world of things" is therein disclosed or that it is only or primarily of one kind.[47] The selection of books could thus "draw out relationships of context" and, by extension, contexts of relationships.[48]

Many of the publishers I knew described a deep connection between how they experienced themselves and the act of collecting. James told me once that "to either collect or produce work within a narrow but tenderly maintained area of interest is to ask yourself – is this something I would like to see in the world, either to discover or to bring about? My hunch is that the smaller the operation, the closer you get to this condition of collecting." For his part, James saw his compulsive attraction to particular figures as activating a "spectral network." When I asked him if he could think of an example, he described the experience of his latest book, which he recently sent me in the mail, along with instructions to read the afterword first. "In the afterword to each of the books I've translated you find names recurring, which was deliberate but also kind of inevitable," he explained. As James first became familiar with Wilhelmine writers whom he dedicated Rixdorf to publishing, he found his mind "pinging with new and exciting input and I couldn't wait to share what I had discovered." With Else Lasker-Schüler and Franziska zu Reventlow, it was the parallels in their lives that caught his initial attention, the similarity in their dispositions and their stories. But things took on new intensity after he visited an exhibition on Reventlow's life in 2011:[49]

> It is only a small exaggeration to say that I started Rixdorf to issue Reventlow's work. It was always a given she would be on the roster, and initially I had settled on a book called *The Money Complex*, which is very much drawn from her life, displaying her deadpan humour and that winning sense of irony. Out of a sense of duty more than anything else, I read *The Guesthouse at the Sign of the Teetering Globe* (1917), a set of short stories which was the last book she issued in her lifetime. The secondary literature is much more reticent about it than the prior four books, and I was effectively reading it so I could discount it from selection. But almost as soon as I started, I realised it was something very special and I knew I had to translate it.
> 
> I was reading it on the bus to Tegel Airport to pick up a friend at the airport; she had lost her luggage and I had just been reading one of the uncanny stories in the book in which a set of luggage basically develops a personality of its own and rebels. But there was more; the title story mentions a "correspondence association" which puts people together based on their interests rather than location or profession or other traditional categories. She's basically describing social media, but a century ago. And the guesthouse itself is – I believe – a metaphor for the old European order. It is slowly sinking into the ground taking its querulous inhabitants with it. This was at the height of World War One; Reventlow actually died in the last summer of hostilities, so she was describing an outcome of history she wouldn't actually live to see.
> 
> I really went deep with Reventlow – buying first editions, reading her diaries, her letters, biographies, visiting the little mountain village on the island of Corfu where she lived for a time. She became very close to me;

as I engaged with her life I felt like I was living through every high and the more frequent lows. I was determined to do what I could to make her better known, or even known, in the English-speaking world. My failure to do so to any appreciable extent is one of the great disappointments of this whole venture. Strategically it was perhaps not the best choice to issue short stories, which are harder to reach people with than novels, but once the idea of translating *The Guesthouse at the Sign of the Teetering Globe* had taken hold, *not* issuing it was simply no longer an option. That's the nature of compulsion, I guess.

Persons arise in James's account and exert pressure through their relations, with him, with one another, with other people and things in the world, his and theirs. What he calls his compulsion might be described as a process of collecting relations, one where each connection also potentially reconfigures other sets of relations. Collections don't remove an item from circulation. Instead, adding someone or something to the collection compels the production of new relations. Not a list of objects only for acquisition, but which allows for "intersecting circles of circulation."[50] To feel compelled by a book, or an author, or a story, for James, is a desire to "see it in the world." In this way, the recurrence of idioms of kinship, that is, of "relations of relation to one another,"[51] here and throughout this book, is wholly unsurprising. And yet, as Strathern reminds us, relations can also obscure relations. Sometimes we have to let them go, and sometimes we endure them. They can disappoint, unravel, express conflict or rivalry, and worry.[52] In the time I have known James, he has been coming ever closer to a crossroads with Rixdorf. It has become increasingly difficult for him to see a way forward. Not because it is too time-consuming or because of the financial situation (a real but not definitive pressure). It is the disappointment he feels at having not made for Reventlow or Lasker-Schüler more connections, his concern that he had let them down. A decision will have to be taken whether to continue pressing on.

Compare James's story with the one I heard from Mary who, along with her son Matthias, had been struggling to maintain a publishing imprint dedicated to translating books from and about India – her deceased husband's great passion, but which neither Mary nor Matthias shared. We met through a mutual friend and bonded over a love for similar books, but when she learned about my interest in German Indology, she was eager to tell me about her husband, though it often pained her. Roland's love of India was very deep, she said, "he loved books already as a young child, but at his father's behest initially studied physics." During his studies, he became friendly with a visiting student from India and who inspired a nascent interest in philosophy. Roland soon discovered he had little passion for physics and he took a break from school to work a series of short-term jobs, including as a tram driver, before returning to initially to study Germanistik. By chance, there was a teacher at the university offering a course in Sanskrit, and he quickly signed up. After school, Roland started working for a small publisher that had once been quite well-known and which now existed as a private imprint. There he began editing books and translating, first from Russian and eventually from Sanskrit, on topics ranging from architecture to theatre. But he wanted to be able to decide for himself which projects to take and not; "he always wanted to have more influence, and the opportunity came during the Wende, and he founded his own publishing house shortly thereafter."

He began with collections of short stories, since novels were hard to come by. In the East German regime, he was able to spend time travelling through India, first in 1979. As he travelled through Rajasthan taking photographs for a book he envisioned publishing, Mary explained, he came to know many authors throughout the country. Some, like Nirmal Verma, he met at literary events in Germany. Mary herself was never in India. "I had my job, and two children, and Roland had more time for his things." "The Verlag never really had much money," Matthias chimed in. "Exactly," Mary answered him:

> It was papa's passion also during the DDR time, Indian literature. He didn't add much to the family budget, but I approved, I said "We're getting by on my salary and he's doing something good." That state should actually finance that, because it is something very important, because he wanted arrogant Europeans to find out about cultural achievements from other parts of the world.[53]

At that time, Mary explains, "literature was the window to the world when people couldn't get out," and so he found a small group of interested friends to help move books in Germany. Books that had "anything to do with the world were bought and read immediately. It was of course a bit disappointing after reunification that there was simply such an oversupply of literature and that he was no longer able to play that role." The opening up of the former East to Western markets ultimately curtailed business, in part by weakening the position of the curator of texts. "Before the Wall," Matthias added, "it was rather difficult to convince publishers to pick up projects, but when it was done, it pretty easily found an audience, since the publishers had a certain standing and people were curious and were confident that what was on offer was of quality. After the fall of the Berlin Wall, readers had more freedom to decide for themselves what to do and which authors to publish, but it was difficult to get into the market. It's even more difficult to find an audience." For Matthias, quality in diversity was restricted by the opening of the trade to market forces, even as (or because) it democratized access to publishing that flooded the field of reception. But in their case, these difficulties were also compounded by illness. Roland had an accident that led doctors to uncover underlying Parkinson's disease:

> He was able to work fully until 1999 and then he had an accident – that actually accelerated it, you could say. I suspect that it made Parkinson's much more severe, progress faster. Three years after the diagnosis, he could no longer walk, he was in a wheelchair. It is usually 15 years after diagnosis. It is said that way. He did not want to admit he had the disease and was still doing projects, and in 2006 there was another book fair where India was the guest country, and there he did eight book projects that he could not actually realize himself. The whole family worked there to somehow get it done at the last moment. He couldn't even go to the book fair anymore. My daughter and I, we went to Frankfurt together and then met a few authors there.

Roland and Mary's daughter Susi, a graphic designer by trade, offered to help at that time. But Roland was what Mary calls an "extreme solo-fighter, a go-it-aloner" [Einzelkämpfer, Einzelgänge]. "He was not able to initiate people [into the work], in a way that they could work with him on a project on equal footing. I think he had more information about his condition he kept to himself, so others wouldn't know exactly what was going on. For example, it was so bad too, he really wanted to do the whole layout himself for one book." Roland's motor skills and vision quickly deteriorated. "He would stand in front of the computer all night, not sitting, leaning forward, somehow trying to use the mouse to position things for the layout." Susi offered help again and again, but he continued to refuse. He wanted to do it himself, and so found himself constantly up against deadlines, under increased pressure. She had made up her mind to join the business, if he would let her. "She is very pragmatic, and at some point, she realized it doesn't work," Mary told me. "After reunification, I was unemployed, I had some time. I also went to the Institute for a while and worked as a volunteer [she had been a physicist in East Germany], but I could just as easily have done something for the publishing house with him. I would have loved to do it. But it didn't work either."

When Roland died, things became complicated in other ways. Susi and Matthias agreed that it would be a shame for all their father's relationships with authors and his ideas to fall away. There was still much to be done, and all that he'd accomplished, they felt, would be lost little by little. Matthias finished a doctorate in theoretical chemistry and returned to Berlin. The siblings at first decided to work together to keep the house open. They travelled to India to meet authors. Susi brought in two friends – one who had a background in publishing and another in social science. They played with the idea of forming a publishing collective, each responsible for their own projects, but Matthias was the one who took it on full time while others continued to work other jobs. "Soon, we found we were in each other's hair, because we had different ideas about where to go, and we were all very emotionally attached to it, but at the same time, our ideas were increasingly difficult to reconcile. It was very personal, but there were also political ideas at stake, then suddenly we were colliding quite a bit. And then it became a crisis, and then an argument, and I ended up doing it on my own." Since the press continued to earn very little, he worked part-time as a coder and moved back into his mother's house. A decision would have to be made soon. This was as far as the conversation could go that day – he couldn't bear to talk about it anymore.

∽

The philosopher Sandra Laugier has argued that as works of popular culture accompany us, often over many years, integrating into our everyday lives, they are also become a source of moral education. Through our attachment to and care for characters who live in public view, whom we share with others, discuss, love, hate, and worry about, "this intertwining of the private and of modes of constituting a public translates into new modes of subjectivation by the public."[54] In a closely related essay, Cavell describes the mind as a kind of theatre where we witness characters acting in scenes, expressing human emotions, sometimes appearing in the light, sometimes the dark, sometimes expressing joy, sometimes pain, and that these "provide precisely impressions or perceptions of myself, revelations of myself, of what I live and die for, wherein I catch myself."[55] Such impressions are not of "simple, stable things," but possibilities, even opportunities, for self-discernment, in that they occasion my discovery of the story unfolding in the scene or the identity of the characters, and with them, my own role in the plot.[56] If the self has often been described in philosophy as a collection of things, it is, for Cavell, the narration of these scenes that holds the collection together.

The characters in stories I heard from Mary and from James included not just those contained in the pages of the books they have read or published but also the authors of those books, other publishers, neighbours, and kin. I noted earlier that this was the register in which I understood James's suggestion that bookmaking was an act of collecting. The boundaries of the collection didn't stop at the backlist. It was the force of juxtaposition, of new connections and reconfigurations, that gave it life. Cavell suggests that collecting is a form of human life; our relationship to which proposes something about our relationship to the world of things. It is usually supposed this means the aspiration to completeness, to finishing the series, to the total library, or conversely, as signalling the impossibility of completeness, the never-ending work of collecting. James's and Mary's lives in bookmaking were shadowed by a concern with how the collection would come to an end. But might this have something to say about coming to an end itself? Collections, writes Cavell "may not exempt themselves from the knowledge they impart, that they are to be left." Our words, our books, our passions are to be abandoned to the care of others. Philosophers have sometimes worried that collections have nothing to offer but a desire for conformity and equivalence, hence commodification, that they have nothing to teach us about resisting the weight of conformity. But if anything, these stories show that in selecting books, in making them and sharing them, in exchanging words, we decry the fantasy of fixing objects in the world. Books tell us something important about importance, about what we have allowed to matter to us. And in this sense, the process is instructive:

> Don't take it as a matter of course, but as a remarkable fact, that pictures and fictitious narratives give us pleasure, occupy our minds. I know of no better initial tip in matters of aesthetics. You are advised to consult yourself as to whether a thing you have taken into your mind, have consented for that time to bear upon your life, gives you pleasure, or perhaps otherwise disturbs you, and if not, to demand of yourself the cause, whether the thing that solicits you is not remarkable or whether you are coarsened in what you can remark, allow to matter to you. Why do we put things together as we do? Why do we put ourselves together with just these things to make a world? What choices have we said farewell to? To put things together differently, so that they quicken the heart, would demand their recollecting.[57]

This is perhaps not where one expects to end up. In trying to account for the value or passion of bookmaking, I have focused on the concrete relations established between people living together, rather than starting from very large, classical questions about the relationship between value and values, or art and commodity under capital in a modern city. And yet the former show themselves to be "like shadows"[58] of latter. Learning to live with books and their characters, selecting and collecting them, involves learning a whole world in which they are commodities and gifts, friends and enemies. This means too learning how I am implicated in this world, discovering what matters for me in putting things together – and eventually in letting it be.

## Chapter Six

# Life in a Net of Language: Literature, Translation, and the Feel of Words

To speak a language is to take on a world.

– Frantz Fanon

In the preceding chapters, I described examples from a network of uses of the concept of literature I found in Berlin. In each case, this has involved describing how words moved; how they passed one another, cut, skipped, shook, and vibrated, in time (as in the palpable presence of multiple pasts) and in space (for instance, in their assignment to geographical locations by discursive regimes). This has also entailed, perhaps too subtly, a variety of ways of picturing movement in or among language(s) and social location(s), as well as the relationship between the two. What I hope to have shown through these descriptions is that in everyday life, and in contrast to a prevailing linguistic ideology, such movements do not proceed from a certain prior fixity.[1] Locations in social worlds and in language are, in Nancy Munn's words, "meaningful forms in process rather than ... static givens, since their existence is ongoingly subject to the varied ways they enter into human practices – into people's actions, expectations, pasts, and sense of their pasts."[2] Movement is not necessarily an aberration from a usual stillness but can itself be another normal condition of life in language.

The most conventional way movement is expressed in European linguistic ideologies is through its assimilation to translation, understood through the idea of a trajectory between languages: an origin and a target.[3] This book has argued that this manner of picturing movement is intertwined with the way people describe the trajectories migrants are said to follow, as well as the sense that history always marches in one direction. Translation (and mistranslation) across time and space takes on a particular valence in these contexts, moreover, because of a pervasive assumption: that, usually, life in language is constituted by life in *a* language, at least until we encounter others with their own languages in our daily lives or in literature. The same power-laden apparatus similarly distinguishes which languages counted as foreign languages and which were said to belong within the same family. But if multilingualism is a "new public idea" in the West,[4] this sense of newness is itself the result of long-standing supposition in Europe of normative monolingualism. In this chapter, I offer some reflections on the implications of these different ways of picturing movement in language, taking my cue from literary sources and their reception which I think provide important lessons for current debates in anthropology. I am led through these experiences to ask how one might challenge the assumption behind particular ideas of what language at bottom is and, by extension, what literature is – its anxieties over where one language stops and another begins – and in so questioning, open up new ways of thinking about human movement more broadly.

Berlin has historically played an outsized role in the invention and promotion of dominant theories of translation. But how – and when – we tell origins stories is symptomatic of present commitments and can at times end up reproducing their vocabulary, or even naturalizing the assumptions it means to undo.[5] The story in this case is often tracked to a moment of renewed nationalist sentiment: debates about what Germany is or ought to be and which are often resolved into different practices of reading other parts of the world.

In the first quarter of the nineteenth century, Berlin found itself at the centre of an explosion in Orientalist scholarship and art focused on India, Persia, and the Near East, that, at least in the case of Indological projects, far outpaced the rest of Europe by the end of the century. As Saverio Marchignoli writes, while the "phenomenon of migration of texts is undoubtedly very ancient ... the German culture of the late eighteenth and early nineteenth centuries constituted an absolutely unprecedented context for textual assimilation since, in order to solve a self-conscious crisis, it considered its own essential task as being that of reshaping itself through the integration of 'foreign' texts." By the end of the century, there were more Indologists working in Germany than in the rest of Europe and America combined,[6] and though this did not necessarily translate into institutional cultures like durable course enrolments, scholarship on Sanskrit had a central role in the emerging "cultural politics of the state."[7]

While rival textual traditions emerged elsewhere in Germany, notably in Bonn and in Leipzig, the long shadow of the Humboldt reforms to the education system – which included the promotion of Weltbürgertum (world citizenship) as the ideal of self-cultivation[8] – gave the city's

# Life in a Net of Language: Literature, Translation, and the Feel of Words    151

Orientalist projects a unique character. Franz Bopp was appointed to a chair in Sanskrit in Berlin in 1821 at Alexander Humboldt's recommendation, and Bopp's own emphasis was on the possibility of comparison and not, as philologists had earlier advocated, on isolated languages and literatures. His hope was to establish a procedure for using texts to guide scientific inquiry into elemental parallels across linguistic systems, rather than to offer a manner of interpreting texts. As with Georg Friedrich Creuzer's comparative mythology before him, the enterprise threatened to supplant a philhellenic account of human origins.[9] Berlin came to be associated thereby with the study of the language of texts because of the promise they held for establishing linguistic and cultural equivalences, giving birth to what some scholars have described as "a version of historical and cultural relativism as well as a universality framework for cross-cultural comparisons."[10]

It was also in Berlin, in 1825 and 1826, where Wilhelm von Humboldt gave a series of influential lectures at the Königlich-Preußische Akademie der Wissenschaften on the poetic and philosophic achievements of the *Bhagavadgita*. The lectures spurred a contemptuous and now famous response from G.W.F. Hegel, who, at the time, was the ascendent doyen of philosophy in the city. Humboldt's comments were guided by his reading of August Schlegel's recent translation of the Gita into Latin (published in 1823).[11] By translating the text into Latin in a critical edition, Schlegel was attempting to treat the Gita "in the same way texts from Greek antiquity were treated."[12] Schlegel chose this particular episode of the *Mahabharata*, he explains in the preface to the translation, because of its philosophical content, especially for those interested in the history of ancient thought outside Greece. Schlegel conceived of translation as a "creative aesthetic act" that manifested fidelity to the original text through its capacity to transform, add, and rearrange – not despite it. Translation for Schlegel required anticipating "a measure of embellishment and amelioration, but the rendering might also display the sheer impact of trying to transpose one language into another: the target language will sometimes be strange, reflecting the foreignness of the original language being conveyed."[13] Linguistic grammar could be recruited in service of smoothing the process – Latin, Schlegel felt, was better suited to bringing Sanskrit texts to Europe than, say, German, because unlike agglutinative languages, it shared in some of the inflectional flexibility and complexity of the "original."

It was the implication of these claims, both about the merits of the Gita and the nature of language, that Hegel's 1827 review of Humboldt's published lectures sought to undermine.[14] Marchignoli argues that Hegel, who had no knowledge of Sanskrit himself, rejected the very possibility of appropriation (Aneignung) by means of translation as a (involuntary) mystifying misinterpretation. Translations of the Gita had "*deceived* Europeans as to the contents of the poem in that they had surreptitiously rendered them familiar to European minds by 'Europeanizing' them." For Hegel,

> It is certainly contrary to the nature of things to expect that an expression in the language of a people, who have a particular sensitivity and a culture opposed to our own – if such an expression does not concern the objects of the senses ... be rendered with an expression in our language that fully corresponds to it in its determinateness. A word of our language gives us a determinate representation of such a thing *which is particular to us*, and hence not particular to the other people, who not only have a different language, but also different representations.

Because Hegel believed the content of understanding (the determination of species-class relations) was given in Geist, in common to humanity, it lay "beyond the sphere of the confrontation of languages,"[15] and the differences that arise therefrom "can only be a relation of a content to its genus ... what we find in dictionaries as different[16] meanings of a word are mostly different determinations of the same basic element." Hegel's racist rejection of Indian thought as "mere" religion[17] is enabled by a critique of Schlegel and Humboldt's translation practices and predicated on a philosophical anthropology that takes the human itself as a given, providing him access to the truth of the Gita without access to its language. In this way, "one the one hand, Hegel preserved 'the other' in its difference and individuality, against its assimilation or domestication; but on the other hand, he denounced Humboldt's idea of a possible endless approximation (unendliche Annäherung) to it, as inconsistence." The process essentializes and substantivizes differences, while rejecting the idea that the others it produced and racialized could carry any knowledge alien to Europe because of its proximity to universal reason expressed in "World History." As Ranajit Guha puts it, this allowed "concreteness to be drained out of the phenomena which constitute the world and its historicity." By abstracting into the domain of universal concepts, the "concreteness of the human past" is "converted by an act of superseding into philosophy." Guha writes, "What is presented there as the subject of World-history turns out, on closer look, to be no more than a region claiming to speak for the world as a whole."

The conflict between Humboldt and Hegel is emblematic of a broader difficulty that stems from the fact that despite their differences, these alternatives share common criteria for what can be said or asked of language. These questions continued to resound in the Berlin in which I lived in the ways people spoke about the movements of people and texts. Often, this history was claimed directly in public discourse, and in explicitly cosmopolitan nation-building projects (which regularly championed the return of a Humboldtian worldview) or, more subtly, in the paternalism of human-rights talk.[18] But scholarly literature too often remains in the grip of a Western ontology of language, as does much writing about the current discourse, whether on migration or historical memory, that grows from it. This is clearest in the ways it furnishes the categories through which we think about what constitutes a basic question, and in many cases still proceeds according to paradigmatic oppositions that assume the boundaries of social words are given; that some regions of language hew closer to the world than others (as in conventional semiotics); or that translation is an activity primarily of experts rather than a normal feature of what it is to live in language. Some "precipitation of cultural authenticity"[19] seems to linger behind the need to ask, for example, whether Hegel's or Humboldt's interpretations really captured the hidden meaning of the text, or whether readers who do not consult "regional" sources can be *genuinely* influenced, or even moved, by the texts they read – as if the status of literary works in the places they "originate" were not already power-laden, as if they emerged somehow from unitary and well-bounded linguistic systems, or as if translations or, for that matter, other movements in language only began when texts reached the shores of Europe or when Europe came to them. Or that texts *belonged* necessarily elsewhere and that elsewhere was "outside" the world in which "we" live. Are there always originals? Did reading in the metropole simply license a free play of imagination, such that another text might have done just as well? If the discourse produces its object without regard for reality on the ground, is there anything left to be said about the force of the text itself? Must our capacity to provincialize European really be limited to the finding of equivalences or local examples? Or might language itself really be experienced differently?[20]

There are other ways of picturing movements in language and the sense of strangeness that arises while trying to make myself intelligible to others and to myself, and them to me.[21] One way forward might be to ask a related question that has reappeared in different ways at various points throughout this book: How do we come to know a writer in their words? Why do we say we can read others, for instance, like an open book?[22] How is it that I come to think of this voice as a familiar one? What happens when I read a sentence on the page, and then again in another language? Or hear it on the radio? Is the "look of a word …

familiar to us in the same kind of way as its sound?" Is it something like the way we learn to read letters on a page, feeling an almost causal connection between the shapes of the words and what we utter out loud or in our heads?

To venture some initial steps along these lines, I describe something of my experience of becoming familiar with the work of one Berlin-based writer, critic, and translator, whose words continue to inspire and challenge my thinking about how we live in language. At the end of a research stay in the city, I was discussing books with a friend in a park near my apartment. She told me that she had been reading Yoko Tawada, and that she was writing in ways that "loosened the hold of all the usual manners," not through very grand gestures of formal repudiation but through a subtle style of verbal play. I learned that Tawada's texts took a range of prose and verse forms, but that each experimented with how to describe the feel of words in normally multilingual contexts. Tawada, I read in local news articles, was born and educated in Japan, studied Russian literature, and came to Germany for a writer's residency in 1982 after a ride on the Trans-Siberian railroad, ultimately submitting a dissertation in Germanistik to the University of Zurich. She had been living in Berlin for many years, but I had never had the chance to hear her read or talk with her about her work in person before then. I did however find several recent interviews in print where she described new methods she'd been developing – for example, one called "continuous translation," which involves writing a manuscript simultaneously in two languages. "People sometimes ask me where I really live because I travel so much," she told Bettina Brandt in an interview from 2008. "I think I live in the languages. Or maybe I should just say that one small, simple word sometimes can be enough of a place to reside in ... to me, a word might be a place where different thoughts and people meet each other."

Unlike many of the authors I have discussed in this book, I came to know Tawada primarily through her public presence, her publications, panel appearances, and interviews. I take this too however to constitute an ethnographic approach to the voices in books, or on a screen, or over a sound system, where in this context at least, very intimate sorts of exchanges regularly take place in full public view. After all, to read a novel, or a memoir, or to listen to poetry, is to engage in a social practice; it is among other things a way people come to know one another, neither higher nor lower than any other ordinary use of language. Reading (with) Tawada became an education in reading Berlin and its neighbourhoods of language.

# Life in a Net of Language: Literature, Translation, and the Feel of Words    155

It wasn't until a year after I first encountered her on the page that I heard Tawada's voice in an interview with a local cultural organization. I anticipated her wordplay – both since my friend had alerted me to it and because by then I had begun to read her writing. But hearing her in that moment, what struck me most was the intimacy with which she described her experiences with the strangeness of language, especially the fears, hopes, joy, and disappointment that could arise in such moments. In that first interview, I heard an unnamed, offscreen interviewer asks Tawada whether there were things that her work with language had revealed to her. Tawada paused for a moment and looked up before replying that, particularly in German, she had discovered many things. "For example, in the Japanese language, there are many words for 'I,' depending on whether one is man or a woman, or which situation, official or private, or how one talks, there are many words, and what that means – I never thought about that in Japan but that means that this 'I' – the Japanese sign for 'I' – is some kind of a description, as a third person … the definition of 'I' is always determined in a public way … encounters with language bring up a lot of new questions like that." Here was a picture of language not as a curtain thrown over an inner world of private experience, not a discovery of something hidden, but where even the capacity to say who I am depends on shared language. And there was, even in just these few lines, also a sense of what sort of potentialities reside in languages that are activated by their proximity to other languages as we move through the world.

As I became more familiar with her work, reading and listening to Tawada helped unfurl a series of thoughts about what it means to live with literature and in language. Within so much talk about translation lies the idea that language is primarily about the meaning behind our words, a world into which our languages may be hooked inadequately. Because languages pick out different objects in different ways, situations in which we are speaking multiple languages are assumed to imply questions about how we know the objects others, especially those speaking other languages, intend. The paradigmatic case is the usual colonial anthropological scene of arriving on the shores of a place where one does not yet speak the language, seeing someone ostensibly point to an object and utter an expression, and then trying to parse out which object or quality or action is being pointed out, as in W.V. Quine's standard example of a rabbit entering into view and hearing someone say "gavagai." In such a situation, the reference of the utterance is inscrutable since it depends on the background ontological commitments of the speaker. Does the utterance pick out the colour? Or the action? The whole of the animal or just a part? It is sometimes assumed that this implies there are objects of thought indicated by the expression that I do not know or to which I do not have access?[23] For Quine, this could also be said of conversation among "closely related" languages or even intralingually. "Radical translation," he writes, "begins at home." The philosophical trick of course is to disallow context, to remove gesture and the next steps in a conversation.[24] The picture begins to look quite different when we begin from other coordinates. "I imagine a radical translation," Tawada wrote in 2015, as itself a crossing over into poetry: "There, you don't have to compromise to find an answer, but can leave all open questions open … proximity is sometimes more difficult than distance." Describing a movement in language as an act of translation is a complex affair. But at a minimum, I came to find that what is conventionally understood as translation cannot be an activity that relies on an entirely separate set of procedures and operations.

If being at home is usually taken to imply a singular mother tongue, Tawada's writing is filled with scenes where being at home in language takes ongoing work in multiple languages. Her descriptions make clear that the question cannot be about the existence or inexistence of objects hidden by our words; translation and mistranslation appear as normal activities always already underway, and indeterminacy as something we learn to accept we live with. The movements often described as translation are no longer figured as external pressures but instead figure as something where a potential already within the grammar springs to life. This meant too that coming into language is not only a process of learning to name objects in the world, asking for and providing ostensive definitions, and communicating about them: it is a training in how it is we live with our words and objects. Rather than fixing the referent, when we learn to use words, we learn at the same time a whole set of practices that go along with them and which allow us to use the same word in contexts beyond the one in which we first hear or see it. This means learning not only that there are rabbits in the world and that we have a name for them but also that some people hunt and eat them, that they bring eggs to children once a year, they accompany the goddess of the moon, or that one wears a blue jacket with brass buttons. Learning a language entails entering into a whole form of life, and this is a lifetime's work. It means taking risks and making leaps, trying and failing, and having elders rebuke and encourage our attempts, and through this process discovering how far our words can go.[25]

This first step implies the next several. Language is sometimes thought to be usable (meaningful?) primarily by means of the definitions of words and rules for combining them into sentences we use to represent experiences. But for Tawada, words are not, to borrow a phrase from Wittgenstein, "mere threadbare representations of the *real* experiences." They are themselves an experience.[26] They have a physiognomy, a texture, smell and taste, in addition to a look and a sound. Her books are filled with small moments where a character doesn't quite know the definition of the word or know how it is being used in a particular expression, and yet it has sense, it takes hold, it moves, it vibrates, it means something for them. So while learning another language is sometimes said to be like entering a form of life the way a child does, this cannot be the case in every respect, since one already has language (if not this one) and so makes use of bits of language by testing their similarities and differences, by exploring the ways they encounter one another; though, at some stage, this is what children do too. Where these movements come to be at odds in turn tells us something about the extensibility of our own ontological commitments.

**Stolen Words**

The first book of Tawada's I was able to find in my local bookshop was an English translation of *Kentoshi* (献灯使) as *The Emissary*, which was published first in Japanese in 2014. The novel is set in the aftermath of global catastrophe that remakes human bodies so that the very old have strong bodies and the young are so fragile as to border on death. Because everything seems a potential threat, a strict isolationism comes to govern the Earth, disrupting trade, including in language. After national borders are tightly sealed, "foreign words fall into disuse," and new words are created. Singing songs in a foreign language in public was prohibited, as was the translation of novels. The plot centres on Yoshiro, a writer who is now quite old and a member of an underground association that smuggles children out of the country to participate in an international research project into Japanese children's health. Yoshiro also cares for his great-grandson Mumei, a frail and inquisitive child.

Several short scenes in the novel describe how different characters experienced words against this background. One consequence of the catastrophe was that "foreign" words that fell out of use often meant objects disappearing between generations. Dry cleaners nearly go extinct, for instance, "until someone got the idea of writing it in Chinese characters meaning 'chestnut-person-tool.'" One morning, we find Mumei wrestling with his clothes. "Though cloth was not necessarily ill-tempered, it didn't bend easily to his will, and as he tried rubbing it, smoothing it over, folding it, but generally having a hard time, bits of brightly colored paper – orange, blue, and silver – began to sparkle in the grey matter of his brain." He wonders whether despite the appearance of two legs, perhaps an octopus lives inside him. Pulling off a pant leg, he worries momentarily that he's pulled one of his legs off with them. When he hears his great-grandfather's voice call – "Are you dressed yet?" – the octopus disappears. Mumei says to Yoshiro that he wishes he had some work clothes. "Work clothes? Oh, you mean *tsunagi*. People used to call tsunagi overalls ... but *overalls* is a foreign word, so you'd better not use it." The phrase "better not use it ... never sounded right" to Mumei's ears. While his great-grandfather knew many words "he never uses lots of the words he knows; he teaches me words he never uses; then he tells me never to use certain words he tells me about ... Could clothes still be there, just as they were, even after the words for them had disappeared? Or did they change, or disappear, along with their names?" Mumei wonders.

In another scene, we learn that what used to be called German bread became Sanuki bread even though "people don't seem to remember that *bread* is a foreign word," as a local baker explains to Yoshiro. "Bread reminds you of faraway lands," he replies, "that they exist, I mean – that's what I like about it. I'd rather eat rice, but bread sets you dreaming." The baker then replies that baking bread is hard work and his muscles and tendons hurt. Yoshiro answers that there's a class on loosening up at the aquarium, "you reminded me of it when you mentioned *tendons* just now, because the Chinese character for *octopus* looks so much like it." Yoshiro replies that perhaps humans were evolving to be more limber, to which the Baker wonders, "so in anther hundred thousand years we'll all be octopi?" – "In high school I used to envy people with bodies like Greek statues. I was trying to get into art school, you see. Don't know when I developed a liking for entirely different bodies – birds, say, or octopi. I'd like to see everything from an optical point of view." – "Optical?" – "No, I meant octopi. I want to see through the eyes of an octopus."

> Long ago, this sort of purposeless running had been referred to as *jogging*, but with foreign words falling out of use, it was now called *loping down*, an expression that had started out as a joke meaning "if you lope your blood pressure goes down," but everybody called it that these days. And kids Mumei's age would never have dreamt that adding just an *e* in front of it the word *lope* could conjure visions of a young woman climbing down a ladder in the middle of the night to run away with her lover.

In each of these examples, we find moments of play with words, where some potential is actualized – perhaps animals do not live in the wild, but they exist in my limbs. Others at times respond by offering a small correction, whether or how to use a word, or about which word is meant.

As Mumei learns to use a word, he also learns also what one does with it. Learning language is anything but a linear process, a passage from not knowing to knowing for sure, or even one process in particular.[27] He learns a word in one context but finds he can project it into new ones, not because the same context reappears, but rather through his play, he tests it out in different situations. As Josephine Stebler has argued, learning language doesn't just happen when the child sits down to read or is shown a word and given a definition (this is but one possible relevant language-game). They might experience something like the character or a figure – say, in Mumei's case, "octopus" – by playing a role or in a script or as sound. It can show up in many different parts of life.[28]

Animal names are a recurrent theme for Mumei, since in the world he inhabits there are very few wild animals to be seen, if any at all, and so each name occasions a flight of imagination, until he learns a bit more – that is, if the opportunity arises. In an early scene, a dentist remarks that there have been debates about how best to get the necessary calcium for children's teeth to grow properly, and there are now shops selling ground Naumann Mammoth bones for that purpose. By chance the next day Yoshiro and Mumei see a poster announcing a lecture by a university professor about the mammoth. The words "cast a spell" on Mumei. For him "the words themselves were an animal that would start moving if only he stared at it long enough." He even jumps with excitement despite his weakness. The incident reminds Yoshiro of a German girl he met while travelling as a young student, who told him "the only wild animals in Japan are spiders and crows," a statement that woke him with a jab and which, now that the country was closed, one could not hear. The contrast highlights the degree to which the actualization of possibilities in language is tied to context. In the scene where Mumei is getting dressed in the morning and wrestling with the pants of his clothes (a function also of his weakened body), Mumei sees himself as an octopus in a way that in one sense Yoshiro can only hope to do. For the child the possibilities remain rather more open. What does strike Mumei as odd is a word that cannot be used, like the word "overalls" that Yoshiro teaches and then seems to take back, which calls into question the object itself. Part of learning language is learning to accept what those teaching language "say and do as consequential," but this also means they have to accept, "even have to applaud, what I say and do as what they say and do"[29]; said otherwise, when Yoshiro tells Mumei not to use the word "overalls," Mumei's difficulty has to do with the fact that the forms we rely on in "making sense" are human in nature, which is to say they impose limits on what can and cannot be said that can be recognized by others.[30]

It is important here that the child does not live in a world or a time when different languages are normally seen in the same neighbourhood, though they linger in the background for the older adults. Their absence and spectral presence account for what each of the speakers perceives. It is not just that the child does not yet have a word for "eloping" and, because of this, no scene of a young woman escaping her parents' house to find her lover arises in his mind. It is also that a particular kind of play, where jogging might turn into the sort of situation in which blood pressures are liable to rise all around, is not available to him. The feelings that accompany interlingual puns are ones he cannot imagine. This is the first blush of a difference between the child who is coming into language as opposed to another language – a difference that Tawada wants to destabilize when made too sharply. For the child, the myriad possibilities that come about through crossings of languages doesn't seem all that odd, nor does it occur to him to think that a particular word like "overalls" belongs in this language rather than that one. The absence of animals, or foreign words, takes on a very different character for the adults, who become in turns nostalgic and anxious on behalf of the children. But it is interesting that if there is a note of lament in Yoshiro's sense that if only there were animals to be seen it would set Mumei's heart on fire, the latter is perfectly capable of conjuring them up from "mere" words. The two live in proximity even as the possibilities are not entirely the same.

Something similar might be said about the narrator, the author, and the characters in the novel. While the narrator appears at times omniscient, there are in fact subtle shifts in their alignment with different characters, at times speaking in the voice of Mumei and at other times, and more frequently, Yoshiro; sometimes with this one's memories and partial knowledge, sometimes with that one's. Rather than an Archimedean point of view, the narrator has an indefinite relationship with the characters, both those within and outside the text – the novel is less a closed text and more a shifting relation or set of relations. Something similar might be said about the author and her alignments with characters, or plots, words, and scenes. The frame is always available to be shifted, remade through interactions. Each of the speakers plays with the frame.

**Language Experience**

These themes led me to two collections of short writings where Tawada thinks about the different ways we experience languages in proximity to one another. This time I read in the company of literary criticism, and

# Life in a Net of Language: Literature, Translation, and the Feel of Words 161

I was quickly gripped by Yasemin Yildiz's account of Tawada as a critic of the trope of the mother tongue. One essay from *akzentfrei*, carrying the potent title "Writing in a Net of Languages" [Schreiben im Netz der Sprachen], poses a question of how to think not only about the usual figurations of language crossing, like code-switching, but also about the force of contingently proximate languages, as in the case when one is riding the bus or the subway, or overhears a conversation in a restaurant, and "two sentences ... one right after the other penetrates my ear by chance don't yet occupy a common space."[31] One often sees nowadays, she writes, different words and even different worlds "standing next to each other" (Nebeneinanderstehen)[32] but for which we do not yet have a "corresponding frame." Consider one crucial example:

> When I hear two words that sound similar, from Japanese and from Germany, gathered together, they needn't be historically related. A kind of noodle soup is called for example in exactly the same way as the German word "Rahmen." A restaurant where one can buy these noodles, could be called "Rahmenhandlung." These two words have of course nothing to do with each other historically. Therefore such a phenomenon is not taken seriously and dismissed as coincidence ... people with stiff brains would ask me: why do you have to busy yourself with such a word game?

Yildiz points out that the coincidence of the sounds and the simultaneous use of interlingual homonyms (like ramen and Rahmen) and intralingual ones (like the noun Handlung, which can be an act, the plot of a story, or shop) point to an experience of the indeterminacy of meaning[33] that results from our simultaneous perception of the possibilities in a word; it makes it possible to listen in different ways to the same sentence. Multiple aspects are preserved in this case because the distinction is not marked inflectionally or morphologically, and yet there is a shift in what it is possible to perceive thanks to the twinning of sounds. Yildiz helpfully suggests that example itself also theorizes the situation. Rahmenhandlung, as it is used here, can also mean a framing story or narrative. The connections that arise do not dissolve into pre-existing frames, then, but rather create and are created by a frame – their coincidence and surprise generates new kinds of conditions and new perceptions, or "poetic correspondences," through the crossings of words or sounds from many different languages. They acquire depth in this way, Tawada says, quite different from the idea of depth uncovered by historical or philological points of mutual derivation.[34] The story that emerges helps us to see the connections between adjacent words and images; it turns out to be itself what Yildiz calls a "medium of connection," where Rahmen connotes both the opening and closing of certain possibilities.³⁵ In contrast, then, with the usual idea of language change through historical derivation, in this case, Tawada writes, "new chain of words offers possibilities for associations that have a lot to do with the present and in which the elements from different cultures and realms come together in a surprising way." It is not in such situations that the words and linguistic grammatical structures are changed but their perception, an experience that Yildiz says is "affectively akin to experiencing a 'second childhood.' This new perception is not limited to one language alone but listens for new meaning and words both within and across languages." I want to hold this question of childhood in abeyance for the moment, to think a bit more first about these experiences of language.

The pun "tips or goads to us to read with subtlety and activity."³⁶ Punning through iconicity of sounds is a common feature of poetic play in many contexts and, it has been noted, often highlights the difficulty with translation.³⁷ The twinning of sound that makes a pun work is often lost in translation,³⁸ as are sometimes the reduplications that give the point to a text.³⁹ And where the twinning occurs interlingually, as it does in the example cited above, it can have a range of political implications, like when an unintended vowel slip provides fodder for gossip when it is offensive or amusing or morally instructive. (Perhaps this is why we feel "a grammatical joke to be deep."⁴⁰) This means too that play with words provides "tools for learning grammar,"⁴¹ but also a way of "continuously recreating grammar."⁴² The same string of signs might appear now as a joke, now an insult, now a sign of a slide into madness.

Part of what is so compelling about Tawada's descriptions is the sense we get that language is something we experience and not only a representation. Using a word with right is less a matter of our capacity to give a definition and more an intuition, one that also transforms meaning in use. Where words move among multiple languages, these possibilities of sense are alive alongside one another in the pulse of language. This is so much the case that we find that words have sense for listeners and speakers even when they can't produce a rigid definition at all.⁴³ This view is reminiscent of Wittgenstein's insight that meaning *is* physiognomy, not in the sense of a "process which accompanies a word," but rather that it is an actual likeness of its meaning, that it pertains to our attachment to words and that there could be human beings to whom all this is alien, in the sense that they might not have the same attachments.⁴⁴ To experience words in my attachments to them is an experience of their meaning *for me*; that is to say, their interestedness, their significance, how much they matter.[45] This touch of words can also burn, and it can be lost.

One of the recurrent images Tawada employs is of the digestion of words. Tawada and her characters talk about chewing on words, swallowing, and incorporating them into the body. Consider this example where she describes German words sitting in her stomach and becoming part of her skin:

> The skin is, of course, something that is very close to us ... These words are outside of my body and I eat them, I consciously eat them. I can put them into my mouth and then they enter my body; but they are not part of my body. Sometimes these words turn out to be indigestible and then you easily can get a stomachache. These foreign words, though, can also slowly transform themselves and become meat and then, ultimately, they can become my flesh. Although sometimes this process does not work and then the foreign word remains something in between, in between my own body and the foreign body ... this bodily image is also quite concretely linked to the feeling that I get when I pronounce words in a foreign language. Then I am working with my tongue, just like when I am eating.[46]

Unlike in other sources and contexts, where the image of digestion might function as a metaphor of analytical breakdown into components that are easier to pass, here it is something that remains at the level of the body; I have nothing, or very little, to say about the outcome, it is not something intentional, but I am left with a sense that a particular word does (or perhaps more viscerally, does not) sit well. The proof is in the act of swallowing the words.[47] Some words become part of the flesh, and some do not. Notice too how it is when the "the process does not work," when something is indigestible, that some words feel strange, that I am pronouncing a word in a "foreign language," that they remain as if somehow between myself and another, but even in this case not like a skin, which is more like a sign of a word having been taken up, made part of me. This image deeply disturbs the usual picture of an economy of inner and outer worlds since the tongue is both the means of taking in and expelling. Meaning words is figured as the particular attachments I have to them (or them to me), in my very being, and so in the movements of words, it is our attachments to them that are complicated, nudged, surprisingly rearranged, reforged, transformed, wiggled, so on; however, that they have a feel is not something that ceases to hold "outside" *this* language. We have myriad relationships to words. They can bless and curse. They can be alive or dead for us. And in this way, as Cavell writes, "our attachments to our words is allegorical of our attachments to ourselves and to other persons."[48] I take this to mean that in attending to the physiognomy of words we also come to see another, not as it were from the outside and not as matter of "mere knowing." The body, the skin that is made up of digested words, doesn't merely represent the soul of the person I am looking at it, whose physiognomy I am reading, and who I see "according to my reading"; it is an expression of it.

This is a very different picture of language than the one we arrive at through an exclusive emphasis on linguistic grammatical rules. The next book of Tawada's I read was a collection of essays called *Talisman*. In the opening pages, Tawada writes how in her first year in Germany, she found herself sleeping more than usual to recover (erholen) from the impressions of everyday life. She describes daily routines at the office as a series of enigmatic scenes (Kette rätselhafter Szene) in which particular words made certain impressions on her, sometimes replacing other words. The word Bleistift was one such example. On the one hand, a German Bleistift does not differ so very much from a Japanese Enpitsu, she observes, except that she found herself writing with a Bleistift and not an Enpitsu,[49] and this, she came to find, meant making do with another "object" (Gegenstand). At first, she is shadowed by a slight pang of discomfort for her attachment to Bleistift, which she says is like being called by a new name after one is married. Even this short thought about public renaming, so intimate, struck me as the sort of utterance that might not be intended for everyone, that some would pick it up and others let it pass, by design. Something about the shift in the word had *that* sort of character; it had a public quality, an expression of hers, somehow uneasy, especially because of how naturally it could roll off the tongue.

A few pages later she recalls one of the words that stood out and continues to stand out, many years on. The situation is one where the singular, neuter, third-person pronoun "es" is used to fill the need for a grammatical subject. One says in Germany, "es ist kalt," "es geht mir gut" or "es regnet."[50] Tawada's grammar book noted that the word itself meant absolutely nothing (gar nichts bedeutet), that it merely filled a grammatical gap; without the pronoun, the subject of the sentence would be missing, and this was impossible, since sentences require subjects. "But I did not see," she writes, "that a sentence had to have a subject."

> Moreover, I did not believe that the word "es" had no meaning. In the moment in which one says that it rains, there arises an "Es" that pours water from the sky. When it is going well for someone (wenn es einem

gut geht), there is an Es that has contributed to it ... Es never had a proper name. But it always worked diligently and effectively in many areas and lived modestly in a grammatical gap.[51]

In these few lines, Tawada puts several issues on the table. Is it right to say the third-person pronoun has no meaning in a sentence in use, while meaning the statement? What can we make of Tawada's insinuation that the meaning of the pronoun is that something must be pouring like rain from the heavens, or that makes things go well with me? We could of course read her as making a straightforward critique of the metaphysical claims embedded beneath the surface of German grammar. But it reads to me like she is pointing to something rather different. First, it highlights the difficulties that come about as a result of a confusion of linguistic for philosophical grammar. The peculiar feeling that arises from scrutinizing a structure like the requirement of a grammatical subject that seems to mean "absolutely nothing" is akin to taking a statement about one's belief to be an assertion about an inner state that comes then to be projected onto language, as opposed to something where the two are learned together. In the present case, this might lead us to ask whether we should more carefully distinguish the use of the "es" to fill grammatical roles in a sentence reporting about the weather – where if one were to ask, I can quickly confirm by looking out the window – and a sentence like "es geht mir gut," about which my status as a report is quite different, even if the grammar of "believe" is in each case a report about a mental state. But this is not, as is sometimes argued, because there are some inner states without physiognomic accompaniments, as if linguistic differences were "intrinsic differences in the content of experience."[52] Rather, this mode of questioning asks us to consider the ways I am in a position in each case to ask and to say.

The sentence "es regnet" (it is raining), has long been associated with a reputed problem in philosophy known as Moore's paradox, where the question arises whether there is in the sentence an implied use of the first-person present indicative of "belief" ("ich glaube, es regnet"). While I may not believe it is raining and it may be the case that it is, it would be nonsensical to say, "It is raining, but I do not believe it." The issue similarly arises for Wittgenstein in the course of a discussion of whether the same expression can be used differently in different language games. "Do I always talk with a very definite purpose?" he asks, "and is what I say meaningless because I don't?" Wittgenstein reformulates the paradox by pointing out that while the sentence "ich glaube, es regnet" is used as an assertion, the conjecture that I believe it to be the case that it is raining is not in this situation used as a conjecture.[53]

Moreover, while "ich glaube, es wird regnen," I believe it will rain, is similar to the assertion "It will rain," the same cannot be said of the sentences "I believed then, it would rain" and "It did not then rain." While I may well mistrust my senses, I cannot say I mistrust my belief. "If there were a verb that meant 'to believe falsely' it would not have any significant first-person present indicative."[54]

But perhaps more pressing, the example highlights the fact that our attachments to words are not zero-sum games. They can be weaker or stronger, and this is in part what enables different kinds of verbal play. A relatively loose attachment might make it easier to play. We can pick something up, try it out, see how it stretches, in ways that are different perhaps from the ways of others, who feel, perhaps, more "attached" to a certain likeness of meaning. The question shows itself in what strikes one as curious, or whether something does.[55]

*A Language, Only Not This One*

Unlike the child initially learning language, many characters in Tawada's work, as I said earlier, already have a language, even if not *this* one. This can be both where possibilities for newness enter in or where one has a feeling that they do not quite have a footing in language.[56] As bits of the language we have are tried out in combinations with new words, objects, and grammatical or aesthetic forms, the question of whether something works in an utterance (or what does) has less to do with mastery over rules than with the feel of the horizons of possibility it opens. This what Tawada often describes as poetic correspondences effected by movements in language: namely, where some connection between words takes hold and takes us in a new direction. This use neither reproduces a linguistic grammatical or cultural rule, nor does it break with the philosophical grammar of what is usually called "the original." Here a word or phrase or an image shows itself to be charged with possibilities that come to life in different moments, cropping up and disappearing – the examples correspond in that they speak to one another in all sorts of ways.

In one of her most widely cited essays, Tawada recounts reading Paul Celan first in translation and wondering what it was that made it translatable.[57] Tawada learns from a friend that for the translator of the Japanese volume of Celan's poetry, one particular radical (the indexing component of a character) was especially important in making the translation: 門, which is used for "Tor" in German (door in English). While some ideogrammatic characters have multiple components, some, like this one, consist only of a radical. This radical, she notices, seems to arise

Life in a Net of Language: Literature, Translation, and the Feel of Words  167

at crucial moments throughout the collection. For instance, Tawada sees in the character "hear" – 聞 – in the poem "Ich Hörte Es Sagen" (I Heard It Said) an ear beneath the Tor; "according to this sign, to hear means to stand on the threshold like an ear." Tawada writes that the ideogram recalls a saying:

> It goes: Monzen no kozoo narawanu kyoo o yomu ["The boy who lives before the gate of a temple can recite the prayer without learning it"]. For me, the boy who doesn't go into the temple and remains standing at the gate embodied the person who is hearing. But now that I have begun to think in German quite frequently, I most often associate the verb to hear ["hören"] with to belo to ["zugehören"] so that when I hear something I feel the need to hurry after the unfamiliar voice and not remain standing on the threshold … The more intensely I read, the stronger my impression became that Celan's poems were peering into the Japanese.

Celan's third poem *Leuchten* ["Gleam"] is titled using the ideogram 閃, a component of which is the radical for gate, or Tor. The character pictures, Tawada writes, "a man 人 standing beneath a Tor 門," which she had never considered could produce a gleaming, though it strikes her that "perhaps someone who stands beneath a gate [or on a threshold] will be particularly receptive to a gleam from an invisible world."

> In addition I sensed something that strongly linked the German word *leuchten* ["gleam"] with this ideogram: It struck me that the word *ich* ["I"] briefly appears in the middle of the German word *leuchten* when you speak it aloud clearly. The word *ich* does not otherwise appear in this poem, there is only *mir* ["to me"], *du* ["you"] and *uns* ["to us"]. Only in this gleaming does the "I" appear in a quick flash, for one brief, fragmented moment.

In these passages, something is opened up in the poem in its movement, not in a way that totally transforms the text but rather in its capacity to activate a potential already within it. It is there in the lines of the text, both in the image of a person standing at a threshold receptive to light (though hard to see at first in leuchten when read in isolation) and in the ideogram itself, in its connection with the phrase that places a boy at a gate of the temple, learning. The movement offers what Naoki Sakai calls an optic on the text in which the putative unity, countability, and coherence of the language in its cartographic representation is shattered.[58] In other words, here German, there Japanese. To say the poem is at home in Japanese is to say something very different from fidelity to the original or simply the generation of new meaning because something of a shared criteria must be there prior to the assignment of national-linguistic borders. This play continuously recreates *this* grammar, not only through creation of new lexical possibilities as we see in mixed languages, where speakers can find ways to "indicate a new identity vis-à-vis the two dominant languages,"[59] but also in the philosophic sense, of what we do with words. Tawada writes,

> If I imagine a poem as a receptor for rays of light, it becomes meaningless to look for something "typically German" in a German poem. For what it picks up is always foreign to it and never the poem itself. Perhaps there are also German poems that have been made of German soil. But the poems that most interest me are the ones that correspond to constellations of foreign languages and ways of thinking that they had not previously encountered at the time of their composition.[60]

In 1998, Tawada was in Tübingen in for a series of lectures in which she described the difficulty she encountered when she tried to get lost in books in German. She told the audience that as a child, she entered a book like one enters a house, dashing in until you no longer see the door – or words – in front of you. But something about the alphabet system resisted her, and she found herself lingering over particular words until there was just silence, and meaning disappeared. "Maybe you need a vehicle to drive across the landscapes of the alphabet. The rhythm of a language, for instance, could serve as such a vehicle." For this reason, she prefers to listen to the language on the radio, where the rhythm helps words forget their definitions and become pictures. Phonetic-script readers, she muses, must read in the opposite direction, perceiving pictures that they form into words. "When I read Japanese, I do not convert the ideograms into phonemes. I recognize a sign as a picture and understand its meaning." The questions raised earlier by the materiality of sounds in multiple languages is thus connected to the materiality of the script.[61] In this case, difficulties are related not to comprehension but to the feel of words. "The body of an ideogram is not mysterious," it hides nothing, though its meaning can be painted over again and again, accumulating layers. A letter, by contrast, is not normally the seat of meaning. But this is also what makes it "lively." "You are not allowed to look at it, but rather have to translate it into a sound and makes its linguistic [scriptural] material disappear. If you do not do so, the letter will become alive, jump out of the sentence and change into an animal." The possibility of combining them in different ways is what gives them a "slippery" or "lively" texture. "It can be risky to send a letter into the world since the author or rather the typesetter cannot ever know what will become of it."[62]

The claim is not that she has some better command of ideograms, or that they are any easier or harder to use, nor that they are any less bodily, but that their experience takes different qualities. Tawada recounts a well-known story of the origin of the Chinese script in which the characters are patterned on the way the footprints of birds and the landscape seemed to meet. These imprints are then sorted by the inventor of the characters, who further experiments with their possibilities for recombination. When it comes to alphabet systems, Tawada sees in the cracks and crevices of nature, "on the surface of a scorched dirt road, on a wood door, or on a leather bag," a range of alphabetic signs that give the impression that they can be read directly from the world or even on the surface of her own body. "Sometimes I look at my hand and try to find all the letters of the alphabet on the surface of my skin. This is palmistry in the literal sense of the word." The thought occasions a story about how deep meaning goes. She describes her first time reading aloud a story to an audience where she talks about words or place names with two "o"s, as in Airolo, and says that it reminds her of a tunnel, which in turn helps her to see that she wanted to return to Göschenen, which one arrives at by driving northward through the Gotthard tunnel. Someone in the audience pointed out that her name also has two "o"s:

> Upon hearing this I experienced the power that the alphabetic script had over my body that now ran the risk of turning into the letter O. Two tunnel entrances were piercing their way through the text into my body. In that instant I swiftly rewrote my name in ideograms as if this gesture were a new self-defense technique: that character name for "yo" means "a leaf of a tree," and "ko" means "child."[63]

Tawada observes that "letters cannot be translated. In the end it is not so much the text that one can never translate, but the script." But this sentiment is oftentimes read too strongly as an indictment of the practice; the lecture in general read as a comment on a linguistic lack in alphabetic languages or that German is just too strange for her. Her argument though is that a literal translation, which she takes to be a literary act, "should take untranslatability as the case and face it rather than eliminate it." The untranslatable is a sign of what is in fact accomplished in language, where it can give a "feel for the existence" of another language. Where friction occurs is also where transformation is liable to take place, in literature and in everyday life. "Isn't it an interesting displacement, a refreshing twist, or a manic shift into one's own language rather an accomplishment of a translation?" The danger is just as much in too-easy praise heaped on translations when they are too smooth. What such experiences do is "palpate the surface of the text." Surface is not in this case something superficial, but something like the forms language takes, which Tawada distinguishes from the nucleus.[64] As Gizem Arslan has argued, Tawada's play with does not "instrumentalize textual surfaces to reach the depth of meaning, but can address materiality in its own right. This in turn yields modes of reading the illegible in contexts of translation, readings that hinge on the immediacy of contact and encounter with purportedly illegible subjects."[65] We might connect this insight, as Tawada does herself in her lectures, with the curious thought that perhaps there are translations without originals or for which an original would have to be invented.

The question of translatability points to a difference between the feel words have within forms of life and their conventional hermeneutic sense. The narrator in "Das Fremde aus der Dose," which Tawada's English translators render as "Canned Foreign," offers a description of the difference: "I failed every time I tried to describe the difference between the two cultures: The difference was inscribed directly on my skin like a foreign writing, that I could feel indeed, but I could not read." For Tawada, these are spaces of invention, in which relations between words and between people are recast, and which, by the same token, are susceptible to breakdown. It seems to me that were it to be the case that words had no feel to them, then perhaps we have reached the point at which our differences cease to be criterial.[66] But this is precisely not what happens in these the examples.

We come then in this roundabout way to see just how problematic is the assimilation of these figurations of linguistic mobility in Tawada's work to tropes of migrant itineraries or intercultural experience, as was often the case in German reading publics.[67] Several critics have argued that by adopting a "mock ethnographic tone," Tawada expresses profound doubts about the possibility of reading or writing "authentic others" created by the ethnological imagination. One of Tawada's translators, Chantal Wright, has argued persuasively that the author, the texts themselves, and the speakers in them "deliberately cultivate misunderstandings and are frequently misunderstood by others."[68] Wright takes a series of provocative examples. The first, from the novella *Ein Gast*, tells of a woman from Japan who recounts the experience of going to a German-speaking ear doctor, who, blushing, announces, to the narrator's surprise, "You are pregnant." Interpreting his reddening face as annoyance that she had not sought out an obstetrician, she asks him to look again: "Maybe you've confused a flea with an embryo?" But she had no sense that the sentence that she heard as a declaration of fact was in this situation an interrogative, meant to be distinguished by intonation rather than inflection. In both German and Japanese, she learns, the word order is preserved in this kind of shift, but the latter introduces an interrogative participle, "ka." As Wright points out, the misfire also marks a shift in the narrative. When the doctor looks again into the ear, he sees women on stage dressed in kimonos, which the narrator recognizes as a scene from *Madame Butterfly*, another sort of misunderstanding, this time on the part of the culturally ignorant doctor.[69]

For Wright, these misunderstandings issue from the arbitrariness of the linguistic sign or from ignorance about cultural others. She reasons that a listener might not have access to the meaning of the word given by the conventions that bind signifier and signified. On this view, meaning appears to stand behind words. But in the account I have been developing, it is not so much meaning in the sense of ostensive definitions that is at stake in these scenes but the feel of words. In each of these cases of misunderstanding, the speaker uses words with right, even without justification.[70] If the word has a sense, in what way do we say we do not know its meaning? How else to take the emphasis on the motivation of these lexical crossings? How do we understand the fact that she writes so painfully from *within* language? Travelling in language, we find that even very ordinary movements can bewilder, or disorient, or clarify. Writing neither offers an answer to the desire for perfect intelligibility nor suggests a hermetic closedness of one to the other. Tawada does away with the very terms of opposition by pointing to the awkward condition of being at home in language; which is to say, both our longings for home and for an escape.[71] Perhaps what is at work in these moments is not a question of truth and error, but a "poetics of misrecognition," a way of passing on of the "force of attachment" to a word, a thought, a thing.[72]

In "Das Fremde aus der Dose," Tawada tells a story about her arrival in Germany and recognizing the alphabet on posters and signs but feeling she did not yet know what the words meant. She would stare at individual letters and practice the sounds they tokened: "I repeated the S sounds in my mouth and noticed that my tongue suddenly tasted odd. I hadn't known a tongue, too, could taste of something." This short quip draws a very subtle and important distinction by taking advantage of the ambiguity in "tongue," that it is not only "foreign words" that taste peculiar, but also the tongue that pronounces them itself.

Moreover, while the sensation of new words felt in many cases disagreeable, the experience also produced in her a feeling that her "native tongue" also did not automatically have the right words. She compares this sensation to the scrutiny to which people in Germany seemed to subject her face. "In those days I often found that people became uneasy when they couldn't read my face like a text." Their desire to "discover a familiar face behind the strange one" led such people to ask the usual questions that began "Is it true that the Japanese ..." or "In Japan do people also ..." At the bus stop she becomes acquainted with a woman called Sasha who, to the contrary, "accepted all forms of illegibility ... she didn't want to read things, she wanted to observe them in detail." Sasha would often buy soap for her girlfriend in the local supermarket, and the packaging had a picture of a phoenix and the word "soap" on it, but Sonia couldn't read it. Tawada wonders aloud whether the letters don't somehow try to fix the contents of the packaging, as if without them, the soap might transform and fly away. Later, she herself goes to the market and buys a can with a Japanese woman painted on the side – when she arrives at home, she discovers it's a can of tuna fish. "The woman seemed to have change into a piece of fish during her long voyage."

> This surprise came on a Sunday: I had decided not to read any writing on Sundays. Instead, I observed the people I saw on the street as though they were isolated letters. Sometimes two people sat down next to each other in a café, and thus, briefly, formed a word. Then they separated, in order to go off and form other words. There must have been a moment in which the combinations of these words formed, quite by chance, several sentences in which I might have read this foreign city like a text. But I never discovered a single sentence in this city, only letters and sometimes a few words that had no direct connection to any "cultural content." These words now and then led me to open the wrapping paper on the outside, only to find different wrapping paper below.[73]

The thought that foreignness can be canned is striking in the way it captures both the desire to fix the feeling of foreignness through abstraction (by bringing it under the logic of equivalence and exchange) and the worry that something might always slip out and be transformed, that words might fly away.[74] It captures something of what Cavell described as an inevitable temptation "to force our ordinary words to do what they, as they stand, will not do."[75] What is foreign, what we render foreign when we treat others as objects of knowledge, my doubts about which we sometimes imagine can be secured, is *our* language. The same language that produces an accord

Life in a Net of Language: Literature, Translation, and the Feel of Words    173

that is natural to us – a naturalness elided by conventionalism's insistence on the arbitrariness of language's "abutment to the world"[76] and that is reconfigured by poetic correspondence, which at the same time relies on it for its feel.

**Context and Conflict**

Tawada's writing provided an occasion for thinking about how words from various languages are perceived within shared (if contested and vulnerable) human forms of life. These movements are not always smooth. They are often occasioned by difficulties. But what resists movement, and when does it obtain more easily? Where do difficulties arise, and what should we say about them? When are they morally instructive, and when ontological?[77] If we are speaking different languages, how do we identify the object of someone's thought, particularly when we feel as though they live in other times, or other worlds?[78] If, as Tawada suggests, writing with Bleistift means learning to live with another sort of object and doing different sorts of things with it, does this mean, prior to learning the word, the object did not exist *for her*? When Mumei hears the word "overalls" does a new object appear? Does the word "soap" or the image of the phoenix fix the contents of the container in the supermarket? How do we move among languages if the things we pick out with our utterances differ?

In one of the short stories in *Überseezungen*, "Die Botin," a student named Mika returns to Japan after having abruptly given up music study in Germany. When she learns that a friend is travelling to Munich, she sends along a message to her teacher, explaining why she left. In a bid to hide the reason from the teacher's wife, she begs her friend to whisper the message. But her friend speaks no German and the teacher no Japanese, so Mika has her friend memorize a long string of words in Japanese, taking advantage of German homophones to convey a message. Critics have suggested that, in part because Tawada chooses to render the message in German transliteration, the secret of the code is hidden, inscribed as a secret that cannot be unlocked, or that at a minimum, would need to be back-transcribed into kanji to be read as though in German, but that as it stands, the text string is nonsense.[79] But is the message strictly speaking nonsense?[80] Isn't the point that precisely nothing is hidden, that everything, including the private intimations and even the fact of the secret, is in full public view? Or else, that one *can* read the surfaces of words, signs, images, sounds in multiple languages simultaneously? There are in this case no nonsense words, even if read directly in German. And there is also no absence of syntax when read homophonically. Nonsense arises only from a disjuncture in the expectations one might have about the category of the terms as they appear in the sentences, as though words carried with them those categories no matter the context, from reading according to such a view.[81]

In moments when things become jarring or slippery or strange, the sense words have does not always obey the location assigned to them by a certain picture of "inside" or "outside" this or that language. And yet radical misunderstanding always remains a real possibility, that our words might acquire the "feeling of nonsense," a worry that shadows each line, every utterance, that they "might betray a manner of leaving our common conceptual world"; common, that is, by virtue of our languages being *human* languages, and not because we have ready-made equivalents for every word or concept.[82] Such moments test how far our concepts can be extended and where and when they cannot, how far our moral vision goes, how we "measure our distance" from others. These are not just differences of opinion or belief – say, about whether a writing instrument is capable of crying – differences that depend, at another level, on agreement in criteria, in grammar. It is also a question of whether this is the sort of thing we can imagine a person might say, not in virtue of their argument per se but in the sense that we discover the sense the use of the word has or does not have. While this is certainly a quality literature, of reading and writing and listening that allows us to explore our capacity for imagination, it is not a special capacity of it; rather, these are possibilities built into our "ordinary human responsiveness to words."

Nonetheless, in instances where two seemingly irreconcilable or contradictory ways of speaking meet up, reality can be on the line. And yet, Cora Diamond argues, since the logical shape of the contest involves a conception of reality "not internal to either of the two forms of thought that provide the initial understanding of the conflict-situation," the space opened up could not have been given in advance. It is the meeting that "gives the *space*":

> ... there are ways of thinking of what is real and what is not that are deeply connected with our responses to conflicting modes of thought ... there does not need to be, before the conflict, some "universe of discourse" with its logical space, which provides standards to which you can appeal ... our understanding of what is real and what is unreal can be in part shaped by how we take such conflicts and by how we reason in response to them.[83]

Our very agreements in those shared forms of life from which our criteria are grown, our sense of what is real and unreal, are not only threatened by these difficulties. They are also transformed in their playing out by the manner in which they play out. Context is not something we refer back to in order to secure our statements, it is not prior, independent, and invariable but rather emerges with movement. What counts, by extension, as context is less group affiliation and identification, the borderlands of languages (especially those produced by hegemonic discourses), and more the forms of life that are disclosed in the practices of those who live in proximity to one another, "breathing the same air, frequenting the same businesses, coveting the same partners," who love and detest, indeed, who misunderstand one another – call it a neighbourhood or a Kiez – and out of which one can also fall.[84]

Robert Walser once described Berlin as an "ill-mannered, impertinent, intelligent scoundrel," over which waves of intellect wash, some things being picked up, others tossed aside: "An artist here has no choice but to pay attention." The artist has no hope of stopping up his ears but must rather "pull himself together like a human being":

> Berlin never rests, and this is glorious. Each dawning day brings with it a new, agreeably disagreeable attack on complacency, and this does the general sense of indolence good. An artist possesses, much like a child, an inborn propensity for beautiful, nobel, sluggardizing. Well, this slug-a-beddishness, this kingdom, is constantly being buffeted by fresh storm-winds of inspiration. The refined, silent creature is suddenly blustered full of something coarse, loud, and unrefined. There is an incessant blurring together of various things, and this is good, this is Berlin, and Berlin is outstanding.[85]

It is, for many of the same reasons, a city that can prove lonely. "The metropolitan artist" Walser writes, "has no dearth of opportunities to see and speak to no one at all." But though lives throttle up and down these possibilities, many of the people I have known found themselves in the grip of the city and its restlessness, perhaps most of all for the ways it kept possibilities alive in the dark. For none was literature a sphere of social life set apart, sealed away from common life. Nor was it something that picked up and patched over our failures of and in language, failures to understand or make ourselves understood. If anything, it helped recover (our confidence in) ordinary language, a confidence undermined by the view of literary language as rarefied or ideal, the idea that without it, there would be no way to speak or listen.⁸⁶ Language can become obscure to itself. (We can become obscure to ourselves in our language.) Literature offers one way of responding, of finding out what it is we can do with the words we experience; in other words, what matters. It is one form of recovery of our capacity to word the world, a "transformative capacity ... of *having a language*,"⁸⁷ a human life with language; that is, of accepting, living with the fact that language might become obscure, that our words might fail. And it is often in these moments that we see anew the possibilities for expressivity.

# Notes

## 1. Introduction: Berlin, City of Letters

1. The romantic notion of the fragment at play here is one that has found a life in recent anthropological writing, because it gives us a way of describing relations without recourse to the logic of parts and wholes (Das 2007; Garcia 2020). See also Herzfeld (2009) for a slightly different interpretation.
2. Ahmed 2013.
3. Boyd 1990, 196.
4. Nabokov 2017, 374. In thinking about the Berlin that emerges in these stories, I was inspired by Jenya Mironava's insightful digital installation, entitled *A Guide to Nabokov's "A Guide to Berlin"* and hosted by Harvard's Mapping Cultural Space across Eurasia project. See also Smith (2021).
5. C.f. Emery 2002.
6. Nabokov 1963, 330.
7. Boyd 1990, 447.
8. As Schiller and Çağlar (2018) point out, "there is still insufficient research and theory that explores the relationship between projects to rebrand and regenerate cities with different degrees of political, economic, and cultural power, on the one hand, and the everyday sociabilities and social citizenship practices of city residents, on the other." See Gerstenberger (2008).
9. In recent literary theory, this point has been made specifically about the status of characters. For some of contours of this debate, see Felski, Anderson, and Moi (2019).
10. This is the more or less the position of Nigel Rapport (2007, 215) for whom also literature "fosters a sense of individual uniqueness and separateness, experientiality and integrity, providing testimony to human diversity and perversity."

11 Greenblatt 1997.
12 Gal 2002.
13 Schiller and Çağlar (2011, 4) note that "despite the scholarship detailing the social construction of difference and the challenge to write 'against culture,' migration studies continue to approach migrants' relationships to economic, social and political forms of urban incorporation through an ethnic lens." See also Conrad (2010) on the nation as "centre of gravity" in German historical discourse.
14 Pollack (2006) famously calls this process literarization. The wide use of spatial metaphors only serves to entrench this sense of separation. After all, spatial imageries are automatically thought to characterize social locations, since "linguistic conventions seem to be spatially distributed." As Blommaert et al. (2005) argue, space and spatial metaphors "organize regimes of language."
15 Perhaps the best-known version of this view is put forward by Iser (1991).
16 Trouillot 2002.
17 Povinelli 2002. See also Herzfeld (1997) on the "strategic deployment of ideal types"; James Scott (1998) makes a similar point about the "simplification" entailed in making legible to the state.
18 Basso 2009.
19 Morrison 2017.
20 In 2010, Bundeskänzlerin Angela Merkel made international headlines when she made this statement, which, while part of a longstanding political rhetorical strategy in Germany, was taken in this context to mirror a sentiment expressed by Thilo Sarrazin, whose book *Deutschland schafft sich ab* argued that migrants were lowering the intellectual environment. The move was seen as a gesture to the right, which had been critical of what it took to be an overly "soft" position on immigration earlier in her term. As recently as 2007, the state has started tracking a new category it adopted from earlier studies on youth welfare: Germans with a Migrationshintergrund or migration background, which initially included "foreigners born in Germany," or who had a parent that was not born a German citizen, and now legally only refers to the latter, though its common usage is more ambiguous (Will 2019).
21 See Chin 2017; Pautz 2005.
22 Sassen 2005. The city emerges in this literature as a site of contradictory forces and the enactment of a global ecumene (Soysal 2004; Hannerz 1992, 217–63). On the limits of this language and its service to the re-inscription of racialized violence, see Kiliç and Petzen (2013).
23 Krätke 2001; Kulke 2003. For Sassen (2001; 2005), major cities emerge in a new strategic role in the transforming global economy as 1) "command points" of transnational flow, 2) as centres in financial and specialized

service industry, 3) as "sites of production" at the leading edge of industrial innovation, and 4) as markets for these new products. Such a shift in the structure of economic circulation, Sassen hypothesized, meant also that the economic fortunes of the city became untethered from the hinterlands or national economic landscapes (2001, 30). To take just one data point, unlike most other modern capitals, Berlin is a drag on national GDP per capita. If earlier research on the "global" treated globalization as a universalizing process that, while expressed within national boundaries, nevertheless transcends such local designations, making the local expressive of world-wide relations and processes (Kearney 1995), I ask how we might take specific histories and urban practices as not the touching point but the very grounds for the emergence of forms of globality.

24 Yildiz 2017, 206.
25 In 2005, the parliamentary coalition led by the centre-right Christlich Demokratische Union (CDU) launched an initiative called Deutschland – Land der Ideen ahead of the World Cup's return to Germany the following year. When Bundespräsident Horst Köhler came into office in 2004, he declared that this would be the motto of the Federal Republic. Among the moments and exhibitions hosted around Berlin, perhaps the most familiar was the Ideengang (Walk of Ideas), including a twelve-metre-high sculpture of books outside the Humboldt Universität, near where Nazi youths had tossed books in the streets to be burned. The monument, Der moderne Buchdruck (Modern Book-Printing), boasted seventeen names stretched from the base to the top, from Goethe to Grass, celebrating the heights of German literature that could be recuperated. After 1945, historians had publicly debated whether a Sonderweg, a special path, had led German history inevitably to Nazism and thus tainted all earlier achievements. If these concerns still lingered, the monument was clearly an effort to reclaim a national literary history. It was on these terms that the German state explicitly sought to brand itself to the world. Its impact was compounded when German spectators publicly and en masse wrapped themselves in their flag during the games for the first time since the end of the Nazi period. The tournament itself, the theme for which was "Die Welt zu Gast bei Freunden" (loosely, "the world visit friends"), was preceded by several racist attacks: in a slew of incidents, groups of white men shouted fascist slogans and, singing the national anthem, assaulted people with dark skin. In the aftermath, Uwe-Karsten Heye, a former government official in the Schröder administration, described the region around Berlin as a hotbed of racist violence, and advised anyone with a "different skin colour" of certain "no-go zones" from which they might not "make it out alive."

26 Partridge 2010a. See also Jurgens (2012) on the increasing incorporation of marginalized figures in the production of national memory. The situation – as the recent critical discussion of Borneman and Ghassem-Fachandi's work on "welcome" in Berlin makes clear – requires considerable effort to disaggregate, and anthropological intervention, if it is to be meaningful, must resist a quick ascent to monolithic descriptive categories. Important work has examined the connections between dominant cultures of memory in Germany and the politics of globalization (Graves 2014), as well as the violent anti-migrant politics that marginality has produced (Shoshan 2016). Supposedly European experiences, like those of the Jewish writer in exile, are often made into yardsticks against which all other experiences of displacement and suffering are measured. This is especially salient for German youth who grew up in the shadows of Historikerstreit – public debates among intellectuals in popular newspapers and the urgency of working through the past – and for whom there is an ever-present worry that the guilt of their grandparents will begin to feel more settled or even onerous. The metaphysical exemplarity of the Jewish victim, I argue in chapter three, leads both to a masculine desire to know the pain of the other, impossible to satiate, and to a wielding of that figure against primarily Muslim writers today. On the ways decolonization also set the context for galvanizing Holocaust memory, see Rothberg (2020); Özyürek (2018) has likewise written on the ways Muslim-Germans' relationship to Holocaust memory is scrutinized. See also Doughan and Tzuberi (2018).
27 See also Moses (2007).
28 Rothberg and Yildiz 2011.
29 Boyer 2005. Dominic Boyer has helpfully read this turn inward as a sign of the transposition of the intellectual's "indifference" to the world onto the nation. But it could also be interpreted as a type of colonial reason that draws the world inward. A romantic nationalism was combined with a cosmopolitan, universalizing impulse, in which an imagined future Kulturstaat (a cultural state) emerged from a world-historical process mediated by a translocal estate of the educated. This was a feature of the original conception of world literature, but also of practices of world history, philology, and anthropology that serviced the interests of a rational modern desire for intellectual mastery over the world by measuring, classifying, and organizing; in this case, by managing the exchange of substantivized and interchangeable ethno-national identities as cultures. The institution, they hoped, would replace the aristocracy who had formerly aligned themselves with the industrial bourgeoisie, not with the merchant class, as had been the case in the bourgeois revolution in France. On this difference and the role of the cultural bourgeoisie see,

for example, Föllmer (2002), Kocka (1992), Blackbourn and Evans (1991), Fehrenbach (1994), Giesen (1998), Frevert (1989), Hohendahl (1985), Tatlock (2010), and Breuilly (1992).
30 McGetchin 2009.
31 Leavitt 2014.
32 Germana 2009.
33 They are assumed, Susan Gal (2006) writes, "to be nameable (English, Hungarian, Greek), countable property (one can 'have' several), bounded and differing from each other, but roughly inter-translatable, each with its charming idiosyncrasies that are typical of the group that speaks it."
34 As cited in Cassin et al. (2014). If in France and England translators insisted on the universality of European languages and therefore on the domestication of "foreign" texts, German romantics sought to "foreignize" translations to highlight their unique and separate character. See Berman (1984); on this history, see Leavitt (2010).
35 As cited in Friedrich (1986).
36 Mani 2016.
37 Ibid. In a letter to A.W. Schlegel in 1797, Novalis argues that Germany manifests a national inclination to translation, an irresistible impulse that Germany owes to its cultural emphasis on Bildung (cultivation), a quality it shares only with late Roman literary culture (Kultur). "Germanness is a cosmopolitanism mixed with the most vigorous individualism. Only for us have translations become expansions ... One translates out of love for the beautiful and for the literature of one's home country." The romantic "will to translate everything," on my interpretation, expressed a national desire to bring the world home.
38 It also extends beyond material borders, administrative offices, and documentary practices, into what Mariam Banahi (2020) describes as an imaginative geography that produces identity in ordinary conversations and everyday encounters. See also Giordano (2008).
39 Blommaert 2010.
40 Malkki 1995.
41 Holmes and Castañeda 2016.
42 Cabot 2019.
43 See Söderström et al. (2013), Randeria (2016), and Conrad and Randeria (2002).
44 Ticktin 2011.
45 Björgvinsson at al. 2020.
46 In this way, the concerns of my interlocutors often reflect similar debates in academia, about the recuperation of cosmopolitanism or its combination with a critical attitude (Robbins 1998; Schiller & Irving 2017).
47 On the earlier history of this moniker, see, for example, Kiaulehn (1997).

48 The book was publicly presented for the first time at prestigious Internationales Literaturfestival Berlin (ILB), which had declared the refugee crisis one of its annual themes. The ILB the premier event in the city founded ten years earlier by Ulrich Schreiber with help from the German UNESCO committee and the state as "the most international of all international literature festivals," which organizers described as a "lively, polyglot forum by and for literature enthusiasts" and a place where literature serves as "bridge between cultures." (As quoted in Janzen 2017.)

49 A large body of scholarship in Germany, particularly in political sociology, has tracked these legal regimes and the protest movements that have emerged in response. See, for example, Steinhilper (2017) and Schwiertz (2016). See also the text of Asylverfahrensgesetz, §85.

50 As Janzen (2017) notes, the book itself, the festival, and the reviews all serviced a story about cultivated Weltoffenheit, "awareness" and "openness" to the world, a would-be counter-point to the various barriers raised against voices of those excluded by the migration regime but which was really oriented toward the "self-formation" of the European audience.

51 I owe this thought to Fred Moten (2017; 2003) and especially his reading of Hartmann (1997).

52 It is worth briefly situating these recent developments against the backdrop of historical shifts in the dynamics of law, class, and cultural practice (Narotzky and Smith 2006). Jan-Jonathan Bock and Sharon Macdonald (2019) have recently provided an overview of these trends, emphasizing changes in language in light of changing economic conditions. In the introduction to their recent book on the "welcome" of refugees, they trace how the West German Wirtschaftswunder, built on currency reform and low rates of inflation, created renewed demand for industrial labour. In response, Gastarbeiter (guest workers) agreements were intended to be temporary-stay accommodations primarily for men, and by end of the period, BRD had the highest net migration of any country in the region. The state was explicit that it had no intention of providing a pathway to citizenship for labour it considered temporary. Provisions were dismal in swelling cities. Initially, the state responded to labour shortages by encouraging migration of so-called "ethnic Germans" fleeing Soviet pogroms, though their integration was plagued by "problems" of religious difference and scarce resources. Germany had lost its colonies before the war, unlike France or England where labourers primarily moved from the postcolony to the metropole where they could claim citizenship and which provided considerable new labour.

Bock and Macdonald trace how East Germany also suffered a labour shortage after the war, and the Soviet's relocated workers from other communist countries (Vertragsarbeiter, contract workers) but kept them strictly divided from German labourers – though this population was comparatively small. In the West, there soon emerged a discourse of Überfremdung (over-foreignization), cast in terms of the potential for social disharmony or unrest. (Bock and Maconald 2019; see also Herbert 2001.) This lead the West German government to form a (strategically underfunded) new department in the 1970s to administer integration. This moment was marked by a subsequent linguistic shift, both among guest workers themselves and in the rhetoric of national political parties. Earlier, the assumption had been that if migrants stayed, they would ultimately become indistinguishable from Germans – workers would either assimilate (anpassen) and stay or return home. The worry became that integration would preserve cultural difference, threatening to overtake "German" culture.

This latter change also coincided with a long period of centre-right rule, during which CDU politicians campaigned on the assertion that Germany was "no country of immigration" (kein Einwanderungsland), even as some legal protections were extended for labour migrants. German industry could still not afford to rely on citizen labour alone, and competition for wages created structural antagonisms that further advantaged capital. An attendant exponential rise in the number of asylum cases during the 1980s and 1990s was met with public warnings about "hordes" and "waves" of migrants and an increase in violence at asylum processing centres, as well as constitutional reforms supported by all parliamentary parties that restricted the rights of petitioners and long-term residents. A growing number of citizenship claims were also made under provisions for naturalization by descent by Spätaussiedler, late-returners from the former USSR, who were in turn attacked for an assumed unfamiliarity with the German language and local custom – a position that complicated ideological support for limiting right of citizenship ius sanguinis that had been formally instituted in 1913 (Brubaker 2009).

One fascinating consequence of this situation was that in the East, in addition to the attacks, political rhetoric, and strong right-wing votes, a number of former DDR residents converted to Islam (see Özyürek 2014). In 1998 the situation changed again. A centre-left coalition was elected and the government extended possibilities for applying for citizenship beyond blood descent. Then-chancellor Gerhard Schröder called for a commission to investigate the status of long-term migrants and their integration, and an official policy of "multiculturalism" was adopted by major parties. Liberal commentators in Germany often considered this to be the first moment in which a modern German government took stock of the fact of durable migrant communities in its midst and that return could no longer reasonably be assumed. But it was the political right that successfully polarized debate, stoking fears about citizenship reform. One campaign slogan, for example, called for "[German] children rather than Indians." The shift toward "knowledge work" throughout Germany but especially in Berlin effected further realignments of race and class. Within a broader post-industrial "colonization of life by work," labour done by upwardly mobile migrants was simultaneously seen as desirous and discounted (Amrute 2016). While some forms of such labour, such as IT work, might have been predicated on particular cognitive faculties of labourers and yet signified as "universal" and "unmarked," literary and cultural labour worked in the opposite direction – marked and particular despite the underlying assumption of universality.

53 De Genova 2017.
54 As is the preoccupation of Jacques Ranciére's (1998; 2000; 2011) influential body of work.
55 "Refugee-helper."
56 Cole 2019.
57 Ataç et al. 2015; Wilcke and Lambert 2015. After the Second World War, the West German constitution established a broad asylum provision explicitly as a reparation for German crimes and which was in effect until re-unification, when it was amended to include a provision, called 16a, that denied protection when an applicant had crossed another safe country on their way to Germany. This provision has been important in light of debates about "burden" sharing among European Union member states, and has been used to send petitioners back through endless circuits within the European Union. It is also used to deny the claims of those fleeing states deemed "safe." In particular it allows the state to activate the temporality of "crisis" to determine whose claims are most pressing and deserving of entry. The Ausländergesetz, the law that had governed West German migration policy since 1965 and was adopted by the unified government, expired in 2004 and was replaced by the Aufenthaltsgesetz. The old law, re-affirmed in 1990, granted limited voting rights and made it possible for children of guest workers (and long-stay guest workers themselves) to eventually apply for citizenship. The new law did away with fine-grained distinctions among residency permits and more sharply distinguishes temporary and permanent settlement. Asylum seekers, and those who were given temporary stays of deportation (Geduldete, tolerated) found themselves curtailed by the Residenzpflicht, administered by local Ausländerbehörde, foreign

offices. In the years since, the state has declared which countries of origin would be "safe" for return and has overturned earlier court rulings that guaranteed quality of living standards for asylum seekers.
58 Webster 2012.
59 Smith 2021b.
60 But inhabitants of the former East Berlin have increasingly been displaced by new economic and linguistic conditions this attraction in part produced, not least a demand for English-language competence and changes in credentialing expectations. If the initial public erasure of signs of the DDR cleared out a space for the emergence of a palpable nostalgia for the East, often called Ostalgie (Cooke 2003), the clearing out of so-called "real Berliner" opened up further possibilities for resignification by the time I arrived. Debates about memorialization of Berlin's Soviet past lingered, but at least in the city's centre, these were increasingly marginalized by those for whom the memory of the DDR was less immediate. Areas at the centre of ambitious Soviet housing projects were re-signified as peripheries and associated in newspapers with racist and anti-Semitic violence committed by the Wendeverlierer (transition losers) produced by global shifts in production. As Daphne Berdahl's ethnographic work in Berlin in particular documented (Berdahl 1999; 2009; 2010), re-unification brought with it an explosion in the Ostalgie industry, the products of which could be put to both hegemonic and oppositional uses (see also Eidson 2000). On notions of community and sanctioned commemorative practices in this period, see Blum (2004) and Enns (2008).
61 These figures are according to state census. Numbers have changed in relatively equal measure for those coming Africa and North America, though at a slightly greater rate from Asia and within the European Union. Migration from Turkey specifically, at the same time, has declined.
62 Estimates vary on the percentage of the economy dedicated to creative industries, from 10 per cent to as high as 25 per cent of regional GDP. Most sources however agreed that the percentage is far higher in Berlin than in any other part of Germany. At the time of my fieldwork, more than 220,000 people were reportedly employed in the sector.
63 Wurtscheid 2021.
64 Lowe and Lloyd 1997. "However dominant a social system may be," writes Raymond Williams (1979, 252), "the very meaning of its domination involves a limitation or selection of the activities it covers, so that by definition it cannot exhaust all social experience, which therefore always potentially contains space for alternative acts and alternative intentions which are not yet articulated as a social institution or even project." The problem is the idea of fixity and resolution. The problem isn't that the possibilities have been exhausted, but that they have

been fixed; rather than reach another shore, taking steps into the future figures as a return to everyday life, "to be continuously and surprisingly surprising, discovering surprise where you least expect it, in the banal." As Frantz Fanon (2008) writes at the end of *Black Skin, White Masks*, "I should constantly remind myself that the real leap consists in introducing invention into existence. In the world through which I travel, I am endlessly creating myself."

65 Berlant 1991.
66 Augé 1995.
67 Warner 2002a; 2002b.
68 Anderson 2006.
69 On some relevant antecedents of contemporary practices, for example, see Felsmann and Gröschner (1999), Hertz (1979), and Hundt (2000).
70 C.f. Susana Narotzky's (2011) view of the relationship between class, memory, and future orientation of collective imaginaries.
71 "Berlin should be/is no longer cool."
72 "the line went straight to the middle of the heart."
73 Left-wing activists have been mobilized especially on housing reform, squatting in buildings they painted with slogans of resistance and advocating expropriation policies that will convert hundreds of thousands of privately owned buildings to public housing. In 2012 and 2013, a number of high-profile incidents saw stores and apartment buildings graffitied with phrases parodying anti-immigrant and anti-Semitic language, repurposed against the Schwaben, southern Germans who were assumed to be upper-class drivers of gentrification and displacement of lower-class residents. In 2016, one of the Berlin's most famous squat projects, Rigaer 94, was raided by police by riot gear under a very broad city safety ordinance, leading to lengthy court battles and public debates over whether the city government should purchase the properties to de-escalate tensions. Urban studies research (Bodnar and Molnar 2010) has tracked also how the state's relatively prolonged involvement directly in the house market, and it's huge over-estimate of population growth after the fall of the Wall, affected the market. Public subsidies for multi-family dwellings, however, quickly ran dry in the 2000s. As high as 87 per cent of the city's residents are renters. Despite the high numbers of non-citizen residents, the real estate market remains (in part because of this structure) resilient to globalization.
74 Jorg Braunsdorf, who owned Tucholsky Buchhandlung on Tucholskystraße, received wide attention for founding a resident's group, three hundred strong, to counter march. Heinz Ostermann, who started a similar group, had his car burned outside his bookshop in Neukölln. In 2017, violence similarly erupted at the stall of a far-right publishing house at a major

national festival; the inclusion of the same neo-Nazi imprint led to the withdrawal four years later of prominent Black author Jasmine Kuhnke, who refused to share a venue with an organization that called for her deportation.
75 Çağlar (2016) observes that despite the important critical uses of this language, it has its own chronotopes that require unpacking. While artists have been at the forefront of these efforts, for an example of scholarly work on this perspective, see Attia et al. (2018).
76 Otoo, who came to Berlin from London, made headlines when she won the Bachmann Prize for her short story "Herr Gröttrup setzt sich hin." At the annual Tage der Deutschsprachigen Literatur, of which the Bachman awards are a major component, Otoo delivered a memorable speech entitled "Dürfen Schwarze Blumen Malen?" (Can Black Flowers Paint?), a searing critique of the enduring exclusion violence directed at Black people in Germany, including in its literary circles, much to the consternation of some members of the jury.
77 Part of global protests following the killing of George Floyd in 2020.
78 Cavell 1979; Moran 2011; Das, Jackson, Kleinman, and Singh 2015.
79 Webster 2020.
80 Methodologically then this book builds on insights from scholarship on a wide range of linguistic practices without trying to elide their differences. This includes work in the ethnography of reading (Boyarin 1993; Rosen 2015) as well as ethnographic research ostensibly focused on other kinds of practices, but where reading and engaging with literary work is an integral part of everyday life – in newspapers in teashops (Cody 2011; 2013), in the course of learning of religious texts to fight legal battles over property (Khan 2012), or in the passing of bits of poetry written on court documents in a prison (Hakyemez 2017).
81 For example, Caton (1990), Bush (2020), Webster (2016), Furani (2012), and Abu-Lughod (2016), among others. While less common, there is also a burgeoning body of scholarship on the ethnography of "migrant literature" (Olszewska 2015).
82 Though certainly its iconicity is a matter serious political consequence.
83 See Blommaert (2010) on the ways globalization has forced a rethinking of categories in sociolinguistics. At times, this takes the form of a "linguistic market," but it can take other forms as well.
84 I am reminded of Bahktin's observation that people argue with Dostoevsky's characters.
85 Alworth 2016. While I share Alworth's concerns about these senses and elisions of the site, we take this issue forward in very different ways.
86 Wittgenstein 1954, 567.
87 West 1989.

88 Schielke and Shehata (2021) make this point nicely when they say literature should be "described in historical context" rather than "defined."
89 Das 2020.
90 Language has been described as an "activity in a particular context, co-evolving along with that context, in part constitutive of it." See also Felski (2008) and Debaene (2010).
91 Cavell 1979, 52.
92 I take this exploratory quality of a life in language to be a major theme of Marco Motta's recent work (2019; 2021). Like Motta, I do not take this to suggest by this that the concept of literature lacks any inner constancy, that it could made to do anything, according to a private interest.
93 Wittgenstein described these connections as "family resemblances," a "complicated network of similarities overlapping and criss-crossing: sometimes overall similarities, sometimes similarities of detail." Cavell (1979, 185) writes elsewhere: "Any form of life and every concept integral to it has an indefinite number of instances and directions of projection; and that this variation is not arbitrary. Both the 'outer' variance and the 'inner' constancy are necessary if a concept is to accomplish its tasks – of meaning, understanding, communicating, etc., and in general, guiding us through the world, and relating thought and action and feeling to the world."
94 See Das et al., forthcoming.
95 Guetti 1993, 4.
96 Gal and Irvine 1995; 2018.
97 It is our vulnerable agreements in forms of life – and not our agreement in opinion, for instance, about what literature is and is not, what is real and what fictive – that provides the background against which I am able to see or make sense of any particular expression, or action, in this case, for instance, as literary (Wittgenstein 1954, 567). "Criteria are 'criteria for something's being so' not in the sense that they tell us of a thing's existence," Cavell writes (1979, 45), "not of its being so, but of its being so." Or, as Wittgenstein says, "It is not something that is represented, but is a means of representation." Said otherwise, the grammar of these agreement underlies our very understanding of what counts for us as the furniture of the world we inhabit and orients us to their bounds. Because we cannot appeal backwards to a prior region of rules to define phenomena, we know neither where any given literary project will lead nor that it will work out in the end.
98 Talal Asad (2020) writes that "the objects expressed by grammar aren't only palpable, bounded things, but also social arrangements, moral judgments, attitudes, feelings, actions, and the concepts by which they

are known. Getting to know grammar is learning the intelligibility of words – of discourses in worldly situations. It is to engage with the world in and through language even as a child learns to engage with it and live in it. And with the child's (and adult's) always incomplete learning of language, and through her emplacement in the tradition that tells her not simply that she is doing something wrong or right but what it is she is doing, the child acquires not only the skill to use language but also the 'self' that she develops and modifies through life." See also Moi (2017) on the relationship between this notion of grammar and our attunement to one another.
99 Chatterji 2021.
100 Hutchinson and Reed 2017.
101 Following Michael Lambek (2010), my view is that ethics is not a separate domain of social life or one that is only expressed in particular moments of rupture or judgment.
102 Paul Friedrich (1986) once wrote, "Poetic language is actualized in all domains of life … the poet, then, alchemizes through a special process from the prodigious skills that are mastered by every native speaker and used by everyone every day."
103 Diamond 1983: "I want to claim that ideas about particularity and its role in our lives, in our moral thinking and our moral responses, cannot be brought to awareness if we restrict ourselves to language conceived in certain sorts of ways. We need texts like literary texts … we need to be aware of them as the kinds of texts they are, aware of the language they use and what it does, if we are to hear the appeal to particularity." For Laugier (2022), literature is an important site of moral perception, which "achieves its aims by creating a background that makes the significant differences between life forms appear in bold outline."
104 Ibid.
105 Crary 2011, 250.
106 Asad 1986, 149.
107 See also Lambek (2021).
108 Perloff 2004.
109 Zumhagen-Yekplé 2020.
110 "Voice implies a claim," Laugier (2015) explains, a search for the right tonality, "an alignment between the individual voice and a linguistic community; that is, on the basis of the rightness or fit of agreements in language."
111 Leavitt 2010.
112 As Diamond (2012a) puts it, "There does not need to be, before the conflict, some 'universe of discourse' with its logical space, which provides standards to which you can appeal … our understanding of

what is real and what is unreal can be in part shaped by how we take such conflicts and by how we reason in response to them." This doesn't entail holding out for a space of encounter not laden with power.

113 I take this to be one of the central points advanced by Veena Das (2020) in her masterful *Textures of the Ordinary*. As Das makes clear, while we can describe these forms of life as culturally particular, we can also describe them as human forms of life. To speak of human forms of life is not the same as taking the human as a given, as an ontogenetic metacontext that secures the gathering up of local illustrations. When we speak in a human voice, it is always from within particular genres and codes. Enlightenment, colonialism, and capitalism share the presumption that certain forms of life, by virtue of their very location, are the repository of universalizing potential, that they can be naturalized as the human, whereas thought produced elsewhere is bound to local soil.

114 Cavell 1988, 40. "With each word we utter we emit stipulations," says Cavell, "agreements we do not know and do not want to know we have entered, agreements we were always in, that were in effect before our participation in them. Our relation to language – to the fact that we are subject to expression and comprehension, victims of meaning – is accordingly a key to our sense of our distance from our lives, of our sense of the alien, of ourselves as alien to ourselves, thus alienated." See also Mani (2017) on rethinking cosmopolitanism as a claim that subverts or challenges the nationalist ethos dominant in the contemporary "global political force-field."

115 Laugier 2015. At the same time, agreement can always be repudiated; or rather, language can always repudiate itself. Inquiry cannot stop at who is excluded or included but leads to the grammar of inclusion and exclusion itself.

116 Das 2020.

117 On this point, see Benoist's (2020) response to James Conant on alien forms of thought.

118 "We also say of some people that they are transparent to us," Wittgenstein (1954) tells us, but it is as important "as regards this observation that one human being can be a complete enigma to another. We learn this when we come into a strange country with entirely strange traditions; and, what is more, even given a mastery of the country's language. We do not understand the people. (And not because of not knowing what they are saying to themselves.) We cannot find our feet with them. 'I cannot know what is going on in him' is above all a picture. It is the convincing expression of a conviction. It does not give the reasons for the conviction. They are not readily accessible."

119 Laugier 2015; Moi 2017.

120 Das 2020, 44.
121 Schiller et al. 2006; Schiller 2008; Çağlar 1990; 1997; Newendorp 2020; Römhild 2004; 2010; 2014.
122 Jackson 2013b.
123 Laugier 2000, especially Chapter 8.
124 Friedrich 1986, 16.
125 "Kranz von Fragmenten," a phrase Friedrich Schlegel (1798) once used to describe conversations. A project, he goes on to say, "could be called a fragment from the future." Each is meant to be fragmentary in this sense. This approach could be said to embrace a romantic methodological mood (see also Khan 2020), an openness to the ways fragments of experience might reappear in new contexts or in a different register, sometimes unexpectedly. Life in language begins to look a bit circular, observes Cavell (1988) in the sense that words "in turns must be given over to the reaction of an other … as if we must at each step be prepared to be taken by surprise … and find ourselves in separation, exhausted of words." This is a picture of the world and language arising together in a constant activity of turning around – a life in language that remains to be discovered, and not as a book of rules that charts the way forward in advance. This picture of life in language as circular stands in stark contrast to the usual philosophical scene of knowledge, the "Platonic image of walking out of the Cave as going alone, and upward," as Cavell (1988) puts it, "this is for me an image not alone of the resolution in each step of a journey and in each term of a series or of an expansive concept, but of the condition of a certain sociality or congeniality." Fragments tend to arise at cultural crossroads, Cavell reminds us, "characteristically marked by the recurrences of a word, as if the thought were turning in on itself" (ibid.).

## 2. The Prosody of Social Ties: Poetry and Fleeting Moments in a Workshop

1 Haxthausen and Suhr (1990) argue that the city's "ethos" is "relentless self-renewing modernity." Webber (2008) similarly reads the twentieth century as one in which the topoi of the city, their spatial configurations of internality and externality, became especially entrenched, becoming layered with different times and affects. In the words of another novelist, Berlin is a city that attracts people because of its "weirdness, perpetual incompleteness, and outlandishness," an ugliness that "gives newcomers the feeling that there is still room for them … it is this peculiarity that makes Berlin the capital of creative people from around the world today" (Schneider 2014, 8). Or, as Scheffler (1910) put it a century ago: Berlin wird. Berlin will be.

2 Jones 2015.
3 Platthaus 2017. Others describe such events as places where "Middle Eastern poets rub shoulders with Indian short story writers, and novelists from European countries converse with their contemporaries from the Far East" (Kiesel 2009).
4 Before 1989 the neighbourhood had been associated with the subversive brands of literature that defined late-DDR underground culture. The economic downturn of the 1970s and weakening surveillance regimes lead to a youth counter-movement effected through secret meetings and "unofficial" publications run through small-batch printers, mirroring the rise of anarchistic politics in the West (Arnold and Wolf Gerhard 1990; Dahlke 1997; Dalhke et al. 2000). The circulation of French post-structuralist texts helped foster a sense not only of the possibilities for leftist, anti-statist literary forms but also the kinds of sociality such a project demanded (Boyer 2001b). This reputation, coupled with cheap housing, made Prenzlauer Berg especially popular early in Berlin's transformation.
5 In the 1990s, spoken-word and slam poetry made its way to Berlin from the United States (Westmayr 2010).
6 Masomi 2012.
7 Ibid., 62.
8 For Jakob (2013), this situation allows producers to "advance market positions" and to create opportunities for coalitions. Others have shown how experimental artists aligned with state interests. (On the enduring imaginary of DDR poetry in German lyric after the Wende, see Dahlke 2011.)
9 Çağlar 1998.
10 See also Strathern (2020) on how different ways of measuring time exposes different kinds of relations.
11 Ringel 2018. I foreground these experiences not because they are "representative" and not in order to evaluate whether they are borne out in everyday life, but rather as a response to Caroline Humphrey's call for taking seriously "whatever other frameworks of analysis" arise within the condition we are describing, which in her case is postsocialism (Humphrey 2002). Ringel writes, "Do we as analysts simply combine these heterogenous local metaphysics by constructing a metacontext or by choosing between them – and if so, on which analytic, political or ethical grounds? To avoid establishing a dominant narrative treat them as ethnographic objects – to choose among them and thereby to rarefy would be to miss out on 'diverse local meanings and situational uses of (contextual) knowledge and specific narratives and stories'" (Ringel 2018, 47–8, citing Humphrey).

12 Cruikshank 1997.
13 Anthony Webster (2016), for example, has shown how the sound of poetry, its muscularity and physicality, is tied to the difficulty of translation. It is no coincidence, he argues, that those who argue that "all forms of human communication" are infinitely translatable into one another also tend to relegate sound to a secondary position, even taking it to be inessential for meaning. What happens in poetic systems where ambiguities of reference are essential to meaning? "Resolving the ambiguity of poetry is not to translate poetry, but to convert it into *not poetry*," Webster writes. "Many of these discussions of translation are predicated on a language ideology (or, perhaps, an entailed semiotic ideology) that denies the materiality of languages." See also Tedlock (1996; 2002).
14 Hopefully it will be clear that I do not take prosody to be only a metaphorical description of the textures of social relations. As Goffman long ago noted, at a minimum, prosodic elements rather than syntactical elements are implied in shifts of footing, alignment of set stance or posture.
15 C.f. MacKendrick 2016.
16 I see a parallel with Piper's (2009, 76) discussion of the "whisper" as a drama of the move of the artist's control of the subject from "immediacy to semiotic and technological mediacy." The channel's embodiment by the speaker stands in stark relief against the larger economy of sound, wherein noise confounds the audience. The moment of the utterance is both hyper available and dislocates the reference, such that the material is made moveable – the uncanniness of speech reveals that the utterance can be moved.
17 Lotman 2009. The disenchantment of modernity has been extended through the commoditization of sound for middle-class listeners. Hearing, however, appears in the history of literature too as "nothing less than a bodily form of sympathetic vibration," in which a "telephone discourse" of simultaneous intimacy and distance is reinforced (Picker 2003, 87). The voice appears also with an excess of jouissance, thus levelling thought – as object of the scopophilic drive (Dolar 2006). The mediation of the soundscape has appeared as a site for articulating ethical self-formation (Hirschkind 2009) and of colonial control (Peake 2012), perhaps in response to, among other things, the kinds of subversion made possible through poetic speech.
18 Cavarero 2005.
19 This is my translation from the German translation.
20 When Sophie died in 2022, friends and frequent visitors to the shop took to social media to share their grief. Another bookseller to

whom Sophie had lent space for a time described how the "untidy," "magical," "rambunctious" shop was a home, that made it possible to form connections when people first arrived in Berlin, and that it was impossible to separate it from its proprietor's person.

21 Cavell 1979, 368–9.
22 Das 2015.
23 Shuster 2010.
24 This status of the durable is itself predicated on the privileged position of the message at the expense of the effects products by sound, or the text at the expense of the performance, particularly in once ubiquitous Gestalt theories of language. For example, if, as the Prague Circle claimed, a performance amounts to the addition of, at minimum, some element(s) to the realized pattern of speech (which may even distort or ignore the pattern prescribed by the text), then no "real science" of rhythm could be based on parole (Warren and Wellek 1956, 158–9; see also Majetka and Titunik 1984). At the same time, sound patterns could not be wholly divorced from meaning if we assert the integrity of the work of art, as Wellek and Warren famously do, such that even when we hear a language we do not speak, some measure of semiotic effect is produced in us purely through intonation. What Russian formalists called sound patterns (or figures) could be linked into more or less meaningful units of repetition, or else to structural oppositions, but which can have variable if characteristic relationships with meaning. For contextualist semiotics the sound of voices could be credited with only "slight" importance, due only to "hypnotic effects" of "rhythm and rhyme" (Ogden and Richards 1986, 236). For earlier anthropologists, the assessment of distinctions between the real and fictive was maintained across the shift from the time of *mythos* to time of *historia* and *logos*; but there was as well a certain rigidity and endurance of the structures available in a given repertoire of myths, so the concern with narrativity might arise only out of writing cultures. Histories, Jack Goody famously argued, even personal histories, organized narratively are "rare, and without documents, fragmentary" (Goody 2006, 18). Longer recitations would require particular ritual settings to meet the demands of attention; the triviality of fiction means long narratives might, like short fairy tales, be better fit for children. The memory practices of oral cultures, therefore, are not attuned to the verbatim repetition of a string of signs but to creative internalization. Oral memory appears as "experience reworked" – "performance is transmission" not exact forms, but through innovation (Goody 2000, 40, 44; 1987; see also 1986; 2006). And this seems quite true for the symbolic code. As Goody aptly pointed out, literacy was able thereby to underwrite the movement to empire and "civilization." The

historical scholarship on the book has adopted similar insights about the relationship between memory for the text and the persistence of social organization, in particular as it relates to the Thamousian distinction between the "dead" memory of grammata and the living memory of anamnesis (Detienne and Camassa 1988). Such interventions, to varying degrees influenced by anthropological sensibilities, have tended toward either the codification of the law or the scene of poetic pedagogy as the principal sites through which to think about this relation (Martin 1988).

25 Barber 2007.
26 Silverstein and Urban 1996.
27 For example, the nascent Multigraph Collective (2018).
28 I borrow this sensibility from Bate's (2009) *Tamil Oratory and the Dravidian Aesthetic*, shifting of the paradigm of division from Ferguson's diglossia to Bahktinian heterglossia, as structures of correspondence between speech genres and distributions of power.
29 Classically, much scholarship on memory has assumed that the primary aim of such practices was the recollection of narrative details (e.g., Carruthers 2008; Yates 1966). Others, like Carlo Severi (2015) have more recently argued that the ephemerality of the artifactual records associated with oral performances, and which earlier anthropologists thought to be indicative of disordered thought (and thereby, vulnerable memory), are better read as mental artifacts of a chimeric imagination. They are material traces of a process of imagistic condensation that encode memory for objects other than those necessary for the recollection of orders of events (cf. Bloch 1998).
30 Faudree 2012.
31 Weidman 2014.
32 Bauman and Briggs 2003.
33 Harkness 2013.
34 Das 2007.
35 Caldeira 2012. Where visual and public forms of art are often the primary media through which claims on urban space are articulated, literature has enjoyed a privileged status in Berlin. Dippel (2015) makes a related case for the ethnography of literature in Austria.
36 Schipsal and Nichols 2014.
37 Laugier 2015.
38 Simmel 1903.
39 Debord 1967.
40 de Certeau 1984.
41 Augé 2002.
42 Hall 1973; Radway 1991.
43 Felski 2008.

44  Anderson 2006.
45  Warner 2002a.
46  Ibid., 58.
47  Other public forms (e.g., national fantasy) point to a set of relations prior to the textual encounter, "an explication of ongoing collective practices, and also an occasion for exploring what it means that national subjects already share not just a history, or a political allegiance, but a set of forms and the affect that makes these forms meaningful" (Berlant 1991, 4). Such fantasies are made corporeally, leading to a tension between the individual, subjective experience and the collective. The everyday appears as the source of its own fantasies, and the distancing of the living body from those fantasies of social totalities has been the tactic of domination, as well as a mode of hope (193). Rather than read such fantasies as inferior forms of intimacy in the face of growing restrictions to face-to-face relations in the liberal public sphere, and in tightening proscriptions of behaviour, might literature offer "a different mode of being in the world" full of "potentially more vital relations" and enabling "unfamiliar or illicit forms of social intercourse" (Silverman 2012). For a view of this literature from anthropology, see Cody (2011).
48  Ibid. See also Fraser (1992).
49  One might be drawn instead to thinking of such scenes as points of intersection not only of multiple forms of publics, but also the production (and consumption) of cultural commons. In line with recent Marxian theories of the city, literature certainly appears in Berlin as both a "product of labour and the means of future production" (Hardt and Negri 2009) and so creates a social world which is both theoretically open and contentious. But if many especially in urban anthropology have been interested in the forms that claims to the city take, the commons also reminds us of how enclosures protect the commons not from overuse (as in the case for arguments about the scarcity of natural resources) but banalizing abuse (Harvey 2003). In other words, we have to be vigilant in our attention to the particular ways it is threatened by (or really, shot through with) bourgeois logics of property. Moreover, ethnographic use of this contradictory language should be on guard not to elide the very different implications of power that constitute the field – for instance, by imagining a future open commons as emancipating by overcoming a particular relation of production without overcoming alienated labour itself (one would also need a more robust account of these multiply intersecting relations), or that a cultural commons is a domain conceivably set apart from others on which it might impinge.
50  wa Thiong'o (2012), for example, has argued that recent interest in the oral aesthetic is motivated not only by a desire to overcome the rigid

boundaries between forms but also because of its "social function," in the assumption that its spontaneous openness to the world might lead to a mindset given to connecting socially. This inversion echoes Socrates's (and Aristotle's) claims to the animacy of speech in order to subvert the "aesthetic feudalism" inherent in the primacy of written language – a play which ultimately stages the drama of (post)colonial knowledge. He extends this criticism, following Gabriele Schwab, to chide Lévi-Strauss for not recognizing himself, a master of writing, as the subject of play in the hands of the Nambikwara chief, the master of oratory. The encounter stages for Thiong'o a drama of postcolonial power; my own interest is, however, in its playfulness. It is a play that mirrors, in Thiongo's own language, the fluidity of the relation between prosaic and poetic logics. Its aesthetic, moreover, derives its relation to "social function" by means of "intimate relationship(s) and involvement with society" (ibid., 73). Reviewing his own work, and Bekederemo's writing on the Ijaw epic *Ozidi*, he says, succinctly: Drawing from the "spontaneity and liberty of communication inherent in oral transmission – openness to sounds, sights, rhythms, tones, in life and the environment" – could lead to a mindset "characterized by the willingness to experiment with new forms": in short, a willingness to connect.
51 Bachelard 2013, 58.
52 Muriel Rukeyser (1996) likens this to a lightning flash, a moment of energetic exchange – not a discrete event but a manner of "*going through an experience.*"
53 Bachelard 2013, 59.
54 Baudelaire, on the other hand, seizes on the instant more tranquilly. Baudelaire writes, "When I was a child, my heart used to be haunted by two contradictory feelings: the horror of life, and the ecstasy of life." In an instant they are brought together, leading Bachelard to the shocking pronouncement that *all morality is instantaneous.* This is not to say that it arrives from a singular event of judgment, however. His opposition to Bergson's *la durée* is, to be precise, a challenge to continuity. It is an endeavour to think of the intimate ambivalence of the moment without falling into a melancholic longing for the past or a foolish desire for the future.
55 Kearney 2008.
56 As cited in Kearney (2008, 41).

### 3. Exile in Translation: The Politics of Remaining Unknown

1 Liao 2010a.
2 Liao 2010b.
3 Liao and Wojak 2019, my translations.

4 Blommaert et. al. 2017. The case they describe is the asylum office, but I want to extend this issue to other related social situations in the wider context of migration politics.
5 It hopefully goes without saying that most migrants in Germany are not marked as "exiles" or "refugees," nor are they considered "writers," and there are serious problems with the weighty "categorical fetishism" that is taken for granted in much academic literature (Crawley and Skleparis 2017). And as Holmes and Castañeda (2016) argue, such categories are both legal instruments and value-laden descriptors, often used to shift blame from structural causes to the displaced; i.e., by distinguishing the "deserving" refugee from the "undeserving" migrant with dire, often life and death, consequences. The greater portion of migrants historically entered Western Germany under the Gastarbeiter (guest worker) program, or to a lesser extent, as Vertragsarbeiter (contract worker) in East Germany – temporary labour who in both cases filled major post-War shortages in both East and West Germany, but who were always expected to eventually "return home," which the state was late to realize would not come to pass. Growing resentment among the white citizenry framed migrant labour as a threat to national identity and cohesion, while labourers themselves had no pathways to citizenship or political representation. By the 1980s through the end of the 1990s, the governing centre-left SPD tried to resist the discourse of assimilation (Anpassung) by de-coupling cultural identity from "integration," where the latter became primarily a matter of economic independence (a view still prevalent in Berlin's city-state official migration policies). Many former guest workers were themselves unwilling to assimilate and uninterested in citizenship, especially those from Turkey who intended to eventually return (Hunn 2005). In 1998, citizenship requirements were loosened by the coalition government – a fact that drove subsequent right-wing backlash in the 2000s against the "failure of multiculturalism," and ultimately its replacement by a resurrected language of Leitkultur – the idea that a "dominant set of values, views and behaviours – a culture – that should guide or lead, and be shared by, all members of a given society" (Bock and MacDonald 2019, 24).
6 My emphasis.
7 Webster 2010; Agha 1998.
8 Silverstein 2003.
9 Webster 2010. In the case of intercultural performances among Navajo poets, one way of complicating this exchange is through code-switching around terms considered "incommensurate" with target languages in the Navajo case; for example, Webster shows, personal names and place names, where there is a marked tension between Indigenous place-naming practices and Euro-America inscriptive practices.

10 While a number of scholars have pointed to the considerable role played by Turkish "migrants" in increasingly diverse fields of cultural production, especially in poetry and cinema, this has greatly been predicated on the relatively stable opposition of identity categories (and their subversions) as terms of engagement or encounter (see also Kosnick 2007) – if popular art forms associated with minority identities have often been imagined to make possible "new spaces of identification," this has by and large contributed to the re-inscription of their essentialized "cultural difference" (Çağlar 1998; 2016). "In this discursive environment, in which cultural difference is dichotomized and social activists have denounced multiculturalism as a policy that encourages the maintenance of a parallel society," Katherine Pratt Ewing (2006) argues, "a popular solution to the problem of integration has been a celebration of hybridity." These hybrids valorized "culturally 'in-between' spaces, such as the Turkish girl who takes up boxing or the successful German-Turkish entrepreneur." But because this language fails to capture the ways that individuals "manage inconsistency," Pratt Ewing contends that "an ideology based on the assumption of cultural difference and the celebration of hybridity as a strategy for the mediation of this difference actually makes the process of integration more difficult. Not only does it posit and constitute homogeneous collective identities that hamper recognition of the actual heterogeneity of those who fall within the category of this collective identity; it also exacerbates miscommunications between Germans and Turks and between generations within the immigrant community because of very different perspectives on what constitutes an acceptable mediation or hybrid" (Ewing 2006, 267; see also 2003). I would add that part of the reason for the German discourse's insistence on the trope of hybridity in these cases is the pervasive association of the Turk (and by extension the Muslim in general) with unskilled labour and as "bad migrants," whose culture is anti-liberal and thus unfit for assimilation, evidenced in fact by their unwillingness to assimilate ("They don't try to learn German"), in contrast to those "good" migrants, who are associated with high levels of educational achievement or who are more likely to be marked as intellectuals and artists, and thus whose "foreignness" is worthy of being preserved. Whereas for labour migrants, learning German is seen as requisite to integration, for refugee poets, for example, retention of the recognizably foreign quality of language is essential. And yet fluency is often treated as a receding horizon for "Turks," even those who were born and raised in Germany, whereas "good" migrants are often commended for their efforts.

11 The writer in exile, writes Edward Said (1996) in his reflections on Theodor Adorno's life in America, "exists in a median state, neither

completely at one with the new setting, nor fully disencumbered of the old; beset with half-involvements and half-detachments; nostalgic and sentimental on one level, an adept mimic or a secret outcast on another." For the writer, he continues, exile "in this metaphysical sense is restlessness, movement, constantly being unsettled, and unsettling others." This is why Adorno's writing is so "fragmentary ... jerky, discontinuous," his "failure to acclimate" a kind of political project of destabilization.

12 As Cristiana Giordano (2008) observes through her fieldwork with ethno-psychiatrists in Italy, complex practices of translation, effected by expert cultural mediators, strive to make the migrant "intelligible," a process she describes as a mode of citizen-making.
13 Mufti 2016.
14 Allan 2016.
15 The levelling-down characteristic of this imaginary "transnationally translatable monoculture" relies for Apter (2011; 2014) on prefigured pseudo-differences. Some languages nevertheless are more likely to be subject to "forcible transformation in the translation process" than others. It is unsurprising, therefore, that critical theory has offered some of the most powerful tools with which to begin to understand how cultural production in a globalized marketplace like Berlin relies on these translations to effect an abstract domination, where literatures encounter one another as things and mediate thereby an abstract social relation. Raymond Williams (1977) points out that the modern concept of literature itself, which only arises in the Middle Ages, achieves an impressive ideological feat in this way. Whereas it initially was associated in Europe with general literacy and with consumption, starting with the industrial revolution literature was increasingly seen as specialized labour and opposed to "abstract and generalizing modes of other 'kinds' of experience" like society or culture. The greatness of concrete works was thought to work *against* abstraction, even as they are predicated on an essential abstraction from the particular, resulting in a remarkable fetishization.
16 In this way, Allan (2016) argues, literary practice emerges as a site not just of traffic between geographical sites of enunciation, but as world-making.
17 Apter 2014.
18 Particularly over whether or to what extent its promise is recuperable for modern heuristics of translation studies, Since the 1990s, public and academic discourse alike have seen renewed interest in the category of world literature (see especially Damrosch 2006; 2018; Damrosch and Spivak 2011 on its relationship to the discipline), including a marked turn toward its critique (Apter 2014; Allan 2016; Cheah 2014). Many

trace origins to J.W. Goethe's appeal to Weltliteratur as "the universal possession of mankind, revealing itself everywhere and at all times" – a statement often invoked in liberal cosmopolitan spaces in Berlin. In the definition Goethe offers in a letter to Eckermann, he goes on to say that "while we thus value what is foreign, we must not bind ourselves to some particular thing, and regard it as a model." Rather than a set of texts, as Damrosch shows, Goethe's concept has been taken to imply a traffic in a network structured like a market mediated by practices of translation. Or else, to Marx and Engels famous statement on cosmopolitanization: "The bourgeoisie has through its exploitation of the world market given a cosmopolitan character to production and consumption in every country."

19 Hanks and Severi 2014.
20 I am inspired on this point by the work of Emily Apter, Barbara Cassin, Anthony Webster, and others who have made a powerful case for foregrounding the symptoms of difference that emerge from this networked traffic. Such a view would not take mistranslation as a pure antithesis of translatability but as marking the work of translation as always in motion and would treat mistranslation as also worthy of attention. If we give up the search for ultimate resolutions, for a guarantee that our communication will work out, then we can start to be attentive to what happens in the moments where a problem arises, indicated, for example, by the need to generate new words or the reactivation paleonymic dimensions of language. Failure, in other words, is not a problem to be overcome, certainly not once and forever. I am reminded of Paul Friedrich's (1986) remark that the fact that "even simple tokens are pregnant with poetry jumps to reverberating life as soon as we juxtapose and, inevitably, fail to translate 'a little girl' into 'ein kelines Mädchen,' or 'une petite fille,' or 'una muchachita.'" "The relativity of translation," he says provocatively, "suggests the heteromorphism of all languages."
21 Within legal discourse, this is also the limit case. Among the only laws that referred explicitly to the status of exiles (Vetriebenen, or expellees) in the German legal context is the Bundesvertriebenengesetz (BVFG), the Federal Law on Expellees, or more completely the Gesetz über die Angelegenheiten der Vertriebenen und Flüchtlinge (Law on the Affairs of Expellees and Refugees). The BVFG was signed into law in the former West Germany eight years after the culmination of the Second World War as a means of regulating the return from exile of Germans who fled the Nazis from the eastern territories. According to the text of the BVFG, the noun "exile" (Vertriebener) refers to those German citizens or ethnic Germans (deutscher Volkszugehöriger, lit. those who belong to the German people)

who were either forced out of Germany because of political opposition to National Socialism, were relocated due to diplomatic arrangements with non-German nations, or were unable to exercise their profession in exile, and later those who, prior to reunification in 1990, were forced from "Germany" (that is, the state in the West, not geographically) by virtue of their living in an area under Soviet occupation. (This law also applies to the spouse of any of the above.) This group is distinguished from Heimatsvertriebener (expellees from the homeland), those who left prior to 1937. German-ness is avowed by linguistic, cultural, educational, or other (largely undefined in the present context) markers, and can, importantly, be claimed by those who are the descendants of the expelled during the period of the war or subsequently, until reunification. This is significant because of repatriation laws that have sought to reincorporate especially Jews into German citizenry while systematically denying claims by non-ethnic Germans who have resided in the country even for generations (notably, the "ethnic Turks"). A special clause of the German constitution (Article 116, section 2) marks out the Jewish German exile in particular, allowing for reclamation of German citizenship by ancestors of those excluded by racial laws from 1933 until 1945.

22 I avoid the language of "liminality" here, despite its popularity in anthropological studies of refugee conditions, because, as Georgina Ramsay (2017) points out, "approaching the displacement of refugees uncritically as a liminal condition implies a linearity of experience whereby resettlement, by virtue of providing refugees with a recognized national identity, then resolves the 'problem' of their displacement."

23 See also Motta, forthcoming.

24 Das 2020.

25 Basso (2009) describes this as inability "to successfully play the game of social trickstership (following the rules of ritual communication and multiple personhood)."

26 Foucault 2004, 15.

27 Webster (2021) describes a lingual life history as "discursive acts of remembering, so too of attending to those traces of prior interactions. We come to know, in a variety of senses, through such acts of remembering." See also Kroskrity (1993).

28 I suspect that this making-equivalent may also issue from the desire to free certain aspects of German history – in this case, Germany's pretence to world literature – from of the taint of the Sonderweg: the idea that a special path had led Germany inevitably toward Nazism, and which therefore implicats the whole of German history prior to 1933 as well.

29 On the "bearable" life, see Hage (2019).

30 Schuenke and Struzyk 2013.

31 "Mein Weg führt in die Nacht, / wälzt / den Rest Kummer / ins Künftige. // Zwei Geschwister rufen / meinen Namen: / Zigarette / und vage Ahnung. // Ich zermalme den Gedanken / mit den Zähnen / und spucke ihn / schmerzerfüllt / auf die quirlige Straße. // Optimisten / schieben Wagen vor sich her / mit ihrer Zukunft, / tuschelnd, / die Augen leer, / recken sich ihre Nasen / nach dem Jasminzweig. // Die Sonne färbt ihre Lippen / dunkel / wie jede / glückliche Frau." My translation is from Leila Chamma's German translation of the Arabic. Published in the collection *Meerwüste*.

32 As recent anthropological research on the politics of difference in adjacent fields such as theatre and cinema in Germany has shown, creative practices are often thought to provide models for social life more generally. Katherine Ewing (2006) for instance argues that the circulation of cinematic images through Berlin "are particularly powerful when they consistent with other forms of knowledge that are tied to governmentality" As the major source of funding for filmmakers, the state exerts control over aesthetic guidelines that reflect its interest in producing certain kinds of citizen-subjects, staging questions about the "problem" of integrating Turks, or the "plight" of Muslim women. In his work on "postmigrant" theatre in the Ruhr Valley, Jonas Tinius (2016) suggests that this ready availability of public funding allows the time and space needed for experimental projects that problematize and critique political structures – as public institutions, municipal theatres theoretically have more direct access to policy-makers and are able to call attention to supposedly undertheorized domains of political life. In this way, theatre becomes a crucial site for developing political expertise, including by extending participation to marginalized groups and disciplining diversity into a vision for a "unified" cultural arena, even as something generated by creative praxis occasionally manages to escape prefabrication. (See also Tinius 2017.)

33 I read these scenes, to put it another way, as touching on the relationship between what Cavell identified as two forms of scepticism, namely concerning the external world and other minds. For Cavell, while doubt about the external world relies on the imagination of another for whom the facts could be known with certainty (i.e., someone who knows something I do not know, or about which I might well be wrong), this possibility seems less tolerable with regards to my own mind or subjectivity. "What I feel, when I feel pain, is pain," Cavell (1979, 418) writes, "so I am putting a restriction on what the Outsider can know. He can know something about another's pain that I cannot know, but not something about mine. He is not really an Outside to me. If he exists, he is in me."

34 The Shoah is only the latest incarnation, Seyla Benhabib (2018) argues, of this figuration of the Jew as the "eternal half-other," one which she takes to represent the supreme "political paradox of modernity."
35 Cavell (1979, 436, 437) describes the issue thus: "The problem of the humanitarian is not merely that his acts of acknowledgment are too thin, mere assuaging of guilt; but that they are apt, even bound, to confusion … it is apt to perpetuate the guilt it means to assuage." The thought comes in the course of Cavell's astounding reading of King Lear, in which Lear offers Edgar shelter and, in that moment, "he sees him as an exemplar of humanity, rather than as an instance of it." Why in Edgar, the outcast? Because he "exemplifies the restriction of society, that there is that in the human creature which is undefined by social station, or by any property; he is bare, laid bare. Call him an outcast … to have acknowledged him would have meant acknowledging himself as one who casts … The confusion is produced by an avoidance of the two choices open to him: either to reveal himself as one who casts out, or to cast himself out … But the surmise that I have not acknowledged about others, hence about myself, the thing there is to acknowledge, that each of us is human, is not, first of all, the recognition of a universal human condition, but first of all a surmise about myself."
36 This is an issue that Sandra Laugier (2015) has aptly described as a myth of inexpressiveness.
37 Some experiential acts are purely "solitary" while some are essentially social – they are directed in such a way that they require another "intelligent being" to pick them up (Moran 2018).
38 On this point, see especially Floyd (2007).
39 As cited in Garloff (2004).
40 Langer 1993.
41 Huyssen 2003. I am paraphrasing Alaida Assmann's (2006; see also 1999) reading of Koselleck against Bernard Giesen in her classical essay on the "long shadow of the past." For her, "the absence of such a body defines our remembrance." Assmann's introduction of the trope of the shadow was intended to nuance this scholarly presentism "by emphasizing the aspects of involuntariness and inaccessibility in the experience of those who engage with the traumatic past." C.f. Anson Rabinbach's (1997) sense of writing as a witness not for "mastery over the traumatic experience, but to write from the point of its historical caesura."
42 As cited in Cassin (2016).
43 Ibid.
44 I will take up in greater detail there the worry that the particular forms of talk about the past have become caricatured or cliched and thus an obstacle to a more just future. But my intention here is to first highlight

a common sense that there is a need for bringing to light to not just "the facts" but also the mechanisms of prejudice, a turn toward the illumination (and reintegration) of the subject to address its underlying malady would then lay the groundwork for the "captivating spell of the past" to be broken (Adorno 2005, 103).

45  For Gabriele Schwab, this incommunicability shows up in "symptoms" that through "hauntings" shift the burden to the next generation, who have a political or ethical obligation to carry them forward (Schwab 2010; Hirsch 2012; Friedländer 1987), like Sebald's Max Aurach. (C.f. Han and Brandel 2020.) The pressure to narrativity I describe here is to render otherwise fragmentary experience intelligible to those outside subjective experience, as if stories were somehow distinct from experience itself (Brandel and Bagaria 2020).

46  Adorno (1959) named a concern about the appropriateness of then-pervasive talk of Germany's "guilt complex" because it presumed that the "healthy and realistic" person is the one who could move on from the past. "Consciousness of historical continuity is atrophying in Germany," he observed, "a symptom of societal weakening of the ego." Adorno argued that that reality's frustrating of narcissistic individual drives led to a substitution of individual fulfilment with an identification with the (likewise narcissistic) collective. The eventual loss of National Socialism, the frustration of that attachment, however, was dealt with "merely" factually and its root causes never brought into consciousness. And "this is the social-psychological relevance," he writes "of talk about an unmastered past," that the wounded collective narcissism can affix to new nationalisms and material conditions, and so any would-be process of "working-through" the past has "degenerated into its own caricature." Without facing the conditions that produce bourgeois mentality, we are doomed to repeat ourselves.

47  Eric Santner's (1990) work is particularly relevant in this case, so let me take him as an example. Santer emphasizes a distinction between Trauerarbeit, the work of mourning the loss of a cathected object for its intrinsic qualities, from melancholia, where the object is loved for its mirroring of the ego. The outcome of a process of Trauerarbeit, he says following the Mitscherlichs, is ultimately the uninhibited re-integration of the ego, and the capacity to cathect new love objects. It was the latter, the reconstitution of the sense of self from its traumatic fragmentation (following the narcissistic compunction of Nazi society, the identification with the ideal leader) that should have preoccupied a healthy post-war Germany, but which was interrupted by communal defence mechanisms, not least the identification with the victim. The labour of working through this narcissistic pattern is deferred by the defensive identification

because "the capacity to feel grief for others and guilt for the suffering one has directly or indirectly caused, depends on the capacity to experience empathy for the other *as other*."

Santner notices that within a popular form of literary critical discourse (not least, in deconstruction) an "ethics of impossibility or undecidedability" is read into the labour of mourning of the Shoah. Postmodern pastiche and practices of translation emerge as stratagems for working through blockages of ego integration, the kind that would enable Germans to assume "postmodern, post-Holocaust selves." Trauerarbeit comes to be instituted as "the paradigm of translation, reading, and being (a speaking subject)" in general – a gesture that drains the encounter of affect, and evacuates particularity, making it impossible to distinguish any particular victim from another. He argues that for the postmodern critic, any use of language bears within it a "dispossession" of experience in favour of the signifier, a loss or wound that language is then imagined also to heal. In this way, deconstruction "represents an attempt to situate the study of literature, as poetics rather than aesthetics or hermeneutics, *beyond the pleasure principle*." The speaking subject, in other words, is *always* in mourning (of the referent), of the always already shattered world. The invitation to mourn the loss inherent in language in general allows or enacts, however, a particular mourning, the "coming to terms with one's complicity, however indirect or ambivalent, in a movement responsible for the extermination of millions."

Santer's position is compelling for the ways it reveals a bourgeois postmodernism's tacit reliance on a philosophical anthropology it claims to trouble. But his vision retains a sense that there is a way out of the bind, at which point "German cultural identity" will have successfully reconstituted itself. This requires, for Santer, a "good enough" empathic witness, "if it is not to become entrapped in the desperate inertia of a double bind, if it is to be integrated into a history." In denying the human, postmodernism had mistakenly denied "interpersonal rapport." For those of us in post-war generations, the task of "saying '*wir*' in an emphatic sense" again requires carving an "alternative legacy out of the archive of symptoms and parapraxes that bear witness to what could have been but was not." Catching a glimpse of what could have been allows for an excavation of what remains recoverable from the past. In coming to know more about the archive, in bringing to light those lost opportunities, something like a return to a state of healthy play becomes possible again.

48 Han 2020.
49 And historically specific. In fact, any effort to arrest the movement would, Adorno also argued, constitute reification. I am in Charles Clavey's debt on this point.

50 Han 2020.
51 Jackson 2013a. For Arendt – who is herself often made into a paradigmatic figuration of the persona of the exiled writer – narrative storytelling is a supremely political act of claiming what has remained in the shadows; what remains in the private realm is "deprived of the reality that comes from being seen and heard by others."
52 Rechtman 2017, 138.
53 Postcolonial literary criticism since Said (1983) has, on the other hand, suggested that the exilic consciousness of the intellectual breaks narrative through irony, through its unwillingness to be absorbed. "By virtue of living a life according to different norms, the intellectual does not have a story, but only a sort of destabilising effect; he sets off seismic shocks, he jolts people, but he can neither be explained away by his background nor his friends."
54 Buch Segal 2016; Mookherjee 2015. As Han and I earlier argued, "It is only after the fact that these circumstances become 'traumatic events' rendered in narrative form. Fragments of experience, however, may not fit this chronological narrative. They cannot simply be absorbed – or re-narrativised – into the categories of psychiatry, trauma theory, or local idioms of distress."
55 Ordinary ethics investigates efforts to "renew life, to achieve the everyday," especially under conditions "that erode the very possibility of the ordinary" (Das 2012).
56 There is an arresting moment at the outset of Audre Lorde's 1979 interview (1984) with Adrienne Rich, in which Lorde reflects on a feeling that one thread in her life has been the effort to "preserve my perceptions." "I kept myself through feeling. I lived through it. And at such a subterranean level that I didn't know how to talk. I was busy feeling out other ways of getting and giving information and whatever else I could because talking wasn't where it was at. People were talking all around me all the time – and not either getting or giving much that was useful to them or to me." Lorde describes how writing, how poetry became a response to the fact of people not listening when she spoke.

> ADRIENNE: Like a translation into this poem that already existed of something you knew in a preverbal way. So the poem became your language?
> AUDRE: Yes. I remember reading in the children's room of the library, I couldn't have been past the second or third grade, but I remember the book. It was illustrated by Arthur Rackham, a book of poems. These were old books; the library in Harlem used to get the oldest books, in the worst condition. Walter de la Mare's "The Listeners" – I will never forget that poem.
> ADRIENNE: Where the traveller rides up to the door of the empty house?

AUDRE: That's right. He knocks at the door and nobody answers. "'Is there anybody there?' he said." That poem imprinted itself on me. And finally, he's beating down the door and nobody answers, and he has a feeling that there really is somebody in there. Then he turns his horse and says, "Tell them I came, and nobody answered. That I kept [...]"

57 Naiko Saito (2009) explains how "finding a language is a matter of inheritance as much as invention, and how finding his own self is not a matter so much of the articulation and identification of that self but of encountering, persevering and acknowledging the rift within the self. He identifies this process as one of 'stealing' – in the sense both of the child's voice being stolen (the 'theft of selfhood, psychic annihilation' as he is moulded by or incorporated into the received language) and of the child stealing his voice from his parents (appropriating words for himself, against their apparently settled meaning in the vocabulary he inherits)."
58 Conant 2005.
59 Laugier 2015, 68.
60 Das 2007, 39.
61 Ibid, 45.
62 On the capacity of literature to move blockages, see also N. Khan's (2012) analysis of how writing provides an "orientation to striving" in Pakistan.
63 Das 2007, 48. Acknowledgment for Das and for Cavell does not function as an alternative to knowledge, as if it were capable of extinguishing worry that I will not be understood. It is an interpretation of it. While knowledge is normally posed as a solution to scepticism, by securing (circumscribing) the event or object, acknowledgement points to a recognition that I live my scepticism.
64 As Wittgenstein puts it succinctly elsewhere, "Nothing is hidden! Everything is open to view."
65 Das 2007, 47.
66 Cavell 1996.
67 Laugier 2015; 2018.
68 Das 2007, 5.
69 Here the "marriage" event that gives shape to the narrative is extended through the notion of the ordinary. "If some image of human intimacy, call it marriage," he writes, is, or has become available as the fictional equivalent of the ordinary, "then it stands to reason that the threat to the ordinary ... should show up in fiction's favourite threats to forms of marriage, namely in forms of melodrama" (Cavell 1996).
70 Cavell goes on to say "the woman's father, or another older man (it may be her husband), is not on the side of her desire but on the side of law, and her mother is always present (or her search for or loss of or

competition with a mother is always present), and she is always shown as a mother (or her relation to a child is explicit)."
71 See Cavell (1996, 85–100).
72 Cavell's reading of Emerson inverts not the relation between the masculine and the feminine, but instead between the child and mother. "Do not think the youth has no force, because he cannot speak to you and me," Emerson writes – the child's innocence, her openness to change, reveals to us that "one's subject position" does not "exhaust one's subjectivity" (35). It is the child's gaze upon her mother that Cavell opposes to Brecht's description of exile as a tension between two cultures – the woman's position in the melodrama is not a problem of "not belonging" but of belonging on the wrong terms (213). On drama in Brechtian guise in relation to the question of exile, the dialogical, and the problem of the "authenticity" of experience, from which Brecht distances himself, see, e.g., Feilchenfeldt (1986).
73 Cavell 1996, 9.
74 Berlant 2011.
75 Cavell 1996, 213.
76 Ibid., 34–6, and the lecture on *Stella Dallas*.
77 Ibid., 37.
78 The similarity between the scepticism that inheres in everyday life and these "scenes of excess," strikes Cavell as one reason for the popularity of melodrama, but here perhaps appears as an inversion of what Rancière calls an "excess of words."
79 Henderson 1992.
80 Kramatschek 2015.
81 Cixous 1976, 879–80, 883.
82 Das 2007.

## 4. In the Footsteps of a Flaneur: A Grammar of Returning (to a Street)

1 On the double senses of "bearing" the weightiness of history, see Lambek (2016; 2019).
2 Bonilla 2011.
3 Irving 2007, 193.
4 Augé 2002.
5 Augé 2009. Assmann (1988) notes the potential dangers that issue from this fact where memory is tied very closely to identity discourse.
6 Chatterji and Mehta 2001.
7 Debates about the once popular idea of the Sonderweg, the "special path" that lead Germany from the height of civilization to the worst human catastrophe, had long since done away with the possibility of

straightforwardly reclaiming even once seeming accomplishments. For decades, public debate had raged about how best to keep memory of Nazi crimes (and later, memory of East Germany) alive. By the time of my fieldwork, there was a renewed sense that for all the talk about memory that had ensued, little had really been done – Fabian once told me that in his view, with the exception of a brief moment in 1968 during student protests, few Germans had taken the time to think through their own emplotment in those fights (to accuse, as he put it, their own parents and grandparents of crimes) and so had learned how to express guilt without necessarily meaning it. If, on the one hand, it was considered necessary to continually mark national shame, the usual ways of looking back also seemed in many cases to carry the threat of becoming banal and thus ineffectual. In the 1980s and 1990s, and then again in the 2000s, professional historians and philosophers took to national newspapers to criticize one another over the means of public memory, a contest commonly known in popular parlance as the Historikerstreit. At the time, those on the political right, like Ernst Nolte, Michael Stürmer and Andreas Hilgruber argued the Holocaust was not an exceptional historical event, that moral comparisons could be drawn with Allied bombings, and that the root of German fascism lay in a response to the gulags. For Nolte in particular, the fact that the past would not pass away left the present unable to address more pressing concerns. On the liberal-left, Jürgen Habermas chastised this conservative apologetics as revisionism, and for treating genocide as an action that was regrettable, but understandable. If anything, for Habermas, Germany was all the more guilty because of its modernity, and so comparisons with other parts of the world were misguided. These tensions have even earlier roots. For Adorno (1959), "processing the past" (Vergangheitsbewältigung) has to be distinguished from, "working through the past," (Aufarbeitung der Vergangenheit) which carries a double burden of a public and psychodynamic consciousness. Working-through moves towards painful awareness and confronts it. This attitude of confrontation, he argues, inheres in a theory of self-cultivation handed down from the "Enlightenment" – indeed the structure of the essay is meant as a kind of parallel to Kant's essay on the meaning of Aufklärung. He goes on to argue that the term also offers a critique of processing the past, that is, its dialectical antithesis. This antithesis suggests a "wishing to turn the page, and, if possible, wiping it from memory." The aspiration is for a victim's forgiveness through forgetting. Yet this forgetting allows the past to live onward, even intensely – its life in the present is not an apparition of violence that is no longer with us, but a living presence, one that is manifest not just in the corners of society but everywhere.

Where working-through is conscious, critical (in the technical sense), self-reflexive, direct, and an act of *public* Enlightenment, processing is the disavowal or deflection of guilt, the wilful denial or forgetting, a misguided universalism. It is in this register of the disavowal of guilt that Adorno assess the "psychopathology" of the "general social situation." Thus he writes, "the idiocy of all this really does testify to a lack of psychic mastery and an unhealed wound – although the thought of wounds is more appropriate to the victims." Adorno's diagnosis is not of a guilt complex, but rather of repression. He wants to, "point out one of the tendencies covered up by the slick facade of everyday life before it overflows the institutional dams that formerly contained it … Enlightenment about what happened in the past must work, above all, against a forgetfulness that too easily goes along with and justifies what is forgotten."

8 See especially Jürgen Zimmerer (2011) and Dirk Moses's (2021) essay "The German Catechism" and the debates it inspired. Moses argues that the catechism involves an insistence on the singularity of the Shoah and the genocide of Jews, the historical claim that fascism marked a Zivilisationsbruch, a civilizational rupture, and that as a result of both, Germany owed Israel and Jews special allegiance. The German press immediately responded with bitter outrage and feigned shock. Jennifer Evans has curated an excellent set of essays thinking through the responses on the online forum *New Fascism Syllabus*.
9 Rothberg 2020.
10 As Tiffany Florvil (2020) shows in her groundbreaking work on the Black German movement.
11 Ibid.
12 Brandel 2022.
13 Didi-Huberman 2008
14 In the 1980s, for example, the influential "Prenzlauer Berg Scene" of artists and writers, as Dominic Boyer (2001b) shows, used a poststructuralist register gleaned from new printings of Foucault and Lyotard, to describe "the state's 'everyday language of power' and its 'empty rhetoric of talk.'" Their aim, he writes, was to subvert a structure whereby the state, obsessed with production, "functionalized all public language" by "exposing the fictions of 'linguistic continuity,' the limitations of linguistic order, and by continuous probing play into the structures and potentials of language." The writer Klaus Michael describes their efforts as mobilizing "the excluded real … against the forbidden and taboo realities fostered by the prevailing thinking."
15 These are concerns that shadow contemporary scholarship as well, as David Berliner (2005) warns, where the concept of memory is sometimes

overextended and thus deshistoricized. (See Antze and Lambek 2016 for one attempt within anthropology to re-contextualize the emergence of "memory" and its relationship to the formation of "imagined communities.") In his book on neo-Nazi youth in Berlin, Nitzhan Shoshan (2016) describes how in Germany, political categories like "right-wing extremism" are often deployed to "institutions and formal scripts meant to 'tame' anxieties, the return of the repressed" to camouflage the inherent tenuousness of political distinctions, and to restore a semblance of stability. In Germany, today's right-wing extremists appear as concrete incarnations of more general forms that continue to haunt the present. Yet the relation between the extreme right and the collectivity that defines itself, as it were, against it is not a simple, external dialectic between two separate terms that constitute each other through their differences. More precisely, as a political category, right-wing extremism operates in Germany as what he thinks of as a constitutive outside (Mouffe 2000, 21). Viewed in this light, right-wing extremism is at once incommensurable with and the condition of possibility of the collectivity, at once radically external to and fundamentally constitutive of it. It reveals, then, not so much what one is not but rather the nature of deep anxieties about the potential of becoming – or, indeed, already being contaminated by – one's nightmares; hence, the profound discomfort and angst that physical proximity to right-wing extremist "things" seems to provoke among many Germans. Of course, this unbearable intimacy has everything to do as well with the fact that, far from being reified as an "object," nationalism surfaces as a "subject" within virtually every German family in the form of ancestors. The loved ones of one's bloodline thus too often slip into the material of one's nightmares. The perpetual "return of the repressed" in such encounters produces enormous strain. It calls for institutionalized mechanisms and formulaic scripts in order to tame the anxieties that it incites, to camouflage the inherent tenuousness of political distinctions, and to restore a semblance of stability. This book explores some of the many social institutions that participate in this working through of a national neurosis. Perhaps not surprisingly, a prominent place is reserved in this enterprise precisely for repressive methods.

16 Nietzsche (1997) is describing how, from a Platonic point of view, the inadequacy of concretes lives to human ideals leaves us in dualist bind. These are the unpleasant memories cast out by the Saints. Compare with Adorno and Horkheimer (1997): "A constant sameness governs the relationship to the past as well ... Yet for this very reason there is never-ending talk of ideas, novelty, and surprise, of what is taken for granted but has never existed." Adorno and Horkheimer are of course

speaking here about the emergence of a phase of mass culture: "One might think that an omnipresent authority had sifted the material and drawn up an official catalogue of cultural commodities to provide a smooth supply of available mass-produced lines. The ideas are written in the cultural firmament where they had already been numbered by Plato – and were indeed numbers, incapable of increase and immutable."
17 Diamond 1991, 6.
18 Anscombe 1991, 119 (my emphasis).
19 Constantin Fasolt (2014) describes how such a view might be seen as a corrective to common kinds of mistakes scholars make in regards to history: "One form consists of believing that objective facts cannot conceivably depend in any way on how we learn to ascertain such facts, but must exist in some kind of 'reality' of things in themselves, which can then be imagined to be either material or ideal. Another form is based on the 'discovery' that the 'reality' of things in themselves can never actually be known. It consists of believing that there are no objective facts at all. Yet, different though these forms appear to be, they complement each other perfectly and lead into the same wilderness. They show how a confused relationship to our language results in a bad dialectic that makes us shuttle back and forth between equally nonsensical forms of hyper-objectivity and hyper-subjectivity … the essence of the Middle Ages is expressed by the grammar we master when we learn how to study the Middle Ages. The essence of the Middle Ages is nothing like an object existing out there in the past, much less a Platonic idea. It is a matter of the grammar that tells us what kind of thing the Middle Ages are. Grammar gives us the concept 'medieval.' Without agreement on the judgments that make something 'medieval,' we are in no position to communicate with each other about the Middle Ages, let alone their nature or existence."
20 Anscombe 1991, 116. One might object that this view commits us to saying that the past is fungible. Not so, says Anscombe. "The reason for thinking this," she responds, "is that if one states the criteria for saying something one may be claiming, or may seem to be claiming, to give a translation or analysis. It would follow that a change in the things that were the criteria for a statement about the past would entail a change in the truth of the statement. But if one gives up the idea that to give the criteria is to give a translation, then this no longer follows. And it is certain that we do use present criteria for statements about the past, and also that no change would make us say 'it used to be the case that Brutus killed Caesar, but since such and such a time it has been the case that Caesar killed Brutus.'"

21 The point here is not to answer sceptical doubt about knowledge of past events, where this would imply that the truth-condition of an utterance relied on a real but inexpressible, immediate or non-inferential experience, what John McDowell (2001, 299–306) termed a truth-linked realism. Such a view would not hold up the anti-realist charge that these conditions could not obtain for past events in the present (or, for that matter, the experience of another person's suffering). A better realistic view of linguistic competence involves, on McDowell's account, the claim that there are "some occasions when circumstances justify assertive utterances of sentences" about past events, "when their *truth*-conditions – which may on other occasions [be] hidden from us – make themselves [known]." There are detectable circumstances that justify assertions on the basis of their availability to consciousness, like those ones in which we learn to use a word, and there are those that do not. What counts for the realist is the "detectable obtaining of the circumstance that consists simply in such an event's having occurred: an instance of a kind of circumstance that is available to awareness, in its own right and not merely through traces going proxy for it, on some occasions, including this one, although, on other occasions, the obtaining of other instances can be quite outside our reach."

22 Fabian's educational background is clearly inflected in his deployment of the language of technique, as it carries shade of the Platonic notion of techne as productive of reflexive knowledge, and the Aristotelian association with disposition (*hexis*), as that which brings into existence as a form of reasoning, come hand in hand with Foucault's recalibration of techne as technology, as the governance of practical rationality by conscious end.

23 One thinks perhaps of Taussig's sketch-meditation on Benjamin's Denkbilder, simultaneously producing and describing "culture," not to mention the move to "story-telling as analysis" (Taussig 2012). It is coproduction with the people who lived there, not so far from reality enhancing collaborations (Povinelli 2011) that remake contemporary landscapes through the prism of the past.

24 Sharp et al. 2005.
25 Zukin 1995.
26 For example, the powerful work of Caldeira (2012).
27 Bourriaud 2002.
28 Chatterji and Lall 2014.
29 Harvey 2003, 14.
30 Seale 2005.
31 Buck-Morss 1986, 104.

32 Bäcker (2008) argues that despite their affinities, the two adopt different narrative strategies: "Hessel is Flâneuring [*Flanieren*] in space and Benjamin is 'Flâneuring' in time."
33 Already by the 1890s, Berlin had grown into the site of *Große Berliner Gewerbeausstellung*, a worlds-fair-like exposition that celebrated the considerable technological, scientific, and commercial advancements associated with the city.
34 *Die Welt von Gestern: Erinnerungen eines Europäers*. Zweig (1942) means it critically – he felt all "moral restraint had melted away" and was replaced by decadence.
35 Kracauers 1930.
36 De Certeau 1984, 161.
37 The significance of such a historical position, however, comes to light in the development of Benjamin's approach to texts, in particular with the break from a historiographic analysis that levels down revolutionary events in favour of a story of natural progress. The turn to the dialectical image in the 1930s (the textual practice whereby a certain present meaning of the past appears in a lightning strike) runs on parallel tracks to the encounter with Baudelaire. Literary physiognomic types arose in the city alongside panoramic representations of the *Tableaux parisiens* to ease anxieties about a social world that erased individuality, inevitably contributing to the phantasmagoria of Parisian life, a condition born of the commodity fetish and the covering-up of reality through the suggestion of the "real." Drawing together Ernst Bloch's language of "nonsynchronous contradictions" with Susan Buck-Morss's reading of Benjamin's *Passagenwerk*, Michael Taussig (1986, 166) suggests such contradictions "come to life where qualitative changes in a society's mode of production animate images of the past in the hope of a better future." Paraphrasing Bloch on the rise of German fascism, Taussig cites the "impoverishment of the Left in regard to revolutionary fantasy" that "made it an accomplice in its own defeat," and from which Germany might learn a lesson, if it were to put to better use the utopic images that, while "stimulated by the present, refer to the past in a radical way" thereby making possible the transfiguration of the promise for a future otherwise blocked by present conditions (167). The space of redemption is thereby shifted from the individual to what Rochelle Tobias (2012, 665, 679) calls the "mystical now and punctual present," a possibility she reads as located in the "shining (*das Scheinen*) in the night sky [that] symbolizes for Benjamin the possibility of freedom from all semblance (*Schein*) in a realm beyond art – in life or the ethical sphere." The possibility for a future rests (first with the poet and then the historical materialist) in the fanning of what Benjamin calls "the spark of hope in

the past," "signs of a life that is not constrained by the representations of art or the political order" (Tobias 2012, 680). Thinking revolution thus takes on a very different character.
38 Benjamin 1991, 537–69.
39 2013, 9.
40 "Fairytales sometimes speak of passages and galleries that are full on both sides with stalls with temptations and danger. As a boy I was familiar with such a road; it was called Krumme [Crooked] Street. Where she had her sharpest bend, lay her darkest back room: the swimming pool with its red glazed brick walls ... I made myself in front of store windows and nourished my ancestry from an abundance of worn out things in her hat ... The sidewalk was beleaguered with thrift stores with their household wares. He [it] was the line also on which the monthly wardrobes were hung at home ... Where the Crooked Street came to an end in the west, there was a stationary store. Uninitiated glances in the window began at the cheap Nick Carter booklets. But I knew where I had to look in the background for the offensive writings. At this point there was no traffic. I could spend a long time looking through the discs, beginning with the account books [etc.] to create an alibi for myself, but then suddenly venture into the bosom of the papery creations. The drive divines what will prove to be toughest in us ... Rosettes and lanterns in the shop window celebrate the embarrassing event. Not far from pool was the municipal reading room. With his iron lofts he was not too high and not too frosty. I sensed [smelled] my true territory. For his smell preceded him. He waited as if under a thin, sheltering film in the damp, cold, who received me under the stairwell. I pushed open the iron door shyly. But once in the room, the silence of my strength began to take over ..." (Benjamin 2013, 56–87, my translation).
41 Eiland 2007.
42 Benjamin 1991, 325–6.
43 Ibid., 326–7.
44 Huyssen 1995; 2003.
45 Huyssen 2003.
46 Litzinger (1998) develops this term in light of Yao Chinese cultural politics, to emphasize the ways in which the past becomes "objectified in different cultural forms" (226) but includes among these land and the body.
47 Huyssen 2003, 6.
48 Weszkalnys 2010. The emphasis on making place has also been shown to be shot through with forces that produce difference, like race (Lewis 2001), allowing for various extremes of political possibility, from the

democratization of publics to the covering up of structural violence. Interestingly, the anthropology of memory has also inherited much of literary studies' emphasis on the problematique of transnationality as constituted in knowledge practices that were conventionally thought principally a site of national imaginaries (e.g., Schwenkel 2006).

49  Till 2005.
50  Unlike research in other parts of the world, ethnographic work on memory in Berlin almost exclusively focuses on the built environment, and the lives that have produced the new urban landscape. At the same time, literary studies such as Huyssen's, which overcome this emphasis on processes such as memorialization, can be complimented by the sensitivity to life that that ethnography brings. At the same time, the most well-known and nuanced ethnographies of Berlin (Boyer 2005; Borneman 1992; 1997) are grounded in an entirely different moment in the development of the city and its practices of history writing, the period of reunification, which, while reverberating still, bear now a different relation to the broader category of past that is under scrutiny here – especially since in the last decade the population of the city has become considerably younger, and their memories of the Wall more reliant on secondary accounts. And while the best anthropology of Europe in the age of "post-socialism" has poignantly unpacked problems of the ownership of history and the refractions of large political oppositions (Herzfeld 1991; Watson 1994; Verdery 1996), I have resisted beginning from such determined narratives in hopes of taking the Flaneur's ordinary, literary politics as seriously as I can to allow concepts to emerge from the encounter.
51  Huyssen 2003, my emphasis.
52  This palimpsestic nature has always, Huyssen suggests, been an inalienable feature of literary works. For Huyssen, the literary nature of the palimpsest need not mean we read the city as text but the concept can instead be taken from literature and applied to the nature of urban space.
53  For example, Daniel Libeskind's work on the Jewish Museum in Berlin, and the Denkmal für die emordeten Judens Europa – and the general shift away from "triumphalist" to "apologetic" architecture characteristic of the 1980s and 1990s – has been read as a "countermemory," an effort to make present (as a void) the memory of Jews in the city and marks the impossibility of such gestures (and at the expense of its crossing with other histories of migration) (Ackan 2010; Leggewie and Meyer 2005).
54  As cited in Cassin (2016).
55  Ibid.
56  Rechtman 2021.
57  Ibid.

58 Compare with an early anthropological account of the stereotype in Malinowski's (1924) treatment of the Oedipus complex, not in the contemporary sense but rather in Jung and Freud's, as "Klischee," related to the production of imago. I owe my awareness of this antecedent to Charles Clavey.

59 After Jakobson and Benjamin, Boym (1994) argues that an "archaeology of everyday life" would reveal what remains untranslatable in the particular meaning of banality in different contexts – rather than assume, with Arendt, that banality is evil.

60 Das 2007, 39. For example, in her incredible ethnography of the wives of political martyrs and prisoners in Palestine, Lotte Buch Segal (2016) describes how, "in complex ways, the standing language shapes what kinds of suffering can be put into words, and acknowledged, before the limits of agreement about what it means to be human in contemporary Palestine are reached." There were no words to account for the women's feelings of, say, betrayal, not because they are inexpressible, but rather because a question arises of whether they fit or not within the grammar on offer. She finds, for instance, that "the experiences of the prisoners' wives cannot be embodied in the standing language" tied so closely to the martyr: "There are simply no words for what it means to be in their situation."

## 5. Selecting, Collecting, Connecting: Making Books and Making Do

1 See Huneke (2022). See also Marhoefer (2022) on the history of how Hirschfield "fashioned the 'homosexual' out of existing ideas about 'the races,' about empire, and moreover about Jews and about disability" (5).

2 Estimates vary on the percentage of the economy dedicated to creative industries, from 10 per cent to as high as 25 per cent of regional GDP. Most sources however agreed that the percentage is far higher in Berlin than in any other part of Germany. At the time of my fieldwork, more than 220,000 people were employed in the sector.

3 Shoshan 2012; 2014. But inhabitants of the former East Berlin have increasingly been displaced by new economic and linguistic conditions this attraction in part produced, not least a demand for English-language competence and changes in credentialing expectations. If the initial public erasure of signs of the DDR cleared out a space for the emergence of a palpable nostalgia for the East, the clearing out of so-called "real Berliner" opened up further possibilities for resignification by the time I arrived. Debates about memorialization of Berlin's Soviet past lingered, but at least in the city's centre, they were increasingly marginalized by those for whom the memory of the DDR was less immediate. Areas

at the centre of ambitious Soviet housing projects were re-signified as peripheries and associated in newspapers with racist and anti-Semitic violence committed by the Wendeverlierer (transition losers) produced by global shifts in production).

4  This figure is increasingly dominated by English, as high as 64 per cent market share, followed distantly by French (~11 per cent). These data are according to the Frankfurter Buchmesse, one of the most important institutions in the German book-trade landscape and a member of the Börsenverein (1998). Throughout this chapter, I rely on the Börsenverein's calculations, from internal documents, and conversations with staff to determine these figures, though there is some discrepancy. In the same year, the United States – the largest publishing industry in the world – produced fewer than 30 billion in trade total (with stagnated growth over the past several years). Among the most important points of comparison: e-books in the United States market for the past several years account for a quarter of all sales and less than 1 per cent of sales in the German market. The relative composition of the market is also distinct, in terms, for example, of total market share of literary fiction as compared to young-adult serials and self-help products, back catalogue as a percentage of revenue, bestsellers.

5  Stevenson 2017.

6  Rosenbaum's (2019) work with writers in Cuba offers a fascinating comparison on this point.

7  Compare with Augé's (1995) description of proliferating "non-places."

8  Arnold and Wolf 1990; Dahlke 1997; Dahlke, Langermann, and Taterka 2000.

9  All told, the industry generates 1.4 billion euros in revenue annually, according to the city promotions office.

10  "Berlin – Eine Stadt für Verlage." *Project Zukunft*, Senate Department of Economics, Technology and Research for ICT, Media, and Creative Industries in Berlin.

11  On the condition that the business guarantees jobs for a minimum of five years.

12  Backhaus and Hansen 2000.

13  Sweden, which opened its book industry to market in 1970, has had to enact subsidies to keep publishers afloat; the United Kingdom has seen prices as high as 10 per cent over the consumer price index, but an increase in sales among the poor for bestsellers (because prices have dropped). To combat this condensation, in 2000 a group of one hundred independent publishers formed the Kurt Wolff Stiftung, named for the innovative Leipziger publisher famous for supporting avant-garde poetry, for large advertising campaigns using then-new media,

and "creative" packaging tactics like rebinding unsold copies as new editions or printings (which in the wake of the First World War and rapid inflation, came to be seen as unseemly and elitist). The Stiftung describes its mission as standing for "diversity in book culture" (Vielfalt in der Buchkultur); in addition to awards for particularly important books, one of their most visible projects is a catalogue, "es geht um das Buch" – "it's about the book" – sent widely to booksellers to promote lists of small presses, distributed at the Frankfurt Book Fair annually, and supported financially by the minister of state for culture. In one recent edition, compilers lament that "the book trade landscape has changed a lot in the last 20 years. Unfortunately, some excellent publishers no longer exist in this form. We are committed to ensuring that a diverse publishing and book trade landscape can still exist in the future ... we are presenting you with pearls in a sea of books." At an event marking an increasing in state contributions and announcing a new federal study of literary market viability, Minister Monika Grütters described changing market conditions as "threatening a loss of publishing diversity, a loss of votes in public discourse, and losses for the culture of debate and democracy." The language of "diversity" here is meant to signify corporate participation without regard for the nature of the books in print, their authors, or readers – or at least, treating those as downstream effects of corporate interest.

14 As in the "labour in the abstract" behind commodity exchange, and which is "inexorably embroiled in the production of difference, particularly the spatialized difference that is produced by ("national") state borders" (De Genova 2019). De Genova goes on to say that "in a world social order that delegates the expressly political tasks of subordination and coercion to more localized formations of more or less organized violence, the parameters of which are customarily demarcated by the borders of 'national' state formations the global movement of homogenized, abstract labour is finally embodied in the restless life and death of labour in a rather more 'concrete' form – which is to say, actual migrant working men and women."

15 Writing from the US context, Laura Miller (2006) thinks of these as expressions of "ambivalence" about rationalization and different systems of value-making. This idea of the contrast between aesthetic or "cultural" value and economic value, or perhaps value and values, is a major preoccupation of economic anthropological literature as well. Graeber (2001; 2013), for example, argues that value clues us in to the ways in which various different *wholes*, "total universe[s]," are traversed in individual lives, because it is the imaginary "as-if" quality of the social forms that recognize the value of my labour that count (229). For

Graeber, the problem of the relation between this "potentially endless series of little worlds" need not be simply addressed through a system of metavalue, value of values (as he says, in good Dumontian fashion), but is better understood through a system of interior values he calls *infravlue;* they are the means by which one pursues values within a particular register.

16 Godelier 2011.

17 Most standard approaches either have tried to show how social organization and objective position determines aesthetics, or how the movement of art objects produces forms of social relations. On the one side, an important strand in anthropology and sociology after Bourdieu has been to focus on the social determinants of taste as abiding heteronomous or autonomous principles of hierarchization, the intersections of which are determinant of a field of power; the goal then is situate the pursuit of different forms of capital (symbolic, financial) within the social field. According to this view, the selection and production of a particular work, even its aesthetic qualities, reflects structural positions as homologies. "Taste classifies, and it classifies the classifier," Bourdieu (2018) writes, it makes distinctions, in the field of artistic production between the beautiful and the ugly, for example, which enable social subjects to mark themselves out on the basis of the distinctions they make. A more restricted field grants the author greater symbolic power to wield (rhetorically) against the bourgeois order; symbolic power then yields economic returns. On the other, classics of social theory have shown how systems of exchange like print capitalism undergird the maintenance of strange socialities like the nation, for instance through the formation of "reading publics" (Warner 2002a). While both efforts are instructive, as an ethnographer I have two worries: first, that the rush to very large concepts to sometimes elides the particularities of use in context; and second, that our view is sometimes limited by these schemas to a narrow set of social relations. For example, while the point about mass circulation of texts to communities united only by attention to them is well taken, I am more interested in how such social forms intersect concrete, face-to-face networks. For Bourdieu, "the notion of cultural objects has a contingent history of problematic use – a problem, as it were, in the grammar of objectifying the aesthetic" (Mangrum 2015). Against this backdrop, only criticism enables us to see clearly the conditions that count, and which are always prior to, or behind, determinations of aesthetic or value. These determinations are both conventional and objective and there is no reason to take for granted such putative distinctions. No special domain of exists to offer a vantage outside of the contingent conditions of human life, and it is not only

economic activity, or exchange, but also literary tastes that carry a sense of necessity, and it can "put its own naturalness into question," opening up a space from which remake those conditions. As Benjamin Mangrum (2015) puts it, "to construe the kinds of exploitation of late modern capitalist societies as *taking advantage of the arbitrary meanings of human conventions* (as opposed to objectifying what is otherwise not an object, or being a bankrupt framework for embodied relationships) is itself based on a denial of the shared criteria that these practices (along with their criticisms and the very notions of 'exploitation' and 'power' employ)." This would be, in effect, to deny our capacity to remake the world. The circulation of literature both gives birth to resources for reality but is itself born from that soil. For another approach to literary value in a Cavellian spirit, see Bowman 2014. For a critique of Bourdieu's figure of the cultural intermediary, see Nixon and Du Gay (2002), Du Gay (2004), Negus (2002), and Pareschi (2015). See also Bourdieu (1992).
18 Das 1977.
19 The still all-too-common drive to typologize circulation often relies on too quick an extension of these concepts from ideal types to elide the actual practices and the specificities of their use. This is true also of the way anthropology tends to receive "basic" concepts like distinction between commodity and gift – an opposition still in many cases taken for granted. One type of exchange always ends up looking like the "negative imprint" of the other (LiPuma and M. Postone 2020). Literary life involves an economy in which one finds commodities where "one might expect to see gift" and gift "where one might expect to see commodities" (Chaganti 2021), kinship obligations where one might expect clientelism, and neighbourly duty where one expects competition. In a classic essay, Jane Guyer (1993) writes that for comparative purposes, "the critical attributes are less the distinctive contrastive features of transaction types than the powers implicit in them; the capacity of commodities to become separated from their origins (alienability), the power of valuables to evoke time and space … the power of singularity." In other words, the powers associated with commodity exchange – such as alienability and contract law – and those associated with gift economies – say, authorship and inalienability – are not "mutually exclusive, completely contrastive systems." In the case of the equatorial economies she studies, wealth-in-people involved dynamics of both alienability and authorship. In the case I have described here too, the boundary between modes of circulation is not merely porous: the essential play between these realms is *constitutive* of the life of literature. Because those powers also operate according to different scales, what counts as "local" or "concrete" would have to be rethought without taking spatializing tropes for granted, by looking at

the particular relationships between production and domains of social reproduction in specific situations (Meillassoux 1981).
20 Barber 2007.
21 See also Susan Gal (2013).
22 Anouk Cohen (2016; 2017) for instance, has called for more sustained ethnographic attention to the multiple processes that constitute the material life or lives of the book (and not only its textual existence or in its "finished state"), as well as its myriad attendant practices, forms of know-how, modes of interaction and valuation, and dispositions. "This approach to the book 'in the making' leaves no actor aside."
23 See, for example, Puett (forthcoming), on how Confucius's arrangement of the fragments of *Spring and Autumn Annals* can be read through the language of utterance and gesture selection. I have argued elsewhere (Brandel 2020) selection does not necessarily imply a desire for durability, as is sometimes the assumption when talking of writing.
24 And it is only from within particular ideological stances that properties seem to abide naturally in objects.
25 Strathern 1999, 13.
26 I am reminded of how Guyer and Samuel M. Eno Belinga (1995) used the term wealth-in-knowledge to provide a lever through which to understand on economic terms the position of social relations as the ultimate unit of the measure of value in many African systems of exchange. What Guyer and Belinga so innovatively pointed out as that categories like "knowledge" can be as important for understanding these systems as social organizations like kinship or material culture – knowledge, they write, "in a sense ... defines the human endeavour in general," as a "key 'resource'" (117). The struggle, however, was that as an object of analysis, knowledge was neither diffuse like "culture" nor strictly specialist, as a closed system controlled by Meillassoux's esoteric expert. Instead, it functioned as an "open repertoire and an unbounded vista" (93), dispersed throughout the collective body but distributed on the basis of individual capacities. As with the problem of literary art in the European context, "social mobilization," was determined by differential mobilization of bodies at knowledge, situated at the intersection of individual talents and collective reservoirs of material. The benefit of this picture is that it accounts for the simultaneous accumulation of more elements and composition of different elements, two axes which account respectively for the features like clientalization on one hand, and the shifting spatial shapes of social networks on the other (118). This model seems especially important also for the ways it opposed the ideal systems conventionally assumed to pervade European societies.

27 Tennant 1996; Wenzels 1996.
28 Myers 2004. One well-known historical divergence, however, is worth mentioning, which emerged as a result of a several-centuries-long German market preoccupation with Shakespeare (see Brandl 1913; Jones 1923) – the product of this event is so ubiquitous it is often taken for granted by German readers. Shakespeare's plays first crossed the channel in the eighteenth century; thanks in great part to its influence on the Sturm and Drung authors, his complete works were already translated by the 1780s, and by the early nineteenth century, many of Germany's most prominent literary figures were producing translated editions. At the same time, access to quality literary books was for the first time beginning to open up with the expansion of the middle classes – Shakespeare's work, however, like Goethe's, was under the control of powerful houses who artificially drove up prices, preventing their circulation from matching step with demand. The convergence of these forces drove the German Confederation to begin shifting policies on author-rights. In 1867, the Deutsche Bundesversammlung became law, opening texts to the public domain thirty years after the death of the author. The day after the new regulation came into effect, the Reclam publishing house began printing its *Universal-Bibliothek* – familiar, cheaply printed little books sold for pennies and guaranteed by the publisher to remain in print in perpetuity. The desire to put personal home libraries within reach of all social classes lead to such a marked shift in German culture that historians have called the book policy "the turning point of the century" (Wittman 1991, 247; Meiner 1942).
29 Weiner 1992. Annette Weiner once said of the Kula ring that they were "imbued with the intrinsic and ineffable identities of their owners which are not easy to give away," and which was held among concrete relations, held within families or other social groups. "Because each inalienable possession is subjectively unique," she writes, "its ownership confirms difference rather than equivalence ... in this way, inalienable possessions are the representation of how social identities are reconstituted through time." For Weiner, it is the possession that has the power to define who one is in a historical sense, rather than the other way around, since they make person's genealogical past present. While this can appear as a conservative tendency toward strict reproduction of the social order, maintaining difference rather than equivalence takes on additional signification in this context, where the proliferation of difference was seen as a sign of national accumulation of (cultural) wealth. Even the notion of possession implied by things such as copyright is perhaps insufficient – one popular metaphor we already encountered in chapter three is the

likening of begetting a book and a child, "notion of creation that goes beyond the idea of property as possession or commodity."
30 Genette 1991.
31 The more general economic situation in Berlin is one of the conditions of this structure. While housing prices have risen, they are still considerably cheaper than any other major European capital, and the costs of living amount to as little as half of comparable localities. As of 2015, basic utilities cost roughly 180 euros on average (for a 900 square-foot apartment), rent is approximately 400 euros (880 in Paris; 715 in Munich); average monthly salary is more than 1,700 euros (after tax). A gallon of milk costs 2, 60 euros (3,67 in Paris) – a carton of eggs 1,50 euros. (This data is from *Numbeo's* registry of user/resident-submitted data.) My friend Liza was a prime example of the ramifications of this economic context for a literary life; she and her partner each worked a few days a week, mostly translating between English and German – together they spent roughly 60 Euros a month on food, and another few hundred on shared rent. The rest of Liza's time was dedicated to a small literary journal in which they published mainly the writing (translating themselves or, occasionally, with the help of others) of a group of friends they had made in the city. They sold the journal out of the back of a member's car, to local establishments, at events for friends, launch parties, and occasionally online (especially for new readers interested in back catalogues). The prices were calculated with the intention of recuperating investment – sales were never intended to do more than break even, to provide just enough revenue so that the magazine could reproduce itself in a subsequent issue. As their financial manager put it, "We need just enough to keep going."
32 See also Herzfeld (2009) for comparison with the situation in Rome, where cosmopolitan growth increasingly marginalized artisans in Monti, who preferred to form social alliances within kin networks. It is worth noting how in both cases one could detect expressions of simultaneous "pride and exasperation" about gentrification but also the very different ways that the nation was mapped onto these process. This double character was also reflected in the way people spoke about language. One important example was the discourse of Sprachplefge, or language care – an anxiety about changes in language, usually through "contact." Typically, within European linguistic ideologies one expects to find that the ascription of "mixing" among languages that supposedly share genetic affinities is marked as socially acceptable (e.g., German and English) and distinguished from languages that are socially maligned (like Turkish). But recent linguistic work on attitudes toward Kiezdeutsch, the German spoken in the Kiez, has shown how

because English is also seen to serve as a lingua franca among those racialized as non-German, complaints about German-English mixing, even ostensive complaints about the homogenizing effects of the global hegemony of English, become a "socially accepted" proxy for other forms of xenophobic speech (Presau 2020).

33 "wir danken Ihnen für die vielen schönen gemeinsamen Momente im vergangenen Jahr und freuen uns auf die kommenden. Berlin, Charlottenburg und damit auch der Savignyplatz verändern sich. Ladenflächen stehen frei und hoffentlich keine Filialisten in Startposition. Danke, dass Sie an 'support your local dealer' glauben. Wir haben ein gutes Gefühl, dass sich am Platz auch zukünftig Einzelhändler und Gastwirte mit ungewöhnlichen Einfällen niederlassen werden. Das ist doch unser aller Kiez, in dem wir uns wohlfühlen wollen."

34 See Klinkenberg (2001).

35 "Für die Stärkung des Besonderen und Essentiellen stark machen, Literatur als Kunst einen geschützen Raum, Weltliteratur eine neue, unbedingte Heimat geben."

36 Kaufmännlich, lit. salesmen-ly.

37 The word originally in English.

38 Linguistics have argued, for example, that language practices more generally are sometimes understood as a context-bound, "responsive, intertextual" domains of social action; in other words, as dialogical sites where "conflicting ideologies and the systemic constraints of grammar are resources for the combination of voices," i.e., where space could be opened up for critical consciousness to emerge.

39 Janzen 2020.

40 Another of her interlocutors, Thedel von Wallmoden, the founder of Wallstein Verlag, an academic press that more recently moved into literary trade books, shared that of their four million euros in revenue (just below the bar to count in Germany as an independent publisher), one-quarter came from public subvention. Wallstein's editors served as jurors for literary prizes (of which there are more than 1,200 in Germany) and recruited young authors from prestigious writing programs in hopes of winning a prize – an achievement that was essential to bolstering sales.

41 Setrag Manoukian (2012), for instance, has shown how in bookshops in Shiraz, the debates that ensued around history books could be a way of locating oneself in a national story.

42 Reed 2019; Reed and Bialekci 2018.

43 Ivry (2007, 50) suggests that for Benjamin, things move perhaps in the other direction, that the fate of the collection is "indexed" to the collector

and is bound up in the object's relation to the whole and its "metonymic power to evoke the collector's past to himself."
44  Baudrillard, as cited in Reed (2011).
45  Reed 2011, 74.
46  Cavell 2020.
47  Cavell 2020, 38. As Cavell reads him, "Benjamin's writing is at once confessing in its existence as traces the guilt of its privilege and at the same time declaring that its obscurity is necessary if it is not to subserve the conditions that insure our guilt toward one another. But the direct allusion to Marx ('[the collector] conferred on [things] only a fancier's value, rather than a use-value'), hence to Marx's derogation of exchange value as a realm of mystery, suggests a mystery in the living of the life of traces that cannot be solved by what are called detectives … I take Benjamin's portrait, or function, of the collector as the true inhabitant of the interior to suggest that the collector himself is without effective or distinctive interiority, without that individuality of the sort he prides himself on."
48  Ibid., 79.
49  "That kind of figure from cultural history," he explained "who rejects the script prepared for them to live a self-authored life – this is something I find inexhaustibly fascinating. Both Lasker-Schüler and Reventlow left security behind in pursuit of bohemia. They were around the same age (born 1869 and 1871, respectively), they each had an illegitimate son, they started out as artists, and they were central figures in the bohemian circles of their respective cities (Berlin and Munich). They encountered great hardship and neither fell back on self-pity, although their strategies differed; Reventlow had a highly modern sense of irony about herself and her misadventures, while Lasker-Schüler responded with what the writer Judith Kuckart calls a "militant ecstasy which is awakened when the writer bangs her head against reality."
50  Cavell 2020, 61.
51  Strathern 2020, 186.
52  See also Lambek 2011.
53  Here Matthias also says, "I would like to say that this was very special to him, and it is why he was able to establish so many honest, friendly contracts … he did not go in arrogance, but with a wealth of knowledge, about European culture and literature in Europe, but also had acquired a lot about Indian literature, culture, film, theatre, and with a real curiosity, and a joy in others, not from above but at eye-level … that is why sometimes he ran through open doors, and sometimes not."
54  Laugier 2020, 220.
55  Cavell 2020, 45.

56 See Das (2015) and Brandel and Bagaria (2020).
57 Cavell 2020, 70.
58 Das 2007, 4.

## 6. Life in a Net of Language: Literature, Translation, and the Feel of Words

1 Dawson and Rapport 2021. Michael Jackson (2013b) writes, "This is not a matter of being between two worlds, but of being dis-membered – no longer being fully integrated into a familiar community. And so the migrant is obliged to remember himself, to constantly piece together, like a bricoleur, new *assemblages* from the various aspects of his past and present [and, we might add, future] selves."
2 Munn 2003.
3 Glissant (1997, 195) says that the relation is expressed not in a "procession of trajectories, itineraries succeeding and thwarting one another, but explodes by itself and within itself." This relation is also expressed in movement, "for movement is precisely that which realizes itself absolutely. Relation is movement."
4 Gramling 2021.
5 In this way, Fields and Fields (2014) argue, we "remain under the yoke of yore."
6 McGetchin 2004.
7 Sengupta 2004.
8 "*Mobilität, europäische Zusammenarbeit, Weltbürgertum* ... Soviel Welt als möglich in die eigene Person zu verwandeln, ist im höheren Sinn des Wortes Leben."
9 Marchand 2001; 2003; McGetchin 2009.
10 As cited in McGetchin (2009); Dharwadker (2003).
11 The *Bhagavadgita* was not his only such project, however; with financial support from the Prussian government, he founded a scientific journal (*Indische Bibliothek*) and oversaw a number of critical editions and translations.
12 Marchignoli 2003.
13 McGetchin 2009.
14 Hegel wrote a slightly more congenial review in January 1828.
15 Marchignoli 2003, 260.
16 As cited in Marchignoli (2003).
17 Interestingly, as Marchignoli points out, Hegel associated "modern morals" with "that Indian principle as such" in the sense that moral duties did not flow from them – in this way, he draws together the philosophy of the Gita with Kant's formalism.

18 One of the most visible examples was the Stadtschloß, the city palace project built on the footprint of the winter residences of the Prussian royal house. After sustaining considerable damage in the Second World War, it was rebuilt and rechristened the Palast der Republik, a new home for the parliament of East Germany, only to be deconstructed again in the years after re-unification. Though conceived originally as a state project shortly after the fall of the Wall, firm plans for the site wouldn't be announced for more than a decade, when designs were unveiled and temporally displayed in the Humboldt-Box, a large, glass structure near Museum Insel. The palace itself, which would boast three original facades and one modern, was now to be the home of a forum bearing the name of Alexander von Humboldt. It would boast museum collections dedicated to the diversity of human culture, beginning in 2020 with the Ethnological Museum. It was to be cultural centre for interactive exhibits highlighting the interconnectedness of the world, an explicit nod to what Humboldt in his Berlin Lectures on the "Kosmos," the motto of which was a call to recognize "unity in diversity" of natural phenomena, including human culture.

   One museum official described the forum as integral to the recreation of the city centre as "a place of universal enlightenment, a place of global art and global competency through Berlin's state museum as the largest existing encyclopaedic museum." The ambition was to foster an Erinnerungskultur, a memory culture, premised on and attentive to what was described as a "national narrative of diversity," by creating a place for "dialogues between cultures of the world," as if on equal footing in a public sphere. The decision to mobilize colonial collections, including looted objects and human remains, to that end drew substantial criticism and public condemnation from activists like Joshua Kwesi Aikins, Tahir Della, and Christian Kopp, who argued that the forum amounted to a continuation of the colonial project. The forum's defenders argued at the time that Berlin's ethnographic collections were part of a "pre-colonial," liberal vision that should be recaptured for a future Germany. But what is "pre-colonial" about Humboldt's vision of cosmopolitanism, a comparative linguistic practice premised on the figure of Europe as the master mediator? As many have pointed out, the elision of German colonial history was bound to the elevation of other histories, one that also could have been an opportunity to open new apertures on contemporary oversights and oppression.

19 Navaro-Yashin 2020.

20  In other words, what I find instructive about these debates is that for all their disagreement, many of these questions share a sense that what is at stake is a matter of whether a statement about a particular piece of literature, or an author, or a society, is true or false; that is to say, whether an expression is adequate to reality, as though the two were normally at some distance from one another. "It is what human beings *say* that is true or false," Wittgenstein (1954) writes, however, "and they agree in the *language* they use. That is not agreement in opinions but in forms of life." They are indicative, in this way, of a certain grammar of talk about language they share, a way of speaking about what language or literature *does*. But this is not the *only* way of picturing them.

21  Many of these difficulties arise because language is seen as the thing that holds out possibility of community and as a "barrier to that world, seeing language, even our form of life, as empty of whatever it is we think necessary to establishing a satisfying connection to that world." (See also Bertacco and Gibson 2011.) We are met everywhere by disappointment in our efforts to ground the relation of language to the world. "The *practical* difficulty of pegging the mind to the world, and especially to the social-political world, the world of history; and the psychological difficulty of it in the world of religion," Cavell writes (1979), "are main subjects of modern literature … the gap between mind and the world is closed, or the distortion between them straightened, in the appreciation and acceptance of particular human forms of life, human 'convention.' This implies that the *sense* of gap originates in an attempt, or wish, to escape (to remain a 'stranger' to, 'alienated' from) those shared forms of life, to give up the responsibility of their maintenance. (Is this always a fault? Is there no way of becoming responsible for that? … The usual approach is to fill the gap by appeal to metaphysics, or to bridge it by means of universals. And these 'solutions' tend to draw sharp distinctions between my knowledge of myself and of others." As my colleagues and I ask elsewhere (Das, Puett, and Brandel, forthcoming): Can we think instead of the potential and the manifest? Can we think of languages as always already in the company of other languages?

22  See Érard, Layla Raïd, and Joséphine Stebler (2021).

23  This has been a major debate in analytical philosophy between so-called metaphysical realist and anti-realist camps. My own view, following the work of Benoist and others, is that one can reject correspondence theories of truth and nominalism and remain committed to a realistic account through an appeal to context. One of Tawada's key insights is that languages are quite normally found in the company of other languages. As they run together, cross, mingle, spill over and transform one another, they can help us to accept, to live with the fact, that the use of language

always carries this indeterminacy (not just in special cases), and there is conversely no way to ground its relationship to the world and fend off, once and for all, doubt from creeping in.
24 Brandel, Das, and Puett, in press.
25 Brandel and Motta 2021, 14–16; Cavell 1979, 171–7.
26 Wittgenstein 1954, 649.
27 How do I know, after all, when I have learned to read? Perhaps I get stuck on a particular word – there are always unknowns in any language, so how do we come to say we understand a language? The question is instead how I get to the confidence to know that this word is something potentially understandable.
28 Stebler 2020. See also Erard (2017).
29 "We do not know in advance what the content of our mutual acceptance is, how far we may be in agreement. I do not know in advance how deep my agreement with myself is, how far responsibility for the language may run. But if I am to have my own voice in it, I must be speaking for others and allow others to speak for me. The alternative to speaking for myself representatively (for *someone* else's consent) is not: speaking for myself privately. The alternative is having nothing to say, being voiceless, not even mute" (Cavell 1979, 28).
30 Cavell 1979, 29.
31 Tawada 2016.
32 This is often translated "juxtaposition" but I've here tried to preserve the image that arose in my mind of people standing on a street corner.
33 Quine 1960.
34 Brandt 2005.
35 Yildiz 2013.
36 Cavell 1992.
37 Webster 2006a; Webster and Sherzer 2015. On the "joke" in this context, c.f. Boog (2017).
38 Woolard 1998; Webster 2015. The idea here is that a single sound or a string of sounds might belong fully within multiple languages experienced simultaneously, as opposed to, say, a situation where code-switching moves between different linguistic systems.
39 Becker 1995.
40 Wittgenstein 1954.
41 Mannheim 1986.
42 Sherzer and Webster 2015.
43 Meaning, it follows moreover, does not belong to the utterance outside its use in context (Das 2020).
44 On the figure of the feel of the "alien," see Maehl (2015); on the proximity of Tawada and Wittgenstein's thought, see Perloff (2010). While most

people who have noticed this closeness focus on language-games, my own impression is that the question of physiognomy gets closer to the connection. Wittgenstein writes in the *Philosophical Investigations*: "And how are these feelings manifested among us? – By the way we choose and value words. How do I find the 'right' word? How do I choose among words? Without doubt it is sometimes as if I were comparing them by fine differences of smell: That is too ... that is too ... – this is the right one. – But I do not always have to make judgments, give explanations; often I might only say: 'It simply isn't right yet.' I am dissatisfied, I go on looking. At last a word comes: 'That's it!' Sometimes I can say why. This is simply what searching, this is what finding, is like here." The use of a word in a particular context, and our capacity to continue using it with a degree of constancy, relies on its "face" (Geschlecht). When we draw another example, the net of uses speak to each other in so far as this or that feature resembles the others, but neither in a way that the initial context is determinant or has to be reproduced, nor in that is any one feature common to all members of the family of uses. In this way, different contexts seem "right" for the same word: appearances "have no one thing in common which makes us use the same word for all, – but that they are related to one another in many different ways. And it is because of this relationship, or these relationships, that we call them all 'language' ... [like] the various resemblances between members of a family: build, features, colour of eyes, gait, temperament, etc. etc. overlap and criss-cross in the same way." In these cases, who "we" are is complicated by the fact that we are moving among languages, among, that is, forms of life. These faces are not, as Wittgenstein writes elsewhere, the outcome of an "inner process." If one were to keep a diary to record the recurrence of a sensation for which I had no natural expression, and write down a sign to coincide with their attention on the experience, would this be to establish a meaning of the sign? One could say that I recall the connection in the future, but there would be no criteria for its rightness. What we have in such a case is something like a criteria for which I "appear to understand" but which no one else understands. But what then would I mean by expressing it? When Tawada speaks of the impressions (Eindrücken) made by words on her, we should not read this therefore as akin to impressing (prägen) "private experience" onto a sign, as if to create a private language.

45 Cavell 2010. This attachment, Cavell argues, is precisely what metaphysicians want to deny. Hence, when Wittgenstein writes about "aliens" here, Cavell reads him as making a joke at the expense of philosophers.

46 Brandt 2005.

47  On the body in Tawada's work, see, e.g., Weigel 1996; Redfield and Singer 1954. Tingting Hui (2020) likewise picks up on the language of skin, though with a rather different interpretation, and of edibility (2019).
48  Cavell 1979, 355.
49  "Until then," she writes, "I was not aware that the relationship between me and my Bleistift was *sprachliche*, linguistic."
50  "it is cold"; "it is going well (for me)"; "it is raining."
51  Tawada 1996.
52  Das 2020.
53  Wittgenstein 1954.
54  This scrutiny highlights the fact that one can in such situations confuse linguistic for philosophical grammar, as in the requirement of the subject; for instance, where one takes a statement about one's belief to be an assertion about an inner state that comes then to be projected onto language, as opposed to something where the two are learned together (Das 2020). We might therefore need to carefully distinguish the use of the "es" to fill grammatical roles in a sentence reporting about the weather – where if one were to ask, I can quickly confirm by looking out the window – and a sentence like "es geht mir gut." But this is not, as is sometimes argued, because there are some inner states without physiognomic accompaniments, as if linguistic differences were "intrinsic differences in the content of experience." (Ibid.) Rather, what this mode of questioning asks us to consider is in what ways I am in a position in each case to ask and to say.
55  When I shared this example with a friend, she told me it reminded her at once of a case she had read in Bateson of a patient who complained that he was an "end-table made of manzanita wood." The patient had been refusing food, and the psychiatric institution had tried to force it on him. Bateson intervenes by separating eating from the clinic, taking him to a restaurant to have a meal, after which the patient sits back and says "Man's an eater. If the circumstances were resolved, he would." For Bateson, one long-standing concern was how the metacommunicative frame "this is play" was conveyed – that is, the message that takes the form "these actions, in which we now engage, do not denote what would be de-noted by those actions which these actions denote … the playful nip de-notes the bite, but does not denote that which would be denoted by the bite." The interest for Bateson was in the movement between "degrees of abstraction," whereby some action (of play) denotes, or stands in for, another (not-play). Of course, it is not always clear whether or not one is playing, and this, Bateson argues, is how it comes to be, seemingly paradoxically, that through play, in which an action is not meant *in this way*, the metaphor might be meant, where the wine *is* blood –

Bateson takes for example the situation where one experiences the "full intensity of subjective terror" watching a film, or in our case, reading a novel. He reads "Manzanita wood" as a metaphor for what the speaker means. As Anthony Wilden (2013) puts it in his classic reading of the case, "playing around with words" is not something where simply anything goes. Rather, even the distinction between metonymy and metaphor, or their relationship with psychological processes like disavowal and repression, schizophrenic logic or hysteria, are context bound. They depend, in other words, on the level of analysis: "If we change the level of analysis, the polar relation we began with in order to distinguish the processes within a certain level, can be applied to distinguish levels." The distinction itself has meaning only in context. If the nip is the metonymic sign of the bite though not the bite itself, it becomes eclipsed by the metaphor in the new code (Wilden 2013, 59). If it has been assumed that contexts of use are "part, in some sense, of a particular language" (see Davidson 1993), psychoanalytic scenes and those in Tawada's writing each take up cases of everyday multiplicity of language. On this point, see also Tawada's (2000) work on games and the magic of language and their relationship to ethnology.
56 This sense of footing shares with Zumhagen-Yekplé's (2020) account of a picture of rootedness in language a proximity to the question of nonsense.
57 Tawada 2013a; 2013b. As McQuade (2022) points out, for Tawada, "The text's features down to its very physiognomy are not containers" but "openings." The old binary opposition between ideographic and phonetic writing, McQuade shows, falls away in this form of translation, that Tawada here calls "Augen-Übersetzung" – translating with the eyes.
58 Sakai 2020.
59 Sherzer and Webster 2015; Golovko 1994.
60 Tawada 2013a; 2013b.
61 Anderson (2010) describes both of these as surface features of language to which Tawada draws particular attention.
62 Tawada 1998.
63 Ibid.
64 "Transformation" [Verwandlung]. Translation of literary texts, as well as to similar but non-equivalent forms of individual written signs of different writing systems. Compare with the "Western fascination with semantico-referential meanings" (Bauman and Briggs 2003; Webster 2013).
65 Arslan 2019.
66 Das 2020.
67 Kraenzle 2008; 2006.
68 Wright 2013.

69 As translated in Wright 2013. Wright's second short example is from "Der Apfel und die Nase," where a speaker describes an unfamiliar Apple logo on her computer screen and reads it through the biblical story of the fall: "The computer company tempted a woman with forbidden fruit and trapped her inside the computer. You can still see the apple nibble by the woman in the corner of the screen."

70 Wright 2013, 289.

71 Kraenzle (2008) draws here also on the work of Albrecht Kloepfer and Miho Matsunaga (2000) who point to the centrality of a sense of unheimlichkeit. The notion of awkwardness of conditions comes from Cavell's reading of Emerson as an inversion of Kant. (See, e.g., Brandel, forthcoming.)

72 This observation was brought to my attention by Alonso Gamarra at a workshop in which I presented an earlier version of this chapter.

73 Tawada 2007, 90.

74 Benoist diagnoses something similar when, in responding to a question from a colleague about whether there are some things that are in themselves too difficult to think, say too exotic, like "the concept of Africa," he responds by saying that globalization discourse in the West amounts to a belief "that one has the world in all its exoticism at their disposal in their supermarket (one calls it 'ethnic' food) … This is evidently then an adulterated exoticism, both nutritionally and conceptually pasteurized; an exoticism that is *already* entirely, precisely, conceptualized, and as such is integrated into a *conceptual system* … everything is always the same, it is *standardized*." This process results, he argues, from "abstract, poor, conceptualization, that squanders the richness of the reference to the real on which it is nourished." For all the levelling-down characteristic of this imaginary "transnationally translatable monoculture," there is in the end, for Benoist, "no fatality inherent in the concept." Yildiz offers a reading of another story, "Bioskoop der Nacht," from the collection *Überseezungen* as a way forward. In the story, a series of dreams are punctuated by a narrator from Japan who lives in Germany trying to answer a question regularly posed to her about the language in which she dreams. The language she identifies, however, is Afrikaans, and she ultimately travels to South Africa to learn to translate her own dreams, a process that also prompts memories of childhood and learning about the complicity of Japan with the apartheid regime.

75 Cavell 2007.

76 Cavell 2015. See also Laugier (2013, 88–91).

77 In her recent book on reading literature after Wittgenstein, Karen Zumhagen-Yekplé (2020) argues that there are literary and philosophical

uses of difficulty, notably where they are morally instructive. But there are also some difficulties that are ontological, neither resolvable nor, by and large, intentional. Certain genres of literature are especially drawn to such difficulties. For instance, it is part of what a writer such as Virginia Woolf admires in Chekhov or Tolstoy – as Woolf herself writes, "Nothing is finished: nothing is tidied up; life merely goes on." Living with such difficulties is part and parcel of what it means to "at home in our lives and language," that is, if we are to be understood. In "The Russian Point of View," Woolf is responding to a doubt of this kind, that for all our reading of literature, we might remain "to the end of [our] days foreigners." Giving up the effort to secure an end (as in, say, Tolstoy, "nobody thinks of explaining") can leave one with a sense of "bewilderment." "It is difficult to feel sure," she writes of word-for-words translations "in view of these mutilations, how far we can trust ourselves not to impute, to distort, to read into them an emphasis which is false." For Woolf, reading "alien, difficult" texts depends instead on one's capacity to "learn to make yourselves akin to people. I would even like to add: make yourself indispensable to them. But let this sympathy be not with the mind ... but with the heart, with love towards them." Zumhagen-Yekplé's point is that difficulties are morally instructive not because of what they tell us ("there is no single describable lesson we are to extract from them") but because they demand we accept that we live with such difficulties.

78 Since reality is given in language, it is sometimes argued that because the universes of discourse we inhabit are different, because we do not have the same concepts or ways of speaking, because this sound or image fails to take hold of me, this means the skies under which Dante wrote must *be* something other than those contemporary astronomy describes. If certain ways of speaking are not available in a particular universe of discourse, the philosopher Ilham Dilman (2002) reasons then those ways of speaking cannot provide the material objects of thought or action since they do not exist in them. We cannot hope to identify objects across universes of discourse, so we'd best give up trying. In a powerful response to this problem, Cora Diamond takes the example of pointing to a bright object in the sky and teaching a child that it is the planet Venus, drawing on Anscombe's distinction between the intentional objects or action and those at which we materially aim. "If one is talking to a child about the planet Venus, one may pick it out for her as 'that bright thing in the sky,' and so within the grammar of intentionality, the two – what I intend and what in fact I point out – coincide. While the child may not yet have the concept of a planet, and so cannot think about Venus *as a planet*, the phrase 'the planet Venus' nevertheless gives her the material

object of thought. Where one expression provides both the intentional and material object, where they coincide, identity of the material object of the person's thought is not tied to how the thing is thought about" (Diamond 2012b, 191–2). Certainly, she continues, people in Dante's time could have picked out bright objects in the sky, just as we might: "We can say that the medievals believed of (de re) the planet Venus (the material object of thought) that it was a luminous ethereal globe affixed to an ethereal sphere. We can also say that this way of understanding what the luminous bodies in the heavens were, and how they moved, got things wrong. On this account of the grammar of intentionality, there is no impediment to saying that people may have quite different understandings of what the luminous bodies of the heavens are, taking it that different people may nevertheless be speaking of the luminous bodies of *the heavens that we and they see*" (Ibid., 193).

Jocelyn Benoist (2021) develops the issue still further. What are we asking about when we inquire about the *being* of intentional objects in general? The idea that intentional objects exist in general – that is, that they could function as "as *general* features of our thought" – he argues, is an invention of modern European epistemologies. The problem arises as a problem only from the fact that philosophers and anthropologists sometimes take words and world in isolation. Instead, in the examples above, my intending of an object – picking out a bright light from the sky – presupposes its existence. Our ontological commitments, therefore, those embedded in my uses of language, are the "fully disclosed starting point." They are disclosed through use in context. Such questions can only make sense – when they make sense – in context. It is not the words in themselves that tell us what things are, he argues, but our use of them in context that is determinant of meaning. Benoist notes that in this way – in the reluctance to accept uses as "lacking" determination – contextualism stakes out a rather different position from the usual analytical relativism. Said otherwise, a logical relativism assumes a "gap between content and truth false. As such, content may not be enough to go on" (102; 107). For some in anthropology, by contrast, the problem with criticizing from the outside is that the standards by means of which one would judge rightness or wrongness must be provided by one side or the other; "controlled equivocation rather than critical adjudication." This type of relativity is itself only relative "from the outside" – a position it takes as a given. From inside, using this word or that concept doesn't pose any problem. From the point of view of use, there are no "half-words" or "half-contents." "There is no being," Benoist writes, "except *genuine* being – there is no room for *merely intentional being*." But this is often how translation, and metaphors of translation more generally, are understood,

including those commonly deployed within liberal discourse of migration and interculturality, as well as those concerning historical norms and those of the present. Paradoxically, so as are the grounds for their justified critique. Universalism or endless approximation, Hegel or Humboldt.
79 Damrosch 2020, 187. Damrosch develops this thought from Klawitter (2015).
80 Floyd's (2007) discussion of nonsense is particularly clarifying.
81 Diamond 1981, 14.
82 Laugier 2021.
83 Diamond 2012a. This doesn't entail holding out for a space of encounter not laden with power.
84 Rechtman 2021, 12, 144–7. Rechtman writes, "If the ordinary is what presents itself beneath our eyes with evidentiary force, it is also what escapes us regularly; it is taken for granted to the point of being ignored."
85 Walser 2012, 61.
86 Donatelli 2016.
87 Ibid.

# References

Abu-Lughod, L. 2016. *Veiled Sentiments: Honor and Poetry in a Bedouin Society.* University of California Press.

Ackan, E. 2010. "Apology and Triumph: Memory Transference, Erasure, and a Rereading of the Berlin Jewish Museum." *New German Critique* 37(2): 153–79. https://doi.org/10.1215/0094033X-2010-009.

Adorno, T. 1959 (1977). "Was bedeutet: Aufarbeitung der Vergangenheit." *Gesammelte Schriften 10.2. Kulturkritik und Gesellschaft II: Eingriffe. Stichworte. Anhang.* Suhrkamp: Frankfurt/Main, 555–72.

– 2005. *Critical Models: Interventions and Catchwords.* Columbia University Press.

Adorno, T., and M. Horkheimer. 1997. *Dialectic of Enlightenment.* Vol. 15. Verso.

Agha, A. 1998. "Stereotypes and Registers of Honorific Language." *Language in Society* 27(2): 151–93.

Ahmed, Manan. 2013. "Being a Ghost in Berlin." https://www.slowtravelberlin.com/a-ghost-in-berlin/.

Allan, M. 2016. *In the Shadow of World Literature.* Princfeton University Press.

Alworth, D. 2016. *Site Reading: Fiction, Art, Social Form.* Princeton University Press.

Amrute, S. 2016. *Encoding Race, Encoding Class: Indian IT Workers in Berlin.* Duke University Press.

Anderson, B. 2006. *Imagined Communities: Reflections on the Origin andSpread of Nationalism.* Verso.

Anderson, S.C. 2010. "Surface Translations: Meaning and Difference in Yoko Tawada's German Prose." *Seminar* 46(1): 50–70.

Anscombe, G.E.M. 1991. *Metaphysics and the Philosophy of Mind: Collected Philosophical Papers, Volume 2.* John Wiley & Sons.

Antze, P., and M. Lambek, eds. 2016. *Tense Past: Cultural Essays in Trauma and Memory.* Routledge.

Apter, E. 2011. *The Translation Zone.* Princeton University Press.

– 2014. *Against World Literature: On the Politics of Untranslatability*. Verso Books.
Arnold, H.L., and G. Wolf, eds. 1990. *Die Andere Sprache: Neue-DDR Literatur der 80er Jahre*. text + kritik.
Arslan, G. 2019. "Making Senses: Translation and the Materiality of Written Signs in Yoko Tawada." *Translation Studies* 12(3): 338–56. https://doi.org/10.1080/14781700.2019.1600423.
Asad, T. 1986. "The Concept of Cultural Translation in British Social Anthropology." In J. Clifford and G.E. Marcus (eds.), *Writing Culture: The Poetics and Politics of Ethnography* University of California Press.
– 2020. "Thinking about Religion through Wittgenstein." *Critical Times* 3(3): 403–42. https://doi.org/10.1215/26410478-8662304.
Assmann, A. 1999. *Erinnerungsräume: Formen und Wandlungen des kulturellen Gedächtnisses*. C.H. Beck.
– 2006. *Der lange Schatten der Vergangenheit: Erinnerungskultur und Geschichtspolitik*. CH Beck.
Assmann, J. 1988. "Kollektives Gedächtnis und kulturelle Identität." In *Kultur und Gedächtnis*. Surhkamp.
Ataç, I., S. Kron, S. Schilliger, H. Schwiertz, and M. Stierl. 2015. Struggles of Migration as In-/visible Politics. *Movements. Journal für kritische Migrations -und Grenzregimeforschung* 1(2): 1–18.
Attia, I., J.K. Aikins, S. Arnold, N. Beyer, M. Bojadzijev, K. Espahangizi, J. König, K. Kosnick, M. Kulacatan, I. Lenz, and P. Mecheril. 2018. *Postmigrantische Perspektiven: Ordnungssysteme, Repräsentationen, Kritik*. Campus Verlag.
Augé, M. 1995. *Non-places: Introduction to an Anthropology of Supermodernity*. Verso.
– 2002. *In the Metro*. University of Minnesota Press.
Bachelard, G. 1936/2013. *L'instant poetique et instant metaphysique*. Gonthier. Translated as *Intuition of the Instant*. Northwestern University Press.
Bäcker, I. 2008. "Berlin-Bilder von Franz Hessel und Walter Benjamin: 'Flanieren' im Raum und in der Zeit." In *Deutsch-russische Germanistik: Ergebnisse, Perspektiven und Desiderate der Zusammenarbeit*. Moscow: Stimmen der Slavischen Kultur.
Backhaus, J., and R. Hansen. 2000. "Resale Price Maintenance for Books in Germany and the European Union: A Legal and Economic Analysis." *International Review of Law and Economics*.
Banahi, M. 2020. *Between War and the World: Afghans, Borders, and the "Crisis" of Migration in Hamburg*. PhD dissertation, Johns Hopkins University.
Barber, K. 2007. *The Anthropology of Texts, Persons and Publics*. Cambridge University Press.
Basso, E. 2009. "Ordeals of Language." In M. Carrithers (ed.), *Culture, Rhetoric, and the Vicissitudes of Life* (121–38). Berghahn.

Bate, B. 2009. *Tamil Oratory and the Dravidian Aesthetic: Democratic Practice in South India*. Columbia University Press.
Bauman, R., and C.L. Briggs. 2003. *Voices of Modernity: Language Ideologies and the Politics of Inequality* (No. 21). Cambridge University Press.
Becker, A. 1995. *Beyond Translation*. The University of Michigan Press.
Benhabib, S. 2018. *Exile, Statelessness, and Migration: Playing Chess with History from Hannah Arendt to Isaiah Berlin*. Princeton University Press.
Benjamin, W. 1991. *Gesammelte Schriften*. Suhrkamp, Frankfurt am Main.
– 2013. *Berliner Kindheit um 1900*. Hoffmann und Camp Verlag.
Benoist, J. 2020. "Alien Meaning and Alienated Meaning." In *The Logical Alien* (281–92). Harvard University Press.
– 2021. *Toward a Contextual Realism*. Harvard University Press.
Berdahl, D. 1999. *Where the World Ended: Re-unification and Identity in the German Borderland*. University of California Press.
– 2009. *On the Social Life of Post-socialism: Memory, Consumption, Germany*. Indiana University Press.
– 2010. "Good Bye Lenin! Aufwiedersehen GDR." In *Post-communist Nostalgia* (177–89). Berghahn.
Berlant, L. 1989. "Fantasies of Utopia in the Blithedale Romance." *American Literary History* 1(1): 30–62. https://doi.org/10.1093/alh/1.1.30.
– 1991. *The Anatomy of National Fantasy: Hawthorne, Utopia, and Everyday Life*. Chicago Press.
– 2011. *Cruel Optimism*. Duke University Press.
Berliner, D. 2005. "The Abuses of Memory: Reflections on the Memory Boom in Anthropology. *Anthropological Quarterly* 78(1): 197–211.
Berman, A. 1984. *L'Épreuve de l'Étranger*. Editions Gallimard.
Bertacco, S., and J. Gibson. 2011. "Scepticism and the Idea of the Other." In *Stanley Cavell and Literary Theory: Consequences of Skepticism* (106–21). Continuum.
Björgvinsson, E., N. De Genova, M. Keshavarz, and T. Wulia. 2020. "Art and Migration." *PARRSE Journal* Vol. 10.
Blackbourn, D, and R.J. Evans, eds. 1991. *The German Bourgeoisie*. Routledge.
Bloch, Maurice. 1998. *How We Think They Think: Anthropological Approaches to Cognition, Memory and Literacy*. Routledge.
Blommaert, J. 2010. *The Sociolinguistics of Globalization*. Cambridge University Press.
Blommaert, J., J. Collins, and S. Slembrouck. 2005. "Spaces of Multilingualism." *Language & Communication* 25(3): 197–216. https://doi.org/10.1016/j.langcom.2005.05.002.
Blommaert, J., M. Spotti, and J. Van der Aa. 2017. "Complexity, Mobility, Migration." *The Routledge Handbook of Migration and Language* (349–63). Routledge.

Blum, M. 2004. "Re-making the East German Past: Ostalgie, Identity, and Material Culture." *Journal of Popular Culture* 34(3): 229–53. https://doi.org/10.1111/j.0022-3840.2000.3403_229.x.

Bock, J.J., and S. Macdonald, eds. 2019. *Refugees Welcome?: Difference and Diversity in a Changing Germany*. Berghahn Books.

Bodnar, J., and V. Molnar. 2010. "Reconfiguring Private and Public: State, Capital and New Housing Developments in Berlin and Budapest." *Urban Studies* 47(2): 789–812. https://doi.org/10.1177/0042098009351188.

Bonilla, Y. 2011. "The Past Is Made by Walking." *Cultural Anthropology* 26(3): 313–39. https://doi.org/10.1111/j.1548-1360.2011.01101.x.

Boog, J. 2017. *Anderssprechen: vom Witz der Differenz in Werken von Emine Sevgi Özdamar, Felicitas Hoppe und Yōko Tawada*. Königshausen & Neumann.

Borneman, J. 1992. *Belonging in Two Berlins: Kin, State, Nation*. Cambridge University Press.

— 1997. *Settling Accounts: Violence, Justice, and Accountability in Post-socialism Europe*. Princeton University Press.

Börsenverein des Deutschen Buchhandels e.V. 1998. "Erwiderung der anmeldenden Verlage auf die Beschwerdepunkte der Europäischen Kommission gegen die grenzüberschreitende Preisbindung zwischen Deutschland und Österreich – Zusammenfassung." *Sonderdruck zu dem Börsenblatt für den Deutschen Buchhandel* 54(7).

Bourdieu, P. 1992. *The Rules of Art: Genesis and Structure in a Literary Field*. Stanford University Press.

— 1993. *The Field of Cultural Production*. Columbia University Press.

— 2018. "Distinction a Social Critique of the Judgement of Taste." In D. Grusky and S. Szelenyi (eds.), *Inequality: Classic Readings in Race, Class, and Gender* (287–318). Routledge.

Bourriaud, N. 2002. *Relationship Aesthetics*. Les Presses du reel.

Bowman, B. 2014. "On the Defense of Literary Value: From Early German Romanticism to Analytic Philosophy of Literature." In D. Nassar (ed.), *The Relevance of Romanticism: Essays on German Romantic Philosophy* (147–62). Oxford University Press.

Boyarin, J., ed. 1993. *The Ethnography of Reading*. University of California Press.

Boyd, B. 1990. *Vladimir Nabokov: The Russian Years*. Princeton University Press.

Boyer, D. 2001a. "Yellows Sands of Berlin." *Ethnography* 2(3): 421–39.

— 2001b. "Foucault in the Bush: The Social Life of Post-Structuralist Theory in East Berlin's Prenzlauer Berg." *Ethnos* 66(2): 207–36. https://doi.org/10.1080/00141840120070949.

— 2005. *Spirit and System*. Chicago Press.

Boym, S. 1994. "The Archeology of Banality: The Soviet Home." *Public Culture* 6(2): 263–92. https://doi.org/10.1215/08992363-6-2-263.

Brandel, A. 2020. "Literature and Anthropology." In *Oxford Research Encyclopedia of Anthropology*. Oxford University Press.

Brandel, A., and S. Bagaria. 2020. "Plotting the Field: Fragments and Narrative in Malinowski's Stories of the Baloma." *Anthropological Theory* 20(1): 29–52. https://doi.org/10.1177/1463499619830480.

Brandel, A., V. Das, and M. Puett. In press. "Language in Flight: Home and Elsewhere." *Sophia International Journal of Philosophy and Traditions*.

Brandel, A., and M. Motta. 2021. "Introduction: Life with Concepts." In A. Brandel and M. Motta (eds.), *Living with Concepts* (1–28). Fordham University Press.

Brandl, A. 1913. *Shakespeare and Germany*. Oxford University Press.

Brandt, B. 2005. "Ein Wort, ein Ort, or How Words Create Places: Interview with Yoko Tawada." *Women in German Yearbook* 21: 1–15. https://doi.org/10.1353/wgy.2005.0009.

– 2008. "Scattered Leaves: Artist Books and Migration: A Conversation with Yoko Tawada," *Comparative Literature Studies* 45(1): 12–22. https://doi.org/10.2307/25659630.

Brecht, B. 1994. *Kriegsfibel*. Eulenspiegel.

Breuilly, J. ed. 1992. *The State of Germany: The National Idea in the Making, Unmaking and Remaking of a Modern National State*. Longman.

Brubaker, R. 2009. *Citizenship and Nationhood in France and Germany*. Harvard University Press.

Buch Segal, L. 2016. *No Place for Grief*. University of Pennsylvania Press.

Buck-Morss, S. 1986. "The Flâneur, the Sandwichman and the Whore." *New German Critique* (Autumn 1986): 99–140. https://doi.org/10.2307/488122.

Bush, J.A. 2020. *Between Muslims: Religious Difference in Iraqi Kurdistan*. Stanford University Press.

Cabot, H. 2019. "The Business of Anthropology and the European Refugee Regime." *American Ethnologist*. 46(3): 261–75. https://doi.org/10.1111/amet.12791.

Çaglar, A. 1997. "Hyphenated Identities and the Limits of 'Culture': Some Methodological Queries." In P. Werbner and T. Modood (eds.), *The Politics of Multiculturalism in the New Europe: Racism, Identity, Community* (169–86). London: Zed Publications.

– 1998. "Popular Culture, Marginality and Institutional Incorporation: German-Turkish Rap and Turkish Pop in Berlin." *Cultural Dynamics* 10(3): 243–61. https://doi.org/10.1177/092137409801000301.

– 2016. "Still 'Migrants' after All Those Years: Foundational Mobilities, Temporal Frames and Emplacement of Migrants." *Journal of Ethnic and Migration Studies* 42(6): 952–69. https://doi.org/10.1080/1369183X.2015.1126085.

Caldeira, T. 2012. "Imprinting and Moving Around: New Visibilities and Configurations of Public Space in São Paulo." *Public Culture* 24(2): 385–419. https://doi.org/10.1215/08992363-1535543.

Carruthers, A. 2008. *Exile and Return: Detteritorializing National Imaginaries in Vietnam and the Diaspora*. PhD dissertation. University of Sydney.

Cassin, B. 1995/6. L'effet sophistique. Gallimard.

– 2004. Vocabulaire européen des philosophies: dictionnaire des intraduisibles. Éditions de Seuil.

– 2016. *Nostalgia: When Are We Ever at Home?* Fordham University Press.

Cassin, B., E. Apter, J. Lezra, and M. Wood, eds. 2014. *Dictionary of Untranslatables: A Philosophical Lexicon*. Vol. 35. Princeton University Press.

Caton, S.C. 1990. *Peaks of Yemen I Summon: Poetry as Cultural Practice in a North Yemeni Tribe*. University of California Press.

Cavarero, Adriana. 2005. *For More Than One Voice*. Stanford University Press.

Cavell, S. 1979. *The Claim of Reason: Wittgenstein, Skeptcisim, Morality and Tragedy*. Oxford University Press.

– 1988. *In Quest of the Ordinary: Lines of Skepticism and Romanticism*. University of Chicago Press.

– 1992. *Senses of Walden*. University of Chicago Press.

– 1996. *Contesting Tears: The Hollywood Melodrama of the Unknown Woman*. Chicago University Press.

– 1996. *A Pitch of Philosophy: Autobiographical Exercises* (Vol. 4). Harvard University Press.

– 2005. "Stella Dallas." In *Cities of Words: Pedagogical Letters on a Register of the Moral Life*. Belknap Press.

– 2007. "Preface." In V. Das, *Life and Words: Violence and the Descent into the Ordinary* (ix–xiv). University of California Press.

– 2010. "The Touch of Words." In W. Day and V.J. Krebs (eds.), *Seeing Wittgenstein Anew* (81–101). Cambridge University Press.

– 2015. *Must We Mean What We Say? A Book of Essays*. Cambridge University Press.

– 2020. *Here and There: Sites of Philosophy*, N. Bauer, A. Crary, and S. Laugier (eds.). Harvard University Press.

Chaganti, S. 2021. *Geneologies of the Juridical: Law, Land, Property*. PhD. dissertation. Johns Hopkins University.

Chatterji, R. 2012. *Speaking with Pictures: Folk Art and the Narrative Tradition in India*. Routledge.

– 2021. "Myths, Similes and Memory Traces: Images of Abduction in the Ramayana Universe." *Society and Culture in South Asia* 7(2): 232–69.

Chatterji, R., and E. Lall. 2014. "Word, Image, Movement: Translating Pain." In R. Chatterji (ed.), *Wording the World* (69–83). Fordham University Press.

Chatterji, R., and D. Mehta. 2001. "Boundaries, Names, Alterities: A Case Study of a 'Communal Riot' in Dharavi, Bombay." In V. Das et al. (eds.), *Remaking a World: Violence, Social Suffering, and Recovery* (201–49). University of California Press.

Cheah, P. 2014. "World against Globe: Toward a Normative Conception of World Literature." *New Literary History* 45(3): 303–29. https://doi.org/10.1353/nlh.2014.0021.

Chin, R. 2017. *The Crisis of Multiculturalism in Europe*. Princeton University Press.

Cixous, H. 1976. "The Laugh of the Medusa." Signs 1(4): 875–93.

Cody, F. 2011. "Publics and Politics." *Annual Review of Anthropology* 40: 37–52.

– 2013. *The Light of Knowledge: Literacy Activism and the Politics of Writing in South Asia*. Cornell University Press.

Cohen, A. 2016. *Fabriquer le livre au Maroc*. Karthala: IISMM.

Cohen, A (J. Angell, trans.). 2017. "The Distribution of Knowledge and the Material Presence of Books: The Sidewalk Book Vendors of Rabat and Casablanca, Morocco." *Ethnologie francaise* 1: 23–36.

Cole, T. 2019. "On Carrying and Being Carried." Transcript of speech delivered at the HKW, June 18, 2019. https://archiv.hkw.de/en/app/mediathek/audio/70709.

Conant, J. 2005. "Stanley Cavell's Wittgenstein." *The Harvard Review of Philosophy* 13(1): 50–64. https://doi.org/10.5840/harvardreview200513113.

Conrad, S. 2010. *The Quest for the Lost Nation*. University of California Press.

Conrad, S., and S. Randeria. 2002. "Geteilte Geschichten–Europa in einer postkolonialen Welt." *Jenseits des Eurozentrismus. Postkoloniale Perspektiven in den Geschichts-und Kulturwissenschaften* (9–49).

Cooke, P. 2003. "Performing Ostalgie: Leander Haussmann's Sonnenallee." *German Life and Letters* 56(2): 156–67. https://doi.org/10.1111/1468-0483.00250.

Crary, A. 2011. "JM Coetzee, Moral Thinker." In A. Leist and P. Singer (eds.), *J.M. Coetzee and Ethics* (249–68). Columbia University Press.

Crawley, H., and D. Skleparis. 2017. "Refugees, Migrants, Neither, Both: Categorical Fetishism and the Politics of Bounding in Europe's 'Migration Crisis.'" *Journal of Ethnic and Migration Studies* 44(1): 48–64. https://doi.org/10.1080/1369183X.2017.1348224.

Cruikshank, J. 1997. "Negotiating with Narrative: Establishing Cultural Identity at the Yukon International Storytelling Festival." *American Anthropologist* 99(1): 56–69. https://doi.org/10.1525/aa.1997.99.1.56.

Dahlke, B. 1997. Papierboot: Autorinnen aus der DDR – inoffiziell publiziert. Königshausen und Neumann.

– 2011. "Performing GDR in Poetry?: The Literary Significance of 'East German' Poetry in Unified Germany." In K. Gertenberger (ed.), *German Literature in a New Century* (178–96). Berghahn.

Dahlke, B., M. Langermann, and T. Taterka, eds. 2000. *LiteraturGesellschaft DDR: Kanonkämpfe und ihre Geschichte(n)*. J.B. Metzler Verlag.

Damrosch, D. 2006. "World Literature in a Postcanonical, Hypercanonical Age." In H. Saussy (ed.), *Comparative Literature in an Age of Globalization* (43–53). Baltimore: Johns Hopkins University Press.

- 2018. *What Is World Literature?* Princeton University Press.
- 2020. *Comparing the Literatures.* Princeton University Press.

Damrosch, D., and G.C. Spivak. 2011. "Comparative Literature/World Literature: A Discussion with Gayatri Chakravorty Spivak and David Damrosch." *Comparative Literature Studies* 48(4): 455–85. https://doi.org/10.5325/complitstudies.48.4.0455.

Das, V. 1977. (2012). *Structure and Cognition.* Oxford University Press.
- 2007. *Life and Words: Violence and the Descent into the Ordinary.* University of California Press.
- 2012. "Ordinary Ethics." In D. Fassin (ed.), A Companion to Moral Anthropology (133–49). Wiley-Blackwell.
- 2015. "What Does Ordinary Ethics Look Like?" In M. Lambek, V. Das, D. Fassin, and W. Keane (eds.), *Four Lectures on Ethics: Anthropological Perspectives* (53–127). HAU Press.
- 2020. *Textures of the Ordinary: Doing Anthropology after Wittgenstein.* Fordham University Press.

Das, V., M.D. Jackson, A. Kleinman, and B. Singh, eds. 2015. "Experiments between Anthropology and Philosophy." In *The Ground Between: Anthropologists Engage Philosophy* (1–27). Duke University Press.

Davidson, D. 1993. "Locating Literary Language." *Literary Theory after Davidson.* Pennsylvania State University Press.

Dawson, A., and N. Rapport, eds. 2021. *Migrants of Identity: Perceptions of "Home" in a World of Movement.* Routledge.

Debaene, V. 2010. *L'adieu au voyage: L'ethnologie française entre science et littérature.* Éditions Gallimard.

Debord, G. 1967. *La société du spectacle.* Buchet-Chaste.

de Certeau, M. 1984. *The Practice of Everyday Life.* University of California Press.

De Genova, N., ed. 2017. *The Borders of "Europe": Autonomy of Migration, Tactics of Bordering.* Duke University Press.
- 2019. "Migration and the Mobility of Labor." In *The Oxford Handbook of Karl Marx* (425–40). Oxford University Press.

Deleuze, G., and F. Guattari. 1975. *Kafka: Pour une littérature mineure.* Les éditions de Minuit.

Detienne, M., and G. Camassa. 1988. *Les Savoirs de l'écriture en Grèce ancienne.* Presses Universitaires de Lille.

Dharwadker, V. 2003. "Orientalism and the Study of Indian Literatures." In C.A. Breckenridge and P. Van Der Veer (eds.), *Orientalism and the Postcolonial Predicament: Perspectives on South Asia.* University of Pennsylvania Press.

Diamond, C. 1981. "What Nonsense Might Be." *Philosophy* 56: 5–22.
- 1983. "Having a Rough Story about What Moral Philosophy Is." *New Literary History* 15(1): 155–69. https://doi.org/10.2307/468998.

- 1991. *The Realistic Spirit: Wittgenstein, Philosophy, and the Mind*. MIT Press.
- 2012a. "Criticising from 'Outside.'" *Philosophical Investigations* 36(2): 119. https://doi.org/10.1111/phin.12000.
- 2012b. "The Skies of Dante and Our Skies: A Response to Ilham Dilman." *Philosophical Investigations* 35(3–4): 191–2. https://doi.org/10.1111/j.1467-9205.2012.01478.x.

Didi-Huberman, G. 2008. *Images in Spite of All: Four Photographs from Auschwitz*. University of Chicago Press.

Dilman, I. 2002. *Wittgenstein's Copernican Revolution: The Question of Linguistic Idealism*. Palgrave.

Dippel, A. 2015. *Dichten und Denken in Österreich: Eine Literarische Ethnographie*. Verlag Turia + Kant.

Dolar, M. 2006. *A Voice and Nothing More*. The MIT Press.

Donatelli, P. 2016. "Loos, Musil, Wittgenstein, and the Recovery of Human Life." In M. LeMahieu and K. Zumhagen-Yekplé (eds.), *Wittgenstein and Modernism* (91–113). University of Chicago Press.

Doughan, S., and H. Tzuberi. 2018. "Säkularismus als Praxis und Herrschaft: Zur Kategorisierung von Juden und Muslimen im Kontext säkularer Wissensproduktion." In *Der inspizierte Muslim* (269–308). transcript-Verlag.

Du Gay, P. 2004. "Guest Editor's Introduction." *Consumption Markets and Culture* 7(2): 99–105.

Du Gay, P., and S. Nixon. 2002. "Who Needs Cultural Intermediaries?" *Cultural Studies* 16(4): 495–500. https://doi.org/10.1080/09502380210139070.

Eidson, J. 2000. "Which Past for Whom? Local Memory in a German Community During the Era of Nation Building." *In Ethos* 28(4): 575–607. https://doi.org/10.1525/eth.2000.28.4.575. Theme issue on "Subjectivity in History," G. White, ed.

Eiland, H. 2007. "Superimposition in Walter Benjamin's Arcades Project." *telos*, 2007(138): 121–38.

Emery, J. 2002. "Guides to Berlin." *Comparative Literature* 54(4): 291–306. https://doi.org/10.1215/-54-4-291.

Enns, A. 2008. "The Politics of Ostalgie: Post-socialist Nostalgia in Recent German Film." *Screen* 48(4): 475–91. https://doi.org/10.1093/screen/hjm049.

Érard, L.R., and J. Stebler. Lire en l'autre comme dans un livre ouvert. A contrario 2021(1) 31: 3–22.

Érard, Y. 2017. *Des jeux de langage chez l'enfant. Saussure, Wittgenstein, Cavell et la transmission du langage, Lausanne*. BSN Press.

Everett, W., and P. Wagstaff. 2004. *Cultures of Exile: Images of Displacement*. New York: Berghahn Books.

Ewing, K.P. 2003. "Living Islam in the Diaspora: Between Turkey and Germany." *The South Atlantic Quarterly* 102(2): 405–31. https://doi.org/10.1215/00382876-102-2-3-405.

- 2006. "Between Cinema and Social Work: Diasporic Turkish Women and the (Dis)pleasures of Hybridity." *Cultural Anthropology* 21(2): 265–94. https://doi.org/10.1525/can.2006.21.2.265.
Fanon, F. 2008. *Black Skin, White Masks*. Grove Press.
Fasolt, C. 2014. *Past Sense: Studies in Medieval and Early Modern European History*. Brill.
Faudree, P. 2012. "Music, Language and Texts." *Annual Review of Anthropology* 41:519–36. https://doi.org/10.1146/annurev-anthro-092611-145851.
Fehrenbach, E. 1994. *Adel und Bürgertum in detuschen Vormärz*. Stiftung Historisches Kolleg.
Feilchenfeldt, K. 1986. *Deutsche Exilliteratur 1933–1945*. Winkler.
Felski, R. 2008. *Uses of Literature*. Wiley-Blackwell.
Felski, R., A. Anderson, and T. Moi. 2019. *Character: Three Inquiries in Literary Studies*. University of Chicago Press.
Felsmann, B., and A. Gröschner, eds. 1999. *Durchgangszimmer Prenzlauer Berg. Eine Berliner Künstlersozialgeschichte in Selbstauskünften*. Lukas Verlag.
Ferguson, C. 1959. "Diglossia." *Word* 15(2): 325–40. https://doi.org/10.1080/00437956.1959.11659702.
Fields, K.E., and B.J. Fields. 2014. *Racecraft: The Soul of Inequality in American Life*. Verso Trade.
Florvil, T.N. 2020. *Mobilizing Black Germany: Afro-German Women and the Making of a Transnational Movement*. University of Illinois Press.
Floyd, J. 2007. "Wittgenstein and the Inexpressible." In A. Crary (ed.), *Wittgenstein and Moral Life* (177–234). MIT Press.
Föllmer, M. 2002. *Die Verteidigung der bürgerlichen Nation: Industrielle und hohe Beamte in Deutschland und Frankreich*. Vandenhoeck und Reprecht.
Foucault, M. 2004. *Abnormal: Lectures at the Collège de France, 1974–1975*. Picador.
Fraser, N. 1992. "Rethinking the Public Sphere: A Contribution to the Critique of Actually Existing Democracy." *Social Text* 25/26: 56–80. https://doi.org/10.1177/1749975515594467.
Frevert, U. 1989. "Tatenarm und Gedankenvoll? Bürgertum in Deutschland 1807–1820." In H. Berging et al. (eds.), *Deutschland und Frankreich in Zeitalter der Revolution*. Verlag.
Friedländer, S. 1987. "West Germany and the Burden of the Past: The Ongoing Debate." *Jerusalem Quarterly* 42 (Spring). https://doi.org/10.2307/2657347.
Friedrich, P. 1986. *The Language Parallax: Linguistic Relativism and Poetic Indeterminacy*. University of Texas Press.
Furani, K. 2012. *Silencing the Sea: Secular Rhythms in Palestinian Poetry*. Stanford University Press.
Gal, S. 2002. "A Semiotics of the Public/Private Distinction." *Differences: A Journal of Feminist Cultural Studies* 13(1): 77–95. https://doi.org/10.1215/10407391-13-1-77.

- 2006. "Migration, Minorities and Multilingualism: Language Ideologies in Europe." In C. Mar-Molinero and P. Stevenson (eds.), *Language Ideologies, Policies and Practices*(13–27). Palgrave Macmillan.
- 2013. "Texts Are Also Things." *Anthropology of This Century*, Vol. 6. http://aotcpress.com/articles/texts/.

Gal, S., and J.T. Irvine. 1995. "The Boundaries of Languages and Disciplines: How Ideologies Construct Difference." *Social Research*, Vol. 62(4): 967–1001.
- 2019. *Signs of Difference: Language and Ideology in Social Life*. Cambridge University Press.

Garcia, A. 2020. "Fragments of Relatedness: Writing, Archiving, and the Vicissitudes of Kinship." *Ethnos* 85(4): 717–29.

Garloff, K. 2004. "The Emigrant as Witness: WG Sebald's 'Die Ausgewanderten.'" *German Quarterly* 77(1): 76–93.

Gell, A. 1975. *Metamorphosis of the Cassowaries: Umeda Society, Language and Ritual*. Athlon Press.
- 1982. "The Market-Wheel: Symbolic Aspects of an Indian Tribal Market." *Man* 17(3): 470–91. https://doi.org/10.2307/2801710.

Genette, G. 1991. *Fiction et diction*. Seuil.

Germana, N. 2009. *The Orient of Europe: The Mythical Image of India and Competing Images of German National Identity*. Cambridge Scholars Publishing.

Gerstenberger, K. 2008. *Writing the New Berlin: The German Capital in Post-Wall Literature* (Vol. 21). Camden House.

Giesen, B. 1998. *Intellectuals and the Nation: Collective Identity in a German Axial Age*. N. Levis and A. Weisz, trans. Cambridge University Press.

Giordano, C. 2008. "Practices of Translation and the Making of Migrant Subjectivities in Contemporary Italy." *American Ethnologist* 35(4): 588–606. https://doi.org/10.1111/j.1548-1425.2008.00100.x.

Glissant, É. 1997. *Poetics of Relation*. University of Michigan Press.

Godelier, M. 2011. *The Mental and the Material*. Verso Trade.

Golovko, E. 1994. "Copper Island Aleut." In P. Bakker and M. Mous (eds.), *Mixed Languages: 15 Case Studies in Language Intertwining* (113–21). ICG Printing.

Goody, J. 1986. *The Logic of Writing and the Organization of Society*. Cambridge: University of Cambridge Press.
- 1987. *The Interface between the Written and the Oral*. Cambridge University Press.
- 2000. *The Power of the Written Tradition*. Smithsonian Institution Press.
- 2006. "From Oral to Written: An Anthropological Breakthrough in Storytelling." *The Novel* 1: 3–36. https://doi.org/10.1017/CBO9780511778896.009.

Graeber, D. 2001. *Toward an Anthropological Theory of Value*. Palgrave Macmillan.

– 2013. "It Is Value that Brings Universes into Being." *HAU: Journal of Ethnographic Theory* 3(2): 219–43. https://doi.org/10.14318/hau3.2.012.

Gramling, D. 2021. *The Invention of Multilingualism*. Cambridge University Press.

Graves, Tracy. 2014. "Berlin's Museum Island." In J. Diefendorf and J. Ward (eds.), *Transnationalism and the German City* (223–37). New York: Palgrave Macmillan.

Greenblatt, S. 1997. "The Touch of the Real." *Representations* 59: 14–29. https://doi.org/10.2307/2928812.

Guetti, J. 1993. *Wittgenstein and the Grammar of Literary Experience*. University of Georgia Press.

Guyer, J. 1993. "Wealth in People and Self-realization in Equatorial Africa." *Man* 28(2): 243–65. https://doi.org/10.2307/2803412.

Guyer, J., and S. Belinga. 1995. "Wealth in People as Wealth in Knowledge: Accumulation and Composition in Equatorial Africa." *The Journal of African History* 36(1): 91–120. https://doi.org/10.1017/S0021853700026992.

Hage, G. 2019. "Afterword: Bearable Life." *Suomen Antropologi: Journal of the Finnish Anthropological Society* 44(2): 81–3. https://doi.org/10.30676/jfas.v44i2.88985.

Hakyemez, S. 2017. "Margins of the Archive: Torture, Heroism, and the Ordinary in Prison No. 5, Turkey." *Anthropological Quarterly* 90(1): 107–38.

Hall, S. 1973. *Encoding and Decoding in the Television Discourse*. Centre for Contemporary Cultural Studies.

Han, C. 2012. *Life in Debt: Times of Care and Violence in Neoliberal Chile*. University of California Press.

– 2020. *Seeing Like a Child*. Fordham University Press.

Han, C., and A. Brandel. 2020. "Genres of Witnessing: Narrative, Violence, Generations." *Ethnos* 85(4): 629–46. https://doi.org/10.1080/00141844.2019.1630466.

Hanks, W.F., and C. Severi. 2014. "Translating Worlds: The Epistemological Space of Translation." *HAU: Journal of Ethnographic Theory* 4(2): 1–16.

Hannerz, U. 1992. *Cultural Complexity: Studies in the Social Organization of Meaning*. Columbia University Press.

Hardt, M., and A. Negri. 2000. *Empire*. Harvard University Press.

– 2009 *Commonwealth*. Harvard University Press.

Harkness, N. 2013. *Songs of Seoul: An Ethnography of Voice and Voicing in Christain South Korea*. University of California Press.

Hartmann, S. 1997. *Scenes of Subjection: Terror, Slavery, and Self-Making in Nineteenth-Century America*. Oxford University Press.

Harvey, D. 2003. *Paris: Capital of Modernity*. Taylor & Francis.

Haxthausen, C.W., and H. Suhr. 1990. *Berlin: Culture and Metropolis*. University of Minnesota Press.

Henderson M.G. 1992. "Speaking in Tongues: Dialogics, Dialectics, and the Black Woman Writer's Literary Tradition." In J. Butler and J. Scott (eds.), *Feminists Theorize the Political* (144–67). Routledge.

Herbert, U. 2001. *Geschichte der Ausländerpolitik in Deutschland: Saisonarbeiter, Zwangsarbeiter, Gastarbeiter, Flüchtlinge.* CH Beck.

Hertz, D. 1979. *The Literary Salon in Berlin, 1780–1806: The Social History of an Intellectual Institution.* University of Minnesota Press.

Herzfeld, M. 1991. *A Place in History.* Princeton University Press.

– 1997. *Portrait of a Greek Imagination: An Ethnographic Biography of Andreas Nenedakis.* University of Chicago Press.

– 2009. *Evicted from Eternity.* University of Chicago Press.

Hessel, F. 2013 [1930]. *Spazieren in Berlin.* Verlag für Berlin-Brandenburg.

Hirsch, M. 2012. *The Generation of Postmemory: Writing and Visual Culture after the Holocaust.* Columbia University Press.

Hirschkind, C. 2009. *The Ethical Soundscape.* Columbia University Press.

Hohendahl. P.U. 1985. *Literarische Kultur im Zeitalter des Liberalismus 1830–1870.* C.H. Beck.

Holmes, S.M., and H. Castañeda. 2016. "Representing the 'European Refugee Crisis' in Germany and Beyond: Deservingness and Difference, Life and Death." *American Ethnologist* 43(1): 12–24.

Humphrey, C. 2002. "Does the Category of 'Postsocialist' Still Make Sense?" In C. Hann (ed.), *Postsocialism: Ideals, Ideologies and Practices in Eurasia* (12–14). Routledge.

Hundt, M. 2000. *"Spracharbeit" im 17. Jahrhundert.* de Gruyter.

Huneke, S.C. 2022. *States of Liberation: Gay Men between Dictatorship and Democracy in Cold War Germany.* University of Toronto Press.

Hui, T. 2019. "Words That I Swallowed Whole: The Linguistic Edibility of Yoko Tawada's Exophonic Writings." In D. Slaymaker (ed), *Tawada Yōko: On Writing and Rewriting* (199–213). Lexington Books.

Hui, T. 2020. *Melodramas of the Tongue: Accented Speech in Literature, Art, and Theory.* PhD dissertation, Leiden University.

Hunn, K. 2005. *"Next Year We Will Be Back": History of Turkish "Guest Workers" in Germany.* Göttingen.

Hutchinson, P., and R. Reed. 2017. "Grammar." In A. Matar (ed.), *Understanding Wittgenstein, Understanding Modernism* (224–33). Bloomsbury.

Huyssen, A. 1995. *Twilight Memories.* Routledge.

– 2003. *Present Pasts.* Stanford University Press.

Irving, A. 2007. "Ethnography, Art and Death." *JRAI* 13(1): 185–208. https://doi.org/10.1111/j.1467-9655.2007.00420.x.

Iser, W. 1991. *Das Fictive und das Imaginäre: Literarischer Anthropologie.* Suhrkamp.

Ivry, J. 2007. "The Memoirist as Collector: Lyn Hejinian's My Life and Walter Benjamin's A Berlin Chronicle." *ANQ: A Quarterly Journal of Short Articles, Notes and Reviews* 20(2): 47–53.

Jackson, M. 2013a. *The Politics of Storytelling: Variations on a Theme by Hannah Arendt* (Vol. 4). Museum Tusculanum Press.

– 2013b. *The Wherewithal of Life*. University of California Press.

Jakob, D. 2013. "The Eventification of Place: Urban Development and Experience Consumption in Berlin and New York City." *European Urban and Regional Studies* 20(4): 447–59. https://doi.org/10.1177/0969776412459860.

Janzen, M. 2017. "Berlin's International Literature Festival." In K. Bauer and J.R. Hosek (eds.), *Cultural Topographies of the New Berlin*. Berghahn.

– 2020. "Buying Autonomy and Citizenship: The Mischkalkulation in Germany's Literary Industry." In *Die große Mischkalkulation* (33–47). Wilhelm Fink.

Jones, H. 1923. *Shakespeare and Germany*. BiblioLife.

Jones, L.R. 2015. "The Squirrel Principle." *Letters from Berlin*. https://thepigeonhole.com/books/letters-from-berlin.

Jurgens, J. 2012. "Invisible Migrants." In M. Silberman, K.E. Till, and J. Ward (eds.), *Walls, Borders, Boundaries: Spatial and Cultural Practices in Europe*. New York: Berghahn.

Kearney, M. 1995. "The Local and the Global: The Anthropology of Globalization and Transnationalism." *Annual Reviews of Anthropology* 24: 547–65. https://doi.org/10.1146/annurev.an.24.100195.002555.

Kearney, R. 2008. "Bachelard and the Epiphanic Instant." *Philosophy Today* 52: 38–45. https://doi.org/10.5840/philtoday200852Supplement52.

Khan, N. 2012. *Muslim Becoming: Aspiration and Skepticism in Pakistan*. Duke University Press.

Kiaulehn, W. 1997. *Berlin: Schicksal einer Weltstadt*. C.H. Beck.

Kiesel, H. 2009. "Berlin Literature Festival Welcomes Bookworms from around the World." *Deutsche Welle*. http://dw.com/p/Jbdw.

Kilic, Z., and J. Petzen. 2013. "The Culture in Multiculturalism and Racialized Art." *German Society and Politics* 31(2): 49–65.

Klawitter, Arne. 2015 "Ideofonografie und transkulturelle Homofonie bei Yoko Tawada." *Arcadia* 50(2): 328–42. https://doi.org/10.1515/arcadia-2015-0024.

Klinkenberg, R. 2001. "Die 'Löwin' von Kurfürstendamm." In B. Wegner, *Die Freundinnen der Bücher. Buchhändlerinnen*. Ulrike Helmer Verlag. Sulzbach.

Kloepfer, A., and M. Matsunaga. 2000. "Yoko Tawada." *Kritisches Lexikon zur deutschsprachigen Gegenwartsliteratur (KLG)*. Vol 64. Munich Edition Text + Kritik.

Kocka J., ed. 1992. *"Bildungsbürgertum im 19. Jahrhundert*. Klett-Cotta.

Kosnick, K. 2007. *Migrant Media: Turkish Broadcasting and Multicultural Politics in Berlin*. Indiana University Press.

Kracauer, S. 1930. *Die Angestellten*. Surkampf.
Kraenzle, C. 2008. "The Limits of Travel: Yoko Tawada's Fictional Travelogues." *German Life and Letters* 61(2): 244–60. https://doi.org/10.1111/j.1468-0483.2008.00422.x.
Kramatschek, C. 2015. "Ich liebe die Freiheit." *Qantara.de*. 06.07.
Krätke, S. 2001. "Berlin. Towards a Global City?" *Urban Studies* 38(10): 1777–99. https://doi.org/10.1080/00420980120084859.
– 2006. "Travelling without Moving: Physical and Linguistic Mobility, Translation, and Identity in Yoko Tawada's Überseezungen." *Transit* 2(1): 1–15. https://doi.org/10.5070/T721009707.
Kroskrity, P. 1993. *Language, History and Identity: Ethnolinguistic Studies of the Arizona Tewa*. University of Arizona Press.
Kulke, E. 2003. "Berlin – deutsche Hauptstadt und Global City?" *Die Erde* 134(3): 219–33.
Lambek, M. 2010. *Ordinary Ethics: Anthropology, Language, and Action*. Fordham University Press.
– 2011. "Kinship as Gift and Theft: Acts of Succession in Mayotte and Ancient Israel." *American Ethnologist* 38: 2–16.
– 2016. *The Weight of the Past: Living with History in Mahajanga, Madagascar*. Springer.
– 2019. *Island in the Stream*. University of Toronto Press.
– 2021. *Concepts and Persons*. University of Toronto Press.
Langer, L.L. 1993. *Holocaust Testimonies: The Ruins of Memory*. Yale University Press.
Laugier, S. 2000. *Du reel a l'ordinaire*. Librarire Philosophique J. Vrin.
– 2013. *Why We Need Ordinary Language Philosophy*. University of Chicago Press.
– 2015. "Voice as Form of Life and Life Form." *Nordic Wittgenstein Review* (special issue): 63–82. https://doi.org/10.15845/nwr.v4i0.3364.
– 2018. "This Is Us: Wittgenstein and the Social." *Philosophical Investigations* 41(2): 204–22. https://doi.org/10.1111/phin.12197.
– 2020. "The Conception of Film for the Subject of Television: Moral Education of the Public and a Return to an Aesthetics of the Ordinary." In D. La Rocca (ed.), *The Thought of Stanley Cavell and Cinema: Turning Anew to the Ontology of Film a Half-Century after The World Viewed* (210–27). Bloomsbury Academic.
– 2021. "Concepts of the Ordinary." In A. Brandel and M. Motta (eds.), *Living with Concepts: Anthropology in the Grip of Reality*. Fordham University Press.
– 2022. "Wittgenstein and Care Ethics as a Plea for Realism." *Philosophies* 7(4): 86–103.
Leavitt, J. 2010. *Linguistic Relativities: Language Diversity and Modern Thought*. Cambridge University Press.

- 2014. "Words and Worlds: Ethnography and Theories of Translation." *HAU: Journal of Ethnographic Theory* 4(2): 193–220. https://doi.org/10.14318/hau4.2.009.
Leggewie, C., and E. Meyer. 2005. *Ein Ort, an den Man Gerne Geht: Das Holocaust-Mahnmal und die Geschistpolitik nach 1989*. Hanser München.
Lévi-Strauss, C. 1955. *Triste Tropiques*. Plon.
Lewis, L.A. 2001. "Of Ships and Saints: History, Memory, and Place in the Making of Moreno Mexican Identity." *Cultural Anthropology* 16(1): 62–82. https://doi.org/10.1525/can.2001.16.1.62.
Liao, Y. 2010a. "Letter to German Chancellor Angela Merkel." February 5, 2010. Translated by Human Rights in China. https://www.hrichina.org/en/content/3214.
- 2010b. "To My German Readers." March 10, 2010. Translated by Human Rights in China. https://www.hrichina.org/en/crf/article/5397.
Liao, Y., and I. Wojak. 2019. "Für die Freiheit der Anderen Kämpfen." Fritz Bauger Blog of the Buxus Stiftung. https://www.fritz-bauer-forum.de/fuer-die-freiheit-der-anderen-kaempfen/.
LiPuma, E., and M. Postone. 2020. "Gifts, Commodities, and the Encompassment of Others." *Critical Historical Studies* 7(1): 167–200. https://doi.org/10.1086/708255.
Litzinger, R.A. 1998. "Re-constituting the Ethnic in Post-Mao China." *Cultural Anthropology*. 13(2): 224–55. https://doi.org/10.1525/can.1998.13.2.224.
Lorde, A. 1984. "An Interview: Audre Lorde and Adrienne Rich." *Sister Outsider: Essays and Speeches by Audre Lorde*. The Crossing Press.
Lotman, Y. 2009. *Universe of the Mind: A Semiotic Theory of Culture*. Indiana University Press.
Lowe, L., and D. Lloyd. 1997. *The Politics of Culture in the Shadow of Capital*. Duke University Press.
MacKendrick, K. 2016. *The Matter of Voice*. Fordham University Press.
Maehl, S. 2015. "Canned Foreign: Transnational Estrangement in Yoko Tawada." In U. Küchler, S. Maehl, and G. Stout (eds.), *Alien Imaginations: Science Fiction and Tales of Transnationalism*. Bloomsbury.
Majetka, L., and I. Titunik. 1984. *Semiotics of Art: Prague School Contributions*. The MIT Press.
Malinowski, B. 1924. *Mutterliche Familie und Ödipus-Komplex*. Internationaler Psychoanalytischer Verlag.
Malkki, L. 1995. "Refugees and Exile: From 'Refugee Studies' to the National Order of Things." *Annual Review of Anthropology* 24: 495–523. https://doi.org/10.1146/annurev.an.24.100195.002431.
Mangrum, B. 2015. "Bourdieu, Cavell, and the Politics of Aesthetic Value." *Literature and Theology*, 29(3): 260–83.
Mani, B.V. 2016. *Recoding World Literature: Libraries, Print Culture, and Germany's Pact with Books*. Fordham University Press.

- 2017. "'Migrants, Refugees, Exiles': Cosmopolitical Claims beyond Willkommenskultur." *The German Quarterly* 90(2): 219–22.
Mannheim, B. 1986. "Popular Song and Popular Grammar, Poetry and Metalanguage." *Word* 37(1–2): 45–75. https://doi.org/10.1080/00437956.1986.11435766.
Manoukian, S. 2012. *City of Knowledge in Twentieth Century Iran: Shiraz, History and Poetry*. Routledge.
Marchand, S. 2001. "German Orientalism and the Decline of the West." *Proceedings of the American Philosophical Society* 145(4).
- 2003. *Down from Olympus: Archaeology and Philhellenism in Germany, 1750–1970*. Princeton University Press.
Marchignoli, S. 2003. "Canonizing an India Text? A.W. Schlegel, W. von Humboldt, Hegel, and the Bhagavadgita." In D. MacGetchin, P. Park, and D.R. SarDesai (eds.), *Sanskrit and "Orientalism": Indology and Comparative Linguistics inGermany, 1750–1958*. Manohar.
Marhoefer, L. 2022. *Racism and the Making of Gay Rights: A Sexologist, His Student, and the Empire of Queer Love*. University of Toronto Press.
Martin, H. 1988. *Histoire et pouvoirs de l'écrit*. Perrin.
Masomi, S. 2012. *Poetry Slam: eine orale Kultur zwischen Tradition und Moderne*. Lektora.
Matsunaga, Miho. 2000. "'Schreiben als Übersetzung': Die Dimension der Übersetzung in den Werken von Yoko Tawada." *Zeitschrift für Germanistik* 12(3): 532–46.
McDowell, J. 2001. *Meaning, Knowledge, and Reality*. Harvard University Press.
McGetchin, D.T. 2004. "Into the Centre of Sanskrit Study: Ancient Indian Studies and German Culture in Berlin and Leipzig during the Nineteenth Century." In D. MacGetchin, P. Park, and D.R. SarDesai (eds.), *Sanskrit and "Orientalism": Indology and Comparative Linguistics in Germany, 1750–1958*. Manohar.
- 2009. *Indology, Indomania, and Orientalism: Ancient India's Rebirth in Modern Germany*. Fairleigh Dickinson University Press.
McQuade, P. 2022. "Translation with the Eye: Yōko Tawada Reads Paul Celan." *Comparative Literature Studies* 59(2): 316–44.
Meillassoux, C. 1981. *Maidens, Meal and Money: Capitalism and the Domestic Community*. Cambridge University Press.
Meiner, A. 1942. "Reclam: eine geschichte der Universal-Bibliothek zu ihrem 75 Jahring besthen, Reclam."
Miller, L. 2006. *Reluctant Capitalists: Bookselling and the Culture of Consumption*. University of Chicago Press.
Moi, T. 2017. *Revolutionary of the Ordinary: Literary Studies after Wittgenstein, Austin and Cavell*. University of Chicago Press.
Mookherjee, N. 2015. *The Spectral Wound: Sexual Vioelnce, Public Memories and the Bangladesh War of 1979*. Duke University Press.

Moran, R. 2011. "Cavell on Outsiders and Others." *Revue internationale de philosophie* 2: 239–54.
– 2018. *The Exchange of Words: Speech, Testimony, and Intersubjectivity.* Oxford University Press.
Morrison, T. 2017. "The Foreigner's Home." In *The Origin of Others* (93–112). Harvard University Press.
Moses, A.D. 2007. *German Intellectuals and the Nazi Past.* Vol. 61. Cambridge: Cambridge University Press.
– 2021. "The German Catechism." *Geschichte der Gegenwart* 23.
Moten, F. 2003. *In the Break: The Aesthetics of the Black Radical Tradition.* University of Minnesota Press.
– 2017. *Black and Blur.* Duke University Press.
Motta, M. 2019. *Esprits fragiles: Réparer les liens ordinaires à Zanzibar.* BSN Press.
– 2021. "What Can We Learn from Children? A Reading of *The Sound and the Fury.*" *Critical Horizons*, 1–16. https://doi.org/10.1080/14409917.2021.1957358.
– Forthcoming. "The Bewitchment of Our Intelligence: Scepticism about Other Minds in Anthropology." *Anthropological Theory.*
Mouffe, C. 2000. *The Democratic Paradox.* Verso.
Mufti, A.R. 2016. *Forget English!* Harvard University Press.
Munn, N.D. 2003. "The 'Becoming-Past' of Places: Spacetime and Memory in Pre-Civil War, 19th Century New York." *Journal of the Finnish Anthropological Society (Suomen Antropologi)* 29(1): 2–19.
Myers, F. 2004. "Ontologies of the Image and Economies of Exchange." *American Ethnologist*, 31(1): 5–20. https://doi.org/10.1525/ae.2004.31.1.5.
Nabokov, B. 1963. *The Gift.* Weidenfeld and Nicolson.
– 2017. *Lectures on Literature.* Houghton Mifflin Harcourt.
Narotzky, S. 2011. "Memories of Conflict and Present Day Struggles in Europe: New Tensions between Corporatism, Class and Social Movements." *Identities* 18(2): 97–112. https://doi.org/10.1080/1070289X.2011.609431.
Narotzky, S., and G. Smith. 2006. *Immediate Struggles.* University of California Press.
Navaro-Yashin, Y. 2020. *Faces of the State.* Princeton University Press.
Negus, K. 2002. "The Work of Cultural Intermediaries and the Enduring Distance between Production and Consumption." *Cultural Studies* 16(4): 501–15. https://doi.org/10.1080/09502380210139089.
Newendorp, N. 2020. *Chinese Senior Migrants and the Globalization of Retirement.* Stanford University Press.
Nietzsche, F. 1997. *Nietzsche: Untimely Meditations.* Cambridge University Press.
Novalis. 1978. *Werke, Tagebücher und Brief Friedrich von Hardenbergs.* H-J. Mahl and R. Samuel, eds. Vienna: Carl Hanser.

Ogden, C.K., and I.A. Richards. 1986. *The Meaning of Meaning*. Mariner Books.
Olszewska, Z. 2015. *The Pearl of Dari: Poetry and Personhood among Young Afghans in Iran*. Indiana University Press.
Özyürek, E. 2014. *Being German, Becoming Muslim*. Princeton University Press.
– 2018. "Rethinking Empathy: Emotions Triggered by the Holocaust among the Muslim-Minority in Germany." *Anthropological Theory* 18(4): 456–77. https://doi.org/10.1177/1463499618782369.
Pareschi, L. 2015. "How I Met My Publisher: Casual and Serial Intermediaries in First-Time Authors' Publication in the Italian Literary Field." *Cultural Sociology* 9(3): 401–24. https://doi.org/10.1177/1749975515590632.
Partridge, D. 2010a. "Holocaust Mahnmal (Memorial): Monumental Memory amidst Contemporary Race." *Comparative Studies in Society and History* 52(4), 820–50. https://doi.org/10.1017/S0010417510000472.
– 2010b. "Travel as an Analytic of Exclusion: Becoming Noncitizens, and the Politics of Mobility after the Berlin Wall." *Identities: Global Studies in Culture and Power* 16(3): 342–66. https://doi.org/10.1080/10702890902861370.
Pautz, H. 2005. "The Politics of Identity in Germany: The Leitkultur Debate." *Race and Class* 46(4): 39–52. https://doi.org/10.1177/0306396805052517.
Peake, B. 2012. "Listening, Language, and Colonialism on Main Street, Gibraltar." *Communication and Critical/Cultural Studies* 9(2): 171–90. https://doi.org/10.1080/14791420.2012.663094.
Perloff, M. 2004. "'But Isn't the Same at Least the Same?': Wittgenstein and the Question of Poetic Translatability." In J. Gibson and W. Huemer (eds.), *The Literary Wittgenstein* (46–66). Routledge.
– 2010. "Language in Migration: Multilingualism and Exophonic Writing in the New Poetics." *Textual Practice* 24(4): 725–48. https://doi.org/10.1080/0950236X.2010.499660.
Picker, J. 2003. *Victorian Soundscapes*. Oxford University Press.
Piper, A. 2009. *Dreaming in Books: The Making of the Bibliographic Imagination in the Romantic Age*. University of Chicago Press.
Platthaus, A. 2017. "Die lust der deutschen am vorlesen." *Frankfurter Allgemeine Zeitung*. https://www.faz.net/aktuell/feuilleton/buecher/themen/die-lust-am-vorlesen-zukunft-der-literaturbranche-15240369.html.
Pollack, S. 2006. *The Language of the Gods in the World of Men*. University of California Press.
Povinelli, E. 2002. *The Cunning of Recognition*. Duke University Press.
– 2011. *Economies of Abandonment*. Duke University Press.
Presau, L. 2020. *Kiezenglish: Multiethnic German and the Global English Debate*. Peter Lang.
Puett, M. Forthcoming. *A Matter of Detail: Anthropolology, Aesthetics, Philosophy*.
Quine, W.V. 1960. *Word and Object*. MIT Press.
Rabinbach, A. 1997. *In the Shadow of Catastrophe*. University of California Press.

Radway, J. 1991. *Reading the Romance: Women, Patriarchy, and Popular Literature*. University of North Carolina Press.
Ramsay, G. 2017. "Incommensurable Futures and Displaced Lives: Sovereignty as Control over Time." *Public Culture* 29(3): 515–38. https://doi.org/10.1215/08992363-3869584.
Ranciére, J. 1998. *La Chair des mots: Politiques de l'ecriture*. Editions Galilée.
– 2000. *Le Partage fdu sensible: Esthétique et politique*. La Fabrique-Éditions.
– 2011. *Politics of Literature*. Polity Press.
Randeria, S., ed. 2016. *Border Crossings: Grenzverschiebungen und Grenzüberschreitungen in einer globalisierten Welt*. Vol. 42. vdf Hochschulverlag AG.
Randeria, S., and E. Karagiannis. 2020. "The Migrant Position: Dynamics of Political and Cultural Exclusion." *Theory, Culture & Society* 37(7–8): 219–31. https://doi.org/10.1177/0263276420957733.
Rapport, N.J. 2007. "An Outline for Cosmopolitan Study: Reclaiming the Human through Introspection." *Current Anthropology* 48(2): 257–83. https://doi.org/10.1086/510475.
Rechtman, R. 2021. *Living in Death: Genocide and Its Functionaries*. Fordham University Press.
– 2017. "From an Ethnography of the Everyday to Writing Echoes of Suffering." *Medicine Anthropology Theory* 4(3).
Redfield, R., and M. Singer. 1954. "The Cultural Role of Cities." *Economic Development and Cultural Change* 3(1): 53–73.
Redlich, J. 2010. "Reading Skin Signs: Decoding Skin as the Fluid Boundary between Self and Other in Yoko Tawada." In M. Hallensleben (ed.), *Performative Body Spaces* (75–88). Brill.
Reed, A. 2011. *Literature and Agency in English Fiction Reading*. University of Toronto Press.
– 2019. "Reading Minor Characters: An English Literary Society and Its Culture of Investigation." *PMLA/Publications of the Modern Language Association of America* 134(1): 66–80. https://doi.org/10.1632/pmla.2019.134.1.66.
Reed, A., and J. Bialecki. 2018. "Introduction to Special Section 1: Anthropology and Character." *Social Anthropology/Anthropologie Sociale* 26(2): 159–67.
Richie, A. 1998. *Faust's Metropolis: A History of Berlin*. Carroll & Graf Publishers.
Ringel, F. 2018. *Back to the Postindustrial Future*. Berghahn Books.
Robbins, B. 1998. "Actually Existing Cosmopolitanism." In I.P. Cheah and B. Robbins (eds.), *Cosmopolitics* (1–19). University of Minnesota Press.
Römhild, R. 2004. "Global Heimat Germany. Migration and the Transnationalization of the Nation-State." *Transit* 1(1). https://doi.org/10.5070/T711009689.

- 2010. "Aus der Perspektive der Migration: Die Kosmopolitisierung Europas." *Das Argument* 285(1): 50–9. https://doi.org/10.14361/9783839408902-014.
- 2014. "Diversität?! Postethnische Perspektiven für eine reflexive Migrationsforschung." In *Kultur, Gesellschaft, Migration* (255–70). Wiesbaden: Springer VS.

Rosen, M. 2015. "Ethnographies of Reading: Beyond Literacy and Books." *Anthropological Quarterly*, 88(4): 1059–83.

Rosenbaum, M. 2019. *"LiterarySspaces without Readers": The Paradoxes of Being a "Writer" in Havana, Cuba*. PhD dissertation. University of St Andrews.

Rothberg, M. 2020. *Multidirectional Memory*. Stanford University Press.

Rothberg, M., and Y. Yildiz. 2011. "Memory Citizenship: Migrant Archives of Holocaust Remembrance in Contemporary Germany." *Parallax* 17(4): 32–48. https://doi.org/10.1080/13534645.2011.605576.

Rukeyser, M. 1996. *The Life of Poetry*. Paris Press.

Said, E. 1983. "Traveling Theory." *The World, the Text, and the Critic*. Harvard University Press.

Saito, N. 1996. *Representations of the Intellectual: The 1993 Reith Lectures*. Vintage.

- 2009. "Ourselves in Translation: Stanley Cavell and Philosophy as Autobiography." *Journal of Philosophy of Education* 43(2): 253–67. https://doi.org/10.1111/j.1467-9752.2009.00691.x.

Sakai, N. 2020. "Image and the Unity of a Language: Translation and the Indeterminacy of a National Language." In D. Slaymaker (ed.), *Tawada Yōko: On Writing and Rewriting*. Lexington Books.

Santner, E.L. 1990. *Stranded Objects: Mourning, Memory, and Film in Postwar Germany*. Cornell University Press.

Sassen, S. 2001. *The Global City: New York, London, Tokyo*. Princeton: Princeton University Press.

- 2005. "The Global City: Introducing a Concept." *Brown Journal of World Affairs* 11(2): 27–43.

Scheffler, K. 1910. *Berlin, ein Stadtschicksal*. E. Reiss.

Schielke, S., and M. Saad Shehata. 2021. *Shared Margins: An Ethnography with Writers in Alexandria after the Revolution*. De Gruyter.

Schiller, N.G. 2008. "Beyond Methodological Ethnicity and towards City Scale: An Alternative Approach to Local and Transnational Pathways of Migrant Incorporation." In L. Pries (ed.), *Rethinking Transnationalism* (52–73). Routledge.

Schiller, N.G., and A. Çağlar. 2018. *Migrants and City-Making: Dispossession, Displacement, and Urban Regeneration*. Duke University Press.

Schiller, N.G., and A. Çağlar, eds. 2011. *Locating Migration: Rescaling Cities and Migrants*. Cornell University Press.

Schiller, N.G., A. Çağlar, and T.C. Guldbrandsen. 2006. "Beyond the Ethnic Lens: Locality, Globality, and Born-Again Incorporation." *American Ethnologist* 33(4): 612–33. https://doi.org/10.1525/ae.2006.33.4.612.

Schiller, N.G., and Irving, A., eds. 2017. *Whose Cosmopolitanism?: Critical Perspectives, Relationalities and Discontents*. Berghahn Books.

Schipsal, I., and W. Nichols. 2014. "Rights to the Neoliberal City." *Territory, Politics, Governance* 2(2): 173–93.

Schlegel, Friedrich. 1798. *Erstdruck in: Athenäum (Berlin)*, 1. Bd., 2. Stück.

Schneider, P. 2014. *Berlin, Now: The City after the Wall*. Farrar, Straus and Giroux.

Schuenke, C., and B. Struzyk. 2013. *Fremde Heimat: Texte aus dem Exil*. Matthies & Seitz.

Schwab, G. 2010. *Haunting Legacies: Violent Histories and Transgenerational Trauma*. Columbia University Press.

Schwenkel, C. 2006. "Recombinant History: Transnational Practices of Memory and Knowledge Production in Contemporary Vietnam." *Cultural Anthropology* 21(1) 3–30. https://doi.org/10.1525/can.2006.21.1.3.

Schwiertz, H. 2016. "Für uns existiert kein Blatt im Gesetzbuch. Migrantische Kämpfe und der Einsatz der radikalen Demokratie." In *Migration und Demokratie* (229–54). Springer VS.

Scott, J. 1998. *Seeing Like a State*. Yale University Press.

Seale, K. 2005. "Eye-Swiping London." *The London Journal* 3(2).

Sengupta, I. 2004. "Shishyas of Another Order: Students of Indology at Bonn and Berlin." In D.R. SarDesai, P.K.J. Park, and D.T. McGetchin (eds.), *Sanskrit and "Orientalism": Indology and Comparative Linguistics inGermany, 1750–1958*. Manohar.

Severi, C. 2015. *The Chimera Principle*. University of Chicago Press.

Sharp, J., et al. 2005. "Just Art for a Just City: Public Art and Social Inclusion in Urban Regeneration." *Urban Studies* 42(5–6): 1001–23. https://doi.org/10.1080/00420980500106963.

Sherzer, J. 1993. "On Puns, Comebacks, Verbal Dueling, and Play Languages: Speech Play in Balinese Verbal Life." *Language in Society* 22(2): 217–33. https://doi.org/10.1017/S0047404500017115.

Sherzer, J., and A.K. Webster. 2015. "Speech Play, Verbal Art, and Linguistic Anthropology." *Oxford Handbook of Linguistics*. Oxford University Press.

Shoshan, N. 2012. "Time at a Standstill: Loss, Accumulation, and the Past Conditional in an East Berlin Neighborhood." *Ethnos* 77(1): 24–49. https://doi.org/10.1080/00141844.2011.580358.

– 2014. "Managing Hate: Political Delinquency and Affective Governance in Germany." *Cultural Anthropology* 29(1): 150–72. https://doi.org/10.14506/ca29.1.09.

– 2016. *The Management of Hate*. Princeton University Press.

Shuster, M. 2010. "Internal Relations and the Possibility of Evil: On Cavell and Monstrosity." *European Journal of Pragmatism and American Philosophy* 2.II-2. https://doi.org/10.4000/ejpap.901.

Silverman, G. 2012. *Bodies and Books: Reading and the Fantasy of Communion in Nineteenth-Century America*. University of Pennsylvania Press.

Silverstein, M. 2003. "The Whens and Wheres – as Well as Hows – of Ethnolinguistic Recognition." *Public Culture* 15(3): 531–57. https://doi.org/10.1215/08992363-15-3-531.

Silverstein, M., and G. Urban. 1996. *Natural Histories of Discourse*. University of Chicago Press.

Simmel, G. 1903. "Die Großstädte und das Geistesleben." Jahrbuch der Gehe-Stiftung Dresden. Vol. 9, 185–206. Translated as "The Metropolis and Mental Life." In D.N. Levine (ed.), *Georg Simmel: On Individuality and Social Forms* (224–39). University of Chicago Press.

Smith, B.J. 2021. "'Berlin Does You Good': Experimental Art, Place Marketing and the Urban Public Sphere in 1980s West Berlin." *Contemporary European History* 30(3): 414–26. https://doi.org/10.1017/S0960777319000389.

Söderström, O., D. Ruedin, S. Randeria, G. D'Amato, and F. Panese. 2013. *Critical Mobilities*. Routledge/EPFL Press.

Soysal, L. 2004. "Rap, Hiphop, Kreuzberg." *New German Critique* 92: 62–81.

Stebler, J. 2020. *La lecture, un jeu d'enfants: Scènes d'appretissage et d'anthropologie*. PhD dissertation. Université Laussanne.

Steinhilper, E. 2017. "Politisiert in der Migration, vernetzt in der Stadt. Transnationaler politischer Protest von Geflüchteten in Berlin." *Forschungsjournal Soziale Bewegungen* 30(3): 76–86. https://doi.org/10.1515/fjsb-2017-0062.

Stevenson, P. 2017. *Language and Migration in a Multilingual Metropolis: Berlin Lives*. Springer.

Strathern, M. 1999. Property, Substance and Effect: Anthropological Essays on Persons and Things. Athlone Press.

– 2020. *Relations: An Anthropological Account*. Duke University Press.

Tatlock, L., ed. 2010. *Publishing Culture and the "Reading Nation": German Book History in the Long Nineteenth Century*. Camden House.

Taussig, M. 1986/7. *Shamanism, Colonialism, and the Wild Man: A Study in Terror and Healing*. University of Chicago Press.

– 2012. "Excelente Zona Social." *Cultural Anthropology* 27(3): 498–517.

Tawada, Y. 1996. *Talisman*. Konkursbuch Verlag.

– 1998. *Verwandlungen*. Konkursbuch Verlag.

– 2000. *Spielzeug und Sprachmagie in der Europaischen Literatur*. Konkursbuch Verlag.

– 2002. *Überseezungen*. Konkursbuch Verlag.

– 2007. *Where Europe Begins*. New Directions.

- 2013a. "Das Tor des Übersetzers oder Celan liest Japanisch." *Zeitschrift für interkulturelle Germanistik* 4(2): 171–8.
- 2013b. "Celan Reads Japanese." *The White Review*, March Issue. https://www.thewhitereview.org/feature/celan-reads-japanese/.
- 2014. "The Script of a Turtle or the Problem of Translation." In A Nurmi, T. Rütten, and P. Pahta (eds.), *Challenging the Myth of Monolingualism* (171–80). Brill.
- 2016. *Akzentfrei*. Konkursbuch Verlag.
- 2018. *The Emissary*. New Directions.
- 2020. "Laudatio for Uljana Wolf: Erlangener Literary Prize for Poetry as Translation." In D. Slaymaker (ed.), *Tawada Yōko: On Writing and Rewriting*. Lexington Books.

Tedlock, D. 1996. "Towards a Poetics of Polyphony and Translatability." In C. Bernstein (ed.), *Close Listening: Poetry and the Performed Words*. Oxford University Press

- 2002. "Written in Sound: Translating the Multiple Voices of the Zuni Storyteller." In M. Shell (ed.), *American Babel: Literatures of the United States from Abnaki to Zuni*. Harvard University Press.

Tennant, E.C. 1996. "The Protection of Invention: Printing Privileges in Early Modern Germany." In G. Williams and S. Schindler (eds.), *Knowledge, Science, and Literature in Early Modern Germany*. University of North Carolina Press.

Ticktin, M. 2011. *Causalities of Care*. Universities of California Press.

Till, K. 2005. *The New Berlin*. University of Minnesota Press.

Tinius, J. 2016. "Authenticity and Otherness: Reflecting Statelessness in German Postmigrant Theatre." *Critical Stages/Scènes critiques* (14).

- 2017. "Anthropologische Beobachtungen zu künstlerischer Subjektivierung und institutioneller Reflexivität: Das Theaterprojekt *Ruhrorter* mit Geflüchteten am Theater an der Ruhr." In M. Warstat, F. Evers, K. Flade, et al. (eds.), *Applied Theatre – Frames and Positions* (205–35). Theater der Zeit.

Tobias, R. 2012. "Irreconcilable: Ethics and Aesthetics for Hermann Cohen and Walter Benjamin." *MLN* 127(3): 665–80.

Trouillot, M.-R. 2002. "The Otherwise Modern: Caribbean Lessons from the Savage Slot." In M. Knauft (ed.), *Critically Modern: Alternatives, Alterities, Anthropologies* (B220–37). Indiana University Press.

Verdery, K. 1996. *What Was Socialism and What Comes Next?* Princeton University Press.

Walser, R. 1917. *Der Spaziergang*. Leipzig: Huber & Co.

- 2006. *Robert Walser: Berlin gibt immer den Ton an*. Suhrkamp. Translation as *Berlin Stories*. 2012. Suhrkamp.

Warner, M. 2002a. *Publics and Counterpublics*. Cambridge: Zone Books.

- 2002b. "Publics and Counterpublics." *Public Culture* 14(1): 49–90.

Warren, A., and R. Wellek. 1956. *Theory of Literature*. Harcourt, Brace & World.
wa Thiong'o, N. 2012. *Globalectics: Theory and the Politics of Knowing*. Columbia University Press.
Watson, R. 1994. *Memory, History and Opposition under State Socialism*. SAR Press.
Webber, A. 2008. *Berlin in the Twentieth Century*. University of Cambridge Press.
Webster, A.K. 2006a. "The Mouse that Sucked: On 'Translating' a Navajo Poem." *Studies in American Indian Literatures* 18(1): 37–49. https://doi.org/10.1353/ail.2006.0018.
- 2006b. "Keeping the Word: On Orality and Literacy (with a Sideways Glance at Navajo)." *Oral Tradition* 21(2): 295–324. https://doi.org/10.1353/ort.2007.0006.
- 2010. "'Tséyi' First, Because Navajo Language Was Here before Contact': On Intercultural Performances, Metasemiotic Stereotypes, and the Dynamics of Place." *Semiotica: Journal of the International Association for Semiotic Studies*, vol. 2010, no. 181: 149–78.
- 2012. "'Don't Talk about It': Navajo Poets and Their Ordeals of Language." *Journal of Anthropological Research* 68(3): 399–414. https://doi.org/10.3998/jar.0521004.0068.306.
- 2013. "'The Validity of Navajo Is in Its Sounds': On Hymes, Navajo Poetry, Punning, and the Recognition of Voice." *Journal of Folklore Research: An International Journal of Folklore and Ethnomusicology* 50(1–3): 117–44.
- 2015. "The Poetry of Sound and the Sound of Poetry: Navajo Poetry, Phonological Iconicity, and Linguistic Relativity." *Semiotica*, 2015(207): 279–301. https://doi.org/10.1515/sem-2015-0065.
- 2016. "The Art of Failure in Translating a Navajo Poem." *Journal de la Société des Américanistes* 102 (102–1): 9–41. https://doi.org/10.4000/jsa.14602.
- 2019. "(Ethno) Poetics and Perspectivism: On the Hieroglyphic Beauty of Ambiguity." *Journal of Linguistic Anthropology* 29(2): 168–74. https://doi.org/10.1111/jola.12210.
- 2020. "Learning to Be Satisfied: Navajo Poetics, a Chattering Chipmunk, and Ethnopoetics." *Oral Tradition* 34(1): 73–104.
- 2021. "Let Them Know How I Was or Something Like That, You Know": On Lingual Life Histories, Remembering, and Navajo Poetry. *Journal of Anthropological Research* 77(1): 16–34. https://doi.org/10.1086/712286.
Weidman, A. 2014. "Anthropology and Voice." *Annual Review of Anthropology* 43: 37–51. https://doi.org/10.1146/annurev-anthro-102313-030050.
Weigel, S. 1996. "Transsibirische Metamorphosen: Laudatio auf Yoko Tawada zur Verleihung des Adalbert-von-Chamisso-Preises 1996." *Frauen in der Literaturwissenschaft: Rundbrief* 49: 5–6.
Weiner, A.B. 1992. *Inalienable Possessions: The Paradox of Keeping-While-Giving*. University of California Press.

Wenzels, H. 1996. "Die 'fliessende' Rede und der 'gefrorene' Text: Metaphern im Spannungsfeld von Mundlichkeit und Schriftlichkeit." In G. Williams and S. Schindler (eds.), *Knowledge, Science, and Literature in Early Modern Germany*. University of North Carolina Press.

West, C. 1989. *The American Evasion of Philosophy: A Genealogy of Pragmatism*. University of Wisconsin Press.

Westmayr, S. 2010. *Poetry Slam in Deutschland: Theorie und Praxis einer multimedialen Kunstform*. Tectum.

Weszkalnys, G. 2010. *Berlin Alexanderplatz*. Berghahn.

Wilcke, H., and Lambert, L. 2015. "Die Politik des O-Platzes:(Un-) Sichtbare Kämpfe einer Geflüchtetenbewegung." *Movements* 1(2): 1–23.

Wilden, A. ed. 2013. *System and Structure: Essays in Communication and Exchange*, 2nd ed. (Vol. 11). Routledge.

Will, A.K. 2019. "The German Statistical Category 'Migration Background': Historical Roots, Revisions and Shortcomings." *Ethnicities* 19(3): 535–57. https://doi.org/10.1177/1468796819833437.

Williams, R. 1979. *Politics and Letters: Interviews with New Left Review*. New Left Books.

– 1977. *Marxism and Literature*. New York: Oxford University Press.

Wittgenstein, L. 1954 (1999). *Philosophische Untersuchungen in Ludwig Wittgenstein Werkausgabe Volume 1*. Suhrkamp, S.231–485.

Wittmann, R. 1991. *Geschichte des deutschen buch-handels: Ein Oberblick*. C.H. Beck.

Woolard, K.A. 1998. "Simultaneity and Bivalency as Strategies in Bilingualism." *Journal of Linguistic Anthropology* 8(1): 3–29.

Wright, C. 2013. "Introduction: Yoko Tawada's Exophonic Texts." In *Portrait of a Tongue*. University of Ottawa Press.

Wurtscheid. 2021. "Umwandlung von Miet- in Eigentumswohnungen nur noch mit Genehmigung." *Der Tagespiegel*. 03.08.2021.

Yates, Frances. 1966. *The Art of Memory*. Routledge.

Yildiz, Y. 2013. *Beyond the Mother Tongue*. Fordham University Press.

– 2017. "Berlin as a Migratory Setting." In A. Webber (ed.), Cambridge Companion to the Literature of Berlin (206–26). Cambridge University Press.

Zimmerer, J. 2011. *Von Windhuk nach Auschwitz*. Lit Verlag.

Zukin, S. 1995. "Whose Culture? Whose City?" In J. Lin and C. Mele (eds.), *The Urban Sociology Reader* (349–57). Routledge.

Zumhagen-Yekplé, K. 2020. *A Different Order of Difficulty: Literature after Wittgenstein*. University of Chicago Press.

Zweig. S. 1942. *Die Welt von Gestern: Erinnerungen eines Europäers*. S. Fisher Verlag.

# Index

abstract, 61, 200n15, 220n14;
  abstraction, 61, 127, 172, 200n15, 233n55
acknowledge, 62, 91–2, 118, 127, 204n35, 208n63
Adorno, Theodor, 199n11, 205n46, 206n49, 210–11n7
aesthetics, 57, 61, 99, 120, 138, 147, 206n47, 221n17
agreement(s)/disagreement(s), 29–34, 79, 126–9, 174–5, 182n52, 188n97, 189n110, 190nn114–15, 218n60, 230n20, 231n29
alienation, 20–1, 46, 51–2, 78, 109, 127
Arendt, Hannah, 80, 83, 97, 116–17, 207n51, 218n59
authenticity, 10, 34, 42, 62, 83, 118, 141, 170, 209n72

Benjamin, Walter, 3, 105, 111
body, 14, 41, 52, 83–4, 92, 108, 128, 163, 168–9; bodily, 35, 49–50, 163, 169, 175
border, 59, 157
Börsenverein, 20, 59, 128–30, 219n4

Çağlar, Ayse, 177n8, 178n13, 187n75, 191n121, 192n9
capital, 5–10, 19–21, 109, 123–6, 138–9, 148, 191n1, 221n17
care, 14, 137, 147, 225n32
Cassin, Barbara, 116–17, 201n20
Cavell, Stanley: on collecting, 141, 146–7, 163–4, 172; on comedy of remarriage, 56, 85–9
characters, 7–10, 25, 28, 31, 46, 58, 76, 96, 99, 103–4, 112–13, 140–1, 146–8, 159–60, 163, 166, 177n9, 187n84; linguistic, 157–8, 166–9
circulation, 16, 21, 49–53, 64, 126–32, 192n4, 203n32, 221n17, 222n19, 224n28
class, 21, 63, 111
cliché, 116, 204n44
collecting, 25, 102, 111, 128, 142, 144, 148
colonialism, 96, 190n112
commensurability/incommensurability, 9–11, 16, 60
commodity/commodities, 20, 125, 128, 130, 136, 141, 148, 213n16, 220n14, 222n19, 225n29; commoditization, 16, 34–5, 193n17
concepts, 27–30, 35, 62, 80, 174, 217n50, 221n17, 222n19, 236n78
conceptualization, 112, 174, 235n74
context, 23–4, 48–53, 57–64, 83–4, 173–5
cosmopolitan(ism): 8–13, 47, 181n37, 181n46, 190n114, 229n18; cosmopolitanization, 18–21

creativity, 12, 46, 97
crisis, 10, 14–17, 31, 76, 91, 146, 150, 182n48, 184n57
criteria/criterial, 27–30, 56, 152, 168–70, 174–5, 188n97, 213n20, 222n17, 232n44
criticism, 34, 64, 109, 221n17, 229n18; critique, 14, 104, 115, 152, 165, 187n76, 200n18, 210, 222n17; literary criticism, 109, 207n53

Das, Veena, 30, 83–7, 177n1, 190n113, 207n55, 208n63, 218n60, 233n54
DDR (Deutsche Demokratische Republik), 144, 183, 185n60, 218n3. *See also* East Germany
Diamond, Cora, 28–9, 174, 189n103, 189n112, 236n78

East Germany, 16, 58, 63, 94, 139, 145, 183, 198n5, 210, 229n18
ethics, 28, 189n101, 206n47, 207n55
ethnography, 21–2, 115, 187nn80–1, 195n35, 217n50, 218n60
European Union (EU), 10, 15–16, 129, 184n57, 185n61
everyday life, 6–10, 17, 20, 30, 50–1, 62–3, 78–82, 87, 149, 164, 169, 186n64, 187n80, 192n11, 209n78, 211n7; scenes in, 5, 181n38, 209n78; talk/language in, 17–20, 23, 110, 120, 211n14, 234n55. *See also* ordinary life

fantasy, 20, 110, 147, 196n47, 215n37
fiction, 4–8, 81–5, 93, 98–9, 107, 194n24, 208n69, 219n4; fictive, 85, 99, 188n97, 194n24
fixed-pricing, 20, 126, 129–30
forms of life, 9, 27–30, 62, 78–9, 98, 170, 175, 188n97, 190n113, 230n20, 232n44; human forms of life, 23, 30, 173, 190n113, 230n21

Foucault, Michel, 63, 211n14, 214n22
fragment, 1, 4, 31, 63, 81, 98–9, 102–6, 111, 113, 119–20, 167, 177n1, 191n125, 194n24, 200n11, 205nn45–7, 207n54, 223n23
frame, 23, 123, 160–1, 233n54

global: art, 8, 229n18; city discourse, 10–12, 20, 20–2, 114, 127, 131, 178n23; industry, 124–5, 130, 132, 185n60, 219n3
Goethe, Johann Wolfgang, 12, 23, 56, 90, 134, 179n25, 201n18, 224n28
Goethe Institute, 13, 22–3, 90–1, 100
grammar (philosophical), 9, 27–30, 43, 85, 98, 127, 156, 162, 165–6, 174, 188n97, 188–9n98, 190n115, 213n19, 218n60, 221n17, 230n20, 233n54, 236–7n78
guilt, 11, 58, 97, 113–20, 180n26, 204n35, 205n46, 206n47, 210–11n7, 227n47

Hegel, G.W.F., 151–2, 228nn14–17, 238n78
Historikerstreit, 180n26, 210
Holocaust, 78–81, 97, 114, 180n26, 206n47, 210. *See also* Shoah
homogenising, 20, 62, 220n14, 226n32

ideology, 8, 13, 129
impersonal, 19, 52, 115, 131

journalist/journalistic, 16, 33, 40, 64–9, 82, 90, 97–9, 100–1, 105, 118

Kiez, 131–2, 175

Lambek, Michael, 189n101, 209n1, 212n15
language: experience of, 157, 159–63; ideology, 9, 23, 27, 149,

193n13, 199n10; monolingualism, 150; multilingualism, 150, 154; ordinary, 30, 85–8, 100, 117–20, 154, 172, 175
Laugier, Sandra, 79, 146, 189n103, 189n110, 190n115, 204n36
literacy, 51, 194n24, 200n1

markets: 12–13, 19–21, 63, 73, 125, 129–32, 135, 141, 144–5, 172–3, 179n23, 186n73, 187n83, 193n8, 200n15, 201n18, 219n4, 220n13, 224n28; market exchange, 21, 61
Marx, Karl, 72, 201n18, 227n47; Marxist/Marxian, 66, 196n49
meaning, 30, 35, 42–4, 48, 53, 117, 153–8, 162–71, 185n64, 190n114, 194n24, 208n57, 210, 232n44
melancholia/melancholic, 114, 197n54, 205n47
memorial(s), 11, 114, 119, 185n60, 217n50
memory: cultural, 12, 48, 94–7, 104, 180n26, 194n24, 229n18; national, 11, 210, 217n50; poetic/literary, 42, 48–52, 57, 108–18, 195n29, 217n48; technique of, 40–1
migration, 12–14, 19, 22, 150–3, 178n13, 178n20, 182n49, 182n52, 184n57, 185n61, 198nn4–5, 238n78
modernity, 17, 20, 34, 51–4, 80, 98, 109–10, 114–15, 191n1, 193n17, 204n34, 210
movement: artistic, 86, 167–71, 221n17; historical/political, 13, 125, 182n49, 192n4, 194n24, 206n47, 211n10, 220n14; literary, 8, 12, 21, 27–30, 34, 38–40, 44, 49, 55, 83, 154–7, 163, 166, 173–5; migratory, 8–10, 13–15, 61, 87, 96, 125–7, 153; vocal/linguistic, 91, 149–50

Nabokov, Vladimir, 4–8, 30
narrative, 22, 55, 65, 79–84, 87, 110, 113–14, 161, 171, 193n11, 194n24, 195n29, 205n45, 207nn51–4, 208n69, 215n32, 217n50, 229n18; narration, 45, 98, 146; narrator, 67, 95, 160, 170–1, 235n74
Nazis/Nazism, 7, 63–4, 96–7, 101–2, 107, 110, 116–17, 123, 126, 133, 137, 179n25, 201n21, 202n28, 205n47, 210; neo-Nazis, 22, 187n74, 212n15
neighbourhood, 5, 19, 23, 25, 32–3, 47, 75, 95–6, 99, 107, 111, 121–2, 124–5, 130, 192n4; bookstores, 3, 20–2, 131–3; of concepts, 27; of language, 160, 175; neighbours, 5, 10, 19. *See also* Kiez
normativity, 19, 24, 60–2, 84, 150

orality, 49
ordinary life, 13, 17, 54, 81, 93, 115–17, 174, 181n37, 208n69; objects, 6–9; violence, 51

performance: linguistic, 45–52, 60–1, 194n24, 195n29, 198n9; literary, 13, 18, 24–5, 33–5, 39–42, 53–4, 194n24
philosophy, 63, 86, 111, 144, 146, 151–2, 165, 228n17, 230n23
physiognomy, 84, 110, 157, 163–5, 215n37, 232n44, 233n54, 234n57
play, 95, 99–100, 144, 153, 158, 162, 168–70, 175, 197n50, 206n47
pleasure, 136, 147, 206n47
politics/political, 49–51, 105–10, 124, 135–9, 146, 178n20, 183, 203n32; elite, 21, 39, 110; exile, 56–92; far-right, 22–5, 184n52, 202n21, 210, 212n15; literary and linguistic, 39–43, 49–50, 106, 162, 183, 217n50; memory, 114, 180n26; migration, 10–16; translation, 17

popular culture, 34, 63, 87, 123, 146
possibility/possibilities: of the city, 3, 8–9; human, 28–30; literary/linguistic, 25–7, 50, 78, 92, 127–30, 146, 151–2, 159–76; social, 20–3, 87–9, 98, 110, 185n64, 192n4, 230n21
practice: creative, 3, 24–6, 203n32; cultural, 182n52, 185n60, 194n24, 196n47, 199n9; literary/linguistic, 8–15, 18, 23, 28–9, 60–2, 69, 125, 149–56, 170, 187n80, 200n16, 226n38, 229n1; performative/poetic, 35–9, 95, 108, 195n28; violent, 14
public: counter-publics, 52; events, 25, 43, 108–9; experience(s), 8, 15, 39–41, 65, 78, 115, 146; memory, 96, 129; publics (reading), 58, 64, 94; speech, 9, 15, 22–5, 43, 63, 78–80, 116–20, 150–7, 164, 183, 186n73, 200n18, 210, 211n14, 220n13, 229n18

racialization, 11, 23, 30, 79, 97, 152, 178n22, 226n32
real, 4, 8–10, 29, 41, 69, 93, 98–100, 105
realism/realistic, 205n46, 214n21, 230n23
Reed, Adam, 24, 140–1
rent, 22, 94, 124, 225n31
romanticism, 12–13, 112, 177n1, 180n29, 181n34, 181n37, 191n125
rule (following), 14–15, 26, 110

Sassen, Saskia, 178n22–3
scepticism, 87–9, 120, 203n33, 208n63, 209n78
shame, 112–13, 118, 146, 210
Shoah, 5, 11, 65, 77–80, 204n34, 206n47, 211n8. *See also* Holocaust
Shoshan, Nitzan, 21–2, 180n26, 212n15, 218n3
slam poetry, 21, 33, 192n5
soul, 56, 164

spatial(ization), 51, 105, 110, 113–15, 178n14, 191n1, 220n14, 222n19, 223n26
standardization, 10–14, 18, 62, 80, 127–30, 174, 185n57, 189n112, 221n17, 235n74, 237
state, 7, 126–31, 179n25, 182n52, 184n57, 198n5, 203n32, 220nn13–14; institutions/programs, 13, 21, 57, 138, 229n18; owned businesses, 36; Senate, 56, 60–4; welfare/investments, 21, 138, 144, 178n20
stranger (sociality), 21, 49–52, 92, 108
street, 3–13, 20, 31–2, 36–7, 51, 57, 67–8, 73–7, 85–6, 93–121, 137, 172, 216n40

testimony, 48, 62, 77–81, 177n10,
translation, 10–11, 17–18, 20, 23, 34–5, 38, 43, 45, 49, 59–63, 70, 78, 80–2, 85, 90, 108, 124–5, 133–4, 149–56, 162, 166, 170, 181nn34–7, 193n13, 200nn12–18, 201n18, 206n47, 208n46, 213n20, 234nn57–64, 236n75, 238n78; mistranslation, 23, 149, 156, 201n20
trauma (theory), 31, 62, 78–81, 108, 114–15, 204n41, 205n47, 207n54

value, 220n15, 223n26, 227n47; aesthetic and literary value, 20, 48–51, 119, 141, 147–8, 201n18, 220n15, 222n17, 232n44
violence, 16, 51, 57, 77–83, 88, 95–7, 110, 114, 120, 137, 183, 185n60, 186n74, 187n76, 210, 219n3
voice: creative/poetic, 29, 39–51, 104; human, 34, 38, 41, 113, 120, 158; linguistic, 34–5, 38, 82–9, 153–5, 189n110, 208n57; pawning of, 84–6; region of, 63, 87, 91
vulnerability, 15, 22, 173, 188n97, 195n29

walking, 3–5, 10, 13, 15, 27, 37, 93–117, 119–20; tours, 20, 25, 90
Webster, Anthony K., 187n80, 193n13, 198n9, 202n27, 234n64
Wende, 34, 124, 144, 185n60, 192n8, 219n3
witness, 79–80, 108, 120, 137, 204n41, 206n47

Wittgenstein, Ludwig, 26, 37, 157, 162, 165, 188n93, 190n118, 208n64, 230n20, 232n44, 235n77
world, 4, 8–12, 23, 29–30, 60–1, 97, 113, 149; literature, 10–12, 23, 56, 60–2, 136, 180n29, 200n18, 202n28; worldliness, 11–12, 40, 189n98

# Anthropological Horizons

Editor: Michael Lambek, University of Toronto

*The Varieties of Sensory Experience: A Sourcebook in the Anthropology of the Senses*/Edited by David Howes (1991)

*Arctic Homeland: Kinship, Community, and Development in Northwest Greenland*/ Mark Nuttall (1992)

*Knowledge and Practice in Mayotte: Local Discourses of Islam, Sorcery, and Spirit Possession*/Michael Lambek (1993)

*Deathly Waters and Hungry Mountains: Agrarian Ritual and Class Formation in an Andean Town*/Peter Gose (1994)

*Paradise: Class, Commuters, and Ethnicity in Rural Ontario*/Stanley R. Barrett (1994)

*The Cultural World in Beowulf*/John M. Hill (1995)

*Making It Their Own: Severn Ojibwe Communicative Practices*/Lisa Philips Valentine (1995)

*Merchants and Shopkeepers*: *A Historical Anthropology of an Irish Market Town, 1200–1991*/P.H. Gulliver and Marilyn Silverman (1995)

*Tournaments of Value*: *Sociability and Hierarchy in a Yemeni Town*/Ann Meneley (1996)

*Mal'uocchiu: Ambiguity, Evil Eye, and the Language of Distress*/Sam Migliore (1997)

*Between History and Histories: The Making of Silences and Commemorations*/ Edited by Gerald Sider and Gavin Smith (1997)

*Eh, Paesan! Being Italian in Toronto*/Nicholas DeMaria Harney (1998)

*Theorizing the Americanist Tradition*/Edited by Lisa Philips Valentine and Regna Darnell (1999)

*Colonial "Reformation" in the Highlands of Central Sulawesi, Indonesia, 1892–1995*/ Albert Schrauwers (2000)

*The Rock Where We Stand: An Ethnography of Women's Activism in Newfoundland*/ Glynis George (2000)

*"Being Alive Well": Health and the Politics of Cree Well-Being*/Naomi Adelson (2000)
*Irish Travellers: Racism and the Politics of Culture*/Jane Helleiner (2001)
*Of Property and Propriety: The Role of Gender and Class in Imperialism and Nationalism*/Edited by Himani Bannerji, Shahrzad Mojab, and Judith Whitehead (2001)
*An Irish Working Class: Explorations in Political Economy and Hegemony, 1800–1950*/Marilyn Silverman (2001)
*The Double Twist: From Ethnography to Morphodynamics*/Edited by Pierre Maranda (2001)
*The House of Difference: Cultural Politics and National Identity in Canada*/Eva Mackey (2002)
*Writing and Colonialism in Northern Ghana: The Encounter between the LoDagaa and "the World on Paper," 1892–1991*/Sean Hawkins (2002)
*Guardians of the Transcendent: An Ethnography of a Jain Ascetic Community*/Anne Vallely (2002)
*The Hot and the Cold: Ills of Humans and Maize in Native Mexico*/Jacques M. Chevalier and Andrés Sánchez Bain (2003)
*Figured Worlds: Ontological Obstacles in Intercultural Relations*/Edited by John Clammer, Sylvie Poirier, and Eric Schwimmer (2004)
*Revenge of the Windigo: The Construction of the Mind and Mental Health of North American Aboriginal Peoples*/James B. Waldram (2004)
*The Cultural Politics of Markets: Economic Liberalization and Social Change in Nepal*/Katharine Neilson Rankin (2004)
*A World of Relationships: Itineraries, Dreams, and Events in the Australian Western Desert*/Sylvie Poirier (2005)
*The Politics of the Past in an Argentine Working-Class Neighbourhood*/Lindsay DuBois (2005)
*Youth and Identity Politics in South Africa, 1990–1994*/Sibusisiwe Nombuso Dlamini (2005)
*Maps of Experience: The Anchoring of Land to Story in Secwepemc Discourse*/Andie Diane Palmer (2005)
*We Are Now a Nation: Croats between "Home" and "Homeland"*/Daphne N. Winland (2007)
*Beyond Bodies: Rain-Making and Sense-Making in Tanzania*/Todd Sanders (2008)
*Kaleidoscopic Odessa: History and Place in Contemporary Ukraine*/Tanya Richardson (2008)
*Invaders as Ancestors: On the Intercultural Making and Unmaking of Spanish Colonialism in the Andes*/Peter Gose (2008)
*From Equality to Inequality: Social Change among Newly Sedentary Lanoh Hunter-Gatherer Traders of Peninsular Malaysia*/Csilla Dallos (2011)
*Rural Nostalgias and Transnational Dreams: Identity and Modernity among Jat Sikhs*/Nicola Mooney (2011)

*Dimensions of Development: History, Community, and Change in Allpachico, Peru*/Susan Vincent (2012)
*People of Substance: An Ethnography of Morality in the Colombian Amazon*/Carlos David Londoño Sulkin (2012)
*"We Are Still Didene": Stories of Hunting and History from Northern British Columbia*/Thomas McIlwraith (2012)
*Being Māori in the City: Indigenous Everyday Life in Auckland*/Natacha Gagné (2013)
*The Hakkas of Sarawak: Sacrificial Gifts in Cold War Era Malaysia*/Kee Howe Yong (2013)
*Remembering Nayeche and the Gray Bull Engiro: African Storytellers of the Karamoja Plateau and the Plains of Turkana*/Mustafa Kemal Mirzeler (2014)
*In Light of Africa: Globalizing Blackness in Northeast Brazil*/Allan Charles Dawson (2014)
*The Land of Weddings and Rain: Nation and Modernity in Post-Socialist Lithuania*/Gediminas Lankauskas (2015)
*Milanese Encounters: Public Space and Vision in Contemporary Urban Italy*/Cristina Moretti (2015)
*Legacies of Violence: History, Society, and the State in Sardinia*/Antonio Sorge (2015)
*Looking Back, Moving Forward: Transformation and Ethical Practice in the Ghanaian Church of Pentecost*/Girish Daswani (2015)
*Why the Porcupine Is Not a Bird: Explorations in the Folk Zoology of an Eastern Indonesian People*/Gregory Forth (2016)
*The Heart of Helambu: Ethnography and Entanglement in Nepal*/Tom O'Neill (2016)
*Tournaments of Value: Sociability and Hierarchy in a Yemeni Town, 20th Anniversary Edition*/Ann Meneley (2016)
*Europe Un-Imagined: Nation and Culture at a French-German Television Channel*/Damien Stankiewicz (2017)
*Transforming Indigeneity: Urbanization and Language Revitalization in the Brazilian Amazon*/Sarah Shulist (2018)
*Wrapping Authority: Women Islamic Leaders in a Sufi Movement in Dakar, Senegal*/Joseph Hill (2018)
*Island in the Stream: An Ethnographic History of Mayotte*/Michael Lambek (2018)
*Materializing Difference: Consumer Culture, Politics, and Ethnicity among Romanian Roma*/Péter Berta (2019)
*Virtual Activism: Sexuality, the Internet, and a Social Movement in Singapore*/Robert Phillips (2020)
*Shadow Play: Information Politics in Urban Indonesia*/Sheri Lynn Gibbings (2021)
*Suspect Others: Spirit Mediums, Self-Knowledge, and Race in Multiethnic Suriname*/Stuart Earle Strange (2021)

*Exemplary Life: Modelling Sainthood in Christian Syria*/Andreas Bandak (2022)
*Without the State: Self-Organization and Political Activisim in Ukraine*/Emily Channell-Justice (2022)
*Moral Figures: Making Reproduction Public in Vanuatu*/Alexandra Widmer (2023)
*Truly Human: Indigeneity and Indigenous Resurgence on Formosa*/Scott E. Simon (2023)
*Moving Words: Literature, Memory, and Migration in Berlin*/Andrew Brandel (2023)

Printed and bound by CPI Group (UK) Ltd, Croydon, CR0 4YY
31/08/2025

14727212-0002